STRESS, VIBRATION AND NOISE ANALYSIS IN VEHICLES

Papers presented at the Annual Conference of the Stress Analysis Group of the Institute of Physics held at the University of Aston in Birmingham, England

STRESS, VIBRATION AND NOISE ANALYSIS IN VEHICLES

Edited by

H. G. GIBBS AND T. H. RICHARDS

JOSEPH LUCAS LTD AND UNIVERSITY OF ASTON IN BIRMINGHAM

A HALSTED PRESS BOOK

JOHN WILEY & SONS

NEW YORK—TORONTO

PUBLISHED IN THE U.S.A. AND CANADA BY
HALSTED PRESS
A DIVISION OF JOHN WILEY & SONS, INC., NEW YORK

Library of Congress Cataloging in Publication Data

Institute of Physics (1971–   ). Stress Analysis
    Group.
    Stress, vibration, and noise analysis in vehicles.

    "A Halsted Press book."
    "Papers presented at the annual conference of the
Stress Analysis Group of the Institute of Physics
held at the University of Aston in Birmingham, England."
    Includes index.
    1. Motor vehicles—Dynamics—Congresses.
2. Motor vehicles—Vibration—Congresses. 3. Motor
vehicles—Noise—Congresses. I. Gibbs, H. G.
II. Richards, T. H. III. Title.
TL243.I48   1975   629.04   75-14389
ISBN 0-470-29742-5

WITH 28 TABLES AND 261 ILLUSTRATIONS

© APPLIED SCIENCE PUBLISHERS LTD 1975

Printed in Great Britain by Galliard (Printers) Ltd Great Yarmouth

Foreword

The Stress Analysis Group of the Institute of Physics holds annual conferences at various venues in the United Kingdom. The Group has a general policy of informality regarding its meetings and the publication of contributions, in the belief that such informality encourages the expression of views and exchange of ideas. However, annual conferences are built around some theme, and occasionally the chosen topic is felt to be of sufficient interest to merit publication of the proceedings as a whole rather than leaving individual papers to be published in different journals at different times or perhaps not at all. The Group Committee felt that 'Stress, Vibration and Noise Analysis in Vehicles' was such a topic and that publication of the papers presented would constitute a valuable contribution to the literature on the subject, and so the present volume was produced. The discussions remained informal and only the papers themselves have been collected for presentation in this book. No conference of this kind can be fully comprehensive and it transpired that most contributions related to land surface vehicles, but a feature gratifying to the organisers was the balance between contributors from industry and academic institutions: we like to think that this proved mutually beneficial.

The advent of the computer has, of course, had a dramatic impact on design work and one of the most noticeable features which emerged from the Conference was the extent to which techniques such as the finite element method have come to be regarded as natural tools by the stress analyst. It was clear that the use of increasingly sophisticated mathematical models to give a more realistic description of practical situations has been widely accepted as necessary to meet the increased precision called for in design. However, although the swing towards theoretical methods of stress analysis was plain, an account of work on a complicated photoelastic model of a diesel engine frame showed that experimental techniques are still important.

In the field of vibrations the treatment of vehicle structure and suspension dynamics also reflected the practical importance of modern computational methods, but while comparisons between experimental and numerical results gave confidence in computer modelling, limitations were also apparent.

The investigations reported in the various papers presented on noise analysis were valuable examples of how strong incentives, either commercial or statutory, can encourage work yielding dramatic improvements in situations previously regarded as seemingly intractable. In this section, delegates were able to hear convincingly for themselves the magnitude of the noise problem from tape recordings of engine tests.

Delegates to the Conference were welcomed by Professor A. J. Ede, Pro-Vice Chancellor of the University of Aston in Birmingham, and we would like to express our appreciation to him and the University for providing the excellent facilities which we enjoyed.

Although small in terms of numbers, the Conference ran smoothly in a relaxed atmosphere. This admirable state was only achieved by much hard work and preparation by a large number of people and the editors grate-fully acknowledge the help of all those who contributed to the Conference organisation. Those particularly concerned were Mr K. J. Pascoe (Papers Sub-Committee) and Dr J. E. T. Penny (University of Aston).

Our thanks also go to the authors, who are to be congratulated on the high standard of their contributions and to the delegates for their lively discussions both during and outside the formal lecture sessions.

H. G. GIBBS and T. H. RICHARDS

Contents

Foreword v

1. The Application of Stress, Noise and Vibration Analysis to
   Design of Rail Rapid Transit Vehicles 1
   G. J. M. BOTHAM (*Metro-Cammell Ltd*)

2. Finite Element Stress Analysis as an Aid to the Design of
   Automotive Components 21
   M. R. KINGSTON (*Joseph Lucas Ltd*)

3. Static Analysis of a Light Truck Frame Using the Finite
   Element Method 47
   B. MILLS and P. F. JOHNSON (*University of Birmingham and
   Ford Motor Company*)

4. Finite Element Study of a Cast Iron Flywheel with Particular
   Emphasis on Stress Concentrations 75
   P. J. BINDIN (*Perkins Engines Ltd*)

5. Application of the Finite Element Method to the Design of
   Disc-type Wheels 91
   T. H. RICHARDS and C. W. WOO (*University of Aston and
   University of Singapore*)

6. Photoelasticity Applied to Complicated Diesel Engine Models 111
   H. FESSLER and M. PERLA (*University of Nottingham and Stress
   Analysis Ltd*)

7. Torsional Design Aspects of Long Wheelbase Vehicles . . 123
   P. W. SHARMAN (*Loughborough University of Technology*)

8. Noise Reduction of Large Earthmoving Vehicles . . . 149
   D. J. SNOW (*Central Electricity Generating Board*)

9. Automobile Drive-Line Vibration and Internal Noise . . 165
   D. W. PARKINS (*Cranfield Institute of Technology*)

10. Noise Generated at the Tyre–Road Interface . . . 181
    J. C. WALKER and D. J. MAJOR (*Dunlop Ltd*)

11. Control of Noise from Conventional Diesel Engines . . 201
    M. F. RUSSELL (*CAV Ltd*)

12. The Effect of Environmental Conditions on the Noise Level of
    Cooling Fans in Vehicles 217
    J. S. B. MATHER (*University of Nottingham*)

13. A Vibrational Analysis of a Pin–Disc System with Particular
    Reference to Squeal Noise in Disc-brakes 237
    S. W. E. EARLES and G. B. SOAR (*Queen Mary College, London*)

14. Theoretical Analysis of an Active Suspension Fitted to a
    London Transport Bus 253
    M. COTTERELL (*London Transport Executive*)

15. Static and Dynamic Analysis of a Light Van Body Using the
    Finite Element Method 283
    B. MILLS and J. SAYER (*University of Birmingham and London
    Transport Executive*)

16. A Preliminary Investigation into the Structural Behaviour of
    an Underground Railway Coach 313
    A. L. YETTRAM and D. J. SMITH (*Brunel University and London
    Transport Executive*)

17. Application of the Finite Element Technique to the Structural
    Analysis of Road and Rail Vehicles at London Transport . 351
    H. HILLEL, J. SAYER and R. A. PHIPPS (*London Transport
    Executive*)

18. The Optimisation of Undercarriage Characteristics in Transport
    Aeroplanes Using a Hybrid Computation Technique . . 389
    M. R. WHITEHEAD (*Loughborough University of Technology*)

19. A Theoretical and Practical Examination of Engine Shake . 413
    A. EAMES-JONES and C. ASHLEY (*Dunlop Limited and UOP
    Bostrom Ltd*)

20. Application of the WKBJ Approximation Processes for the
    Analysis of the Torsional Vibrations of Diesel Engine Systems 439
    M. S. PASRICHA and W. D. CARNEGIE (*Banares Hindu University
    and University of Surrey*)

21. Simplified Modelling of High Order Linear Systems   .   .   451
    M. COTTERELL (*London Transport Executive*)

22. The Use of Dynamic Strain Records to Estimate the Fatigue
    Life of a Semi-trailer Chassis   461
    P. W. SHARMAN (*Loughborough University of Technology*)

23. Design Data for Heavy Vehicles.   473
    C. C. WOODLEY and B. R. PIGGOTT (*The Welding Institute*)

Index   483

1

The Application of Stress, Noise and Vibration Analysis to Design of Rail Rapid Transit Vehicles

G. J. M. BOTHAM
Metro-Cammell Ltd

SUMMARY

This is a review paper dealing with design developments occurring with the aid of, or as a result of, noise and vibration analysis. To examine the main strength of a vehicle body, finite element techniques now provide a method vastly superior to previous methods, but its cost and complexity cannot always be justified at the present time.

The much simpler framework analysis and approximate methods still have important functions. Comprehensive structural testing employing strain measurement techniques provides not only a final check on a new design but also yields information invaluable in the evolution of later designs. These techniques are applied to produce designs lighter in weight, cheaper in material or manufacturing costs, and hence more economic to the operator, whilst at the same time preserving the reliability and freedom from fatigue required for a vehicle life of 30 years or more.

Increasing public awareness of noise being a form of environmental pollution is leading to greater efforts to produce quieter vehicles, both from the passenger's point of view and with regard to wayside problems. Measurement and analysis techniques show that great improvements can be achieved, often without undue penalties in cost and weight. Attention is given to vibration isolation of the body from track irregularities, rotating machines on the body and to the effect of the body itself as a vibrating beam.

PART 1: STRESS AND VIBRATION

1.1 INTRODUCTION

Railway vehicle design is an evolutionary process. Almost invariably, reliability is given precedence over novelty. The term 'rapid transit' is relatively new and in its broadest sense embraces any form of urban public transport having its own exclusive right of way, but the most common

1

systems are those based on railway design and technology which have been evolved to give high reliability.

Stress, noise and vibration analyses of both a theoretical and experimental nature are playing an increasingly important role in the design of vehicles even where there is a long history of evolution, as for example in the case of London Transport tube and surface line trains. The contribution of stress analysis in achieving reliability becomes more significant as ever more strenuous attempts are made to reduce vehicle mass towards the practicable minimum, so as to meet the needs, born of economic viability and social desirability, of making best use of energy. At the same time, higher standards of passenger comfort and environmental conservation are pressing designers beyond the point where purely subjective means will suffice and specialist activities in noise and vibration analysis are being integrated into the design process.

1.2   MAIN STRUCTURAL DESIGN CRITERIA

In its primary ability to support and transport its own mass, the masses of non-structural parts, such as interior finish and fittings and traction equipment, and the maximum passenger load to be carried, the first consideration in the rapid transit car structure is that stress shall be below the level at which fatigue failure will occur in a life of thirty or more years. Additionally, it must have adequate strength to resist occasional longitudinal impacts arising from coupling operations and to afford protection to passengers and crew in the event, however unlikely, of more serious collision.

The role of stress and vibration analysis, in designing to avoid fatigue failure, becomes clear when the major factors which could contribute to such a failure are examined (Fig. 1.1). Fatigue strength data are largely taken from published references of which the British Standard, BS 153, for steel structures and Code of Practice, CP 118, for aluminium alloy structures are particularly valuable, although it is sometimes judged to be worth while augmenting such knowledge with fatigue testing of component parts or sub-assemblies.

The remaining data need to be assessed in relation to each particular design of vehicle. When the design is novel such assessment must be wholly theoretical or a combination of theory and reference to test results on earlier designs having reasonable relevance.

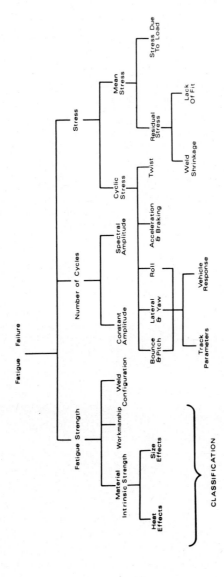

Fig. 1.1. Factors contributing to fatigue in a railway car body.

1.3 THE INFLUENCE OF FINITE ELEMENT ANALYSIS ON BODY STRUCTURE DESIGN

A number of finite element programmes capable of analysing the coach structure in considerable detail now exist, notably the British Rail Research Department's NEWPAC Programme [1]. These represent a sweeping advance over previous methods, the most sophisticated of which was a two-dimensional Vierendeel framework analysis, in which the whole structure of the car was referred to the plane of the bodyside and assemblages of panels and framing members were treated solely as beams.

The application of the finite element method to a complex rapid transit car structure (Fig. 1.2) has been given demonstrable credence by comparison of the results with a comprehensive strain gauge test. Correlation of theoretical and experimental deflections has proved excellent. Stress correlation has been generally good, but with some exceptions, which on close examination can be seen to be due to some disparities between the idealisation and the actual structure.

This method is therefore seen to give real and quantifiable benefits in body structure design in one or both of two ways. It can be used merely as a checking procedure, once the major part of the design drawings have been completed, or it can be applied at the very outset, when little exists on paper but the bare outlines of the car, some reasonable knowledge of its mass and the loads to which it will be subjected and some approximate assessments of the member sizes which will be required.

In the former case the design will have been developed by evolution of previous ones for similar vehicles, most probably checked by simple hand calculations or two-dimensional framework analysis and is likely to be of a conservative nature. It is of course possible that the design will be quite satisfactory without a finite element analysis, but experience has shown that some modification is usually necessary when the prototype or first-off body shell is subjected to a static structural test. This point is illustrated by an unacceptably high distortion of some of the doorway pillars of the London 1967 Tube Car, found when the first-off vehicle shell was tested. If uncorrected it would have caused doors to jam in service, with consequent serious disruption of such service, and hence it was necessary to devise and apply stiffeners, re-test the shell and add the stiffeners to other shells in the course of production. Such modifications at this late stage are far more difficult, costly and disruptive to production than an alteration to design made even a matter of two or three months previously, which could have resulted from carrying out an analysis at that time.

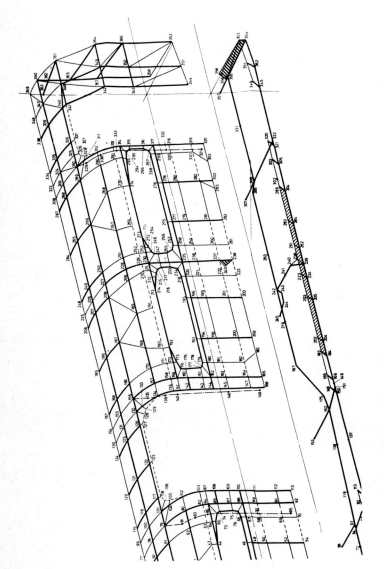

FIG. 1.2. Idealisation for the first finite element analysis carried out on a London Transport tube car.

This in itself is a vast improvement on past methods of checking a design and should, in future, help to remove the constraints on design progression which are present due to considerable uncertainties about its structural behaviour. But the even more exciting prospect is given by the second possibility; that of tailoring a design around an analysis performed at a very early stage. Whilst the current analysis methods demand that the structure be fully defined before the programme can be run, and hence it is not feasible to carry out without having done some drawing work beforehand, this may be confined to some fairly general layout drawings, prepared without total commitment and with all minor section properties having hypothetical although realistic values attributed to them. In the author's opinion this would be commercially most viable if carried out in the spirit of a much speeded-up process of evolution, rather than attempting a completely revolutionary form of design. Whilst much may be attempted towards elimination of redundant mass in the structure, it has to be remembered that this is perhaps only a secondary consideration in relation to accommodation and satisfactory operation of doors, traction equipment, air comfort system, etc. and such matters may well make prior demands on the structural design.

1.4   SIMPLIFIED ANALYSIS

The cost of carrying out finite element analysis on car body structures, comprising computing charges, man time, consultancy charges and incidental expenses, may not always be justified; each particular case must be assessed on its merits. Also, it is plainly desirable that a structure should have the best possible chance of success before a costly analysis is undertaken. The more approximate methods used hitherto are not therefore obsolete.

The most striking feature, structurally, of a rapid transit car is the large cut-outs required for doorways. The degree of criticality will vary according to position of doorway relative to the support points and, since the major influence at such apertures is applied shear force, the most critical location is where it is positioned adjacent to a support and wholly to the side having the greater shear force. Ignoring the elasticity of the structure either side of the aperture enables a quick and simple estimate to be made of the stress and local deformation in the structure above and below the aperture. This provides a ready means of establishing the order of section properties required for the main longitudinal members of the structure.

In order to make any sensible appraisal of the stiffness required of the vertical pillar/panel assemblies between apertures it is necessary to carry out a form of framework analysis. Various means of so doing have been used over the past 25 years, ranging from a method assuming pin joints in all members at the centre of apertures for doors and windows, to make the structure statically determinate (method now obsolete), to the present widely used Vierendeel girder analysis for which computer programs exist at Sheffield University [2] and elsewhere [3].

These programs are relatively quick and cheap to use. The general deflection pattern of the structure is predicted with tolerable accuracy but stresses derived bear little resemblance to measured results, except perhaps in general order. Accuracy relies heavily on individual judgement in producing the initial idealisation.

Despite these shortcomings, the method has been used effectively on many designs, including the London Transport Surface Line C69 Stock, notable for having four large and one small doorway apertures in each side of the car, whereas the 'A' Stock, upon which the design was broadly based, had only three. First computations indicated unacceptably high stresses and deflections. Further cases were immediately analysed with hypothetically increased stiffnesses inserted for vertical and horizontal members, alone and in combination. This clearly demonstrated the importance of having adequate stiffness in the vertical structure adjacent to doorways subject to high applied shear force; the reduction of vertical deflection with increasing pillar stiffness was most marked. Figure 1.3(a) shows some deflected shapes plotted from these calculations, demonstrating how much greater is the effect on vertical deflection of stiffening the uprights, with relatively little increase in weight, than stiffening the horizontals, with a more substantial weight penalty. Applied to the design, this principle could not be fully exploited since an unacceptable increase in quarter panel width would have been required to produce sufficient stiffness. A compromise solution was adopted where as much stiffening as possible, approximately 1·4 times, was applied to the quarters and substantial increase made in the lower horizontal member, resulting in the estimated deflection shown in Fig. 1.3(b), with the measured deflection added to show the good correlation obtained. Strictly, the calculated curve should be read from the adjusted datum, which passes through the true support points.

Some very similar conclusions were independently drawn by Yettram and Smith [4] in an exercise using finite element techniques.

The message to designers of future cars is quite clear; allow sufficient

G. J. M. Botham

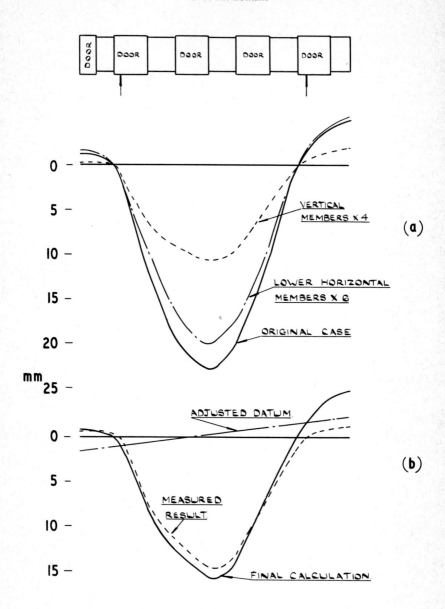

FIG. 1.3. Effect on varying certain member stiffnesses on the vertical deflection of the structure of a London Transport C69 surface line car, determined by two-dimensional framework analysis.

width in quarter panels adjacent to large doorways. Depending on particular circumstances, a width of 0·3–0.5 m appears to be the minimum requirement.

1.5   TESTING OF CAR BODY STRUCTURES

Despite the detailed information on stresses and deflections given by three-dimensional finite element analysis, it is still considered necessary to carry out a series of static structural tests on prototype or first-off bodies. This is for a number of reasons. Due to the size and complexity of the structures, an extremely finely resolved idealisation would lead to an un-handleable amount of data, stress concentrations may not be predicted, and joint behaviour may not be as assumed, particularly in riveted areas. Finally, in some extreme conditions of loading, some non-linear behaviour of the structure produced by local yielding of material may be tolerable when seen in the context of a comprehensive test.

A typical test program commences with mounting a bare body shell on supports representative of its bogies and enclosing it in a rig capable of applying longitudinal compression. Vertical loading is applied in increments, representing shell mass, masses of equipment, interior fittings, etc., passenger loading to an agreed maximum, such as a full-seated load plus standees at a density of $8/m^2$ and a percentage representing vertical impact. There are a number of options for the means of applying this loading, such as with hydraulic or pneumatic cylinders, linked to earth or to suitable masses, water cans or bags, or simply cast-iron weights in handleable sizes. Although this latter method appears at first sight crude and expensive in terms of labour, it does give the advantage of accurate distribution of mass on to the car floor, and the use of roller track inside the shell reduces the physical labour to a minimum. Longitudinal compression is applied by a hydraulic cylinder acting on to the car coupler or a representation of it and this is carried out at the two extremes of passenger loading. A typical requirement for a rapid transit car is that it will withstand, without significant damage, a force of about 800 kN applied in this manner.

Another test which is performed, and which has particular relevance to body panel stability and sliding door clearances, is to subject the laden shell to a torque applied by hydraulic cylinders, acting in the manner of a skew-symmetrical load transfer at the body support positions. Although the amount of twist applied may in the first instance be arbitrarily selected, the torsional stiffness of the shell is measured and the twist angle then related with suspension stiffnesses and known or assumed maximum angle of track twist over which the vehicle will need to operate.

Figure 1.4 shows a typical test in progress, this body shell being for London Transport's 1973 Tube Stock for the Piccadilly Line.

FIG. 1.4. Static structural testing of the body shell of the London Transport 1973 tube car for the Piccadilly line.

Finally a test which has been performed on recent designs consists of vibrating the shell with an out-of-balance mass, driven through an infinitely variable speed gear, as depicted in Fig. 1.5. This enables a measurement of the first natural vertical bending frequency to be made, although it must be realised that, since the body is at this stage on rigid supports, the results are not realistically related to the true service conditions. Nevertheless, it is considered that this simple test is worth doing for information and further work is being done to relate its results to the eventual vibrational behavior of the shells, including performances of the test on finished vehicles mounted on their bogies.

Instrumentation normally consists of electrical resistance strain gauges,

FIG. 1.5. Mechanical vibrator fixed to car underframe consisting of out-of-balance mass, infinitely variable hydraulic drive and electric motor.

at 200–300 locations in the shell and deflection measurements at 20–30 points. Some additional rule measurements are made of such dimensions as bodyside aperture diagonals, sliding door clearances, etc.

It is not easy to quantify the benefits or influence of such testing on design, since the effect of operating vehicles without the modifications introduced as a result of the tests is largely a matter of conjecture. It does not, however, need an over-vivid imagination to picture the effect which may be produced if serious structural deficiencies become apparent after a fleet of vehicles have commenced revenue-earning service. The author can recall only one test in which the car was given a clean bill of health without any modification whatever, whilst at the other extreme, extensive stiffening of the structure was found necessary in some other cases.

As experience mounts in the application of finite element techniques, it may be possible to reduce the amount of data recorded in the testing, although for reasons previously stated it will remain desirable to carry out some form of loading test on new designs at the bare shell stage.

PART 2: NOISE

1.6 ENVIRONMENTAL NOISE

Urban rapid transit vehicle noise has two distinct aspects, viz. the environmental problem of non-travellers subjected to noise in their homes and, secondly, the interior noise levels in the vehicles.

From the environmental viewpoint there is no doubt that railway noise in this country in general engenders few public complaints in comparison with aircraft and motor vehicle noise, despite the fact that peak levels are in many cases as high [5]. One of the reasons for this may be that almost all lines are long established and the majority of affected residents were aware of, and accepted, the situation when moving in.

This does not, however, mean that the question can be completely ignored. The future increase in number and extent of rail rapid transit systems will lead to the construction of new lines in addition to adaptation of existing ones. In the present climate of public reaction to noise as a form of pollution, and reinforced by some successes against authorities in actions such as Stansted and the M6 Motorway through Birmingham, it is quite certain that new systems creating excessive noise in urban areas will not be tolerated.

The control of environmental noise lies largely in the hands of the planners and civil engineers rather than the vehicle builder and Table 1.1

TABLE 1.1.

Parameters of planning and civil engineering having influence on environmental noise and vibration from rapid transit systems

	References
Elevation of track: deep tunnel, shallow tunnel, surface, elevated	6,7,9,11,15
Proximity to dwellings, etc.	6,9,11,15
Climatic conditions	6
Axleload	6,7
Use of sound barrier walls	6,9,11
Tunnel construction and dimensions	7,9,15
Form of track bed: ballast, concrete, asphalt, etc.	6–8,11,15
Form of rail to sleeper and sleeper to track bed mounting	6,7,11
Welded or jointed track: form of joints	6,15
Condition of rail and wheel surfaces: use of rail grinding treatments	6–9,15
Track curvature	6,9,15
Vehicle speed and frequency, acceleration and braking	6–9

summarises the major parameters which have influence. The major noise source from an electric-powered system originates from the rail/wheel contact and noise levels from different rapid transit vehicles passing over the same track will vary only slightly. Comprehensive research in, for example, Germany [6–10] has identified the features of the system construction which influence noise levels and quantified the variations resulting from these; for example, types of track bed, welded or jointed rail, effects of tight curves, rail surface condition, effects of wayside sound barrier walls, effect of over-bridges, etc. Serious noise problems arising on the largely elevated Shinkansen (high speed railway) lines in Japan have caused a massive research programme to be undertaken, resulting in a great deal of knowledge being gained [11].

1.7   VEHICLE INTERIOR NOISE

High noise levels inside vehicles rarely seem to produce complaints from the travelling public. Possible reasons may be: (a) passengers are accustomed to it; (b) passengers are benefiting from the travel; and (c) other passenger environmental aspects, vehicle ride and air comfort, may predominate. This is not, however, seen by the author to form even the makings of an excuse for not attempting to produce systems and vehicles having acceptably low noise levels.

Whilst the influence of the civil engineering factors mentioned previously on noise level experienced by passengers is very great, the design and construction of the vehicle itself is equally important to interior noise levels.

Table 1.2 lists the major factors which can have some bearing on the final result. It is emphasised that these are not given in any order of significance, which will in any case vary from one design to another, but with most designs the final item—sealing the body against ingress of airborne noise—will almost certainly be the first consideration. It would be quite possible to produce a vehicle as quiet as required if all the other conflicting considerations of design, such as low mass, capital cost, etc. were ignored— which plainly they cannot be. The essence of noise control, therefore, is to obtain the desired result with minimum additional mass and cost and to ensure that all the effort spent on obtaining it is not nullified by some relatively minor detail. Examination of Table 1.2 shows that the design of almost every one of the tens of thousands of parts which go to make up the whole can have an effect on the total noise, significantly or otherwise,

TABLE 1.2.

Parameters of vehicle design and construction having influence on interior noise

	References
1. Bogies	
Wheels: type of wheel construction, resilience, material, damping treatment, tread surface condition	6–10,15
Primary suspension: spring stiffness and damping characteristics in all planes	6
Secondary suspension: spring stiffness and damping characteristics in all planes	
Motor and transmission: type, power	6,7
Vibration paths short circuiting suspension	
Brakes: type	6,15
Current collection: type	
2. Bodies	
Form of construction of shell: materials, jointing, etc.	
Interior finish lining: construction, materials, etc.	
Floor: construction, materials, etc.	
Windows: single/double glazed, glass thickness, mounting	12,16
Doors: number, type, construction, materials, etc.	
Heating and ventilating: type, acoustic treatments, vibration isolation (fans)	
Auxiliary machines: noise emission, vibration isolation	7,15
Surface densities of all areas of shell	
Panel damping treatments: extent and material	
Absorptive treatments in structure	
Absorptive materials in interior	
Interior layout	9
Effect of passengers	9,15
Air sealing of body: effect of opening windows, door seals, ventilation inlets/outlets, workmanship and detail design.	

and accordingly every engineer, designer and detail draughtsman concerned with a particular vehicle is in a position to affect the final result.

1.8   DESIRABLE INTERIOR NOISE LEVELS

No international or national specifications have yet been drafted to lay down the noise levels which should not be exceeded inside rail vehicles of any type, and indeed this would be no simple matter. A preliminary move in this direction was, however, commenced in 1969 with the first drafting of an ISO Specification 'Acoustics—measurement of noise inside railbound vehicles', now nearing finalisation of international agreement. Whilst this document does not attempt to specify actual levels, it establishes a method of measurement aimed at obtaining repeatable and comparable measurements, a necessary prerequisite to the specification of actual noise levels.

Some years ago, British Railways tentatively adopted levels not to be exceeded in various types of passenger vehicles, as given by Koffman [12]. These were in terms of ISO Noise Ratings, which were preferred to the more universally used 'A' weighted levels, and for suburban stock a level of N.R. 70 was specified.

The establishment of any sort of generalised noise level specifications for rapid transit vehicles may not, however, have very much practical value. System parameters vary so greatly that noise levels in operation may bear little resemblance to those measured in some standard test conditions, as for example in the ISO draft specification referred to previously. The acoustic performance of a particular vehicle should be considered in the context of the complete transit system.

One possible criterion for assessing a comfortable noise level is by reference to speech interference levels [13]. It may be considered desirable for a passenger to be able to speak to a companion on the adjoining or facing seat without undue effort, whilst at the same time the background noise level prevents the conversation from carrying much further. Taking the distance between speaker and listener to be 0·6–0·3 m the S.I.L. would need to be in the range 59–65 dB (average of the three octaves between 600 and 4·8 kHz). With the shape of sound spectrum usually encountered in rapid transit vehicles, this would correspond very approximately to levels of 70–80 dBA.

1.9 EXAMPLES OF THE APPLICATION OF NOISE ANALYSIS TO ASSESSMENT OF DESIGN FEATURES

Where vehicles are fitted with opening windows or vents, which is fairly common, there can be a dramatic difference in the interior noise levels between the open and closed situation. The effect on the transmission loss obtained from a typical car structure having windows provided with openable top vents, approximately 240 mm deep and opening inwards 90 mm at the top edge, is estimated as shown in Fig. 1.6 for a range of

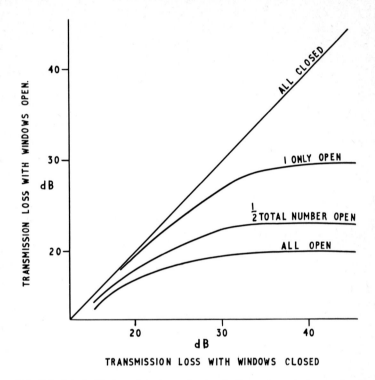

FIG. 1.6. Calculated effect on interior noise level of opening windows related to a range of transmission losses for the sealed body.

'fully sealed' transmission losses. In a series of tests on a number of European systems last year [17], comparable measurements were made with such windows open and closed. The effect is, of course, most pronounced in tunnel conditions, where the sound field around the sides and roof is intensified, and Fig. 1.7 shows one example of such measurement in which a difference of 12 dBA was found.

Another method of comparison attempted, which was not so reliable since it involved measurements from at least two different designs of car, was to assess the performance of 'plug' doors relative to doors sliding within pockets in the bodyside wall. Plug doors sit flush with the outer body panels and open by moving outwards before sliding along the exterior; they can therefore produce a more efficient seal in the closed position.

Measurements were made on the centre lines of cars in both the doorway

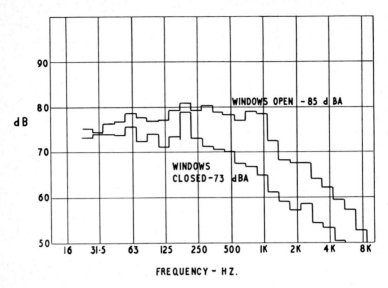

Fig. 1.7. Noise spectrum inside a rapid transit car travelling in tunnel with windows open and closed.

region and away from the doors in a seat bay region. Again, in tunnel conditions, little difference in noise level could be found between doorway and seat bay in a car fitted with plug doors, whereas on cars with sliding doors increases in sound level from seat bay to doorway of from 4 to 10 dBA were measured, thus indicating the degree of benefit expected from the plug door feature.

1.10   AREAS FOR FURTHER RESEARCH

The acoustic performance of a great many existing conventional systems and vehicles is now available through the literature and private reports, etc. The identification of the features of design leading to a particular vehicle being regarded as noisy, or quiet, is less well established although much progress is being made in the quantification of the effects of design variations.

Calculation of the transmission loss of the various areas of car bodies can usually be estimated with sufficient accuracy, but the contribution to overall levels caused by the transmission or generation of noise due to vibration of the structure is largely unknown. Recent work by Bickerstaffe *et al.* [14] on separating the airborne and structure-borne contributions in a Pullman car appears to be a particularly fruitful field of research and it is desirable that such investigations will eventually lead to the ability to make more reasoned assessments of the amount and nature of acoustic treatments required to isolate or suppress structural vibration.

ACKNOWLEDGEMENTS

Grateful acknowledgements are made to the management of Metro-Cammell Ltd, for permission to publish this paper.

REFERENCES

1. Dodd, R. J. M. 'The Application of Finite Elements in Mechanical Engineering Design.' Application of the British Railways finite element program NEWPAC to railway vehicle structures—Applied Mechanics Group, I. Mech. E. Conference (Oct. 1962).
2. Allen, D. N. de G. and Windle, D. W. 'The Use of Aluminium in Railway Rolling Stock'. Stress determination in coach frames by electronic computation—I. Loco. E. and Aluminium Development Assoc. Symposium (May 1960).
3. Anon. 'Strength of Bodies of Passenger Coaches', O.R.E. of U.I.C. Report B7/RP 7/E, April 1972.
4. Yettram, A. L. and Smith, D. J. 'A Preliminary Investigation into the Structural Behaviour of an Underground Railway Coach.' Conference on Stress, Vibration and Noise Analysis in Vehicles, University of Aston in Birmingham (September 1974).
5. Various. Symposium on Noise in Transportation, 8th International Congress on Acoustics, University of Southampton (July 1974).
6. Stüber, C. 'Airborne and Structure-borne Noise of Railways' (Ref. 5 above).
7. Hauck, G., Willenbrink, L. and Stüber, C. 'Körperschall- und Luftschallmessungen an unterirdischen Schienenbahnen', Eisenbahntechnische Rundschau (July/Aug. 1972 and July/Aug. 1973).
8. Anon. 'Physikalish-Technische Bundesanstalt', Bericht über Geräuschmessungen an Schienenfahrzeugen. Gesh. Nr. 5.22-25890/70.
9. Anon. 'Geräuschsituation bei Stadtbahnen', Verein Deutscher Ingenieure—Richtlinien VDI 2716 (Aug. 1973).
10. Bugarcic, H. (Sept.–Dec. 1973). 'U-Bahn-Versuche über das Zusammenwirken von Rad und Schiene hinsichtlich Geräuschentwicklung, Laufverhalten, Stossüberfragung, Reibung, Abnützung und Wellenbildung', *Leichtbau der Verkehrsfahrzeuge*, **17** (5/6).

11. Ban, Y. and Miyamoto, T. 'Noise Control of High Speed Railways' (Ref. 5 above).
12. Koffman, J. L. (1967/68). 'Design for Comfort', I. Loco. E. Pap. No. 696, Vol. 57/5.
13. Harris, C. M., *et al.* (1957). *Handbook of Noise Control*, McGraw-Hill.
14. Bickerstaff, R., Eade, P. W., Hardy, A. J. E., Peters, S. and Woodward, B. 'Internal and External Train Noise' (Ref. 5 above).
15. Berglund, H. (July 1972). Stockholm tackles the noise problem, *Railway Gazette International*.
16. Anon. (June 1970). *The Airborne Sound Insulation of Glass*, Publication by Messrs. Pilkington Bros Ltd.
17. Taylor, R. M. 'Report on Noise Levels of Various European Rapid Transit Systems', unpublished private report by Rupert Taylor & Partners Ltd.

2

Finite Element Stress Analysis as an Aid to the Design of Automotive Components

M. R. KINGSTON
Joseph Lucas Ltd

SUMMARY

The finite element method has been used for the stress analysis of numerous automotive components manufactured within the Lucas Group. The results allowed both failure predictions and suggestions for design improvement to be made for each component. Three specific examples are included for problems arising from basically different areas of vehicle design. A diesel fuel injector nozzle, a handbrake linkage lever and a roller clutch sleeve design are the problems described. The reasons for the investigation, the specification of the problem, and a brief interpretation of the results, are discussed for each case.

General observations are made, from the stress analyst user viewpoint, on the application of a finite element computer program as a design aid to be used directly by any designer or development engineer.

2.1 INTRODUCTION

2.1.1 Stress Analysis in the Automotive Auxiliary Industry

In the automotive auxiliary and accessory industry the components produced may be of very different types and sizes, from flat plates of very simple shape to complex three-dimensional solid bodies. In their operating environments the components may be subjected to various types of applied loading conditions, including centrifugal, pressure and temperature loadings, and prescribed displacements. With the rising costs of materials, over-design and resultant material wastage may be extremely costly for a high volume production item. Failure of the component in service may produce a high service return rate which is extremely undesirable from both the aspects of high replacement costs and damage to the prestige of the product. Stress analysis at the design stage is essential if service failures are to be avoided and near-optimum designs are to be achieved for the specified operating conditions.

2.1.2 A General Stress Analysis Facility—Finite Element Programs

For stress analysis to be performed at the design stage by any designer or development engineer, a general facility is necessary which is straightforward to use and requires no specialised expertise. The finite element method is ideally suited to forming the basis of such a facility and provides a much tried and proven technique for the stress analysis of arbitrary structures subjected to general applied loading conditions.

In the finite element method, the object under examination is considered to be split into a number of smaller component parts, or elements, of simple shape and specific deformation behaviour. Many element types are available for this idealisation procedure, but experience has indicated that the isoparametric class is the most suitable for the majority of applications. The finite element analysis procedure is formed by the solution of a set of simultaneous equations which exactly represent the behaviour of this structural simplification for the component of interest. A comprehensive description of finite element theory is given in the text by Zienkiewicz [1]. The technique is ideally suited to formulation for the digital computer and appreciable computational expertise is required if an efficient solution procedure is to be produced. Many sophisticated finite element computer programs have been developed by different establishments, following various philosophies, and much duplication of effort has also occurred. Following the criteria that a finite element program (a) must be very straightforward to use, (b) must require no specialised expertise, (c) must allow both solid three-dimensional and two-dimensional problems to be analysed, and (d) must allow the application of general loading conditions, the BERSAFE [2] suite of programs has been used to solve numerous stress problems from all areas within the Lucas Group. This program contains a full range of element types, allows for general applied loading conditions and is organised for simplicity in setting up a problem. A major advantage of the finite element approach exists in the facility which allows several load cases to be analysed in one computer run, without appreciably increasing the computing cost.

2.1.3 Performing a Stress Analysis Exercise

In any stress analysis exercise there are three main stages. The engineering problem has to be fully specified, the analysis performed and the results interpreted.

(a) Problem specification

The physical restraints and forces experienced by the engineering component in its normal operating cycle must be translated into specific boundary conditions and applied loads. The finite element program allows displacement restrictions and conditions of symmetry to be imposed directly and simply. This enables problems to be substantially reduced in size to provide accurate results more economically. However, it may be extremely difficult to specify the applied loading and fixing conditions in precise terms.

It is essential, in any theoretical stress analysis investigation, for these applied loads and boundary conditions realistically to represent the physical operating conditions. Components are normally designed to an overload value or safety factor and this provides the loading situation for the required performance assessment.

At this stage it must also be clear which results are required and how they will be used, as this may well influence the problem formulation. If a comparison is required between the performance of two designs, appreciable simplifications of the situation into a two-dimensional form may well be perfectly adequate. This is normally the case with design exercises.

(*b*) *The analysis procedure*

Having specified the problem, performing the finite element analysis is a straightforward process requiring engineering commonsense and a methodical approach. The element idealisation has first to be constructed following the standard rules and then the data prepared for input to the computer program. In general, the finer the element idealisation the more accurate are the results produced. The results will converge towards the true situation as the fineness of the element subdivision is increased, provided that the problem has been set up correctly. From experience, the stress analyst knows the quality of results likely to be achieved from a chosen idealisation but accuracy is also checked wherever possible by examination of the resulting stress at the stress-free boundaries and at the loaded surfaces. The method produces a different accuracy at different regions of the component and a mesh should be constructed to provide relatively accurate results at the areas of interest.

Although very straightforward, the technique is laborious and much scope exists in this area for the development of simpler and more powerful automatic data preparation facilities. A two-dimensional mesh generation program has been developed within Lucas aimed at simplicity of use and this program has been linked with the finite element package on the time-sharing system of the central computer. This facility is available to most design and development areas throughout the organisation.

(*c*) *Interpretation of results*

Most stress investigations are concerned with elastic material behaviour and the results are based on the assumptions of ideal elasticity. However, this still allows some conclusions to be drawn about local plastic yielding of the material. The finite element analysis provides comprehensive displacement and stress information throughout the component being analysed. The program also produces principal stresses and the Von-Mises equivalent stress, which is a combined stress value which may be compared directly to the yield stress when considering possible plastic deformation of the component. The algebraically highest principal stress at a point represents the highest tensile stress experienced at that point and thus should be examined when considering failure.

Before examining the results in any detail it is essential to confirm that a valid analysis has been performed. This may be achieved by comparing any known conditions with the corresponding calculated results. For example, a normal principal stress at a stress-free surface should be equal to zero. Comparing reaction forces with the applied loads also provides a check. Where possible, classical solutions which reasonably approximate to part of the real engineering component should be evaluated to provide some confirmation of the finite element results.

Having established confidence in the analysis, the computer output must be presented in a form suitable for the specific problem, as stress contour plots or surface deformation plots, for example. Again, much time and effort may be saved by programs which aid in the presentation and interpretation of results.

Relating the appropriate stress results to basic material data and to the design specifications allows the required performance prediction to be produced for the component. Depending on the loading conditions, appropriate material-testing information must be available for this interpretation.

2.1.4   Specific Examples

Over recent years, numerous very different types of components manufactured within the Lucas Group have been analysed using the finite element technique. Three specific examples are included for problems arising from basically different areas of vehicle design; a diesel fuel injection nozzle, a handbrake linkage lever and a roller clutch sleeve design are the problems described. For each case, the reasons for the investigation, the specification of the problem and a brief interpretation of results are discussed.

2.2   DIESEL INJECTOR NOZZLE

2.2.1   Background

One factor deeply affecting the performance of diesel engines is the characteristic behaviour of the fuel injection system. The increasing restrictions being imposed on diesel engine manufacturers by exhaust emission legislation and the desire to extract maximum power from existing sizes of engines has produced a requirement for uprated performance from the injectors. In designing injectors for specific engines, it is possible that the fuel injection pressure may be raised and the nozzle and needle tip designs modified to achieve the desired operating improvement.

The injection nozzle, as illustrated in Fig. 2.1, forms a highly stressed engineering component which is subjected to both a pulsating pressure fatigue loading and an impact contact stress loading which is produced by the needle valve seating to provide the necessary sharp cut-off to the fuel flow. It is essential that the stresses induced in the nozzle are at a level such that fatigue failure will not occur.

The investigation described in the following section is concerned with the internal hydrostatic pressure loading. The needle contact stressing problem has been studied by McCallion and Hallam [3] and will not be discussed in this paper.

2.2.2 Problem Specification

Design and test experience with nozzles has indicated that with uprated injection pressures the critically stressed areas would be expected to arise in the region of the nozzle tip and especially near the injection holes. Localising the stress investigation to the tip, a fully three-dimensional analysis is necessary to examine the stress conditions around the holes. However, for the overall stress distribution, an axisymmetric analysis allows a substantially more refined and economical solution to be produced. Both an axisymmetric and three-dimensional analysis have been performed for a typical production injection nozzle subjected to a constant internal hydrostatic pressure.

Under operating conditions, the entire internal surface of the nozzle may not experience the peak injection pressure at the same instant. However, the assumption of constant internal pressure should provide a good representation of the most severe pressure distribution arising in practice. Again, the situation inside the injection hole is unknown but by considering two load cases, one with zero applied pressure inside the hole and the second with the constant pressure also acting inside the hole, two bounds may be produced to the real situation.

The finite element mesh chosen for the axisymmetric analysis is shown in Fig. 2.2 (left). The mesh was constructed by hand, following the usual rules, and was expected to produce results of a fairly high order of

M. R. *Kingston*

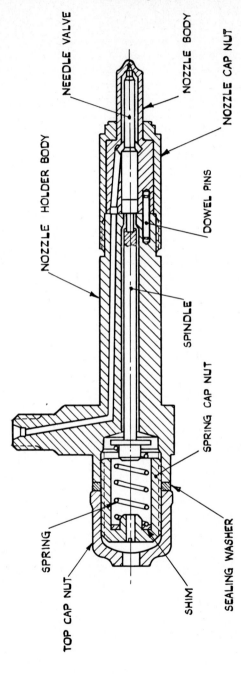

NEEDLE VALVE

NOZZLE BODY

NOZZLE CAP NUT

NOZZLE HOLDER BODY

DOWEL PINS

SPINDLE

SPRING CAP NUT

SPRING

TOP CAP NUT

SHIM

SEALING WASHER

Fig. 2.1. Typical diesel fuel injector arrangement.

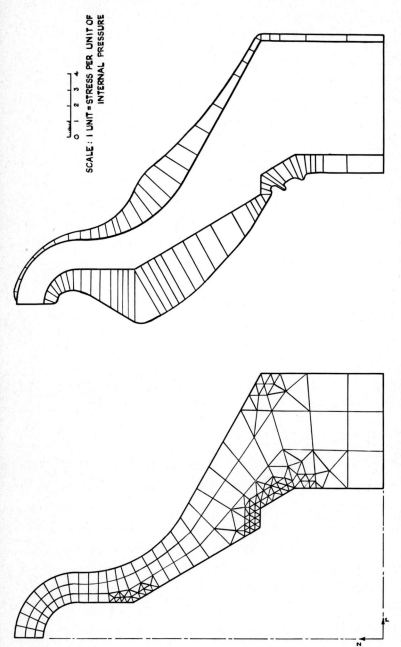

SCALE : 1 UNIT = STRESS PER UNIT OF INTERNAL PRESSURE

0 1 2 3 4

FIG. 2.2. Mesh and stress distribution plotted on nozzle half-sections for the axisymmetric case. (Left) Finite element ideali-sation, fine mesh. (Right) Hoop stress variation at the surface.

M. R. Kingston

accuracy. Considering the fully three-dimensional problem, a specific nozzle with four equispaced and similarly positioned injection holes was chosen for analysis. The holes may be centred on a skew circle whose axis is inclined to that of the nozzle body. In this way the axis of each hole has a different inclination to the nozzle centre line. For the case

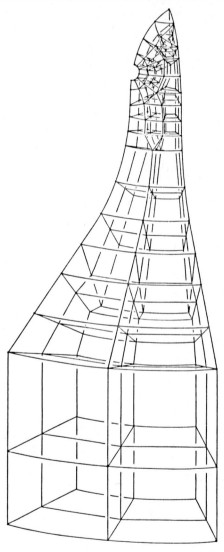

Fig. 2.3. Finite element idealisation for the three-dimensional case.

chosen, symmetry and a suitable choice of boundary conditions allowed the problem to be reduced to considering a one-eighth segment only, as shown in Fig. 2.3.

For both of the analyses, the following restraints were applied:

1. Nodes on the axis at the tip were fixed to the axis and were not allowed any radial displacement.
2. Nodes on the foreshortened end base were fixed to remain on the same Z-plane and hence were allowed no axial displacement.
3. For the three-dimensional case, nodes on the places of symmetry were allowed no normal displacements.

The simplification formed by shortening the nozzle body was expected to have a negligible influence on the stresses in the areas of interest and this was justified by the subsequent results.

2.2.3   Results

In the following presentation of results, diagrams are given of the hoop stress only, for comparison purposes. The surface stresses are plotted on half-section outlines of the nozzle, such that the hoop stress magnitude at a point from which a line emanates is directly proportional to the length of that line. Where possible the lines are drawn normal to the nozzle surface. Figure 2.2 (right) shows the stress distribution for the axisymmetric case and Fig. 2.4 the results for the three-dimensional problem for both of the applied loading cases, with and without the applied pressure inside the hole. Figure 2.4 also shows the stress plot on the section formed by the other plane of symmetry and represents both load cases, as a negligible difference exists between the two sets of results in this area.

A further axisymmetric analysis with a relatively coarse idealisation showed a negligible difference except near the stress concentrations, demonstrating that an acceptable accuracy had been achieved. The three-dimensional mesh at the tip and around the injection hole was also refined and reanalysed, producing little change in the peak stresses at the hole. A photoelastic exercise has also been performed on the same nozzle geometries and the results show good agreement with the finite element work.

Figures 2.2 and 2.4 illustrate that the maximum stresses occur in the seat area but that stresses of the same order also occur at the holes together with a high stress gradient. To relate these stresses to fatigue life, basic pulsating pressure fatigue information is required for thick-walled cylinders composed of the nozzle material. Interpreting the stress results

M. R. Kingston

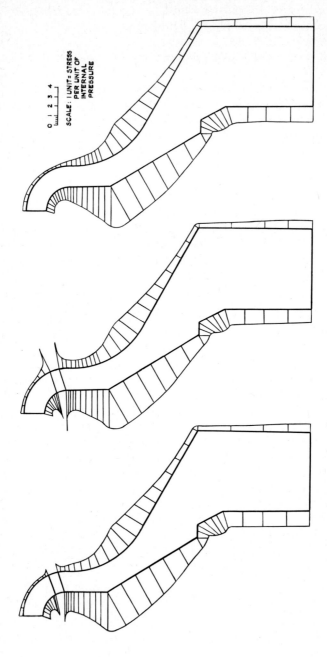

SCALE: 1 UNIT = STRESS PER UNIT OF INTERNAL PRESSURE

0 1 2 3 4

FIG. 2.4. Hoop stress variation plotted on nozzle half-sections for the three-dimensional case. (Left) No pressure in hole, section through hole axis. (Middle) Pressure also in hole, section through hole axis. (Right) Section midway between holes.

in this way, the present normal operating pressure produces stresses which lie well below the fatigue limit for all the nozzle designs which have been examined. If required, the uprated injection pressure, which would be expected to cause nozzle failure, can be predicted.

Design changes which reduce the peak stress values will improve the fatigue life of the nozzle. A comparison between a proposed design of nozzle and a nozzle of known performance will minimise the effects of unknown quantities such as residual stresses and surface finish. In the diesel injection nozzle development program, it was required to assess the performance of different nozzle-tip profiles. This was achieved for each design using basically the same axisymmetric idealisation, distorted by a minimum amount to match the new outline, so as to maintain a consistent accuracy of results and facilitate the required evaluation. The results are not presented but are similar to those shown in Fig. 2.2.

It has already been noted that the load conditions inside the injection hole have a negligible influence on the stress conditions on the symmetry plane midway between holes, and Fig. 2.4 (right) represents both load cases on this section. Comparison of this diagram with the other two curves from the three-dimensional analysis shows only a localised difference at the holes and compares well with the axisymmetric results. It may be concluded that for a general four-hole nozzle with the holes positioned on a skew circle, each hole may be investigated as a separate problem and be simplified to considering a one-eighth segment.

As the axisymmetric idealisation is a relatively easy and cheap problem to analyse, it would be extremely convenient to be able to estimate the peak tensile stress around the hole from these results. The axisymmetric analysis produces hoop and meridional stresses at the position of the injector holes. It has been found that substituting these values into the stress concentration formulae for a flat plate containing a circular hole and subjected to biaxial stress provides a good indication of the maximum tensile stress occurring at the hole.

It may be concluded that the finite element method is ideal for assessing the effect of geometrical design changes on the nozzle stresses produced by the internal pressure acting at injection. An initial axisymmetric analysis should be performed for new nozzle designs to provide a speedy and economical solution which also allows the peak stresses at the injection holes to be estimated. If better accuracy is required at the holes, a three-dimensional analysis should be performed for a segment formed by the plane which cuts both the hole and nozzle body axes and the axial plane midway between holes.

2.3   HANDBRAKE LINKAGE LEVER

2.3.1   Background

A new styling of a passenger car required a modified handbrake
operating system and, in particular, minor redesign of the linkage lever.
Figure 2.5 illustrates the principle of operation of the handbrake linkage

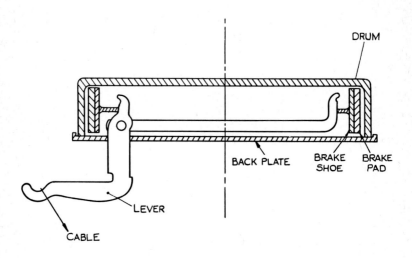

Fig. 2.5. The handbrake linkage assembly.

assembly, where application of the handbrake increases the cable tension,
causing the lever to rotate and so applying the brake shoes. The moment
about the pivot, produced by the cable tension and tending to rotate the
lever, is then balanced by a reaction force at the brake shoe contact surface.

A stress analysis for the lever arm was required so that the likelihood
of failure could be predicted. If failures were expected, possible improvements could be suggested to assist in modifying the design. Restrictions
imposed by the mechanics of the lever and the geometry of other components of the braking system prohibit the improvement of the design in
certain areas. The plate has a certain specified maximum thickness; the
lever arm lengths are prescribed and the shoulders at the lever corner are
defined from other considerations.

The proposed manufacturing technique for the lever is by punching,
which may well induce appreciable residual stresses. Any theoretical stress

analysis cannot allow for such residual stresses which must be determined experimentally and superposed for the full stress evaluation.

2.3.2 Problem Specification

As the lever is a flat plate with in-plane applied loading conditions, a plane stress idealisation provides a good representation of the real situation. The hand-generated finite element mesh is shown in Fig. 2.6 and was

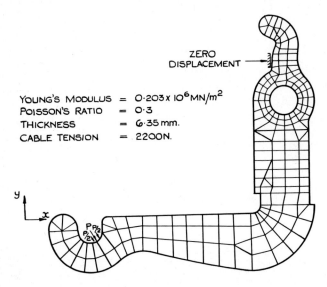

YOUNG'S MODULUS = $0.203 \times 10^6 \, MN/m^2$
POISSON'S RATIO = 0.3
THICKNESS = 6.35 mm.
CABLE TENSION = 2200 N.

FIG. 2.6. Problem specification for the linkage lever.

constructed following the normal rules. It was considered from experience that the area between the pivot hole and the brake shoe seat was the main region of interest and a fairly fine mesh was thus required in this area.

Although the operation of the lever appears straightforward, representing the loading and fixing conditions in terms of specific boundary conditions and applied forces presents an appreciable problem. The following three loading/fixing conditions were introduced to simulate the practical situation: (a) cable tension loading; (b) brake shoe reaction condition; and (c) pivot fixing condition.

(a) Cable tension loading

The value used for the handbrake cable tension of 2200 N is the specified design load which represents a maximum tension developed in the cable at each wheel when the brake is very severely applied. This load was represented by a set of three point nodal forces resolved into components in the two coordinate directions. A normal operating maximum cable tension for a hard pull may be expected to be around 1100 N at each wheel.

(b) Brake shoe reaction condition

This reaction boundary condition is imposed by restricting the nodes at the contact zone to having zero displacement in the x-direction, as indicated in Fig. 2.6.

(c) Pivot fixing condition

As stresses develop in the lever during the application of the handbrake, the lever will deform so as to rotate slightly about the pivot. The physical conditions thus allow negligible radial displacements by limited tangential displacements at the inner surface of the lever pivot hole. This situation cannot be adequately represented by the usual type of displacement

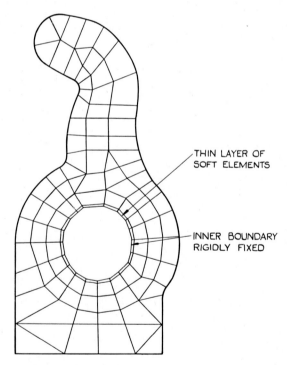

THIN LAYER OF
SOFT ELEMENTS

INNER BOUNDARY
RIGIDLY FIXED

FIG. 2.7. Element idealisation for the pivot fixing condition.

boundary conditions where points on the surface are specified as having zero displacements in one or both of the coordinate directions, as this produces an artificial stress concentration effect.

Using the approach proposed by Cunnell [4], a thin row of soft elements, with the same Poisson's ratio but Young's modulus reduced by a factor of a thousand, was added to the hole surface and the inner boundary of the new elements fixed rigidly. This arrangement is illustrated in Fig. 2.7. The layer of soft elements allows high compressive but negligible shear stresses to develop at the boundary, so allowing the pivot fixing conditions to be realistically represented. The calculated stress distribution in the lever near the pivot should form a good approximation to conditions arising in service.

2.3.3 Results

Having specified the problem, the data were prepared and submitted for analysis by the finite element program, and computer output obtained for the full stress and displacement information. A preliminary assessment of the results indicated that a valid analysis had been performed. The results are illustrated in Figs. 2.8 and 2.9 in the form of contour plots of the maximum in-plane principal stress and the Von-Mises equivalent stress.

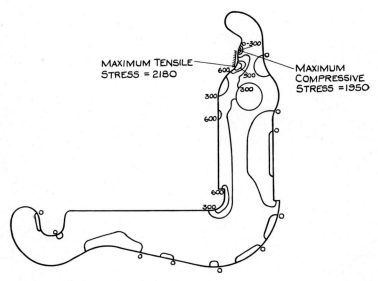

FIG. 2.8. Algebraically highest in-plane principal stress contour plot. (Stresses in MN/m².)

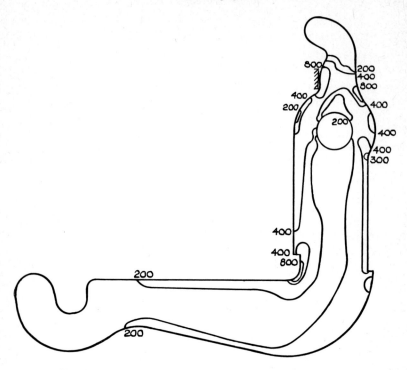

FIG. 2.9. Equivalent stress contour plot. (Stresses in MN/m².)

The following physical properties are representative of the mild steel proposed for the production material for the lever, in the un-heat-treated state: U.T.S. = 540 MN/m²; Yield stress = 350 MN/m².

Comparing the above yield stress value to the contours shown in Fig. 2.9, illustrates that a large area of the lever will have yielded with subsequent redistribution of stress. The contour plots represent elastic material behaviour and do not account for plastic yielding. However, the diagrams indicate that ultimate failure may be expected with the crack initiating from the position of the maximum tensile stress and propagating across to the pivot hole.

As discussed previously, the applied cable load of 2200 N is extremely severe. The stresses may be scaled directly with the cable tension loading, which allows the lever to be assessed for a more realistic operating load. A realistic maximum load of 1100 N produces half the stress values presented. Scaling may also be applied to the results for changes in plate thickness.

The stress situation may be improved by increasing the plate thickness, modifying the external profile of the lever in highly stressed regions and changing the position of the pivot hole. Prohibitive design restrictions, imposed by the mechanics of the lever, the geometry of other components of the braking system, and the vehicle design, do not allow these modifications to be implemented. Changing the material properties by either heat treatment or changing the material, provides the only feasible solution and this approach is being investigated. Scaling the results presented using a reasonable cable tension overload value allows the maximum stress to be estimated which must be less than the design stress level for the material. This would be the fatigue limit for a specified number of handbrake operations. Having defined a required fatigue limit, selection of material and heat treatment can be made.

It may be concluded that a layer of low stiffness elements can allow a realistic representation of a pivot fixing condition. With the proposed material for the lever and the specified cable load, failure would be expected. The required material properties, and hence a range of possible materials, may be evaluated for the lever using the stress results presented and a realistic maximum cable load.

2.4   ROLLER CLUTCH SLEEVE

2.4.1   Background

For a pre-engaged starter motor, the motor torque is transmitted to the engine flywheel by a roller clutch assembly similar to the one illustrated in Fig. 2.10. When the motor is energised, the armature rotates so as to lock up the roller clutch assembly and so apply the starting torque to the pinion and hence also to the engine. As the rollers rotate to lock up the clutch, the sleeve experiences an impact type of loading which is greater than the

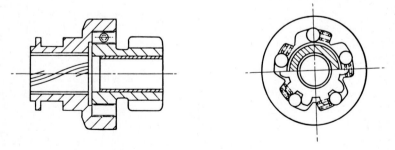

Fig. 2.10. The roller clutch assembly.

loading produced by the static starting torque applied to the locked clutch, by an amount defined by the impact factor for that clutch/motor combination. The magnitude of the impact factor varies from machine to machine and may be reduced by sequentially energising the field coils of the motor.

Although all component parts of a roller clutch are highly stressed, the sleeve forms a particularly severe case for which a detailed design assessment is essential if fatigue failure or material wastage are to be avoided. In the past, new clutches have evolved from the depth of experience acquired from the development and performance of existing clutch designs. A simplified technique was used to design for a required stress level, where the stress-raising effects of spring buttresses and other geometrical irregularities were ignored. Evidently an accurate stress analysis for a realistic applied loading would provide a more critical design assessment. The finite element method of stress analysis has been used to provide this assessment.

There are three main types of sleeve which are of different sizes but of basically similar design. Much experience and practical failure information exists on two of these drive units, but a new design required a full design evaluation. The work was required to assess and compare the performance of the three drive units and to use available failure data to predict the performance of the new design.

2.4.2 Problem Specification

It may be seen from Fig. 2.10 that the sleeves form three-dimensional geometrical shapes, with complex applied loading conditions. The clutch has torque input through the splines on the sleeve and is reacted at the pinion through the locked roller/sleeve assembly. A high contact stress loading is experienced at the rollers, which must equilibrate the torque of the motor.

Although the problem is fully three dimensional, to analyse the sleeve using 3D solid finite elements would necessitate a lengthy and expensive investigation procedure. With most three-dimensional problems, simplifications can usually be made such that an almost identical situation is represented by a simple two-dimensional plate problem or a two-dimensional axisymmetric system. The finite element stress analysis of such 2D problems may be accomplished very rapidly, cheaply and accurately, using the automatic mesh generation facility. This approach is particularly appropriate when a comparison between the performance of different designs is required, where one of the designs has known performance, and thus specific stress values are not required to a high level of accuracy.

The behaviour of the clutch sleeve may be fairly well represented by the correlated results from two independent two-dimensional analyses. A two-dimensional plate analysis on a section at right angles to the axis and through the rollers provides a detailed stress distribution in the region of the sleeve known to be highly stressed and illustrates the stress-raising effects of geometrical irregularities such as the spring buttresses. This analysis, however, ignores the stiffening effect of the back wall and the splined hub. A second investigation for an axisymmetric representation of the sleeve, on a section through the axis, may be compared to the classical thick cylinder solution for the sleeve/roller operating zone to provide a detailed indication of the influence on the stress distribution of the rest of the sleeve body.

(a) *Plane stress analysis*

The stress behaviour of the pinion end of the clutch can be represented by a plane stress simplification, illustrated by the finite element mesh shown in Fig. 2.11. The mesh was constructed manually using plane stress

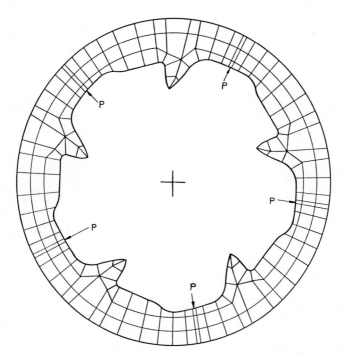

FIG. 2.11. Finite element mesh: plane stress analysis (X100 sleeve).

isoparametric elements and was used for each of the three sleeves, the geometry being changed to represent the correct profile for the three designs. Although the sleeve has repeated symmetry, the complete section had to be analysed due to the Phase I version of the finite element program not allowing this type of boundary condition to be applied.

In setting up the finite element mesh, the applied loading had to be considered such that the roller contact load could be applied in a realistic fashion. This representative loading was applied as a pressure acting over one element face whose side was set up to correspond to the contact area predicted from Hertz contact theory, where the roller force was directly calculated from the geometry of the sleeve cam profile and the motor impact torque.

Boundary conditions for the sleeve also pose a difficulty, since in the real three-dimensional problem, the roller contact force acting on the sleeve is reacted at the splines on the hub of the sleeve. For the pinion end of the sleeve, which the first analysis is considering, the restraint is transmitted through the back wall. Ignoring the stiffening effect of the back wall, which will be considered in the next section, experience has shown that sleeve fixing conditions have a negligible effect. The restrictions used in the analyses allow radial deflections only for the four points on the axes on the outer surface.

(b) Axisymmetric analysis

The stiffening effect of the back wall for three clutches has been examined using automatically generated meshes, as illustrated in Fig. 2.12 for the so called X100 sleeve. In the splined part of the sleeve and in the roller contact area, averaged internal radii were assumed for each case. A relatively fine mesh was used, as fairly accurate results were required at

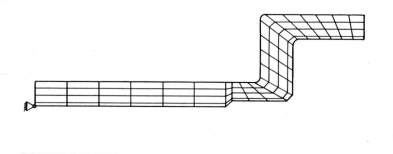

FIG. 2.12. Finite element mesh: axisymmetric analysis (X100 sleeve).

the pinion end of the clutch. The mesh generation program allows any required degree of fineness without any additional data preparation.

The purpose of these analyses was to investigate the effect on the stresses, determined in the plane stress analysis, of the neglected part of the sleeve configuration. This is most easily achieved by performing the axisymmetric analysis with an applied constant pressure loading over the roller contact region and comparing the stress results with the equivalent Lamé's solution. Stress magnification factors may then be deduced and applied to the two-dimensional results from the previous analyses.

For the axisymmetric representation of the sleeve, the only boundary condition required is to prevent the possibility of rigid body axial translations. This is achieved by fixing one point on the sleeve to have zero axial displacements, as shown in Fig. 2.12.

2.4.3 Results

The plane stress results were plotted out in the form of contours of the maximum tensile stress and the Von-Mises equivalent stress and very similar distributions were obtained for the three designs. Figure 2.13 shows these contour plots for the X100 sleeve.

The axisymmetric stress distribution is shown in Fig. 2.14, again for the X100 sleeve. The maximum tensile stress produced in this simplification is 700 MN/m^2 compared to 585 MN/m^2 for the equivalent classical thick cylinder solution, providing a back wall influence coefficient of 1·2. Evidently the geometry of the back wall design will affect this factor. For an X201 sleeve, the coefficient is 1·2 and for the X301 it is 1·28.

The peak values of the maximum tensile stress for the three sleeves, for the particular applied torque loadings specified, are shown in Table 2.1. The table also provides the peak values magnified by the back wall effect. These peak stress conditions occur at the end faces of the sleeves, in the buttress fillets.

TABLE 2.1

Clutch	Applied torque N m	Maximum tensile stress (MN/m^2)	
		Plane stress case	Combined results
X100	47.5	1250	1500
X201	117	1830	2340
X301	102	2300	2940

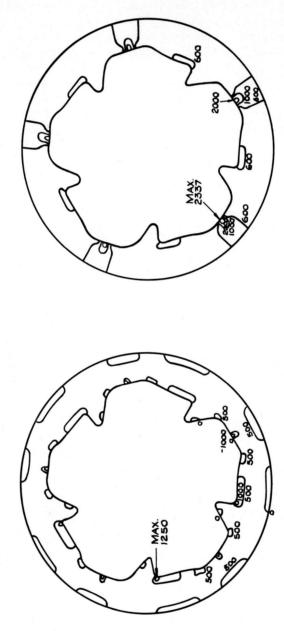

FIG. 2.13. Stress contours for the plane stress analysis (X100 sleeve). (Left) Maximum tensile stress (MN/m²). (Right) Equivalent stress (MN/m²).

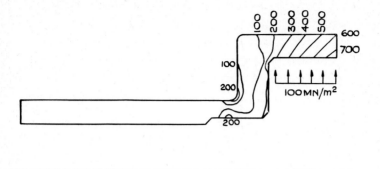

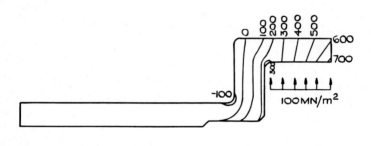

FIG. 2.14. Stress contours for the axisymmetric analysis (X100 sleeve). (Top) Equivalent stress. (Bottom) Hoop stress.

The following material properties are typical for the low alloy steel currently used in production:

1. Fatigue limit (rotating bending) $\pm$ 600–680 MN/m^2.
2. Yield stress 1220–1280 MN/m^2.
3. Tensile strength 2300 MN/m^2 at the case; 1235 MN/m^2 minimum in the core.

These fatigue data may be applied to assess the performance of the sleeves, using a Goodman diagram. However, the results are best used for comparisons between the performance of the different designs.

Component testing experience on the X100 and X201 has shown that for the applications examined, the X100 is completely satisfactory whilst the X201 is just adequate. Using this information, together with the values in the table, it is evident from stressing considerations that the X201 sleeve is well designed, the X100 is over-designed and the initial design of X301 would be expected to fail.

The X301 sleeve should be modified to prevent possible failure, by reducing the peak stress to the same level as for the X201. This may be achieved in various ways, such as thickening up the sleeve section or increasing the buttress fillet radius.

2.5   CONCLUSIONS

It is evident that the finite element technique is ideally suited to forming the basis of a general stress analysis facility which designers or engineers, who may be unfamiliar with both computing and finite element theory, would find easy and straightforward to use. The method can be laborious and time consuming but with suitable input/output aids even complex problems can be set up and analysed easily and quickly, directly from the engineering design areas concerned, using time-sharing computer systems. The interfaces between the engineering hardware and the finite element program, and the program and the interpreted results, offer much scope for improvement in developing the technique as a standard design tool.

In any stress analysis exercise it is essential that in specifying the problem, the defined loading and fixing conditions realistically represent the real physical situation. This area often provides the most difficulty and requires a good engineering understanding of the problem. The success or otherwise of the stress analysis exercise depends on the adequacy of the representation. The examples have shown that adequate simplified representations can be specified for even complex engineering arrangements.

ACKNOWLEDGEMENTS

The author wishes to thank the following: the directors of Joseph Lucas Ltd for permission to publish this paper; his colleagues and associates throughout the Lucas Group for assistance and helpful discussions in the progress of the work; and the CEGB Berkeley Nuclear Laboratories for their help and advice in using the BERSAFE finite element program.

REFERENCES

1. Zienkiewicz, O. C. (1971). *The Finite Element Method in Engineering Science*, McGraw-Hill, London.
2. Hellen, T. K. and Protheroe, S. J. (1974). The BERSAFE finite element system, *C.A.D.* **6** (1), 15.
3. McCallion, H. and Hallam, C. B. (1972). *J. Strain Analysis*, **7** (2), 141.
4. Cunnell, M. D., Ph.D. Thesis, University of Aston, 1974.

3

Static Analysis of a Light Truck Frame Using the Finite Element Method

B. MILLS AND P. F. JOHNSON

University of Birmingham and Ford Motor Company

SUMMARY

A finite element idealisation of a truck chassis frame was created and used to predict deflections under various types of loads. Torsion constants for beams with warping restraints were calculated by a subsidiary programme using plate elements to represent the beams. A test rig was built to support the chassis frame and was designed to avoid indeterminate constraints. Deflections of the frame were measured relative to a specially supported reference frame. Applied loads included out-of-plane bending, torsion, brake torsion, lozenge and lateral loading. Agreement between prediction and experimental values was good for out-of-plane bending and torsion but less satisfactory for in-plane loads.

3.1 INTRODUCTION

The work presented in this paper is concerned with the establishment of a computer-based method of predicting the deflection of a light truck chassis frame under various loading conditions and comparing them with those measured experimentally. The loading conditions comprised:

1. Simple out-of-plane bending for uniform distribution of maximum load, load between axles only and tail load only.
2. Torsional loads about the longitudinal axis of the frame resulting from unsymmetric distribution of payload or from one wheel hitting a bump or pothole.
3. In-plane lateral and longitudinal loads, causing parallelogramming of the frame, arising from unequal braking forces or steering forces during low speed manœuvres.
4. Twisting of individual chassis members by eccentric loads such as cantilever brackets carrying fuel tanks, spare wheels, batteries, etc.

3.2   LITERATURE SURVEY

In the area of experimental tests and analysis of truck frames, recent papers by Sidelko [1], Carver [2], Sherman [3], McNitt [4], Kobrin *et al.* [5] and Fuchs [6] have considered problems including the acquisition of load data during road tests, strength to weight ratios, arrangement of crossmembers and their method of attachment to sidemembers, fatigue properties of the metal and the degree of torsional rigidity. Loading systems considered were mainly out-of-plane bending and torsion, although Sherman [3] does mention lateral loading and Kobrin *et al.* [5] were concerned with stress levels in thin-walled channels subjected to eccentric loads. In his paper, Fuchs [6] considers the provision of torsional rigidity and examines various models built to a one-fifth scale, and concludes that the highest torsional rigidity was obtained with closed section rectangular sidemembers and circular tubing crossmembers.

Recent papers in the area of analytical analysis by Renton [7], Monforton and Wu [8], Tezcan [9] and Brooks and Brotton [10] are concerned with the analysis of space frames. Their papers discuss stiffness matrices for beam elements, the use of finite size joints and methods of allowing for non-rigid joints but warping problems are neglected by most of the authors. Schwabenlender [11] considers a chassis under torsional and bending loads and describes a method of analysis for predicting deflections. All joints are assumed rigid but it is acknowledged that an allowance needs to be made for real joints without saying what basis is to be used for this allowance.

Marshall *et al.* [12], in investigating torsional stiffness of chassis frames, conclude that partial warping inhibition, arising from interaction between crossmember and sidemember, must be included. Sharman [13] presents a design method for ladder frames formed from closed section members only; however, many frames are composed of open section members which react differently from closed section members.

Hessel and Lammers [14] and Petersen [15] present papers using finite element analysis methods applied to automotive structures. Both papers contain programs which suffered from the lack of a variable stress rectangular element and in the latter paper it was acknowledged that errors were due to inadequate idealisation in the joint areas and neglect of warping effects in open section beams.

Ali *et al.* [16], in a recent three-part paper, applied the finite element method to predict deflections, stresses and dynamic behaviour of a car chassis frame. Beam elements only were used and an investigation of the effects of shear, tapered beam elements, manufacturing tolerances and finite joints was made. Agreement between measured and predicted displacements was within 7% but errors in stress predictions were as high as 30% due to departure in the curvature of the predicted displacement curve from that of the experimental curve.

3.3   NOTATION

$[\,]$	square matrix
$[\,]^{\mathrm{T}}$	transposed matrix
$[^{-1}]$	inverse of matrix
a, b, c, d, e	constants in displacement functions
$[B]$	differential of $[M]$
$[C]$	exact value of $[M]$ at nodes
$[D]$	matrix of elastic coefficients
$[k]$	element stiffness matrix
$[M]$	assumed displacement function matrix
$[T]$	matrix of direction cosines
u, v, w	element displacements
x, y, z	element axes
α	rotation about x axis

Subscripts 1 and 0 refer to local and global coordinates, respectively.

3.4   THEORY

The structural analysis of the truck frame was carried out using the finite element method which presupposes that the structure can be broken down into a finite number of individual structural elements interconnected at a finite number of nodes. Beam elements were used for the complete chassis idealisation, while triangular and rectangular elements were used to idealise individual crossmembers to provide torsional stiffness values which then became input data for the complete chassis.

In applying the finite element method of analysis there are two lines of approach available: the force or flexibility method and the displacement or stiffness method. Due to the highly redundant nature of frames the latter method provides the simpler formulation and was used in the present analysis. Several authors, Argyris [17], Petyt [18], Gallagher *et al.* [19] and Turner *et al.* [20], have described the theory for the derivation of the relationship between the loads applied at the node of the element and the resulting displacement. This relationship is expressed in the form:

$$[k_1] = [C^{-1}]^T \int_V [B]^T[D][B] \, dV [C^{-1}] \qquad (3.1)$$

For the beam element used in the complete chassis idealisation the following four independent displacement functions were used:

$$u = a_1 + a_2 x$$
$$v = a_3 + a_4 x + a_5 x^2 + a_6 x^3$$
$$w = a_7 + a_8 x + a_9 x^2 + a_{10} x^3$$
$$\alpha = a_{11} + a_{12} x$$

These functions satisfy the continuity requirements across the beam boundaries.

The triangular plane stress element used was that due to Petyt [18] and has the following displacement functions for in-plane displacements:

$$u = b_1 + b_2 x + b_3 y$$
$$v = b_4 + b_5 x + b_6 y$$

For out-of-plane displacements the triangular element used was that proposed by Clough and Tocher [21]:

$$w = c_1 + c_2 x + c_3 y + c_4 x^2 + c_5 xy + c_6 y^2$$
$$+ c_7 x^3 + c_8 (x^2 y + xy^2) + c_9 y^3$$

The rectangular elements used were those proposed by Zienkiewicz and Cheung [22] and have the following displacement functions for in-plane displacements:

$$u = d_1 + d_2 x + d_3 y + d_4 xy + d_5 y^2$$
$$v = d_6 + d_7 x + d_8 y + d_9 xy + d_{10} x^2$$

and for out-of-plane displacements:

$$w = e_1 + e_2 x + e_3 y + e_4 x^2 + e_5 xy + e_6 y^2 + e_7 x^3 + e_8 x^2 y + e_9 xy^2$$
$$+ e_{10} y^3 + e_{11} x^3 y + e_{12} xy^3$$

In the case of out-of-plane displacement functions for the triangle and rectangle, boundary displacement continuity is achieved but not slope continuity between adjacent elements.

The element loads and displacements are referred from the local coordinate system to the main structural or global system shown in Fig. 3.1,

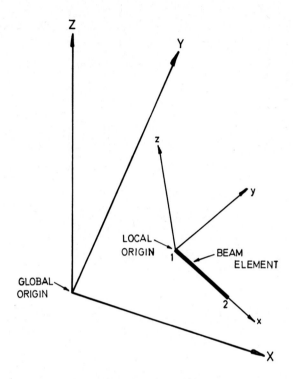

FIG. 3.1. Local and global axes.

by means of a direction cosine matrix $[T]$ and the local stiffness matrix is transformed to the global system using:

$$[k_0] = [T]^\mathrm{T}[k_1][T] \tag{3.2}$$

The beam element global stiffness matrix may have to be modified to take into account the fact that certain joints between elements may not be adequately represented by a single point in space; hence the need to introduce finite size joints. The matrix transformation operation is similar to that shown in eqn (3.2) and further details can be found in Appendix 2 of Ali *et al.* [16].

3.5   COMPUTER PROGRAM

The program used was developed in the Department of Mechanical Engineering, University of Birmingham, and was written in Egtran for use on an English Electric KDF9 machine. It has, since then, been translated into Fortran IV for use on an ICL 1906A machine. Input data to the program consisted of:

1. Introductory data—elastic constants, number of load cases and structural nodes, etc.

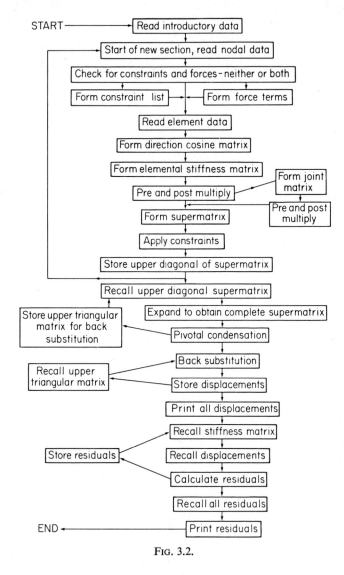

FIG. 3.2.

2. Nodal data—nodal numbers and coordinates, constraints and forces. Unconstrained structural nodes have six degrees of freedom.
3. Element data—separate programs were used to evaluate cross-sectional area, second moment of area, torsion constants and inclination of the principal axes. The end conditions were five in number: encastre at both ends; encastre at end 1 and pinned at 2; encastre at end 2 and pinned at 1; pinned at both ends; and encastre at both ends with finite size joints (see Fig. 3.1).

Output for the computer consisted of a listing of all input data as a preliminary check and the displacements for all six degrees of freedom at all structural nodes. Constrained nodes were stated as such in the displacement list to avoid confusion with zero displacement and the correct list of constraints provided a second check on the data input. The computer conducted a check on accuracy by using the calculated displacements and given stiffness to determine the required input forces. The difference between the required and the actual forces were listed for all degrees of freedom at all structural nodes. Residual forces of the order of 10^{-3} were assumed to indicate successful operation, given that the supermatrix was well conditioned. The program flow chart is shown in Fig. 3.2.

3.6 EXPERIMENTAL APPARATUS AND TEST PROGRAM

The truck chassis frame is shown in plan and elevation in Fig. 3.3 and details of the nature of the various crossmember to sidemember joints are shown in Fig. 3.4. All joints were spot welded except for the rear engine mount crossmember and the front and rear spring brackets, these being bolted because they are normally removable.

The normal road springs were not used to mount the chassis on the support pillars of the experimental straining frame because the magnitude and direction of the resultant forces on the spring brackets would have been difficult to establish. Instead, the road springs were replaced by the rigid beams with pin joints, as shown in Fig. 3.5. The system of rigid beams and pin joints did not contribute to the stiffness of the frame and were considered integral with the truck chassis and could easily and accurately be idealised for inclusion in the computer program.

The experimental straining frame was designed to submit the chassis to out-of-plane bending, torsion and in-plane bending loads. The design was such that no unnecessary or unnatural constraints were introduced, since

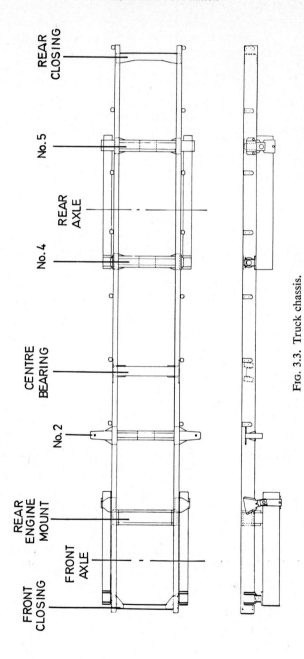

REAR CLOSING

No. 5

REAR AXLE

No. 4

CENTRE BEARING

No. 2

REAR ENGINE MOUNT

FRONT AXLE

FRONT CLOSING

FIG. 3.3. Truck chassis.

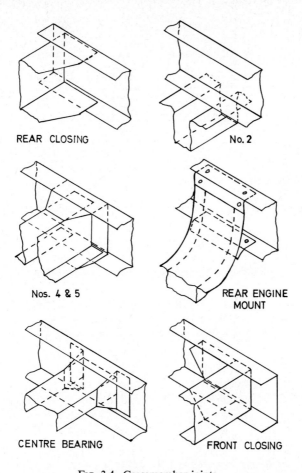

REAR CLOSING

No. 2

Nos. 4 & 5

REAR ENGINE MOUNT

CENTRE BEARING

FRONT CLOSING

Fig. 3.4. Crossmember joints.

these would distort the measured displacements by influencing internal forces in the chassis frame. The straining frame is shown in Fig. 3.6, together with the chassis frame in position and subjected to out-of-plane bending. These loads were applied by hydraulic jacks connected by strain-gauged rods to the float support brackets on the sidemembers of the chassis frame. Torsional loads were applied by rotation of the torsion beam which carried the two support pillars under the front springs. Lateral and lozenge loads were applied by a hydraulic jack through a strain-gauged rod via a derrick system. Axle loads were measured by

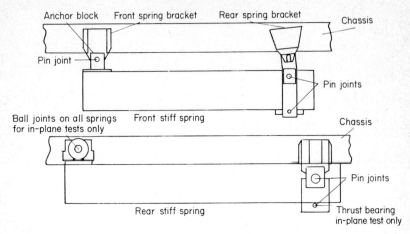

FIG. 3.5. Stiff spring details.

strain-gauged load cells interposed between the stiff springs and the support pillars.

A diagrammatical representation of constraints applied by the rig for the out-of-plane bending, torsion and lozenge loading tests is shown in Fig. 3.7. For lateral loading tests the inverted vee rear support pillar was rotated through 90° and transferred to straddle the torsion beam, as shown in Fig. 3.8.

The vertical deflection of the chassis frame was measured at seventeen positions along one sidemember, using dial gauges with a resolution of 0·0005 in. The rigid body motion of the chassis frame was eliminated by recording the deflection relative to a separate torsionally stiff reference frame freely suspended from the chassis at three points on the axle centre lines, two on either sidemember at the rear axle and one in the centre of the chassis at the front axle. The dial gauges were fixed to the reference frame and their spindles attached by nylon cord and a pot magnet to the sidemembers. Before comparing test results, measured and predicted deflections were corrected to the same datum line, this being the line joining the mid-points of the front and rear springs.

The experimental test programme consisted of seven load tests; three out-of-plane bending, two torsion and two in-plane bending loads as follows:

Load case 1: Uniformly distributed payload; 476 kg over front axle and 4286 kg over rear axle. No account was taken of engine and cab weights [Fig. 3.9 (top)].

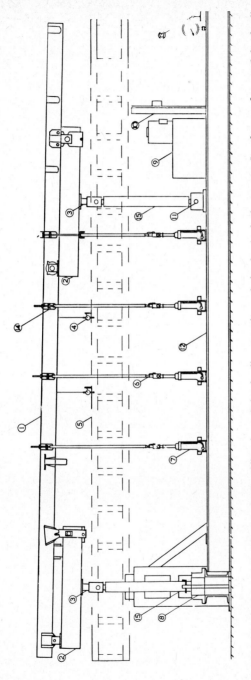

Fig. 3.6. Test rig. 1, Truck chassis; 2, stiff springs; 3, load cell measuring axle loads; 4, clock gauges; 5, reference frame; 6, load cell measuring input loads; 7, hydraulic loading rams; 8, torsional loading beam; 9, hydraulic power pack; 10, hydraulic accumulator; 11, universal joint; 12, loading frame; 13, hydraulic load controls; 14, float support brackets; 15, main support pillars.

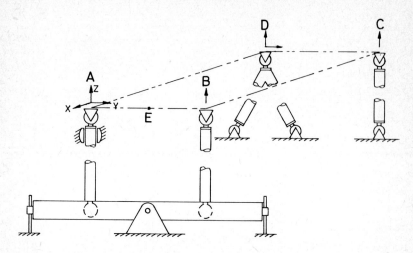

FIG. 3.7. Constraints applied by test rig. Arrows indicate direction of constraint.

Load case 2: Load between axles; 524 kg over front axle and 973 kg over rear axle [Fig. 3.9 (middle)].

Load case 3: Load at rear end; 934 kg at rear overhang comprising −476 kg over front axle and 1410 kg over rear axle [Fig. 3.9 (bottom)].

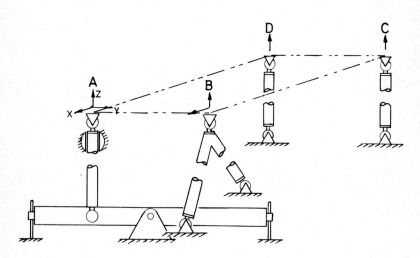

FIG. 3.8. Constraints applied by test rig (lateral loads). Arrows indicate direction of constraint.

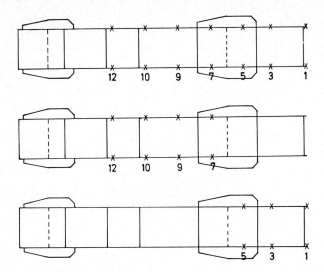

Fig. 3.9. Load input points. (Top) Load uniformly distributed. (Middle) Load between axes. (Bottom) Load at rear end.

Load case 4: Torsion load with all hydraulic jacks disconnected and the torsion beam turned through 3° in either direction.

Load case 5: Brake torsional load with vertical loads of 907 kg applied at the front of each of the four stiff springs, giving conditions equivalent to a brake torque of 4697 N m at each of the front wheels and 5810 N m at each of the rear wheels.

Load case 6: Lateral loading with the rigid springs modified to allow the chassis to flex between spring brackets, as shown in Fig. 3.5. Two loads of 91 and 165 kg were used, each being applied in the plane of the frame along the rear axle centre line and perpendicular to the centre of the sidemember web.

Load case 7: Lozenge loading with the rigid springs in the same conditions as for load case 6. A load of 1035 kg was applied in the plane of the chassis, parallel to the sidemember at the front bracket of the rear spring.

3.7   TRUCK CHASSIS IDEALISATIONS

All structural members were considered as simple beam elements with either pinned or encastre joints. The crossmembers were assumed to lie on their centre lines specified by the position of the joint on the side-members. Sidemembers were assumed to lie on the locus of their centres of gravity. Each idealisation was developed from the previous one with the aim of obtaining one which would give accurate predictions for all load cases. A summary of the idealisations and the extent of their applicability is given in Table 3.1 (see also Figs. 3.10 and 3.11). Idealisations

TABLE 3.1

Idealisation number	Nodes	Elements	Special features	Load case application	
				Actual	Possible
I	54	63	Full model, first representation with few refinements. Nodes at joints only.	1, 2, 3	1,2,3,5,7
II	57	66	Full model with finite size joints. Nodes also on axis of symmetry.	1, 2, 3, 4	All load cases
IIIa	103	112	Full model with finite size joints replaced by short stiff beams.	4, 5, 6, 7	All load cases
IIIb	103	112	As IIIa with warping restraints on crossmembers only.	4	All load cases
IIIc	103	112	As IIIa with warping restraints on crossmembers and sidemembers	4	All load cases

IIIb and IIIc include the torsion constants based on restricted warping, these being derived in Appendix 3.1, page 70.

The boundary constraints used for the various load cases are listed in Table 3.2.

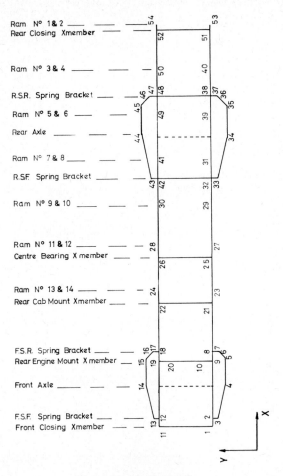

FIG. 3.10. Idealisation I.

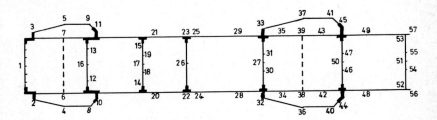

FIG. 3.11. Idealisation II.

B. Mills and P. F. Johnson

TABLE 3.2

Load case	fig. no.	Boundary constraints				
		at A	at B	at C	at D	at E
1, 2, 3, 5 and 7	7	$u = v = w = 0$	$w = 0$	$w = 0$	$v = w = 0$	—
4	7	$u = v = 0$	—	$w = 0$	$v = w = 0$	$w = 0$
6	8	$u = v = w = 0$	$u = w = 0$	$w = 0$	$w = 0$	—

3.8   DISCUSSION OF EXPERIMENTAL RESULTS AND COMPUTER PREDICTIONS

In Figs. 3.12–3.18 inclusive, the various stations at which load is applied and deflections measured are numbered along the abscissa and are identified as follows:

1. Load rams 1 and 2
3. Load rams 3 and 4

2. Rear closing crossmember
4. Rear spring, rear bracket

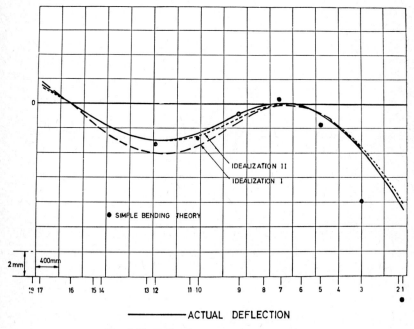

Fig. 3.12. Deflection curves for load case 1.

5. Load rams 5 and 6
6. Rear axle centre line
7. Load rams 7 and 8
8. Rear spring, front bracket
9. Load rams 9 and 10
10. Load rams 11 and 12
11. Centre bearing crossmember
12. Load rams 13 and 14
13. Number 2 crossmember
14. Front spring, rear bracket
15. Rear engine mount cross member
16. Front axle centre line
17. Front spring, front bracket
18. Front closing crossmember

Figures 3.12–3.14 show the measured vertical deflections of the side-member for load cases 1, 2 and 3 respectively, together with values pre-

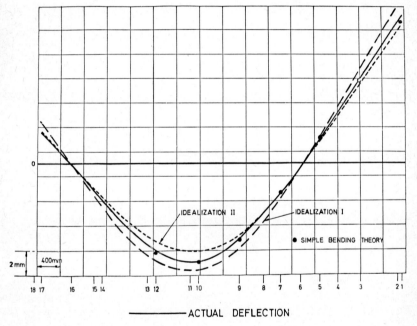

ACTUAL DEFLECTION

FIG. 3.13. Deflection curves for load case 2.

dicted from Idealisations I and II. Idealisation I is clearly too flexible largely due to inadequate representation of joint stiffness. Thus Idealisation II was derived with finite size joints and it can be seen that agreement is much improved. Using Idealisation II the effect of the manufacturing tolerance of ±5% on the thickness of the steel gauge was examined. This produced a change of less than ±3% in the predicted deflections. Also examined was the effect of shear deflections which, according to Roark [23], should not be neglected for span to depth ratios of less than four to

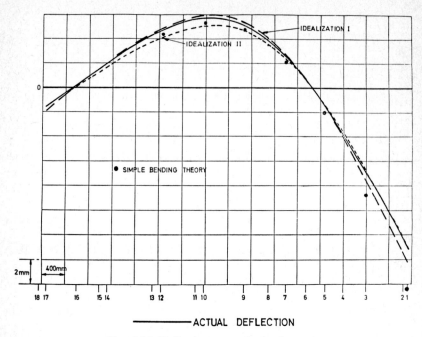

FIG. 3.14. Deflection curves for load case 3.

one. The computer program was slightly modified to neglect shear deflections and this produced less than $\pm 1\%$ difference in predicted deflections.

Also shown in Figs. 3.12–3.14 are the deflections under the loading points calculated using influence coefficients based on the engineer's bending formula, assuming the sidemember to be simply supported at the axle centre lines and neglecting the effect of the crossmembers. Agreement is surprisingly good between axles but unacceptable to the rear of the rear axle when carrying load in that region.

The experimental results for load case 4, the torsion test, are shown in Fig. 3.15, together with predictions based on Idealisations II, IIIa, IIIb and IIIc. Idealisation II shows an overestimation of the actual stiffness of the structure and this is undesirable because an inherently safe idealisation should underestimate the actual stiffness. Idealisation IIIa, in which the finite size joints of Idealisation II were replaced by short beam elements, gave results which underestimated the stiffness. Idealisation IIIb, which introduced warping restraints on the crossmembers only, improved agreement with experimental results while Idealisation IIIc, in which warping restraints were introduced on crossmembers and sidemembers,

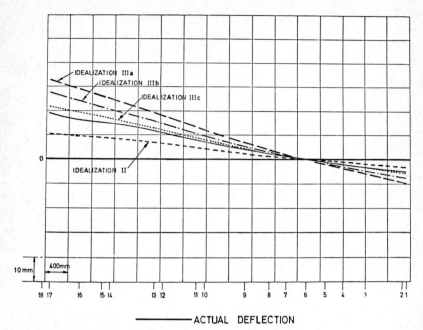

——————— ACTUAL DEFLECTION

FIG. 3.15. Deflection curves for load case 4.

gave the best agreement. Table 3.3 summarises the torsional stiffnesses obtained with the various models.

TABLE 3.3

Actual torque applied	873·4 N m
Actual rotation between axles	2·52 degrees
Actual torsional stiffness	346·6 N m/degree
Calculated torsional stiffness with free warping (using eqn 31 of Ref. 12)	134 N m/degree
Calculated torsional stiffness with restricted warping (using the torsion constants of Table 3.4 and eqn 31 of Ref. 12)	466 N m/degree

Idealisation number	Torsional stiffness (N m/degree)	Rotation (degree)	% stiffness
Actual chassis frame	346·6	2·52	100
Idealisation II	598·2	1.46	173
Idealisation IIIa	203.1	4.30	59
Idealisation IIIb	244.6	3.57	71
Idealisation IIIc	288.3	3.03	83

Figure 3.16 shows the results for the brake torsion test and the predictions obtained using Idealisation IIIa. The results were similar for both sidemembers of the chassis. Idealisation IIIc was also used and gave identical predictions showing that the introduction of warping restraints did not influence vertical bending provided that no direct torsional loads are involved. Also shown are deflection calculations based on the engineer's bending formula and the same comments apply as for load cases 1, 2 and 3.

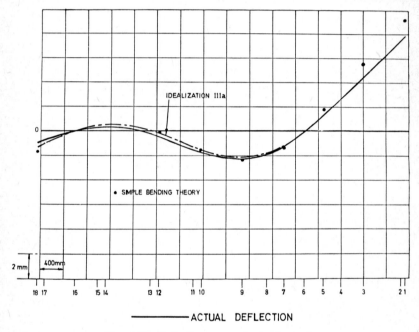

Fig. 3.16. Deflection curves for load case 5.

The experimental results for in-plane bending, load cases 6 and 7, are shown in Figs. 3.17 and 3.18, respectively, together with predictions obtained using Idealisation IIIa. It can be seen that the model overestimates the stiffness of the frame with respect to both lateral and vertical displacements in spite of the fact that this idealisation underestimated the stiffness in previous load cases. It was considered that the idealisation failed to represent the crossmember to sidemember joints adequately. For out-of-plane bending these joints are considered encastre, for torsion

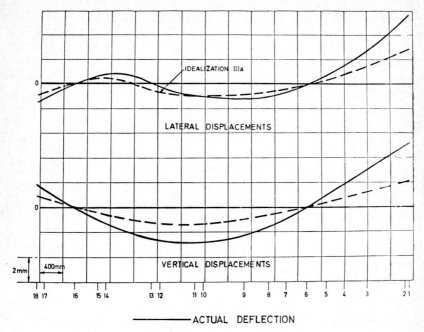

IDEALIZATION IIIa

LATERAL DISPLACEMENTS

0

VERTICAL DISPLACEMENTS

2mm   400mm

18 17   16   15 14   13 12   11 10   9   8   7   6   5   4   3   2 1

———————ACTUAL DEFLECTION

FIG. 3.17. Deflection curves for load cases 6.

loads they are either free or warping inhibited, but for in-plane bending a third type of joint is required which defines the way in which the loads are transmitted. To achieve this the beam element should be replaced by an assemblage of plate elements.

With regard to load cases 6 and 7, one or other of the sidemembers is subjected to compressive loads which are absent in all other load cases. Such loads could lead to incipient elastic lateral buckling and a stress prediction based on the present program showed that the critical stress, assuming the sidemember to be treated as a simple strut, was exceeded in both in-plane bending cases. The present program, however, does not include strut elements, hence lateral buckling displacements are missing from the predictions and therefore an overestimation of the stiffness is produced.

3.9 CONCLUSIONS

The generally good agreement under bending, pure torsion and brake torsion loads between measured and predicted displacements has shown

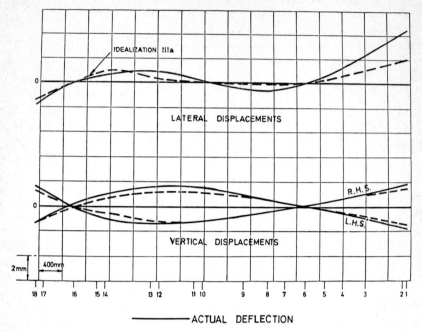

ACTUAL DEFLECTION

FIG. 3.18. Deflection curves for load case 7.

the power of the finite element method of structural analysis. For the chassis frame considered it can be concluded that:

1. Simple beam elements can be successfully used for out-of-plane bending loads.
2. It is necessary to use finite size joints or short stiff beam elements to represent the local stiffening at the joints.
3. If all joints are considered infinitely rigid, an overestimation of the structural stiffness is obtained.
4. Shear deflections are negligible under bending loads but have slightly more significance for torsional loads.
5. Manufacturing tolerances do not produce significant changes in the predicted deflections.
6. Warping restraints should be included in both crossmembers and sidemembers for torsional load cases.
7. An assembly of plate elements can be used to represent open-section members for the calculation of warping restraints.
8. For in-plane bending loads it is necessary to include elastic buckling in the beam elements representing the sidemembers.

ACKNOWLEDGEMENTS

The authors wish to thank Professor S. A. Tobias for the provision of laboratory facilities in the Department of Mechanical Engineering at the University of Birmingham; the Ford Motor Co Ltd for the provision of financial support and the chassis frame, and the Science Research Council for financial support during the computer program development.

REFERENCES

1. Sidelko, W. J. 'An objective approach to highway truck frame design', SAE Paper No. SP276, December 1965.
2. Carver, G. C. 'Application of variable depth siderail to heavy truck frames', SAE Paper No. 690174, January 1969.
3. Sherman, D. W. 'Stresses and deflections in truck siderail attachments', SAE Paper No. 690175, January 1969.
4. McNitt, L. F. 'Truck frame siderail buckling stresses', SAE Paper No. 690176, January 1969.
5. Kobrin, M. M., Kilimnik, L. Sh. and Titov, A. A. 'Investigation of the stress-state and durability of (vehicle) frame sidemember walls at the points of load transfer', MIRA Translation No. 20/70.
6. Fuchs, D. 'Torsional rigidity of commercial vehicle frames in different types of service', MIRA Translation No. 23/70.
7. Renton, J. D. 'Stability of space frames by computer analysis', ASCE Proc. Struct. Div., August 1962.
8. Monforton, G. R. and Wu, T. S. 'Matrix analysis of semi-rigid connected frames', ASCE Proc. Struct. Div., December 1963.
9. Tezcan, S. S. 'Computer analysis of plane and space structures', ASCE Proc. Struct. Div., April 1966.
10. Brooks, D. F. and Brotton, D. M. 'Computer system for analysis of large frameworks', ASCE Proc. Struct. Div., December 1967.
11. Schwabenlender, C. W. 'A computer programme for truck frame design', SAE Paper No. 769D, October 1963.
12. Marshall, P. H., Roach, A. H. and Tidbury, G. H. 'Torsional stiffness of commercial vehicle chassis frames', FISITA Paper No. 3–04, 12th Int. Conf. (Spain, 1968).
13. Sharman, P. W. (1967–68). 'Optimum stiffness-weight design of peripheral and ladder frames', IME Proc. (Auto. Div.) 182, Part 2A, No. 3.
14. Hessel, J. J. and Lammers, S. J. 'Solution of automotive structural problems using the finite element method and computer graphics', SAE Paper No. 710243, January 1971.
15. Petersen, W. 'Application of finite element method to predict static response of automotive body structures', SAE Paper No. 710263, January 1971.

16. Ali, R., Hedges, J. L., Mills, B., Norville, C. C. and Gurdogan, O. 'The application of finite element techniques to the analysis of an automobile structure' (a three-part paper dealing with the static, stress and dynamic properties of a chassis frame). IME Proc., Vol 185, 44/71.

17. Argyris, J. H. (1964). *Recent Advances in Matrix Methods of Structural Analysis*, Pergamon Press.

18. Petyt, M. 'The application of finite element techniques to plate and shell problems', ISVR Report No. 120, University of Southampton, February 1965.

19. Gallagher, R. H., Rattinger, I. and Archer, J. S. (1969) *A Correlation Study of Methods of Matrix Structural Analysis* (Ed. E. E. Agard), Pergamon Press.

20. Turner, M. J., Clough, R. W., Martin, H. C. and Top, L. C. (1956). Stiffness and deflection analysis of complex structures, *J. Aero. Sc.*, September.

21. Clough, R. W. and Tocher, J. L. (1964) 'Analysis of thin arch dams by the finite element method.' Proc. Symp. on Theory of Arch Dams, University of Southampton.

22. Zienkiewicz, O. C. and Cheung, Y. K. (1964). 'Finite element method of analysis for arch dam shells and comparison with finite difference procedures', Proc. Symp. on Theory of Arch Dams, University of Southampton.

23. Roark, R. J. (1965). *Formulas for Stress and Strain*, McGraw-Hill.

24. Vlasov, V. Z. 'Thin walled elastic beams.' Israel Program for Scientific Translations, Jerusalem 1961.

25. Zbirohowski-Koscia, K. (1967). *Thin Walled Beams from Theory to Practice*, Crosby Lockwood.

26. Krajcinovic, D. (1969). A consistent discrete elements technique for thin walled assemblages, *Int. J. of Solids and Structures*, **5**.

27. Timoshenko, S. P. (1945). Theory of bending, torsion and buckling of thin walled members of open cross section, *J. of the Franklin Institute*, **239**.

APPENDIX 3.1: TORSION CONSTANTS

In his book, Vlasov [24], gives a comprehensive account of the properties of thin-walled open section beams and explains why the behaviour of these beams cannot be adequately explained using the theory of thick-walled beams. He introduces the 'law of sectorial areas' as the more general form of the already established law of plane sections. The physical meaning of the forces and properties of thin-walled beams (i.e. flexural twist, bi-moment and sectorial moments of an area) are explained more fully by Zbirohowski-Koscia [25]. In a recent paper, Krajcinovic [26] makes use of the general theory of thin-walled members of open cross section originally developed by Vlasov. He proposes the concept of a seventh degree of freedom at each structural node to take into account the properties of thin-walled beams, but such an approach would entail a lengthy period of development and in the present paper the simpler alternative of representing beams by assemblages of plate elements was taken.

Initial calculations were made using an open section beam of different lengths and various end conditions. A torque was applied at one end and the resulting angle of rotation calculated using both the finite element

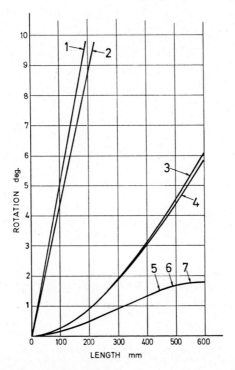

FIG. 3.19. Torsional stiffness of an open section beam.

method and equations from Timoshenko [27]. Figure 3.19 shows the results obtained for the various end conditions and these are summarised below:

Curve 1   Both ends free, finite element model and Timoshenko.
Curve 2   Web restrained both ends, finite element model.
Curve 3   One end encastre, Timoshenko.
Curve 4   One end encastre, finite element model.
Curve 5   Both ends encastre, Timoshenko.
Curve 6   Both ends encastre, finite element model.
Curve 7   Flanges restrained both ends, finite element model.

TABLE 3.4

Beam identification	Cross section	Method of attachment	Torsion constant		No. of nodes	No. of elements
			Free warping	Restricted warping		
Front closing cross-member		TF^a and BF	7 160	75 240	98	78
No. 2 cross-member (middle)			516 000	—	78	64
No. 2 cross-member (ends)		TF	1 190	33 032		
Centre bearing cross-member		W	4 490	5,390	98	78
Nos. 4 and 5 cross-member (middle)			1 460 000	—	66	54
Nos. 4 and 5 cross-member (ends)		TF and BF	1 550	237 267		
Rear closing cross-member (middle)			2 740	—	98	100
Rear closing cross-member (ends)		TF and BF	3 270	195 436		
Sidemember bay 1–2		BF and W–E	10 800	78 767	119	96
Sidemember bay 2–3		E–BF and W	10 800	65 637	98	78
Sidemember bay 3–4		BF and W–W	10 800	26 091	91	72
Sidemember bay 4–5		W–BF and W	10 800	23 649	168	138
Sidemember bay 5–6		BF and W–BF and W	10 800	24 595	168	138
Sidemember bay 6–7		BF and W–BF	10 800	82 009	140	114

^{a} TF = top flange; W = web; BF = bottom flange; E = encastre.

Curve 7 does not differ significantly from curve 6 and this accounts for the high torsional rigidity of channel beams with flange restraints.

Idealisations IIIb and IIIc included warping restraints in the cross-members and sidemembers and for this purpose the torsional rigidities of the appropriate beams were recalculated using a computer program identical to the main program but containing only plate elements. Each member was subdivided into a number of rectangular and triangular elements with end constraints to suit the appropriate joint condition, i.e. flange and/or web restrained. In general, the length to breadth ratio of the rectangular elements was kept below 2 to 1 and the smallest angle in the triangular elements was kept above 30°. Figure 3.20 shows the plate

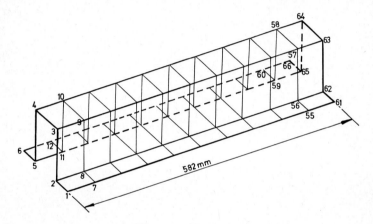

Fig. 3.20. Plate element idealisation of Nos. 4 and 5 crossmembers (66 nodes, 54 elements).

idealisation used for the fourth and fifth crossmember (see Fig. 3.3) and Table 3.4 summarises the torsion constants for all crossmembers and bay lengths of the sidemembers under free warping and restrained warping conditions.

4

Finite Element Study of a Cast Iron Flywheel with Particular Emphasis on Stress Concentrations

P. J. BINDIN
Perkins Engines Ltd.

SUMMARY

The process of deriving an adequately refined mesh in the main area of stress concentration is shown, together with stress variation in adjoining elements and common nodes. This compatibility is taken as a measure of degree of mesh refinement. Compatibility is examined both around the stress concentration and through the bulk material, i.e. along the probable line of fracture.

Having determined a degree of refinement sufficient for solving the immediate problem, the analysis goes one stage further and converges on almost perfect compatibility by considering a very localised mesh with predetermined boundary displacements.

By using the sufficiently refined mesh the problem was analysed and a flywheel speed determined at which the maximum principal stress exceeded the ultimate tensile stress of the cast iron, when failure was assumed to occur.

The results obtained from the above analysis were pessimistic due to the material properties of cast iron (i.e. Young's modulus of elasticity and Poisson's ratio) reducing with increase in tensile stress. Thus, further computer runs were undertaken using varying E and v dependent on average element in-plane stress. By a process of successive iteration the element properties used throughout the mesh coincided with the stresses obtained from the analysis. Thus, a more accurate value of flywheel bursting speed was obtained and the design could be modified accordingly to increase this speed.

4.1   INTRODUCTION

The failure of flywheels due to bursting is almost a classic problem which dates back to the advent of the first internal combustion engines. The need to protect ourselves against this type of failure is still with us, however, and applies particularly to the modern high speed diesel engine.

In typical vehicular applications the engine is often situated in close proximity to the operator and, with the introduction of the syncromesh gearbox, the possibility of engine over-speeding due to inadvertent gear changes makes flywheel bursting a dangerous possibility.

By limiting their speed depending on the outside diameter and material, and supplementing this by the testing to destruction of flywheels which approach the design limit, it is possible to maintain adequate safety factors. When typical cross-sections (see for example Fig. 4.1) are examined it becomes obvious, however, that the flat disc shape is seldom seen in practice and that any simple design rules must err on the conservative side to allow, for example, for bending effects of overhung rims.

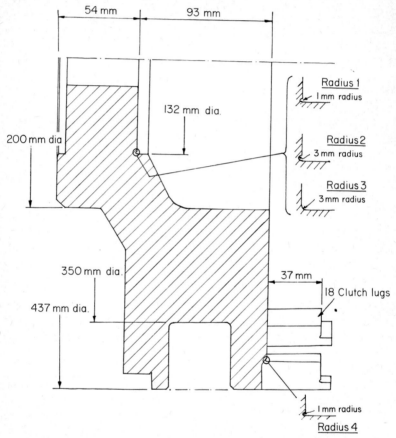

Fig. 4.1. Diagram of flywheel, showing basic dimensions.

This paper will describe how a study was made of a cast iron flywheel, using finite elements, aimed primarily at producing a design which would have a sufficiently high burst speed. A description is also given of the stress concentrations produced by a number of fillet radii and anticipates the effect on the stresses of the characteristic properties of cast iron.

4.2   THE FINITE ELEMENT MODELS

The computer program used for the analyses was the PAFEC suite of routines produced by the University of Nottingham. Two-dimensional isoparametric elements of either the eight noded quadrilateral or the six noded triangular type were used for all the meshes.

The policy of using relatively simple models was adopted and a pilot study was conducted using a coarse axisymmetric mesh. These results were used to highlight the most critical areas. Values of stress from the surrounding elements of various nodes were compared and used to judge where a refinement of the mesh was needed.

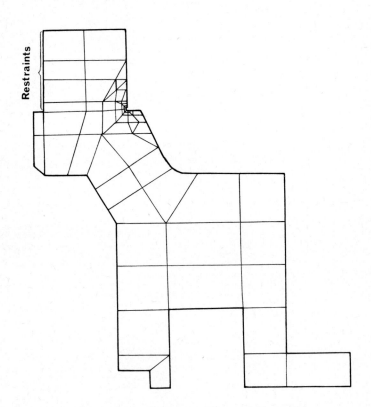

FIG. 4.2. Axisymmetric mesh of flywheel with Radius 1.

Two basic models were used to represent the flywheel: (1) an axisymmetric mesh of the whole flywheel; (2a) a plane-stress model of one of the clutch lugs shown in Fig. 4.1; and (2b) an axisymmetric model of the localised area around the inner fillet undercut radius which used the same mesh as (2a).

1. The axisymmetric mesh of the flywheel is shown in Fig. 4.2 and consists of a relatively coarse mesh with increasing refinement as the fillet on the 132 mm bore is approached. The loading imposed simulated the body forces produced by the rotation of the flywheel and restraints were where the flywheel was bolted to the crankshaft flange. The mesh was altered appropriately in the fillet region to cater for the three different radius conditions shown in Fig. 4.1 and denoted Radius 1, 2 and 3.

2a. The plane stress mesh of the clutch lug is shown in Fig. 4.3 and again consists of a fairly coarse mesh with refinement as the fillet is approached. The loading imposed also simulated the body forces due to the rotation of the flywheel but, unlike the axisymmetric mesh, these loads were derived by applying a gravity field and factoring the density of each element depending on the flywheel speed and the radial distance to the element centroid. The restraints were applied along the innermost base of the mesh.

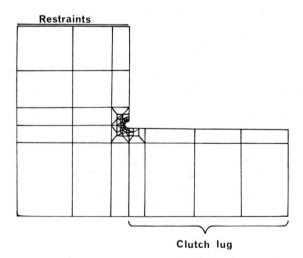

FIG. 4.3. Plane stress model of clutch lug (also used for axisymmetric localised mesh).

2b. The axisymmetric mesh of the localised region around the fillet used the same mesh as (2a), shown in Fig. 4.3, except that the element type was changed. In this case displacements were prescribed around the appropriate boundaries in order to obtain the same strains as the larger model. The mesh was used to assess the effect on accuracy of an increased number of elements around Radius 1. A discussion of results follows.

4.3 THE EFFECT OF MESH DESIGN ON STRESS COMPATIBILITY

Any node in the mesh is shared by several elements each giving its own value of stress and, as might be expected, the finer the mesh then the better the agreement between these values. In the initial phase of the work, when a coarse mesh was used, this agreement, or lack of agreement, was used to decide the critical areas in the flywheel but a comparison has also been made between the results from two meshes in the region of Radius 1 to assess accuracy. The first mesh used four elements around the radius and the variation of stress around the radius is shown in Fig. 4.4. The

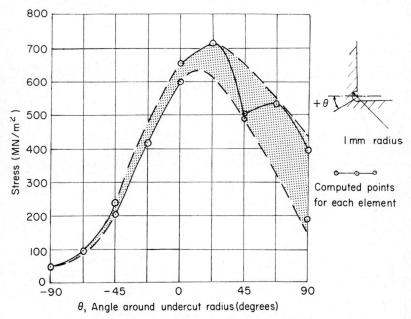

FIG. 4.4. Principal stress variation around Radius 1—four elements.

second mesh used eight elements around the radius and the variation of stress is shown in Fig. 4.5. The upper and lower bounds of the stresses are shown on these diagrams and it is apparent that the finer mesh considerably reduces the scatter band. The mean values of peak stress provide reasonable agreement, however, and for the purposes of this study the four element subdivision around the radius was considered adequate.

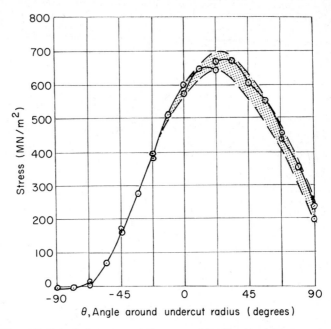

FIG. 4.5. Principal stress variation around Radius 1—eight elements.

Some of the scatter in stress between the 45 and 90 degree positions of Fig. 4.4 may be due to the positioning of the mid-side node slightly off the centre distance between the corner nodes. It has been shown [1] that, when isoparametric and other curved sided elements are used, extreme caution must be exercised when defining the element geometry and that distortion of the sides of the elements can cause considerable errors in deflections and stress. The position of the mid-side nodes at the precise distance between the corner nodes is essential where accuracy is at a premium. The variation of stress for the nodes lying along the line from Radius 1 across the narrowest section is shown in Fig. 4.6. It can be seen that the stress rises sharply as the radius is approached and also that the stress compatibility between elements at each node is excellent for the main bulk of the section, making further refinement of the mesh in these areas unnecessary.

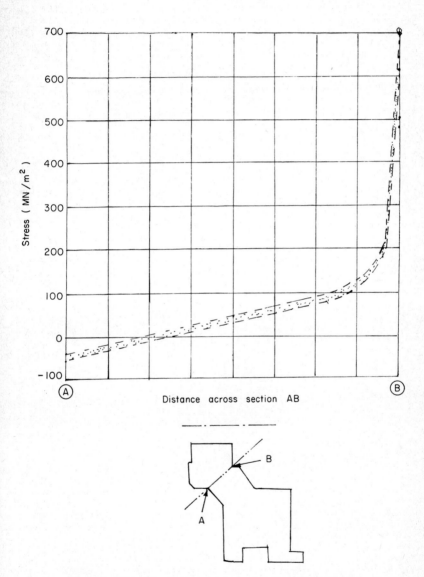

FIG. 4.6. Variation of stress across section through Radius 1.

4.4 RESTRAINT CONDITIONS OF THE AXISYMMETRIC MODEL

Restraints were applied to the main axisymmetric model to simulate the clamping conditions existing between the flywheel and the crankshaft flange. The crankshaft flange was assumed to be completely rigid and two conditions were considered:

1. Where the clamping was perfect and no radial slip occurred anywhere along the face. The effects of this type of clamping can be seen on the contour stress plot of the in-plane principal stresses in Fig. 4.7.

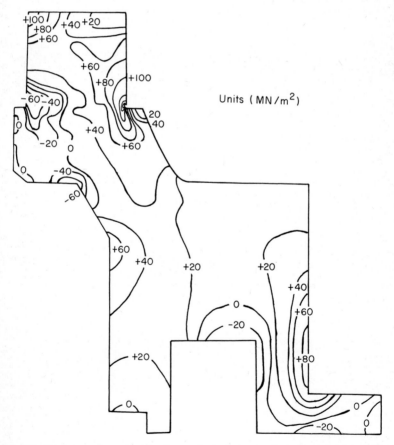

Units (MN /m^2)

FIG. 4.7. Contours of constant in-plane principal stresses for axisymmetric model of flywheel.

The outgoing forces of the flywheel body are causing a 'heeling' about the clamping face with considerable compressive stresses on the outer surface of the face, giving way to even higher tensile stresses on the inner surface.

2. When restraints are modified to allow free radial movement along the face and also unrestrained axial movement at the inner surface of the face, the picture is changed somewhat. The stresses remain very similar from the outer edge to the centre of the face but decrease from 40 MN/m² (tensile) at this position to zero at the inner edge.

As the restraints are removed this also causes a reduction of stress levels at the fillet and this is shown in Table 4.1, where the summarised results at the fillet for some fully and partially restrained cases are given.

TABLE 4.1
Summary of computed results

Description	Stress at 8000 rev/min (MN/m²)	Equivalent speed at 254 MN/m² (rev/min)
Radius 1: Constant Modulus—fully restrained	712	4778
Radius 1: Constant Modulus— partially restrained	656	4978
Radius 1: Modulus varied with average stress—partially restrained	524	5571
Radius 1: Modulus and Poisson's Ratio varied with average stress— partially restrained	493	5742
Radius 2: Constant Modulus— fully restrained	439	6085
Radius 3: Constant Modulus— fully restrained	388	6473
Radius 3: Constant Modulus— partially restrained	359	6730
Radius 3: Modulus varied with average stress—partially restrained	287	7526
Radius 4: Constant Modulus	369	6637
Radius 4: Modulus varied with average stress	295	7423

4.5   ALLOWANCE FOR VARIABLE MATERIAL PROPERTIES

The elements chosen for the analysis were of the popular axisymmetric and plane-stress types. An isotropic, homogeneous material is assumed to exist throughout the element and the stress/strain matrix used to derive the element stiffness can be described with two variables: Modulus of Elasticity and Poisson's Ratio.

The initial run of an analysis assumed these material properties to be constant at zero stress values given for the material [2], Grade 17 Grey Cast Iron, throughout the mesh. The results of this run were examined and the position of highest stress found. Since failure under unicycle conditions was being predicted, this highest stress was compared to the ultimate tensile strength and the stress at the centre of the elements appropriately factored. Reference was now made to data on the material properties of cast iron [2, 3] where the variation of Modulus of Elasticity determining total strain and the variation of Poisson's Ratio with tensile stress were found. The material properties of all the elements were now re-specified where necessary, by using the modified centroidal stress to determine revised values of Modulus of Elasticity and Poisson's Ratio. This procedure typically has to be repeated once more to obtain a 'settled' state of stress throughout the mesh.

Failure was assumed to occur when the maximum computed stress exceeded the ultimate tensile strength of the material and the rotational speed of the flywheel was obtained from the relationship of nominal speed, nominal maximum stress and ultimate tensile strength.

4.6   DESIGN REQUIREMENTS

The speeds reached by the flywheels which are spun to destruction in the test cell have to be related to some criterion in order to judge whether or not the flywheels are acceptable. This criterion has been derived by relating the 'minimum burst speed' to the engine rated speed in such a way that the fatigue strength of the flywheel is also maintained at a necessarily conservative value. The peak speeds that an engine experiences during its life is very much a function of the application to which it is applied. For example, a vehicle engine will experience speeds of 135% of rated speed fairly regularly, whereas an engine driving a stationary generator will rarely exceed this value.

If the minimum burst speed is set to 250% of rated speed, for example, and the material of the flywheel in question is Grade 17 Cast Iron: since stress (σ) is proportional to speed squared and $\sigma = 262$ MN/m^2(UTS) at the burst speed, then $\sigma = 262/(2 \cdot 5)^2 = 42$ MN/m^2 at rated speed.

From a Goodman diagram and using the Wöhler (notched) fatigue limit: Fatigue Reserve Factor $= 3 \cdot 64$ but, allowing for low cycle fatigue in vehicular applications, $\sigma = 262 \times (1 \cdot 35/2 \cdot 5)^2 = 77$ MN/m^2 at 135% of rated speed, and Fatigue Reserve Factor $= 2 \cdot 0$.

The theoretical analysis was therefore aimed at producing a flywheel which would, with minimum design change, be capable of sustaining a speed of 6500 rev/min without failure, since the engine rated speed was 2600 rev/min.

4.7   DISCUSSION OF RESULTS

The overall picture of stresses is shown in Figs. 4.7 and 4.8 which give contours of in-plane principal stress and hoop stress, respectively. The more detailed values of stress around Radius 1 are plotted in Fig. 4.4. All these values are for constant material properties across the mesh and at a nominal speed of 8000 rev/min. The values of stress in the critical regions will be considerably reduced by the effect of variable material properties as discussed previously. One way of explaining this reduction is by considering the case where the local strain remains constant and the Modulus of Elasticity is reduced, with a proportional reduction in stress. In practice, the strain does not remain constant, however, and will vary depending on how crucial the local reduction of elasticity is on the overall deflection of the body. The reduction of material properties also introduces a further complication when we are reminded that an axisymmetric solution is essentially three dimensional, with triaxial strains and material properties.

A comparison of the three fillet conditions, Radii 1, 2 and 3, is given in Table 4.1 and it can be seen that the peak stresses in the radii are 712,439 and 388 MN/m^2, respectively. In practice, the flywheel tested incorporated Radius 3, which has a theoretical burst speed of 7526 rev/min, slightly higher than that of the clutch lug.

The clutch lugs on the flywheel tested were machined to Radius 4 and the stresses produced from this in-plane analysis are shown in Figs. 4.9 and 4.10. Once again the results are for the constant material, 8000 rev/min

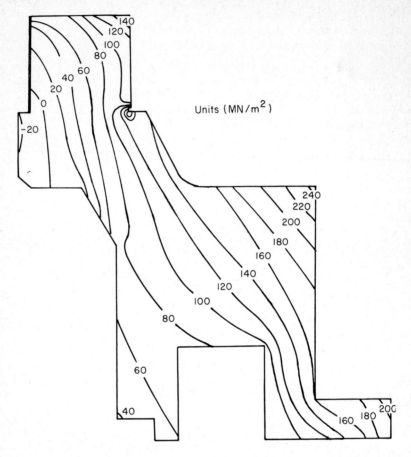

FIG. 4.8. Contours of constant hoop stress for axisymmetric model of flywheel.

case. The theoretical burst speed of the clutch lugs is 7423 rev/min which can be compared favourably, if rather pessimistically, with the actual burst speed of 8000 rev/min.

4.8   BACKGROUND TO ANALYSIS AND DETAILS OF TEST

The analysis was started before the manufacture of any of these flywheels, with the original design showing Radius 1. The results suggested that Radius 3 should replace Radius 1 and this modification was incorporated

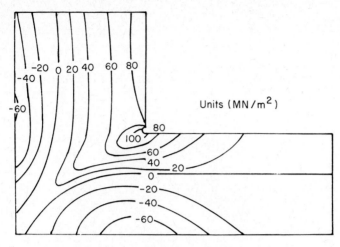

FIG. 4.9. Contours of constant principal stress for plane-stress model of clutch lug.

in the first manufactured flywheels, one of which was selected for testing.

The spin tests take place in a shielded pit and the flywheels are slowly accelerated until a complete fracture occurs. Failure, in the case of this flywheel, occurred at 8000 rev/min when some of the clutch lugs on the extremity of the flywheel detached themselves from the main body of the

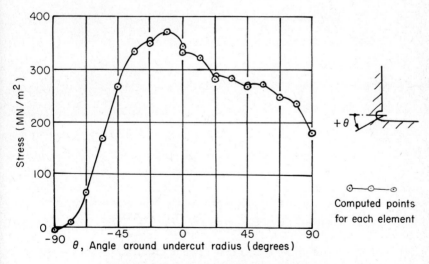

FIG. 4.10. Variation of stress around Radius 4.

flywheel. This resulted in the flywheel becoming unbalanced and subsequent shearing of the fastening bolts allowed the flywheel to drop into the pit. A photograph of the failed flywheel is shown in Fig. 4.11.

Further examination showed that the fractures ran from the fillet radius (Radius 4) at the position of peak stress shown in Fig. 4.10. The material strength was found to be 254 MN/m^2.

FIG. 4.11. Photograph of failed flywheel.

4.9   CONCLUSIONS

Relatively uncomplicated and economical models of the flywheel have been used to predict, with reasonable accuracy, potential and actual areas of failure when subjected to rotational forces. The analysis was performed at the ideal stage of design, namely before hardware had been produced, and the results were used to improve the integrity of the component.

The analysis did, however, reveal certain problems related to representing the non-linear material properties of cast iron without escalating the problem to a three-dimensional, elasto-plastic analysis. A workable technique was evolved but, to obtain more accuracy, further testing would be necessary and elements used which are capable of variable material properties in all three directions.

ACKNOWLEDGEMENTS

The author wishes to thank the Directors of Perkins Engines Ltd for permission to publish this paper, and his colleagues who assisted in its production.

REFERENCES

1. Henshell, R. D., Walters, D. and Warburton, G. B. (1972). On Possible Loss of Accuracy in Curved Finite Elements, *J. Sound and Vibration*, **23** 510–513.
2. Gilbert, G. N. J. *B.C.I.R.A. Engineering Data on Grey Cast Iron*, B.C.I.R.A., 1968.
3. Gilbert, G. N. J. (1961). Stress/strain properties of cast iron and Poisson's Ratio in tension and compression, *BCIRA Journal*, **9**, (3), 347–363, May.

5

Application of the Finite Element Method to the Design of Disc-type Wheels

T. H. RICHARDS AND C. W. WOO

University of Aston and University of Singapore

SUMMARY

This investigation was concerned with determining the stress distribution in various proposed designs of mass-produced disc-type wheels, with a view to the economic utilisation of material. The development of a complete optimisation procedure was beyond the scope of the work, but as a step towards this ideal, the influence of certain salient geometric features on the stress distribution was examined. Since disc-type wheels are bodies of revolution, it is natural, when contemplating a finite element solution, to think in terms of ring-type elements. However, since the loading (which may be prescribed to have axial as well as radial components) is decidedly non-axisymmetric, the displacement models for such elements must incorporate tangential as well as radial and axial displacement components. Expansion of the displacements in terms of series of trigonometric functions of angular position yields a semi-analytic finite element method; this formed the basis for the computation carried out. The so-called effective stress was computed as part of the analysis with a view to comparison with the yield stress in accordance with the Von Mises criterion for yielding.

On the basis of the finite element solutions obtained, a procedure incorporating the use of design curves was devised by means of which suitable proportions of wheel could readily be obtained to meet a given duty. Further, by calculating the effective stiffness of the wheel at the load, an elementary theory could provide some measure of the impact rating for the wheel.

5.1 INTRODUCTION

Solid disc-type wheels have been used in a wide range of situations from railway stock to various factory light vehicles and jockey wheels for trailer caravans. This investigation was concerned with wheels for the latter light-duty kind of application, produced on a mass production scale and having the general form illustrated in Fig. 5.1. The starting point for the study was a basic design of wheel which had been evolved by trial; this had proved adequate for its original duty but, as often happens in such design situations, attempts to uprate the performance of the component highlighted areas of uncertainty regarding its structural behaviour and the need to understand this to allow further progress to be made.

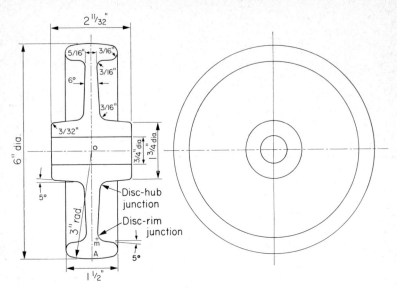

Fig. 5.1. Complex rimmed disc wheel.

From the stress analysis point of view, a loaded wheel, even a solid one with no ribs or cutouts in its disc, presents a formidable problem; the methods of mechanics of materials are not adequate for the purpose and a more rigorous formulation is called for. Elasticity theory comprises a formal body of analysis by means of which greater precision in formulation may be achieved. However, as is the case here, such an approach does not usually yield solutions in the form of formulae for stresses and displacements and one is led to the need for a numerical technique which provides an approximate solution to the properly formulated problem. A number of approaches are available, but the finite element method was chosen for its versatility and ease of application.

When the solution to a stressing problem can be expressed as formulae for stresses or displacements, the influence of a change in some geometric or load parameter is readily apparent and the approach to an efficient design is easily effected. However, when a solution can only be obtained by numerical means, an examination of the influence of parameter changes is more cumbersome; now, any proposed new structure defined by new geometric and/or load parameters must be analysed completely afresh. To determine overall trends in stress and displacement distributions as load and geometric changes occur, a number of new independent structural problems must be solved. Evidently, when resources are limited, only relatively few cases may be treated in this way and a certain amount of compromise is necessary. To make reasonable deductions from limited information, then, requires the exercise of engineering judgement.

These were the circumstances in which the present work was carried out. The finite element method was used to yield sufficient data to allow the formulation of a relatively straightforward design office procedure for determining a suitable size of wheel disc and rim to satisfy a prescribed static load-carrying capacity and to provide some estimate of the wheel's impact rating.

5.2   NOTATION

a, b, c	with subscripts, functions of element nodal coordinates
$[D]$	elasticity matrix
$[g]$	a strain model matrix, defined in Appendix 5.1, page 109
$[h]$	matrix of a's, b's, c's, defined in Appendix 5.1
$[k]$	element stiffness matrix
$[K]$	system stiffness matrix
$[M]$	displacement model matrix
n	integer
P, p	with subscripts, nodal circle force, amplitude
q, Q	generalised coordinate and force
r	coordinate
U, V	strain energy, potential energy
u, v, w	displacement component
z	coordinate
α	parameter
ε	with subscripts, direct strain component
γ	with subscripts, shearing strain component
θ	coordinate
σ	direct stress component
τ	shearing stress component
$[\phi], [\Omega]$	matrices defined in Appendix 5.1

5.3   THEORETICAL FOUNDATIONS OF THE FINITE ELEMENT METHOD

The finite element method is now firmly established and widely described in the literature [1–3] so that, for the purposes of completeness, only a brief summary of the relevant theory is necessary here. We are only concerned with the so-called displacement method as applied to solid continua.

In its most widely developed form the displacement finite element method may be viewed as a piece-wise Rayleigh-Ritz technique used in conjunction with the principle of stationary total potential energy. In this approach to stress analysis, the region of the solid is imagined as divided into sub-regions, called the finite elements, so that the bounding surfaces of the elements generate a mesh, the intersection points of which define nodes. Displacement patterns described by functions incorporating a finite number of adjustable parameters are assumed local to each element; these parameters are identified with element nodal displacement components when interpolation functions are used.

An assumed displacement pattern implies an assumed strain distribution within an element and on the basis of a finite number of parameters one obtains an expression for the strain energy stored in the element in the characteristic form

$$U_e = \tfrac{1}{2}\{u\}_0{}^t [k]_e \{u\}_0 \qquad (5.1)$$

where $[k]$ is a matrix of coefficients the values of which depend on the form of the assumed displacement pattern and which are obtained by integrations over the element volume.

Suitable choices of displacement functions ensure continuity of displacements across interelement boundaries when nodal compatibility is ensured, so that the total strain energy stored in the representation of the solid becomes

$$U = \sum_e U_e \qquad (5.2)$$

For compatibility, the $\{u\}_0$ for the elements are expressed directly in terms of the displacement components $\{q\}$ at appropriate nodes of the whole mesh. The $\{q\}$ comprise the generalised coordinates for the discretised system and if the generalised forces associated with them are $\{Q\}$, the total potential energy of the system is expressible in the form

$$V = \tfrac{1}{2}\{q\}^t [K]\{q\} - \{q\}^t \{Q\} \qquad (5.3)$$

The overall stiffness matrix $[K]$ is generated from the individual $[k]_e$ by means of eqn (5.2) and the q's are the basic unknowns of the formulation.

Whilst the assumed displacement pattern ensures continuity of the displacements so that eqn (5.3) is a valid equation of potential energy for any values of the q's, the true q's, which correspond to an equilibrium configuration, are identified by the principle of stationary total potential energy:

$$\delta V = 0 \qquad (5.4)$$

Equation (5.3) in (5.4) then yields

$$[K]\{q\} = \{Q\} \tag{5.5}$$

which is a set of stiffness equations characterising equilibrium at the generalised coordinates of a finite degree of freedom system: the set is central to displacement finite element analysis.

When these ideas are applied to special classes of problem, the elements are chosen in an appropriate form. Thus, for plane stress or plane strain situations, they are plane figures such as straight-sided or curvilinear triangles or quadrilaterals. The structures of interest in the present work were solids of revolution so that the ring-type elements of Figs. 5.2 and 5.3 were suitable. Here, nodal circles are defined by the corners of the triangle section.

When axisymmetric structures are loaded in an axisymmetric manner, only the radial and axial displacement components relative to a cylindrical coordinate system are non-zero: formulation of the element stiffness properties and the establishment of the appropriate form of eqn (5.5) is a quasi two-dimensional problem. When such a structure is loaded in a non-axisymmetric manner, as in the case of an axle-mounted wheel, the tangential displacement component is no longer zero and all three displacement components are functions of all three (cylindrical) spatial coordinates, and a truly three-dimensional situation obtains. However, if the angular dependence of the displacement components is expressed in terms of series of trigonometric functions, the orthogonality properties of such functions yield a formulation of the problem as a series of uncoupled quasi two-dimensional problems, when the integrations to form the $[k]$'s are carried out. The generalised coordinates of the system are then the amplitudes of the Fourier components [4].

The element used here is shown in Fig. 5.2. There are only three nodal circles per element, so that provided there is a diametral section with respect to which displacements are symmetric, a suitable displacement model for the element is

$$u = \sum_n (\alpha_{1n} + \alpha_{2n}r + \alpha_{3n}z) \cos n\theta$$

$$v = \sum_n (\alpha_{4n} + \alpha_{5n}r + \alpha_{6n}z) \cos n\theta$$

$$w = \sum_n (\alpha_{7n} + \alpha_{8n}r + \alpha_{9n}z) \sin n\theta$$

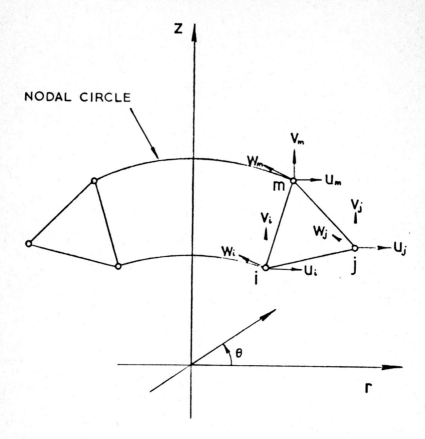

FIG. 5.2. Axisymmetric ring element—diametral section.

or in matrix form

$$\{u\} = \sum_n [\phi_n][M]\{\alpha_n\} \qquad (5.6)$$

where $[\phi_n]$ and $[M]$ are defined in Appendix 5.1. This displacement model is suitable for our case of the loaded wheel.

Equation (5.6) may be used to express the α's in terms of the element nodal u's. After some manipulation, we have

$$\{u\} = \sum_n [\phi_n][M][h]\{\hat{u}_n\}_0 \qquad (5.7)$$

with $[h]$ defined in Appendix 5.1.

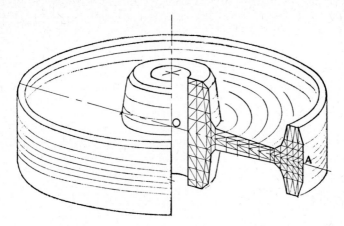

FIG. 5.3. Structural idealisation of a complex rimmed disc wheel using ring elements
(No. of elements, 189; No. of nodes, 126).

The element is in a three-dimensional state of strain defined by the vector

$$
\begin{Bmatrix} \varepsilon_r \\ \varepsilon_z \\ \varepsilon_\theta \\ \gamma_{rz} \\ \gamma_{z\theta} \\ \gamma_{r\theta} \end{Bmatrix}
=
\begin{Bmatrix} \sum_n \hat{\varepsilon}_{rn} \cos n\theta \\ \vdots \\ \sum \hat{\gamma}_{z\theta n} \sin n\theta \\ \vdots \end{Bmatrix}
=
\begin{Bmatrix} \dfrac{\partial u}{\partial r} \\[2mm] \dfrac{\partial v}{\partial z} \\[2mm] \left(\dfrac{1}{r}\dfrac{\partial w}{\partial \theta} + \dfrac{u}{r}\right) \\[2mm] \left(\dfrac{\partial u}{\partial z} + \dfrac{\partial v}{\partial r}\right) \\[2mm] \left(\dfrac{\partial w}{\partial z} + \dfrac{1}{r}\dfrac{\partial v}{\partial \theta}\right) \\[2mm] \left(\dfrac{1}{r}\dfrac{\partial u}{\partial \theta} + \dfrac{\partial w}{\partial r} - \dfrac{w}{r}\right) \end{Bmatrix}
\qquad (5.8)
$$

or

$$
\{\varepsilon\} = \sum_n [\Omega_n]\{\hat{\varepsilon}_n\} \qquad (5.9)
$$

Substituting from eqn (5.7) in eqn (5.8) yields, by appropriate differentiation,

$$
\{\varepsilon\} = \sum_n [\Omega_n][g_n][h]\{\hat{u}_n\}_0 \qquad (5.10)
$$

with $[g_n]$ defined in Appendix 5.1.

For an isotropic material, Hooke's law abbreviated from Appendix 5.1 can be written

$$\{\sigma\} = [D]\{\varepsilon\} \tag{5.11}$$

Then the strain energy stored in an element is

$$U_e = \tfrac{1}{2}\int_{\text{vol}} \{\varepsilon\}^t [D]\{\varepsilon\}\, d(\text{vol}) \tag{5.12}$$

If, on substituting from eqn (5.10) in eqn (5.12) we integrate first with respect to θ, we can take advantage of the orthogonality properties of the trigonometric functions. Uncoupling of the harmonic terms occurs and if U_e is written in the form of eqn (5.1), it is found that

$$[k]_e = \sum_n [k_n]_e \tag{5.13}$$

where the element stiffness matrix for the n'th harmonic is

$$[k_n]_e = [h]^t \left(\int\int [g_n]^t [D][g_n] r\, dr\, dz \right)[h] \tag{5.14}$$

The applied nodal circle forces are also expressed in terms of Fourier components. For symmetry about a diametral section

$$\{P\} = \begin{Bmatrix} P_r \\ P_z \\ P_\theta \end{Bmatrix} = \begin{Bmatrix} \sum_n \hat{p}_{rn}\cos n\theta \\ \sum_n \hat{p}_{zn}\cos n\theta \\ \sum_n \hat{p}_{\theta n}\sin n\theta \end{Bmatrix} \tag{5.15}$$

Then, proceeding as summarised in eqns (5.2) and (5.3), it is found that the overall stiffness matrix for each harmonic can be generated separately. The primary task is then reduced to solving equations of the form (5.5) for each harmonic in turn: the basic unknowns are nodal circle displacement amplitudes with the right-hand sides of the equations being nodal circle force amplitudes.

Having determined the nodal circle displacement amplitudes for an adequate number of harmonics, the strains and stress components are given by eqns (5.9) and (5.11). For the design calculations here, the effective stress

$$\sigma_e = \sqrt{\left(\tfrac{1}{2}\{(\sigma_r - \sigma_z)^2 + (\sigma_z - \sigma_\theta)^2 + (\sigma_\theta - \sigma_r)^2 \right.} \\ \left. + 6(\tau_{rz}{}^2 + \tau_{z\theta}{}^2 + \tau_{\theta r}{}^2)\}\right) \tag{5.16}$$

was computed for use in conjunction with the Von Mises criterion for yielding.

5.4 FINITE ELEMENT MODELLING OF
DISC-TYPE WHEELS

The accuracy of a finite element solution depends significantly on the original finite element modelling of the system; for the procedure used here, this implies the mesh design and the number of harmonics used. For economical working, one needs a minimum number of degrees of freedom compatible with adequate accuracy for the purpose at hand. To provide guidance in this matter, some preliminary computational experiments were carried out on finite element idealisations of two known situations not too far removed from the wheel problem. The diametral compression of a circular disc and the bending of a circular plate were chosen for this purpose and, in the light of the results obtained, the wheel idealisations typified in Figs. 5.4 and 5.5 with 20 harmonics were chosen to obtain the design data. The core store of the computer available for the work was fully utilised with this modelling. The two figures show the distribution of the maximum principal stress; it was the effective stress of eqn (5.16) which was actually used.

Using the mesh of ring-type elements of Figs. 5.4 and 5.5 with relatively few elements, the task of data preparation is eased. It is interesting to contrast this with the number of elements and thus the data preparation effort required for comparable overall accuracy if the wheel is idealised as a plane stress problem with elements of varying thickness. Such a treatment would only be appropriate for in-mid plane loading, of course, and Fig. 5.6 shows the mesh design required with simple constant strain elements. In referring to 'comparable accuracy' above, we were guided by the results of plane-stress and ring-type element idealisations for the case of a diametrally compressed disc.

The design specification required a consideration of three types of load: (a) a purely radial load P_r, as illustrated in Fig. 5.4; (b) an offset load P_0, typified in Fig. 5.5; (c) a combined radial load P_r and axial load P_a, where $P_r = 2P_a$.

Experience with wheels in service had shown that failure usually occurred in the disc near the disc–hub junction. Preliminary finite element calculations showed that such failures were consistent with the effective stress distribution produced by loading condition (c) above. The design calculations which follow consequently relate to the effective stress distribution in the wheel's disc due to loading (c).

A final consideration is the modelling of the conditions at the bore

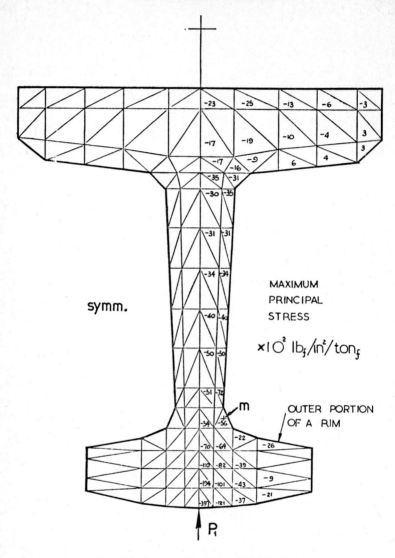

Fig. 5.4. Stresses due to a radial point load.

of the hub. The wheels of interest here were made of a low modulus material and usually the bore of the hub contained a force fit sleeve of metal. The elastic moduli of the wheel and sleeve were of different orders of magnitude, so that it was considered adequate to regard the bore of the

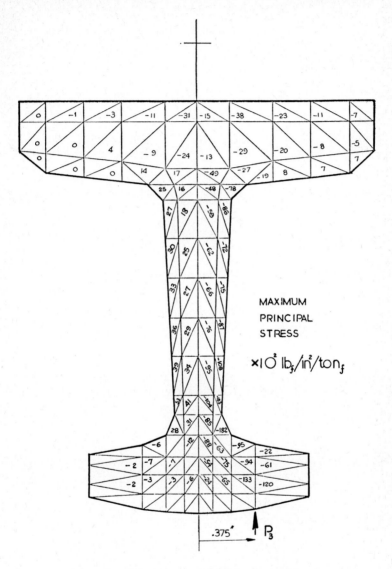

Fig. 5.5. An eccentric radial point load.

hub as rigidly constrained (computation showed that with the interference used, the shrink-fit stresses were negligible compared with those
due to the applied load).

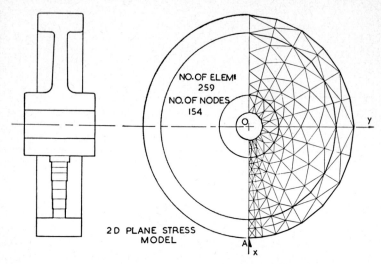

FIG. 5.6. Structural idealisation of a rimmed disc wheel.

5.5   INFLUENCE OF DISC AND RIM PROPORTIONS ON DISC STRESSES

The stress distribution in the disc due to the prescribed loading depends on the disc thickness, the manner in which the thickness varies with radius, the degree of camber if the disc is conical instead of flat and the size of the rim. To study the influence of these parameters on disc stresses, the wheel section was simplified to the form shown in Fig. 5.7.

TABLE 5.1
Dimensions of disc wheels with various rim sizes

Model	c(in)	d(in)	e(in)	h(in)	i(in)	V_{hub} (in³)	V_{dis} (in³)	V_{rim} (in³)	$\dfrac{V_{\text{rim}}}{V_{\text{disc}}} \times 100$
B1	0.50	2.00	0.25	0.25	0.50	3.142	6.627	1.129	17.04
B2	0.50	2.00	0.25	0.25	1.00	3.142	6.627	3.387	51.11
B3	0.50	2.00	0.25	0.25	2.00	3.142	6.627	7.903	119.27
B4	0.50	2.00	0.25	0.50	0.50	3.142	6.627	2.160	32.59
B5	0.50	2.00	0.25	0.50	1.00	3.142	6.627	6.480	97.78
B6	0.50	2.00	0.25	0.50	2.00	3.142	6.627	15.119	228.15
B7	0.50	2.00	0.25	1.00	0.50	3.142	6.627	3.927	59.26
B8	0.50	2.00	0.25	1.00	1.00	3.142	6.627	11.781	177.78
B9	0.50	2.00	0.25	1.00	2.00	3.142	6.627	27.489	414.82

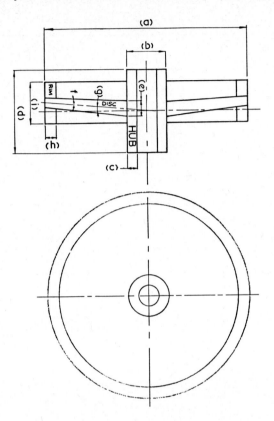

FIG. 5.7. An optimisation disc wheel model.

The effective stress associated with a radial section through the point of application of the load is a maximum at the disc–hub junction. The first set of calculations were aimed at finding the influence of the rim size on this maximum σ_e. Table 5.1 shows the range of plane disc wheels examined and Fig. 5.8 shows how increasing the rim volume reduces the maximum effective stress in the disc (for the purposes of these calculations, the rim was treated as the *extra* material added to an originally plane disc, as shown in Fig. 5.7). Interesting features of the results are:

1. The effectiveness of adding material to the rim decreases as the rim size increases.
2. Within the range of the proportions examined here (which were in

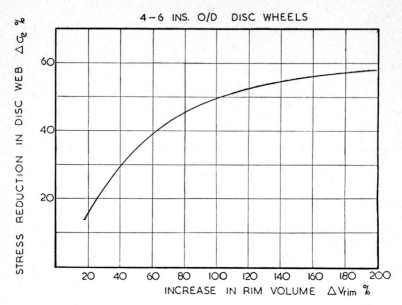

FIG. 5.8. Reduction of stresses due to increase of rim volume.

the neighbourhood of those currently used), the shape of the rim does not affect matters.

3. The wheels of interest ranged from 4 in to 6 in o.d. and the curve of Fig. 5.8 was found to be applicable to them all.

The stress distribution is very uneven in a constant thickness disc, σ_e being very much higher at the disc–hub junction than at the disc–rim junction for the combined load case, so that it is appropriate to consider varying the section of the disc. Figure 5.9 shows the manner in which the stress distribution is more favourably distributed when a taper is introduced. Here, the volume of the disc material was kept constant for the various tapers and a considerable improvement in material utilisation results. Naturally, one would expect the size of rim to influence the stress levels in a tapered disc in a manner analogous to that for a uniform disc. In fact, a few calculations showed that Fig. 5.8 could also be applied to these cases.

The stresses in the disc arise from a combined bending and direct action so that the optimum taper depends on the thickness of an initially uniform disc design. It was found that the relation between desirable taper and initial uniform thickness could be summarised by Fig. 5.10 for the range

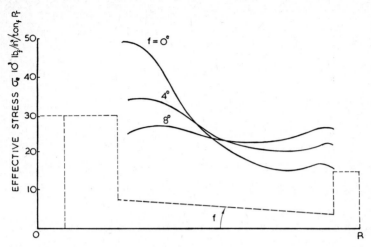

FIG. 5.9. Effect of disc taper. (Rimmed disc model: $a = 6$ in o.d., $b = 1 \cdot 5$ in o.d.).

of wheels of interest and for which a rim volume of about 60% of the disc volume was used.

For certain situations the performance of a wheel under impact could be important. This topic was not examined in great detail, but the few results obtained by means of an elementary theory of impact used in conjunction with the finite element results are of interest.

Using a conservation of energy argument and assuming that the deformed *shape* of a structure due to an impact load is the same as if the load were applied statically, the displacement under load is given by the familiar expression

$$\delta = \delta_{st} \left[1 + \sqrt{\left(1 + \frac{2H}{\delta_{st}} \right)} \right] \tag{5.17}$$

and the stresses by

$$\sigma = \sigma_{st} \left[1 + \sqrt{\left(1 + \frac{2H}{\delta_{st}} \right)} \right] \tag{5.18}$$

The quantities δ_{st} and σ_{st}, corresponding to static load, may be obtained by the finite element method in the case of a complex system; then, eqns (5.17) and (5.18) provide a measure of the effects of impact. Clearly δ_{st} is a measure of the stiffness of the structure, as seen by the load, so that if it can be reduced the impact effect can be mitigated. In this connection it is interesting to find that applying a camber to the disc improves matters considerably. Under a static radial load (with no axial component)

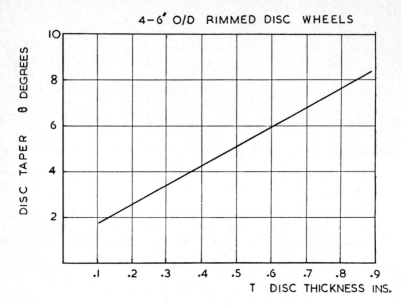

FIG. 5.10. Evaluation of disc taper from disc thickness.

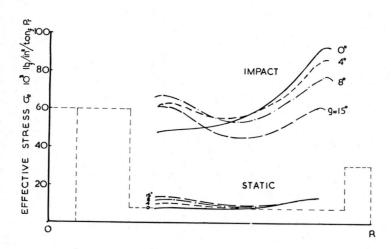

FIG. 5.11. Effect of disc camber (Rimmed disc model: $a = 6$ in o.d., $b = 1 \cdot 5$ in o.d.).

the worst disc stresses are found near the disc–rim junction, so that it is appropriate to apply eqn (5.18) to that station to obtain an estimate of the impact rating for the wheel disc. Figure 5.11 shows how impact performance is significantly improved by the introduction of a cambered disc to wheel B2 of Table 5.1.

The data produced by the investigations described above have been used to provide a very straightforward drawing office procedure to design a wheel disc and rim. This is described in the next section.

5.6 DESIGN OF A WHEEL FOR A PRESCRIBED STATIC LOAD

For our purpose here, a prescribed load always consists of a radial load P_r and axial load $P_a = \frac{1}{2}P_r$, acting simultaneously as described previously. P_r is said to be the rated load of the wheel.

As part of the work described in the previous section, the effective stress at the hub–disc junction was computed for 6 in, 5 in and 4 in o.d. wheels having 1 in, 1·5 in and 2 in o.d. hubs and a number of uniform thicknesses. Using the curve of Fig. 5.8, a desired reduction in the value of this stress can be achieved by the addition of an appropriate rim. For a given volume of rim, it is possible to re-interpret the results in a form more convenient for design. Curves can be produced which relate disc thickness to rated load directly. Figure 5.12 shows such a set for a 5 in wheel for which the rim–disc volume ratio was 60%. Curves, which are very

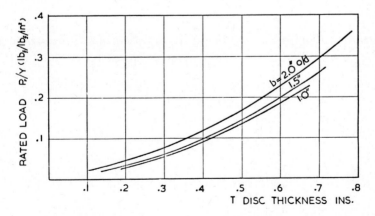

Fig. 5.12. Evaluation of disc thickness from rated load (5 in o.d. wheel).

similar in form, were produced for 6 in and 4 in wheels. The rated load is expressed in terms of a permissible working stress Y. For a uniform disc wheel, this is essentially all that is required but since the stress distribution is uneven, it is desirable to use a tapered disc. We have previously pointed out that the optimum taper required depends on the thickness, and the data obtained may be summarised in the curve of Fig. 5.10 which has been found applicable to the range of wheels from 4 in to 6 in outside diameter. The procedure, then, is to use Fig. 5.12 to yield a suitable constant thickness disc and Fig. 5.10 to derive an optimum taper. Strictly, new curves would be required if different rim–disc volume ratios were used but in view of the shape of the curve of Fig. 5.8, Figs. 5.12 and 5.10 would be adequate for rim–disc volume ratios neighbouring on the 60% used here.

5.7 CONCLUSION

Bringing increased precision to design calculations inevitably means more elaborate design procedures but unless such procedures are easy and convenient to use they may not be adopted. In the problem discussed here, realistic prediction of stresses and deformations requires a very sophisticated analysis tool; we have distilled the data produced by such a tool to yield a very straightforward procedure. Further refinement of this treatment of disc wheels is possible of course, but, as always, only at some cost.

ACKNOWLEDGEMENTS

The authors would like to thank Professor A. J. Ede, University of Aston, for his encouragement whilst this study was in progress and Messrs. Geo. H. Hughes Ltd for providing some financial assistance.

REFERENCES

1. Martin, H. C. and Carey, G. F. (1973). *Introduction to Finite Element Analysis*, McGraw-Hill.
2. Zienkiewicz, O. C. (1971). *The Finite Element Method*, 2nd ed, McGraw-Hill.
3. Pian, T. H. H. and Pin Tong (1969). Basis of finite element methods for solid continua, *Int. J. Num. Methods in Engineering*, **1**.
4. Wilson, E. L. (1965). Structural analysis of axisymmetric solids, *J. A.I.A.A.*, **3** (12).

APPENDIX 5.1

The matrices used in Section 5.3 are defined as follows.
In eqn (5.6):

$$[\phi_n] = \begin{bmatrix} \cos n\theta & 0 & 0 \\ 0 & \cos n\theta & 0 \\ 0 & 0 & \sin n\theta \end{bmatrix}$$

$$[M] = \begin{bmatrix} 1 & r & z & 0 & 0 & 0 & 0 & 0 & 0 \\ 0 & 0 & 0 & 1 & r & 2 & 0 & 0 & 0 \\ 0 & 0 & 0 & 0 & 0 & 0 & 1 & r & z \end{bmatrix}$$

In eqn (5.7):

$$[h] = \tfrac{1}{2}\Delta \begin{bmatrix}
a_i & 0 & 0 & a_j & 0 & 0 & a_m & 0 & 0 \\
b_i & 0 & 0 & b_j & 0 & 0 & b_m & 0 & 0 \\
c_i & 0 & 0 & c_j & 0 & 0 & c_m & 0 & 0 \\
0 & a_i & 0 & 0 & a_j & 0 & 0 & a_m & 0 \\
0 & b_i & 0 & 0 & b_j & 0 & 0 & b_m & 0 \\
0 & c_i & 0 & 0 & c_j & 0 & 0 & c_m & 0 \\
0 & 0 & a_i & 0 & 0 & a_j & 0 & 0 & a_m \\
0 & 0 & b_i & 0 & 0 & b_j & 0 & 0 & b_m \\
0 & 0 & c_i & 0 & 0 & c_j & 0 & 0 & c_m
\end{bmatrix}$$

where

$$\left.\begin{aligned}
a_i &= r_j r_m - r_m r_j \\
b_i &= z_j - z_m \\
c_i &= r_m - r_j
\end{aligned}\right\}$$
Other coefficients by cyclic permutation of subscripts

$$2\Delta = r_j(z_m - z_i) + r_i(z_j - z_m) + r_m(z_i - z_s)$$

$$[\Omega_n] = \begin{bmatrix}
\cos n\theta & & & & & \\
& \cos n\theta & & & & \\
& & \cos n\theta & & & \\
& & & \cos n\theta & & \\
& & & & \sin n\theta & \\
& & & & & \sin n\theta
\end{bmatrix}$$

$$[g_n] = \begin{bmatrix} 0 & 1 & 0 & 0 & 0 & 0 & 0 & 0 & 0 \\ 0 & 0 & 0 & 0 & 0 & 1 & 0 & 0 & 0 \\ \dfrac{1}{r} & 1 & \dfrac{z}{r} & 0 & 0 & 0 & \dfrac{n}{r} & n & \dfrac{nz}{r} \\ 0 & 0 & 1 & 0 & 1 & 0 & 0 & 0 & 0 \\ \dfrac{-n}{r} & -n & \dfrac{-nz}{r} & 0 & 0 & 0 & \dfrac{-1}{r} & 0 & \dfrac{-z}{r} \\ 0 & 0 & 0 & \dfrac{-n}{r} & -n & \dfrac{-nz}{r} & 0 & 0 & 1 \end{bmatrix}$$

Hooke's law is $\{\sigma\} = [D]\{\varepsilon\}$ or, written in expanded form:

$$\begin{Bmatrix} \sigma_r \\ \sigma_z \\ \sigma_\theta \\ \tau_{rz} \\ \tau_{z\theta} \\ \tau_{\theta r} \end{Bmatrix} = \frac{E(1-\nu)}{(1+\nu)(1-2\nu)}$$

$$\times \begin{bmatrix} 1 & \dfrac{\nu}{1-\nu} & \dfrac{\nu}{1-\nu} & 0 & 0 & 0 \\ & 1 & \dfrac{\nu}{1-\nu} & 0 & 0 & 0 \\ & & 1 & 0 & 0 & 0 \\ & & & \dfrac{1-2\nu}{2(1-\nu)} & 0 & 0 \\ & \text{Symm} & & & \dfrac{1-2\nu}{2(1-\nu)} & 0 \\ & & & & & \dfrac{1-2\nu}{2(1-\nu)} \end{bmatrix} \begin{Bmatrix} \varepsilon_r \\ \varepsilon_z \\ \varepsilon_\theta \\ \gamma_{rz} \\ \gamma_{z\theta} \\ \gamma_{\theta r} \end{Bmatrix}$$

6

Photoelasticity Applied to Complicated Diesel Engine Models

H. FESSLER AND M. PERLA

University of Nottingham and Stress Analysis Ltd

SUMMARY

The construction of the frames of diesel engines has become very sophisticated, to meet the demands for the greatest possible power output from a given overall size and overall weight. The frames are highly rated structures, subjected to very complex dynamic loading from many different forces which vary in magnitude and direction. This has led to very complex shapes, as the basic 'boxes' which carry the bearings and cylinder liners, torque reaction and ancillary equipment have been strengthened by changes of shape and the additions of ribs and other reinforcements. The resulting complicated shapes can only be produced economically as castings. The geometric freedom of this method of construction, together with the requirements of the moulding shop and foundry, have brought further complications of shape. These developments, which have occurred in almost all the competing manufacturing organisations, have led to the position where previous experience of successful operation allows 'design by modification' but the structures are far too complicated for even approximate stress calculations. If a major advance is contemplated it is therefore necessary to determine stresses experimentally. At the design stage a model technique is obviously preferable to testing a (non-existing) prototype; this paper shows how photoelastic models can be used to give complete stress analysis of these very complicated castings.

Because the loading is so very complicated and the load paths in the components are only partially understood, simplifications of shape may lead to significant differences between model and prototype stresses.

6.1 INTRODUCTION

Models are useful in stress analysis of engine parts because they can be made to a convenient scale and of materials which allow convenient loads to be used. Results may therefore be obtained more quickly and more cheaply than using engine components, especially for large engines. Diesel engine models are complicated because the engines are complex and sophisticated.

Photoelasticity is useful because much stress analysis is required, as the engines have to be highly rated to obtain a share of this very competitive

market. This means that the components are subjected to large firing
forces and high temperatures as well as large inertia forces due to the
high speeds which are essential to produce the required power in an engine
of minimum length and minimum weight. Stress analysis is carried out
on new projects and to redesign components of operating engines to
allow up-rating or to investigate failures. We have studied engine frames
(bedplates, A frames, bearing caps), crankshafts, connecting rods, piston
pins, valves, cylinder heads and liners.

6.2   ENGINE FRAMES

The construction of the frames of diesel engines has become very sophisticated to meet the demands for the greatest possible power output
from a given overall size and overall weight. The frames are highly rated
structures, subjected to very complex dynamic loading from many different forces which vary in magnitude and direction. This has led to very
complex shapes, as the basic 'boxes' which carry the bearings and cylinder
liners, torque reaction and ancillary equipment have been strengthened
by changes of shape and the additions of ribs and other reinforcements.
The resulting complicated shapes can only be produced economically as
castings. The geometric freedom of this method of construction, together
with the requirements of the moulding shop and foundry, have brought
further complications of shape. These developments, which have occurred
in almost all the competing manufacturing organisations, have led to the
position where previous experience of successful operation allows design
by modification, but the structures are far too complicated for even
approximate stress calculations. If a major advance is contemplated it is
therefore necessary to determine stresses experimentally. At the design
stage a model technique is obviously preferable to testing a (non-existing)
prototype.

Models of engine frames are used for stress and deformation analysis.
The latter is often more important than the former because it is required to
determine the radial and angular stiffnesses of the bearings, which are
necessary to determine crankshaft bending moments.

Deformation analysis can be carried out at room temperature as well
as by using the frozen stress method. Room temperature, 'direct loading'
tests require larger forces than frozen stress ones but are quicker to carry
out and potentially more accurate because several load magnitudes can
be used to obtain the required stiffnesses. However, the positions where

measurements can be made are limited by the loading arrangements. A room temperature loading is shown in Fig. 6.1.

Because the loading is so very complicated and the load paths in the components are only partially understood, simplifications of shape may lead to significant differences between model and prototype stresses. It is therefore necessary to reproduce most of the details of the prototype in the model; this often involves features which cannot be machined and it was therefore necessary to develop a technique of precision casting.

FIG. 6.1. 8-cylinder vee engine frame model arranged for room temperature loading by hydraulic jacks.

6.3   MODEL MANUFACTURE

As for any other casting, a precision epoxy resin casting needs a mould with cores, made from accurate patterns. The technique has been described by the present authors [1]. For the engine frame tests described here it was necessary to make castings of the bedplate, A frame or column and cylinder casings shown in Fig. 6.1. Patterns were made of only half of one bay of this four-bay (eight-cylinder) model; these patterns were each used ten times and each mould was carefully assembled from ten pieces which were cemented with silicon rubber at the joints. The main bearing caps were cast in split moulds which could be used several times.

The resulting castings were proportionally more accurate than the engine castings. Machining was only carried out in the same positions as in the engine. After machining the upper and lower faces of the bedplate and the main bearing, joint surfaces of bedplate and bearing caps, all the necessary holes were drilled and the bearing caps were clamped to the bedplate with the correct pre-tension forces in the bolts before boring the main bearings. The joint faces of the column and cylinder casings were machined and the necessary holes for the connecting 'bolts' drilled. The studs which retain the cylinder casings were screwed into cylindrical steel inserts. The latter were located in holes bored transversely through the stud bosses.

The crankshafts, also made of epoxy resin, were too flexible to be turned from one casting. To achieve the greatest possible accuracy of the frozen test crankshaft, it was built up from individual webs, pins and journals. Precision castings of webs had recesses machined at the required positions to fit journals and pins. One journal and one crankpin were cemented to one web for each throw. These sub-assemblies were inserted into the main bearings and the other web was cemented after the individual crank throws had been accurately aligned relative to one another using standard metrology equipment. The neat fitting crankshaft made in this way could be turned in its five bearings with one hand, showing that it was correctly aligned in the main bearings.

6.4 DESIGN OF EXPERIMENTS

When components are subjected to several concurrent loads, the corresponding model loads must be in the same ratios to one another as the component loads. The engine frames consist of several parts connected by bolts or studs and it is necessary to model the correct stiffness of these as well as their pre-tensions. The order of magnitude of the stresses in the models is limited by the required accuracy of measurements and the acceptable deformations. The strain ratio (model strain/engine strain) which arises from the above considerations has to be fixed before the model is completed if the extents of the contact areas of bearings are to have a predetermined value. The bearing clearances can then be adjusted using Hertzian contact stress theory.

Frozen stress tests can only be carried out with steady load; engine inertia forces must therefore be replaced by boundary forces applied by weights or soft springs. The reactions to these forces must not act on the model but must be carried to 'earth', i.e. must be carried by the 'foundation' on which the model is supported. The same argument applies to the output torque.

As no photoelastic material exists which has required strength and ductility to model the high tensile steel screws used in engines, epoxy screws are usually replaced by small diameter steel bolts and steel coil springs or conical disc springs are used to obtain the correctly scaled model bolt stiffness.

When the engine components are made of different materials it is desirable to make model components in materials having the same ratios of Young's moduli. For frozen stress tests a ratio of 3:1, as occurs between steel and cast iron, can be achieved by altering the composition of the epoxy resin [2].

6.5 LOADING OF MODELS

A room temperature loading set-up for an eight-cylinder vee engine model is shown in Fig. 6.1. The disc springs mentioned above may be seen under the steel nuts in Fig. 6.2. In addition to the bolting forces the hydraulic jack seen near the top of Fig. 6.1 can apply firing or reciprocating inertia forces; for the former it is connected to the top of the cylinder casings of the model, for the latter to the steel 'earth' frame to which the model is bolted (see also Fig. 6.2). These jacks are joined to steel connecting rods which can exert upward or downward forces on the epoxy resin crankshaft. The torque is transmitted to the steel 'flywheel', shown in Fig. 6.1, and measured by the floating proving ring immediately below it.

In frozen stress tests it is necessary to allow the model to expand freely and the frames are therefore suspended from four long pivoted steel rods. Deflection due to self weight is reduced by immersion of the whole model in a dense inert oil during the freezing cycle. The firing and inertia forces are applied by freely hanging lead weights acting through knife-edge pivoted, overhead levers. The reactions to the unbalanced inertia forces and the output torque are also reacted by pivoted rods which do not restrain the thermal expansion of the model.

FIG. 6.2. Detail of model showing method of supporting displacement transducers, disc springs.

6.6　MEASUREMENT OF DEFORMATIONS

For 'neat' fitting crankshafts (i.e. no clearance between journals and bearings) bearing displacements can be obtained from journal displacement measurements. This was done in some of the room temperature tests. After typical, scaled, running–bearing clearances were introduced in the model, direct, room-temperature tests only gave journal displacements. Small linear capacitance transducers were used for this work. Small holes were drilled in the bearings to admit the sensing rods. The bodies of the transducers were mounted on the 'earth' frame by an arrangement of clamps shown in Fig. 6.2.

In the frozen tests significant deformations may occur due to the 'self' weight of the components. To achieve the greatest possible accuracy, self-weight deformations, obtained after a stress freezing cycle without applied loads, were subtracted from the displacements due to the loads. Very careful preparation and great care were necessary to ensure that the model was positioned correctly for these sets of measurements. It is essential that the model is accurately located in a measuring rig which

Fig. 6.3. Bearing bore measurement: front carriage carries reference ring (hidden behind bearing cap); rear carriage supports transducer (shown in bore).

also locates the measuring instruments. The arrangement is shown in Fig. 6.3.

The model was located at six points, defined by 3 mm diameter steel balls cemented to the bedplate. It was supported on three balls near the corners of the foundation surface and pushed against three points on vertical faces of the bedplate, two on one side, one on one end. The three support balls define a $y = $ constant plane, parallel to the accurately ground top surface of the base of the 'earth' frame; all vertical readings are referred to this plane. The two side balls define an $x = $ constant plane used as datum for horizontal measurements. The end ball ensures that the model always rests in the same z position on the base, thus eliminating any positioning errors due to the inevitable flatness defects of the locating surfaces.

To measure the deformations of the main bearing bores, the model was dismantled and the bearing caps were replaced after removal of the crankshaft. A linear capacitance transducer was mounted on a carriage as shown in Fig. 6.3. This carriage has to move axially along the generators of the bearing bores. A kinematic slide was constructed by supporting this carriage on three bearing balls fixed to its (horizontal) base and locating it horizontally relative to the base by two bearing balls fixed to an overhanging (vertical) plate. In operation the carriage is sliding on the y = constant plane on which the model rests (vertical positioning) and along an x = constant plane of the earth frame parallel to that which locates the model (horizontal positioning). The carriage is pressed by a coil spring against the x = constant plane of the base to ensure correct horizontal positioning through constant contact pressure on the two side balls.

Significant displacement of the bores displaces the centre lines of the bores relative to the axis of the transducer movement. Because it would be very tedious to calculate the displacements from eccentric measurements, a second sliding carriage was constructed to carry a reference ring. This steel reference ring is mounted on slides to measure its horizontal (transverse relative to the axis of the bores) and vertical movements accurately when it is aligned to be concentric with one end of each bore in turn. It is then used as the datum for the transducer.

Because the effective coefficient of thermal expansion of epoxy resin ($\alpha_{epoxy} - \alpha_{steel}$) is $4\cdot74 \times 10^{-5}/°C$ between 20° and 112°C for the type used, allowance must be made for variations of temperature of the measurement room before and after stress-freezing. A linear capacitance transducer which measured the thermal difference of expansion directly was found useful and accurate for this purpose. The overall accuracy of location of the model and the sliding carriage on the base and of the linear capacitance measurements was found to be within $\pm 0\cdot0001$ in.

The calculation of the displacements of points in the bearing bores was not simple because the position of a point was defined by the vertical and horizontal positions of the reference ring and by the radial transducer readings in the bore and in the reference ring. The radial displacement of the point due to loading must also take account of the differential expansion of the model and the steel base, reference ring and measuring carriages because there were differences of room temperature at times when measurements were taken.

6.7 DEFORMATION AND DISPLACEMENT OF BEARINGS

Using the above procedures, displacements of the five bearing bores were measured at ten angular and five axial positions in each bore for the time in the engine cycle when the greatest firing forces occur in the second bay.

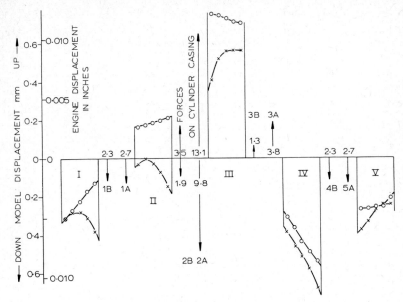

FIG. 6.4. Vertical deformation of bearings and forces on crankshaft, in kg: ◯ = cap; × = bedplate.

The bearing displacements in the vertical plane are shown in Fig. 6.4, together with the vertical components of the forces exerted on the crankshaft, except for the firing forces which are reacted on the cylinder casings. It is not convenient to show the necessary information at the true axial positions. Roman numerals refer to diaphragms, 1A refers to Number 1 cylinder in A bank, etc.

Distances between corresponding ◯ and × symbols show the opening (◯ above ×) or closing (◯ below ×) of the bores in the vertical plane. It will be noted that the greatest openings occur nearest to the firing forces. Curvature of the bearing surface shows how the bearing conforms to the bending of the journal with which it is in contact.

Figure 6.5 shows the corresponding values in the horizontal plane. Because this plane contains the joint surface, it is necessary to measure above it for cap displacements and below it for bedplate bore displacements.

The horizontal components of the forces are very much smaller than the vertical ones. It should be noted that the horizontal displacements are generally smaller than the vertical ones. Positions of greatest vertical opening of the bores described above generally coincide with the greatest horizontal closing, showing that the bearings behave like rings.

120   H. Fessler and M. Perla

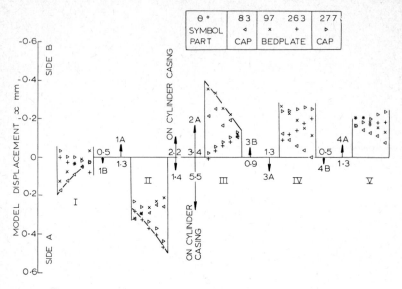

Fig. 6.5. Horizontal deformations of bearings and forces on crankshaft, in kg.

The greatest distortions occur in bearings II and III. All the values for three $z =$ constant planes for bearing III have been plotted in Fig. 6.6. (The values for the other two measured planes have been omitted to avoid confusion, the greatest convenient displacement scale having been used.) The undeformed bores are drawn 1·7 times full size; the deformations are magnified 50 times, leading to 29 times radially exaggerated deformation curves.

When these measuring positions were selected, slipping of the joint surface was not expected and it was believed that ten points would be sufficient to define the deformed shapes. Although there are only five experimental points on the cap and five on the bed, it is reasonable to deduce from Fig. 6.6 that slipping of that joint surface has occurred.

6.8   DISCUSSION

There are two approaches to model deformation studies: (a) actual, critical engine loading conditions may be reproduced in the model and the model measurements may be used to predict whether the corresponding engine deformations are acceptable; (b) individual loads or related

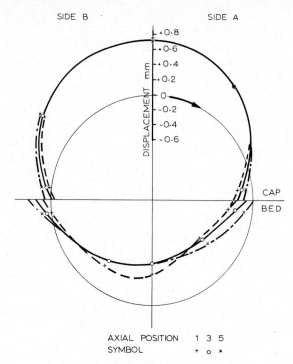

SIDE B   SIDE A

AXIAL POSITION   1 3 5
SYMBOL   + o ×

FIG. 6.6. Deformation of bearing III.

groups of loads may be applied to obtain stiffness factors for use in design calculations. The latter method has limitations due to the non-linear behaviour caused by the clearance of the crankshaft journals in the main bearings (for example, the flexural restraint of a bearing depends on whether the 'clearance has been taken up', i.e. whether the journal touches the bearing on opposite sides at both ends).

Stiffness factors may be obtained for the assembled frame and crank-shaft or they could be obtained for the frame without a crankshaft. The latter requires the correct forces to be applied to each bearing. This may be conveniently done by replacing the crankshaft by a series of straight pins, each of which spans one bay and extends to the centres of the ad-jacent bearings. The necessary loading may then be applied to those pins.

The first approach was taken for the frozen test, as it would have been practically impossible to carry out in the limited time the many different loading modes. The experimental procedure for the frozen test is lengthy and takes approximately 14 days to conduct. One critical engine loading condition was chosen—firing of cylinder B in bay 2 with all the corresponding loads in other cylinders applied.

The room temperature tests were conducted with individual and groups of loads—the second approach to the problem—as each test could be carried out in a relatively short time.

Note. Conventional frozen-stress photoelastic analysis of the main members of the frame was carried out but unfortunately could not be completed in time for inclusion in this paper; it will be published elsewhere.

ACKNOWLEDGEMENTS

This work formed part of an investigation supported by a Science Research Council grant. The authors wish to thank members of the staff of Mirrlees-Blackstone Ltd for their interest in the work and for providing engine information. They also wish to thank the technicians in the photo-elastic laboratory and of the Applied Science Faculty Workshop for their careful, skilled work.

REFERENCES

1. Fessler, H. and Perla, M. (1973). Precision casting of epoxy-resin photo-elastic models, *J. Strain Analysis*, **8**, 30.
2. Perla, M. (1964). 'Epoxy Resins for Composite Models', 5th Conf. Photo-elastic Method of Stress Analysis, Leningrad, p. 126.

7

Torsional Design Aspects of
Long Wheelbase Vehicles

P. W. SHARMAN
Loughborough University of Technology

SUMMARY

Torsional stiffness—does it need to be high or low? What is the effect of suspension roll stiffness? What is the best way of distributing torsion resisting structure? These are some of the questions in the mind of the designer of the vehicle chassis, and this paper examines some of the aspects of designing for torsion.

Four types of torsional loading are identified, covering asymmetrically distributed load, ground plane twist, lateral acceleration due to cornering, turning loads and dynamic response from ground plane ripple.

Two simplified chassis models are considered—the 'backbone', consisting of one or more torsionally resistant longitudinal members; the peripheral frame, in which the two torsionally flexible longitudinal members are connected at their ends by torsionally resistant members; and the ladder frame, in which the longitudinals are connected by many cross-members.

The effect of varying the cross-sectional shape, size and disposition of the torsionally resistant members is examined from the point of view of minimising weight while maintaining a satisfactory stress level. The analyses use both simple structural theory and computer analysis for the more complex structures.

7.1 INTRODUCTION

Torsional stiffness—does it need to be high or low? What is the effect of suspension stiffness? If a torsion resisting structure is needed, how is it best distributed?

These are some of the questions in the mind of the designer of the vehicle chassis, and this paper will examine some of the aspects of designing for torsion—starting with simple loading considerations and leading to the optimum design of ladder frames.

Four types of torsional loading are identified, covering asymmetrically distributed loading, ground plane twist, lateral acceleration due to cornering and static turning forces.

Two simplified chassis models are considered—the 'backbone', consisting of one or more torsionally resistant longitudinal members, and the ladder frame, consisting of two torsionally flexible longitudinals connected by several or many torsion resistant members.

7.2 LOADING CASES

The design of commercial vehicle chassis frames principally revolves around the bending strength required in the longitudinal members [1]. For good structural efficiency, deep beams are used with thin webs and flanges. As these members have low inherent torsional stiffness, cross-members are added to provide some torsional resistance and stability to the structure.

Four principal torsional loading cases may be identified, which may be superimposed in various combinations according to the type of expected operation. They are as follows.

Case 1: Vehicle static with load asymmetrically distributed. This 'dead weight' condition may also be used as a steady velocity case, in which dynamic load factors of between 1·3 and 2 are introduced to account for the operation on bumpy roads and related fatigue criteria [2].

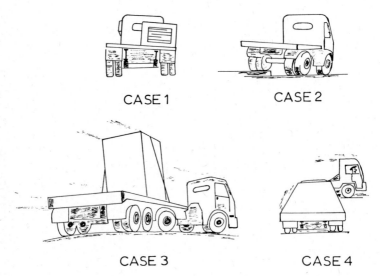

CASE 1   CASE 2

CASE 3   CASE 4

Fig. 7.1. Torsional loading cases. Case 1—asymmetric loading. Case 2—twisted ground plane. Case 3—cornering side force. Case 4—severe turning.

Case 2: Vehicle static with ground plane twisted. The suspension may accommodate the majority of the twist depending on its roll stiffness, but, in so doing, the chassis will be subjected to torsion.

Case 3: Vehicle under steady lateral acceleration, causing cornering. The payload, due to the height of its centre of gravity above the roll axis, causes a large torque which is reacted by the front and rear suspensions. The influence of torsional stiffness on this distribution has been examined in a previous note [3].

Case 4: Vehicle subject to large turning forces at low forward velocity. This is particularly severe in rear multi-axle configurations where, due to tyre scrub, large turning forces are required. In articulated vehicles, the tractor may be at a right angle to the trailer axis during manoeuvring, causing a large torque due to the wheel scrub.

These cases are illustrated in Fig. 7.1.

7.3 TORSION INDUCED BY LOADING CASES

In order to facilitate the calculation of the induced torque, the chassis has been simplified into a single torsionally resistant member, supported at its extremities by the suspension and axle beams which have been represented by a simple rotational spring. Thus the model may represent any conventional commercial vehicle chassis, and in the case of multi-axle configurations each rotational spring would represent the group of front or rear suspensions. For semi-trailers the front rotational spring would be the effective rotational rate at the fifth wheel coupling, thus including the tractor suspension and torsional stiffness. It should be noted that this model is only used to obtain induced torque, and not for structural analysis; thus its crudity will not restrict the derived results. Also, the properties of the model are derived from analysis of realistic representations of chassis.

In terms of the road spring stiffness k_S and the tyre stiffness k_T, the effective rotational stiffness is given by:

$$k = \frac{1}{2/B^2 k_S + 2/B_W^2 k_T} \tag{7.1}$$

where B_S and B_W are the lateral distance between the springs and tyre centres, respectively. For multi-axle groups the stiffnesses represent the total stiffness of each side of the group. This equation is valid only for simple (non-linked) suspensions, such as beam axles, trailing arms, etc.

7.3.1 Asymmetric Load

It frequently arises that, when loading a vehicle with certain payloads (e.g. timber, bricks, etc.), due to pallet sizes and fork-lift truck utilisation, one side of the vehicle is loaded first. Thus a realistic condition is to consider one-half of the maximum distributed payload to be placed on one side of the vehicle. Conditions could conceivably be worse for more concentrated loads, but under these circumstances the operator would probably reduce the payload.

Simple analysis using equilibrium and compatibility gives the fractions of the applied torque that are reacted at front and rear as

$$\frac{T_F}{T} = \frac{L_2 + GJ/k_Fl}{1 + GJ/k_Fl + GJ/k_Rl} \tag{7.2}$$

$$\frac{T_R}{T} = \frac{L_1 + GJ/k_Rl}{1 + GJ/k_Rl + GJ/k_Fl} \tag{7.3}$$

The quantities L_1 and L_2 are the distances of the payload c.g. from the front and rear suspensions divided by the wheelbase, respectively. For a uniformly distributed load over the whole wheelbase, these fractions are both equal to 0·5 and the front and rear torques are then only dependent on the spring rates k_F and k_R. These relationships are shown in Fig. 7.2.

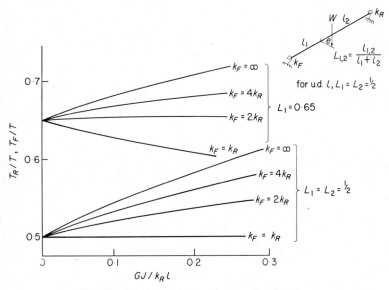

FIG. 7.2. Maximum torque due to offset loading.

Note that changes in the torsional stiffness (equal to GJ/l) only change the torque in the chassis a small amount.

7.3.2 Static Vehicle with Imposed Torsional Displacements

The model of the trailer is much the same as the previous case although the payload itself does not contribute any torque. The ground plane is twisted through an angle α from front to rear, which corresponds to imposing a rotation α at the base of the rear rotational spring. In terms of a single bump raised a distance Δ above an otherwise flat road surface, the relationship between α and Δ is simply:

$$\alpha = \frac{\Delta}{B_W} \tag{7.4}$$

Using a similar method to the previous case, the solution for the induced torque is given by:

$$\frac{T}{k_R \alpha} = \frac{GJ/k_R l}{1 + GJ/k_R l + GJ/k_F l} \tag{7.5}$$

It should be noted that this torque is constant from the front to rear suspensions. Figure 7.3, which shows this relationship, indicates that the torque increases sharply with torsional stiffness.

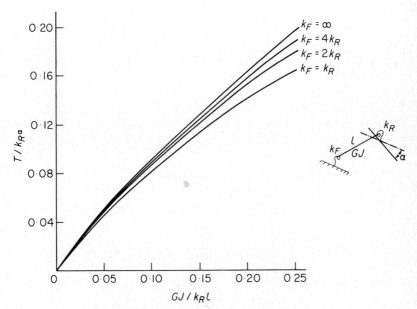

FIG. 7.3. Torque induced by given twist.

There is a limit to the maximum torque sustained by a chassis under these conditions, which occurs when the chassis is so stiff that the wheel, opposite to the one undergoing bump, loses contact with the road. The maximum torque is given by:

$$T_{max} = \frac{L_1 W B_W}{2} \tag{7.6}$$

Another limiting condition occurs when the suspension on the bump side reaches the end of its travel and becomes virtually solid. In this case, the rate of the rotational spring is effectively doubled (one spring is solid). If Δ_S is the maximum travel of the spring from static loaded position to bump stop, then the angle of the ground plane twist at which this occurs may be shown to be:

$$\alpha^* = \frac{\Delta_S}{B}\left(2 + \frac{lk_R}{GJ} + \frac{k_R}{k_F}\right) \tag{7.7}$$

and the corresponding torque in the chassis is:

$$T^* = \Delta_S k_R B \tag{7.8}$$

However, it should be mentioned at this stage that numerical studies have indicated that these limiting conditions seldom occur in practical situations.

7.3.3 Steady Lateral Acceleration

Figure 7.4 shows the geometry of the problem. The centre of gravity of the payload is distance h above the twist (flexural) axis of the chassis, and the payload (assumed as a concentrated mass) is subjected to a lateral acceleration of $n \times g$. This causes the c.g. to move laterally due to the torsional flexibility of the system, although the shift due to lateral flexibility is neglected. The vertical component of payload mass also contributes to the torque, making the problem mathematically non-linear.

If ξ is the rotation of the originally vertical line through the payload c.g. and the flexural axis of the chassis, then the applied torque is:

$$T = Wh(\sin \xi + n \cos \xi) \tag{7.9}$$

The rotation ξ at the payload c.g. may be related to the stiffnesses and the applied torque given by:

$$\xi = T\left\{\frac{(1/k_R + l_2/GJ)(1/k_F + l_1/GJ)}{1/k_R + 1/k_F + l/GJ}\right\} \tag{7.10}$$

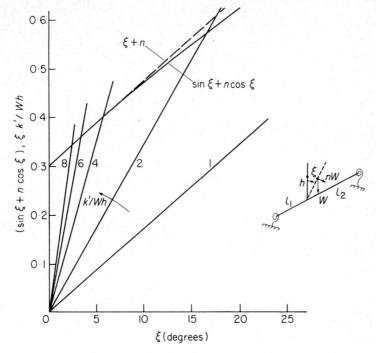

FIG. 7.4. Solution to cornering problem.

Thus the equation to determine ξ is:

$$Wh(\sin \xi + n \cos \xi) = k'\xi \qquad (7.11)$$

where k' is the inverse of the expression in braces in eqn (7.10).

To solve this equation, a graphical technique may be used, such as illustrated in Fig. 7.4. However, in practical situations, the angle ξ is limited to a fairly small value, for instance less than 15°. Thus the linear approximation to the equation may be used with reasonable accuracy:

$$Wh(\xi + n) = k'\xi \qquad (7.12)$$

giving:

$$\xi = \frac{n}{k'/Wh - 1} \qquad (7.13)$$

The form of this equation shows that an instability occurs when the denominator is zero—in other words, there is a critical combination of the parameters at which torsional instability will occur, regardless of lateral acceleration. Above this lower limit of stiffness, small but finite values of the angle may be calculated, from which the applied torque may be found. The resulting torque in the chassis is given by expressions (7.2) and (7.3), with the applied torque given by eqn (7.9). The influence of the non-linear term in the expression for the applied torque may be judged from Fig. 7.5 showing that even at a small angle of 5°, the torque is increased by 20–30% by the shift of the payload c.g.

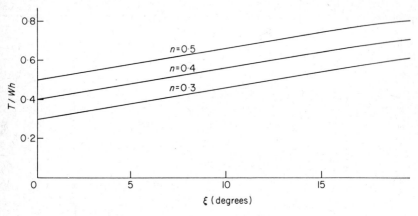

FIG. 7.5. Torque applied during cornering.

The reactions of the wheels on the inside of the corner are of prime significance from the point of view of road-holding, for when one of these reactions is reduced to zero the distribution of the lateral resistance of the suspension changes, which could cause an instability on a slippery road surface. The inner wheel reaction at the rear suspension is given by:

$$R = L_1 W - \frac{T_R}{B_W} \tag{7.14}$$

but

$$T_R = \eta_R Wh(\xi + n) \tag{7.15}$$

where η_R is the distribution factor for the rear suspension, given by the eqns (7.2) and (7.3). Thus:

$$\frac{R}{W} = L_1 - \eta_R \frac{nh}{B_W}\left(\frac{1}{k'/Wh - 1}\right) \tag{7.16}$$

The sensitivity of the reaction to the term in brackets is obvious from the form of the equation, and is illustrated in Fig. 7.6.

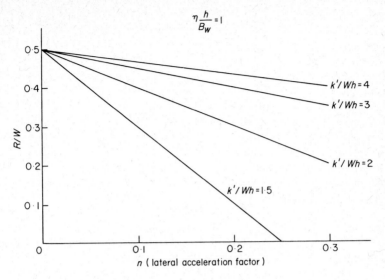

FIG. 7.6. Inside wheel reaction.

7.3.4 Cornering Forces

Two conditions may be envisaged, one of which is a limiting case of the other. The first that will be considered is appropriate to 'rigid' vehicles (not articulated) with more than one rear axle. Referring to Fig. 7.7 it can be seen that if rotation occurs about 0, the slip angles of the inner and outer wheels are given by:

$$\tan \theta_1 = \frac{l_A/2}{\sqrt{(R^2 - l^2)} - B_W/2} \tag{7.17}$$

$$\tan \theta_2 = \frac{l_A/2}{\sqrt{(R^2 - l^2)} + B_W/2} \tag{7.18}$$

Assuming that the side force produced by a tyre is proportional to the slip angle, the constant of proportionality being μ, the total side force on one axle is given by:

$$S = \mu \eta_R \frac{W}{2} \theta \tag{7.19}$$

Thus the side force required at the steered wheels is given by:

$$P = \mu \eta_R \frac{W}{2} \frac{l_A}{l} (\theta_1 + \theta_2) \tag{7.20}$$

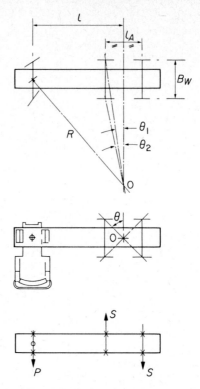

Fig. 7.7. Forces due to turning.

This force is transmitted from the tyre contact points up through the wheel, axle and suspension, and will cause an applied torque to the chassis due to offset between the suspension pick-up points and the flexural axis of the chassis.

For an articulated vehicle, the centre of rotation can occur at the centre of the rear tyre contact points, which is the limiting condition of the rigid vehicle when $R = l$. However, the foregoing analysis is unsuitable because of the large slip angles involved. Both angles are now identical, and given by:

$$\tan \theta = \frac{l_A}{B_W} \tag{7.21}$$

For most common multi-axle configurations, this angle is larger than the limit usually assumed for 'linear' side force–slip angle relationships [4] and thus the side force is simply given by the coefficient of static friction

(μ_0) multiplied by the wheel load. The steering force required at the fifth wheel pick up is therefore given as:

$$P = \mu_0 \eta_R \frac{W}{2} \frac{l_A}{l} \qquad (7.22)$$

This side force is applied to the fifth wheel lateral pivot on the tractor, which has an offset from the flexural axis of the trailer chassis structure, causing an applied torque. Figure 7.8 shows the magnitude of the steering force parameter with radius of turn.

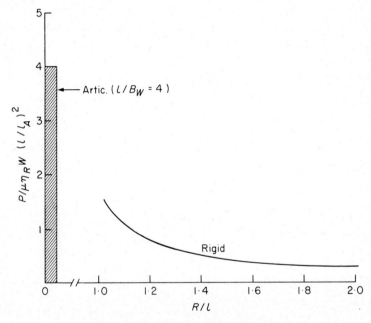

Fig. 7.8. Steering forces for rigid and artic. vehicles.

The side forces at the rear axles are considerably larger than these steering forces and will be transferred to the chassis through the point of side force resistance in the suspension. For conventional leaf springs, this would be the point of side contact between the spring and spring hanger. Such a point will inevitably have an offset from the flexural axis of the chassis and thus a larger input torque will be present. However, this occurs between the axles and will only affect this local region. The detail design of the suspension of multi-axle configurations will radically affect the distribution of torque in this region.

7.4   APPLICATION TO DESIGN EXAMPLE

The design cases so far discussed will be applied to a specific design in this section. No attempt will be made to define an acceptable or satisfactory design, since this is not only dependent on material strength data (including fatigue) but also on design policy, such as safety factors, economic benefits from weight savings, cost of complexity, etc.

As a working basis, a semi-trailer outside the existing regulations was chosen, 9·1 m (30 ft) in length, 30 000 kg (30 T) of payload. The centre of gravity of the payload is 1·5 m (5 ft) from the deck, the spring base is 1·37 m (54 in) (laterally) and the rate of the rear suspension springs is 1·76 kN/mm (10^4 lb/in^2). The fifth wheel rotational spring rate was taken as the same as the rear suspension rotational rate.

As mentioned previously, there are three principal methods of varying the torsional stiffness of a chassis:

1. Increasing the torsional stiffness of the longitudinals, such as making them of box section.
2. Concentrating torsionally resistant material in two members, one at each end (i.e. the peripheral frame).
3. Distributing torsionally resistant material in cross-members throughout the length (i.e. the ladder frame).

Each of these designs will be compared from a stress point of view, and the four loading cases are taken as follows.

Case 1: One-half of the payload will be distributed uniformly over one-half of the width of the deck. Thus, 15 000 kg (15 T) will have an effective offset of 0·6 m (2 ft) giving total applied torque of 88 kN m (30 T ft).

Case 2: With the tractor fifth wheel horizontal, one side of the rear suspension is elevated 152 mm (6 in) above the other side. On a 2 m (80 in) wheeltrack, this gives a ground plane twist of 4·3°.

Case 3: A steady lateral acceleration of 0·3 g will be applied to a concentrated payload equal to one-half of the distributed payload and placed at the centre of the chassis with its c.g. 1·5 m (5 ft) above the deck. For a rigid chassis this is equivalent to a central concentrated torque of 66 kN m (22·5 T ft).

7.4.1   Design with Box Longitudinals

Whilst this type of chassis structure is unusual for commercial vehicles, it was thought worth while investigating, since it represents one method of increasing torsional stiffness while maintaining satisfaction of the longitudinal bending criterion.

Each longitudinal forms a box beam approximately 100 mm × 460 mm (4 in × 18 in), the thickness of the sides is taken as the design variable, starting at 3·2 mm ($\frac{1}{8}$ in) and finishing at 11 mm ($\frac{7}{16}$ in), and the thickness of the flanges is adjusted so that the largest second moment of area of the section remains at a constant value of 208 mm × 16^6 mm⁴ (500 in⁴). This value was found to give satisfactory stresses for longitudinal bending. The torsion constant is calculated from the usual Bredt–Batho theory. This implies that the cross-section is undistorted in its plane and free to warp normal to its plane. Such conditions are the usual assumptions when the cross-members consist of diaphragms which are flexible normal to their plane.

The effect of other cross-sectional sizes has been examined. Generally, deeper sections than that taken decrease the cross-sectional area for the same section modulus in bending and in torsion (the section modulus in torsion is defined as the constant of proportionality in the equation $T = C\tau$). It can be shown that an optimum depth exists, which minimises the cross-sectional area for constant values of the section moduli in bending and torsion. Applying this optimisation to the current design shows that the least area occurs for the thinnest webs. Using 4·8 mm (0·188 in) as a minimum thickness, the optimum depth is 0·54 m (21·2 in), with a cross-sectional area of 7000 mm² (10·8 in²), which is 10% less than the corresponding design used in the calculations.

The stress analysis is elementary when the distribution of twist along the chassis is linear, which is the condition for Case 2. For this mode, the torsion is split evenly between both longitudinals.

With both ends of the chassis constrained to remain level, as in Cases 1 and 3, the twist mode is no longer linear, and a different type of analysis was used. Due to the continuous nature of the longitudinals, and the possibility of a reasonable number of cross-members, a continuum solution to the problem was obtained by assuming a mode of deformation and minimising the total potential energy to evaluate the coefficients.

The results of the stress calculations are given in Fig. 7.9, which shows the shear stress due to torsion for the four loading cases. Also shown in the figure are the values of bending stress induced by torsion, which occur for Cases 1 and 3. The shear stresses are all less than 38 N/mm² (2·5 T/in²) and are thus unlikely to be critical. When the beams have very small torsional stiffness, such as would occur if I beams were used, the bending stress due to torsion is 83 N/mm² (5·4 T/in²) and 196 N/mm² (12·8 T/in²) for Cases 1 and 3, respectively.

P. W. Sharman

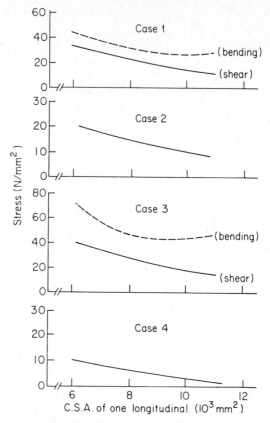

FIG. 7.9. Stress in box longitudinals.

Certain combinations of the four loading cases may be superimposed to give higher stress levels. Figure 7.10 shows a combination of Cases 2 and 3 such as would occur when cornering the ground plane at a constant twist. A further combination shown consists of Cases 1 and 4 such as would occur when manœuvring at low speed with asymmetric load.

Both of these combinations show the same trend—that is, decreasing shear stress with increasing cross-sectional area. The bending stress is similar, with increasing benefit at the larger cross-sections. For the purposes of comparison, let us suppose that the shear stress is limited to 80 N/mm² (5·3 T/in²) in either combined condition. The implication is that the required cross-sectional area of each longitudinal is 9000 mm² (13·7 in²), using the assumed dimensions.

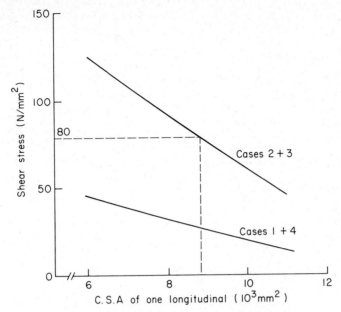

FIG. 7.10. Combined stresses in box longitudinals.

7.4.2 Design with Torsionally Resistant Cross-Members

Most commercial vehicles have a chassis which consists of two heavy longitudinal members, usually of channel or I section, connected by several cross-members, which are sometimes tubular and sometimes open section. The functions of these cross-members are: (*a*) to maintain the shape of the cross-section, particularly under lateral loads, and torsion; (*b*) to support various equipment; and (*c*) to increase the torsional stiffness.

The least number of these cross-members is two, positioned near the extremities of the longitudinals, which has the effect of making the chassis into a 'peripheral frame'. The longitudinals have low torsional stiffness on their own, and, when assembled as described, the structure has finite stiffness under centrally applied and also under end torque. Obviously, increasing the torsional stiffness of these cross-members will increase the torsional stiffness of the structure. However, it does not follow that increasing the size of the cross-members will reduce the shear stress in them. This can be typical of statically indeterminate structures, in which, by adding stiffness to a member, the internal forces in that member are increased, and possibly also the stresses.

The same arguments apply to structures with several cross-members, and the purpose of this section is to examine the effect of the size and number of the cross-members on the stresses induced in them (and the remaining part of the structure), and, to a lesser extent, the torsional stiffness of the structure.

To begin with, it is obvious that a method of structural analysis is required. For a chassis with several or many cross-members, exact solutions are difficult to obtain and cumbersome to use, and thus some approximations are necessary. They are:

1. All cross-members are identical and equally spaced.
2. The longitudinal members are of uniform bending stiffness and zero torsional stiffness.
3. The supports are at the ends of the chassis.
4. The deflection of the longitudinals may be represented by a polynomial expression, with sufficient terms to accommodate all the kinematic and static boundary conditions and including one undetermined coefficient.

This coefficient is found by minimising the total potential energy of the system, which yields a solution which will show the main trends of structural behaviour, and is sufficiently simple to evaluate over a wide range of parameters. In order to integrate the strain energy of the cross-members, it was necessary to 'spread' their torsional stiffness over the whole length of the chassis—a 'continuum' technique well used in the analysis of semi-monocoque structures. However, it was felt that this was unlikely to yield answers of sufficient accuracy when the number of cross-members is low (say 2 to 6). Thus for small numbers of cross-members, an 'exact' method was used, which involved satisfying the condition of compatibility at each junction of cross-member and longitudinal, with equilibrium being satisfied by solving the beam differential equation for the longitudinals. Because of the laborious nature of this solution, it was only applied to chassis with up to 6 cross-members. Full details of the method are given elsewhere [5].

For the purpose of comparison, the 'continuum' theory was also applied to chassis with 6 cross-members and, on the basis that the solution for 8 cross-members lies somewhere between the discrete theory for 6 cross-members and the continuum theory for 10 cross-members, results for 8 cross-members (derived by the 'continuum' theory) were slightly corrected. Figure 7.11 shows these main results.

It can be seen that the two methods have quite a reasonable correlation and thus the approximations are justified, at least for preliminary design work.

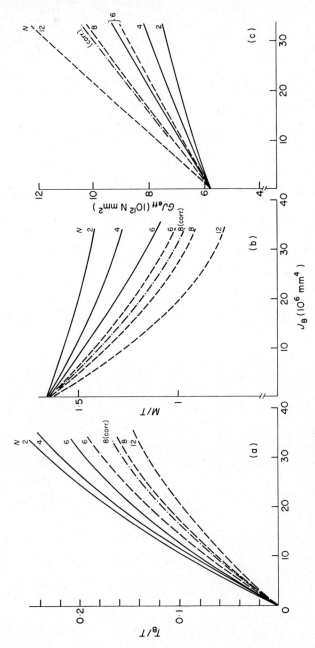

FIG. 7.11. Ladder frame with central torque. (a) Maximum torque. (b) Maximum bending moment. (c) Torsional stiffness. —— discrete theory; ——— continuum theory; —·—·— corrected continuum theory.

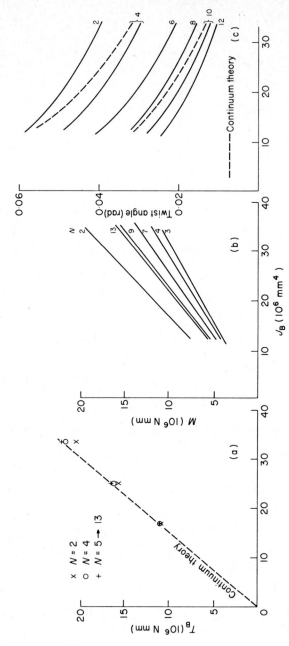

Fig. 7.12. Ladder frame with end torque. (a) Torque in cross-member (twist = 0·074 rad). (b) Bending moment in longitudinal (twist = 0·074 rad). (c) Twist produced by torque of 6×10^6 N mm.

Figure 7.12 shows the results for the ladder frame under end torque—appropriate to Cases 2 and 4. The torque in the cross-members is the major result and computer checks are in close agreement with simple theory. However, the theory is unable to predict the bending moment induced in the longitudinals, by the torque in the cross-members. The position of this bending moment is always at the extremities, and is plotted from computer results.

These two figures were then used as 'design charts' to predict the stresses induced by the torsional loading cases. From the work done in the previous section it is apparent that Cases 1 and 4 are not critical and therefore these were not investigated, due to the complexity of the calculations. Case 3 is significant because it causes large torques in the cross-members and large bending moments in the longitudinals. Case 2 can occur in combination with Case 3 and was therefore also pursued.

The results for Case 3 are shown in Fig. 7.13, in which the torsional shear stress in the cross-members and the maximum bending moment in

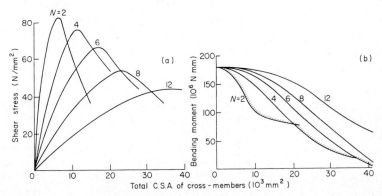

FIG. 7.13. Shear stress and bending moment in ladder frame with central torque. (a) Shear stress in cross-members. (b) Maximum bending moment in longitudinals.

the longitudinals is shown as a function of the number and the area (thus weight) of cross-members. In order to obtain this latter parameter, it was necessary to assume that the cross-members were circular section tubes, of constant (4·8 mm) wall thickness. The effect of other cross-sectional shapes is investigated in Section 7.6. The shear stress increases up to a certain weight of cross-members, then decreases, the position of the maxima depending on the number of cross-members. Thus, there is no 'optimum' design in the usual sense of the word. Increasing the weight of cross-members can be either beneficial or worsen the shear stress in them, depending on which side of the maximum point the design is. The bending moment in the longitudinals is more conventionally behaved, and shows a fairly steady decrease, with increasing cross-member weight. The asymptotes are appropriate to conditions which imply 'fully fixed' conditions at cross-member junctions, and the heavy line indicates the best designs, if the bending moment is required to be minimised.

It is worth pointing out that the position of this bending moment coincides with that of the maximum for longitudinal bending and therefore the stresses may be superimposed, in which case there could be a requirement to reduce the bending moment induced by Case 3.

Figure 7.14 shows the results for Case 2, and as the maximum bending moment occurs at the ends of the longitudinal, it has not been included in this figure. From consideration of the anti-symmetry of this type of loading, the bending moment at the centre is zero, and thus need not be calculated for combination with longitudinal bending or Case 3. As the simple theory predicts, the torque and thus shear stress in the cross-member shows steady increase with cross-member size, and the torsional stiffness of the chassis is steadily increased.

If Cases 2 and 3 are combined, which is quite possible in practice, and

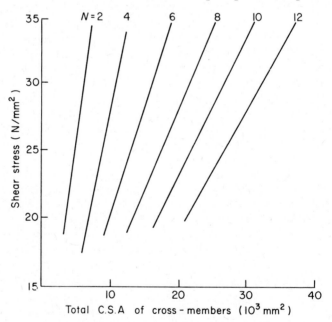

Fig. 7.14. Shear stress in ladder frame under twist of 4·3°.

has been done in Section 7.4.1, the results are as shown in Fig. 7.15. This indicates that the lightest chassis which meets the shear stress limits is one in which there are only two cross-members, i.e. the peripheral frame. However, if more torsional stiffness is required, the best method is to increase the size of cross-members until the shear stress limit is reached,

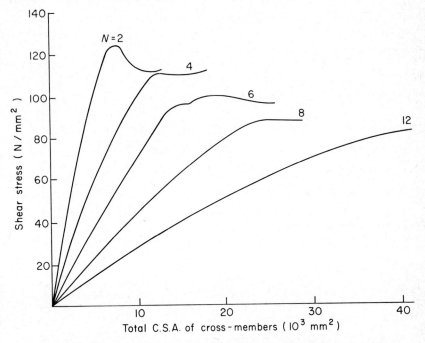

FIG. 7.15. Shear stress in cross-members due to combined Cases 2 and 3.

and thereafter the number of cross-members has to be increased. If the relative severity of the two loading cases is changed, or the relative geometry changed, then this recommendation may change. For instance, if the limiting shear stress was just above the 'flat' part of the curve for $N = 8$, then increasing cross-member size would increase stiffness with no shear stress limitations.

7.5   WEIGHT–STRENGTH–STIFFNESS COMPARISON

The first cost of a vehicle is a basic factor that will determine its potential market, and weight is also of importance. Weight and cost are linked through the price of materials, and thus a reduction in weight will lead to a reduction in cost, if all other things are equal. However, if reduction in weight increases the complexity of production, then the argument is not so strong. In this section a comparison is made only on weight, since cost of complexity is very sensitive to production volume and methods.

Section 7.4.1 concluded that if box section longitudinals were used they need to be of 8100 mm^2 (12·7 in^2) cross-sectional area each, to satisfy torsional loading cases. In order to compare this with the other designs, it is necessary to subtract from this the area required for resisting bending only, leaving the torsion-resisting element for the purposes of comparison. Based on a beam depth of 400 mm (18 in) and a web thickness of 4·8 mm ($\frac{3}{16}$ in), the area required for bending is 5300 mm^2 (8·5 in^2), leaving 2800 mm^2 (4·2 in^2) required for the torsion cases. Since this runs the whole length of the chassis, the volume of material required is 51 × 10^6 mm^3 (3030 in^3), giving a weight of steel as 400 kg (890 lb). The effective torsional constant (*GJ*) of this chassis is 16·7 × 10^{12} N mm^2 (5·8 × 10^9 lb in^2) when subjected to a central torque.

In the design in which the longitudinals have a very small torsional stiffness on their own, it is apparent that the lightest design corresponds to cross-members of zero weight and hence zero stiffness. Under these conditions they do not resist the applied torque, which is carried by differential bending of the longitudinals when a central torque is applied. However, under end torque, the stiffness is practically zero, which leads to large twists under Case 4, and poor stability of a load which may be placed on a corner of the chassis at the fifth wheel end. Thus, some degree of stiffness is required, and to compare with the weight of the previous design we will make the stiffness the same under central torque. Using Fig. 7.12 the size of the cross-members is established which satisfies this stiffness, giving the values shown in Table 7.1.

The final tabulated row is the total volume of cross-members, which should be compared with the previous design of 51 × 10^6 mm^3. It is ap-

TABLE 7.1

N	2	4	6	8	12
J (10^6 mm^4)	520	360	252	200	140
A (10^3 mm^2)	9	7.9	7.1	6.5	5.8
NA (10^3 mm^2)	18	31.6	42.6	52	70
2 bNA (10^6 mm^3)	24·7	43·4	58·5	71·3	96·0

parent that the ladder frames with four and less cross-members are lighter than the previous design, for the same torsional stiffness. However, Fig. 7.15 shows that all of these ladder frames are unsatisfactory with regard to torsional shear stress, and it is not possible to design a ladder frame of these proportions which satisfies the same conditions as the previous design.

The best that can be achieved with the ladder frame, within the limitations of shear stress, and of less weight than the box member longitudinals, is $N = 8$, and a total volume of cross-members of 34×10^6 mm^3, and interpolating for $N = 10$, and total volume of 45×10^6 mm^3. Both of these have a smaller stiffness than the box member longitudinal design, being in the region of $8 \cdot 6 \times 10^{12}$ N mm^2 and 13×10^{12} N mm^2, respectively, in comparison with $16 \cdot 7 \times 10^{12}$ N mm^2.

However, one factor remains unaccounted for in the box member longitudinal chassis, that is the weight of internal (or external) diaphragms, and 'between-longitudinal' diaphragms, which are necessary to ensure that the box members twist as the longitudinals deflect. This is likely to be significant, both in weight and complexity, and is possibly the reason, probably arrived at intuitively, that chassis are not made in this fashion.

Obviously, the manufacturers prefer to sacrifice some torsional stiffness, and therefore payload stability, in order to market a trailer which is competitive in cost and has a reasonable fatigue life.

7.6 INFLUENCE OF SHAPE OF SECTION ON TORSIONAL STIFFNESS AND SHEAR STRESS

The basic function of the cross-members in a ladder frame is to increase the basic torsional stiffness, and therefore the criterion for choice is the maximum value of the torsional constant J for a given cross-sectional area. However, the previous section has shown that increasing J causes increasing shear stress, and thus a further criterion should be considered, namely the minimum shear stress to torque ratio for a given cross-sectional area.

The calculations are easily performed for circular and square section thin tubes, and are shown in Figs. 7.16 and 7.17. It can easily be shown that rectangular section thin tubes show decreasing efficiency in both stiffness and strength, as the ratio of breadth/depth increases.

For the purposes of comparison, the results of calculations on thin open sections of I and channel cross-section, with fully restrained ends, are shown. The theory of restrained torsion warping is quite complex [6], and is strongly dependent on length, which was taken as $1 \cdot 37$ m (54 in),

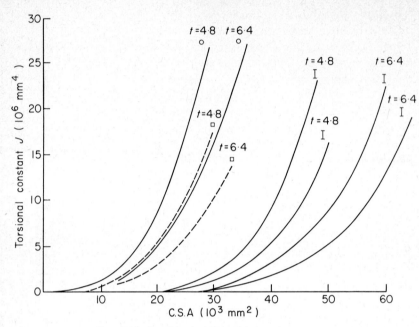

FIG. 7.16. Torsional stiffness of various sections.

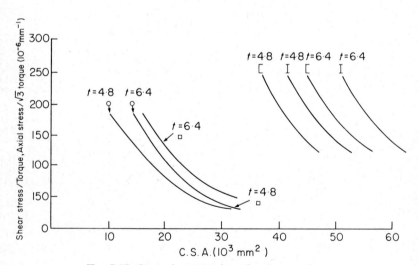

FIG. 7.17. Stress due to torsion of various sections.

appropriate to the example used throughout this paper. The maximum stress in restrained open sections under torsion is an axial stress, occurring at the edge of the flange, where it is attached to the rigid wall. In order to be comparable with a shear stress, this has to be divided by $\sqrt(3)$, in accordance with the Hencky–Von Mises criterion for elastic failure.

As would be expected, the best section is always the circular section tube of the least possible wall thickness. The square section tube is only competitive if its thickness can be made smaller than the circular section. This is unlikely, because minimum thicknesses are fixed from welding and general durability considerations, and also the flat thin walls of the square tube are more prone to shear buckling than the curved walls of the circular tube. The open sections show very poor efficiencies, requiring large cross-sections for reasonable torsional stiffness, and suffering from high stress in localised positions. Clearly, rapid fatigue failure is likely for this type of cross-member.

7.7 CONCLUSIONS

Of the four loading cases investigated, the combination of cornering lateral acceleration and twisted ground plane gave the most severe stresses in torsion-carrying material and also in the longitudinals.

A chassis with torsionally resistant longitudinals can be designed satisfying a conservative shear stress limitation under the above-mentioned loading condition. It also exhibits a high torsional stiffness. However, the provision of diaphragms to ensure its efficiency will cause it to be heavy in comparison with a ladder frame. Complexity of manufacture is also against it.

The ladder frame can be designed to have a similar shear stress limitation, and is considerably lighter in its torsionally resistant cross-members. The lightest frames have the smallest possible members positioned at the extremities, as in the peripheral frame, but their inherent torsional stiffness is low, particularly under linear twist modes. Stiffness can be increased at the expense of cross-member weight, and shear stress limitations can be easily exceeded by merely increasing cross-member size, rather than number. Many cross-members are required to achieve the torsional stiffness of the box member longitudinal design, but the ladder frame is still likely to be an easier manufacturing problem than the other type, at least using conventional production methods.

A treatment of the design of cross-members, considered separately, shows that the circular section thin-walled tube leads to the least weight and stress for a given torsional stiffness. The minimum wall thickness should always be used, if sufficient space exists to accommodate the diameter.

REFERENCES

1. Sidelko, W. J. 'An objective approach to highway truck frame design', SAE Paper No. SP276, Dec. 1965.
2. Sharman, P. W. (1974). 'Fatigue Damage Prediction on a Semi-trailer,' Conference on Stress, Vibration and Noise Analysis in Vehicles, University of Aston in Birmingham, Sept.
3. Sharman, P. W. (1969). The effect of torsional stiffness on cornering performance, *ADE*, **10**, (April).
4. Joy, T. and Hartley, D. (1953–54). 'Tyre Characteristics as Applicable to Vehicle Stability Problems', *Proc. Inst. Mech. Eng., AD*, p 113.
5. Sharman, P. W. 'Some Aspects of the Structural Analysis and Design of Commercial Vehicles', Ph.D. Thesis, Loughborough University of Technology, 1974.
6. Zbirohowski-Koscia, K. (1967). *Thin-Walled Beams, from Theory to Practice*, Crosby Lockwood, London.

8

Noise Reduction of Large Earthmoving Vehicles

D. J. SNOW
Central Electricity Generating Board

SUMMARY

The large earthmoving vehicle can present a noise problem both to the operator and to the general public. In this paper the results of a joint program between the CEGB and the manufacturers are described which ameliorate both effects. The reduction of internal cab noise to an adequate level has been relatively simple although a further reduction may still be desirable.

External noise radiation is quickly reduced in the first instance by fitting effective exhaust silencers which are not always used on this type of vehicle during site work. Subsequent panelling of the engine and transmission units produced a gradual reduction in BS 3425 noise level as it became more complete but it was apparent that a lower limit was being approached. The existence of such a limit was found to be caused by gear noise from the transmission system, the complete enclosure of which was not practicable.

It is concluded that for this kind of vehicle a BS 3425 level of approximately 90 dBA is achievable by simple panelling techniques. However, the CEGB's future requirement of an 85 dBA noise level will require a detailed modification of the engine, transmission and cooling system design whilst care will also have to be taken to avoid any significant increase in maintenance and servicing times.

8.1   INTRODUCTION

The large earthmoving vehicle, used primarily as a coalscraper within the CEGB, is a demanding object for a noise reduction program. The vehicle is over 14 m long and uses two propulsion units each of nearly 300 hp, either of which would normally be adequate for the heaviest of commercial vehicles. The two units, called the tractor and scraper, operate as pull and push partners and are made up from identical engine and transmission units. The front or tractor unit contains the driver's cab and provides the steering capability. A modern vehicle of this type is illustrated in Fig. 8.1.

There are two kinds of noise problem created by this type of machine, which may be simply classified as internal and external, and the paper which follows is essentially a description of a practical attempt to reduce

FIG. 8.1. General view of coalscraper TS.40C.

these problems on a short timescale. Although the particular work described relates to a specific vehicle the more general remarks can be taken to apply to all similar vehicle types, e.g. bulldozers, diggers, etc.

8.1.1 Internal Noise

High internal cab noise levels can offend against the Department of Environment Code of Practice on Noise which sets a maximum level of 90 dBA for a continuous eight-hour exposure. It was already well known that the inclusion of absorbant material within the driver's cab could markedly reduce the prevailing noise level and it was decided to utilise this same line of approach [1].

8.1.2 External Noise

The target external noise level was 86 dBA, though there is still discussion over the finally desired figure. It was shown in Ref. 1 (1969/70) that approximately 70% of normal commercial vehicles exceed this figure when new. The achievement of such a level for the coalscraper which is a much larger and more powerful vehicle therefore represents an ambitious target. Other workers [1–3] have shown that considerable benefit can be achieved by enclosing the engine in conjunction with effective exhaust silencing. The possible alternative approach of detailed design changes to the various machine parts was not contemplated on the timescale available.

8.2   METHODS OF MEASUREMENT

It was decided that all measurements taken should comply with accepted national and international standards where these exist and are applicable.

8.2.1   Cab Noise

The measurement of noise levels under various operating conditions has been proposed, of which the simplest is to run the machine at maximum revolutions in a neutral gear. The machine was in its standard form and the microphone no closer than 300 mm to the cab walls. Other possible conditions are: (*a*) with the engine stalled to represent heavy working, and (*b*) to compute an average or equivalent noise level measured over a representative cycle of work.

Actual tests on machines have shown that, at least for coalscrapers, there is little difference between these various forms of measurement and that far greater variations are to be found between different machines. Thus, the maximum revolutions condition, because of its simplicity, has generally been adopted.

In all of these measurements the 'A' weighted scale is used (dBA).

8.2.2 External Noise

The measurement of vehicle external noise in this country is covered by BS 3425 [4], and this method was generally used, although it was found convenient on some occasions to increase the measuring distance to 10 or even 15 m. It was found that such alterations could reasonably be allowed for by application of the inverse square law and these results are illustrated in Fig. 8.2. It is interesting to note, in the companion graph, that the same conclusion is not true for linear or dBC measurements. A possible reason

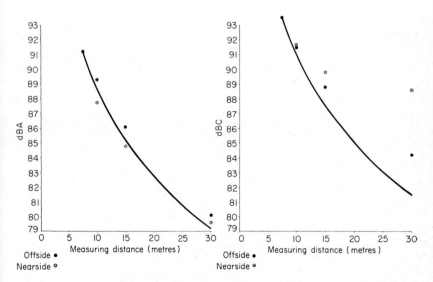

FIG. 8.2. The magnitude of BS 3425 levels recorded at different distances using dBA and dBC filters. The continuous line represents inverse square law decay.

for this difference in behaviour is that the dBC measure is dominated by low frequency exhaust and engine noise which is susceptible to ground interference effects throughout the range of test geometries. On the other hand, near field source effects will have disappeared at and beyond a distance of 7·5 m.

External noise levels were also measured statically so that a better idea of the relative source strengths could be obtained and different machine modifications compared. This was done by measuring along a line 7·5 m from the centre line and parallel with the machine. Thus, a comparison with the mobile test was immediately available.

8.3   NOISE REDUCTION TARGETS

8.3.1   Cab Noise Levels

The cab noise level should neither cause any risk of hearing damage nor necessitate the wearing of hearing protection for long periods. To avoid either possibility the equivalent noise level within the cab should not exceed 90 dBA [5]. A survey of machines showed that reductions in sound level of up to 9 dBA were required.

8.3.2   External Noise Emissions

The defining of target levels for this problem creates rather more difficulty. Regulations such as the 'Motor Vehicles Construction and Use Regulations (S1, 1969, No. 321)' and other recommendations suggest BS 3425 levels from 89 to 92 dBA for a vehicle over 200 bhp. However, these figures have been decided on the assumption of road use rather than site use, where the criterion is that of not creating a noise nuisance at any residential property around the site. To avoid such a noise nuisance one must aim to produce a negligible change in the prevailing background level. The operation of this rule presents no problem at many CEGB sites which are remote from the nearest neighbour, but to eliminate possible complaint at a majority of sites a level of 85 dBA has been proposed by the Standards Committee preparing a CEGB Draft Standard for Coalscrapers.

8.4   MODIFICATIONS TO ACHIEVE TARGETS

Originally coalscrapers were delivered without fitted exhaust silencing and this situation still applies to part of the construction industry. However, the only acceptable conditions under which such a machine could operate would be if the operator wore hearing protection at all times and the machines worked remotely from all habitation. Exhaust silencing can be fitted with little difficulty or penalty and is the single most effective silencing measure. Without exhaust silencing, noise levels measured according to BS 3425 of over 100 dBA were frequently recorded. After exhaust silencing a reduction of the order of 8 dBA in the external noise level results so that a level of 94 dBA is typical for the BS 3425 test on a machine fitted with only exhaust silencing.

A survey of cab noise levels for silenced coalscrapers produced figures varying between 94 and 99 dBA, the benefit of the exhaust silencing being some 3 dBA.

8.4.1   Cab Noise Treatment

For machines fitted with exhaust silencing, sound reductions of up to 9 dBA are required within the cab. This level of reduction can be obtained by lining the cab with a sound absorbant foam. On the particular machine investigated, the foam was fitted to all available surfaces. On the ceiling and

FIG. 8.3. Coalscraper cab treatment.

sides of the cab there was room for a 2 in thick layer, whilst elsewhere only a 1 in thickness could be fitted. The cab roof panel was also stiffened by a pair of struts and the floor covered by heavy rubber matting. After this treatment, a level of 89 dBA was recorded in the cab, at maximum revolutions, representing a reduction of 9 dBA on the original value. An illustration of the modified cab is shown in Fig. 8.3.

It is possible that in the future there will be a requirement for levels lower than 90 dBA. Further reductions could be obtained by improved isolation of the cab from the main vehicle framework.

8.4.2   Engine and Transmission Panelling

After exhaust silencing, a program of engine and transmission enclosure was undertaken. A general view of the enclosed machine is shown in Fig. 8.1, whilst Fig. 8.4 shows detail of the rear section and the panels about to be fitted.

Fig. 8.4. Detail view of rear panelling.

Table 8.1 shows the effect on noise levels of gradually extending the panelling. The initial progress (of tests 1, 2 and 3) was disappointing, particularly for the static measurements. However, by the end of test 4 the

TABLE 8.1

Machine condition	Test	Cab noise max revs	Mobile noise BS 3425	Static noise levels at 7·5 m maximum revs			
				Offside	Nearside	Front	Rear
Front and rear silencers only	1	89	94	92	90	91·5	92·5
As above plus engine panelling and partial rear transmission panelling	2	89	93	89·5	88	91·5	91·5
As test 2 with minor improvements to panelling	3	90	92	90	88	92	92
Improved panelling with complete enclosure of rear transmission	4	88	92	86	86	90	90
As test 4 plus front and rear radiator cowls	5	88	90	86	84	82	83
Addition to front transmission housing	6	88	88·5	86	84	84	85
As test 6 with and without look-up available	7		91 90				
Front engine only	} 8		89·5	86·5	85		
Both engines			92	88	87·5		
Addition of belly panels	9	88	89	85	84		

cab noise had dropped to 88 dBA and the BS 3425 level by 2 dBA to 92 dBA. Also, the target noise levels had been met statically at the side of the vehicle.

At this point it was apparent that the front and rear radiated noise was important, and the wedge-shaped air intakes in Fig. 8.4 were fitted at the front and rear. Like the other panels, these were made of mild steel plate lined on the inner surface with a 1 in thickness of sound absorbant foam; tests (test 5) showed these additions to be very effective. The static noise level now met the target all around the machine and the BS 3425 noise level was lowered to 90 dBA. The front transmission was difficult to enclose satisfactorily because it rotates with the rest of the tractor unit. The fitting of an improved housing to this front unit produced the lowest BS

3425 level measured during this work. However, we were unable to repeat this level of 88·5 dBA and some degradation of the absorbant lining is possible. It was thought that the 'lock-up' mechanism on the transmission unit, which converts the normally fluid transmission into a rigid one when full speed is achieved in each gear, might be an important source of noise. In fact, a 1 dBA decrease in level was recorded with this device out of use but it is not possible to ascribe too much significance to a change of this magnitude.

A final attempt was made to reduce the mobile external noise level by completely enclosing the underneath of the engine and transmission at both front and rear. Because the machine chassis sometimes strikes the ground these panels had to be made from $\frac{1}{4}$ in steel plate, and since they are liable to collect any oil drips from the power unit, the absorbant lining was omitted. These panels were, of necessity, very heavy and therefore difficult to remove and, in conjunction with the other panels, made ready access to the engine from any direction difficult with subsequent consequences for servicing the unit.

In return for these disadvantages, only a small reduction in noise level was obtained. It was concluded that the limit of improvement by enclosures of this type had been reached. Further progress would mean either the use of heavier and better sealed panels or by the redesign of offending components. To identify these the more detailed noise analysis, described in the next section, was carried out.

8.5   IDENTIFICATION OF MAJOR NOISE SOURCES

In Fig. 8.5(b), the timescale has been expanded to show the time trace more clearly and it can be seen that the time between the two peaks is approximately two seconds. During this test, the vehicle speed is in the order of 11·5 mph so that a distance of 10 m is travelled during that time. In Fig. 8.6 the calculated sound field for two omnidirectional sources 10 m apart is shown. The key features are the flat maximum, viz only a 0·5 dB fall-off over a distance of 14 m, followed by a rapid decrease in level at a rate of 0·5 dB/m. Eventually, the normal inverse square law decay would be expected to take over when the distance between the two sources has become small compared with the measuring distance. Also in Fig. 8.6 is shown another expanded time trace, this time for run 3 of Fig. 8.5(a). This particular run was chosen because it shows the most marked discrimination of all the tests between the two peaks. The comparison with the theoretical

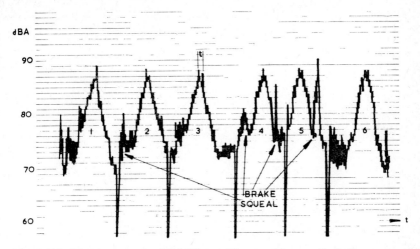

FIG. 8.5(a). The six runs of a BS 3425 test. The nearside runs (1, 2, 3) average at 88·5 dBA whilst the offside runs average at 88·2 dBA. The BS test result must therefore be 88·5 dBA.

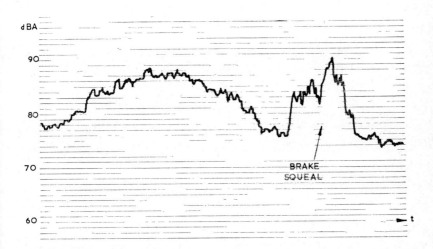

FIG. 8.5(b). A detail of run 5 played at 10 mm/sec. Note the high intensity of brake squeal although this is taking place at a much increased distance. The test speed is nearly 12 mph so that 10 mm on the chart above represents a distance of approx. 5 m passed by the vehicle. The peak sound level, say ⩾87 dBA, can be seen to last approx. 2 sec.

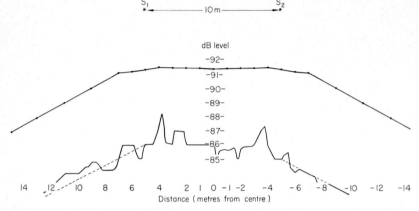

FIG. 8.6. Total sound field given by two sources S_1, S_2 of equal strength, 10 m apart, as they pass in line 7·5 m from the measuring position, at the nearest point. The sources are assumed to be omnidirectional. For comparison a real trace (Run 3 Figs. 8.5a) is shown below.

curve is most interesting. The difference in absolute level is not important, being purely arbitrary. In the theoretical curve the two sources have been chosen such that they would produce a maximum level of 90 dBA individually, so that reinforcement can be seen to contribute approximately 1·5 dB. The general shape of the theoretical curve is duplicated in practice but the detail differences can be explained if the two sources are assumed to be closer together and also exhibit mild directionality. Some directionality is not too surprising but the more useful information is that the two sources appear to be nearer than 10 m to each other. On the vehicle itself the two engines are the order of 11 m apart, whereas the transmission units are the order of 8 m apart. Thus, these tests provided the first non-subjective evidence that the transmission units were the most important noise source on the machine.

This was further confirmed by the BS 3425 test, which produced noise levels in excess of those predictable from the static measurements at full revolutions. In order to investigate further a tape loop was made, using an approximately two-second length of tape, recorded at the peak of the drive past. A 6% (one-twelfth octave) analysis of this tape showed that the band of frequencies between 500 Hz and 2·0 kHz was primarily responsible for the high noise level. To obtain better frequency resolution the recordings were analysed on a Hewlett Packard real time (digital) analyser using a 10 Hz bandwidth. The results, shown in Fig. 8.7, indicate strong tones at fre-

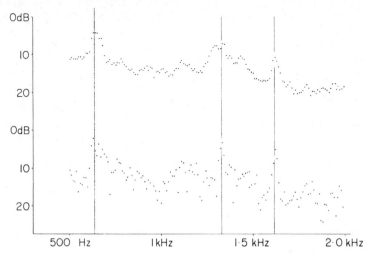

Fɪɢ. 8.7. 10 Hz bandwidth real time analysis of BS 3425 tests (tape 40). (Top) Accumulated average over six runs, 10 samples/run; (bottom) single run, average of 3 samples.

quencies of approximately 640 Hz, 1330 Hz and 1620 Hz. The source of these tones was at this stage unknown and, as a first step in determining their origin, recordings were made close to (0·3 m) the engine and transmission units at the two speeds of 1800 rpm and 2100 rpm in neutral gear. A 6% analysis of these recordings is shown in Figs. 8.8 and 8.9. The use of the 'A' shaping filter helps to reveal the relative subjective importance of various parts of the spectrum. It is clear that the low frequency engine tones, at both firing frequencies and shaft frequencies, are not of great significance. A more detailed analysis of these tones was made by narrow band analysis and Fig. 8.10 shows the results between 500 Hz and 2·0 kHz. This analysis reveals that the tones causing the high BS 3425 level (Fig. 8.7) are also present during the static tests (Fig. 8.10), and the 6% analysis (Figs. 8.8 and 8.9) shows that they emanate from the transmission system rather than the engine.

Because the static noise measurements are made in neutral gear, the possible sources within the transmission are limited to the torque converter, the charging pump with its associated gear drive and the first stage of the planetary gearing. Amongst these sources the charging pump gear train is most likely to be responsible. These gears have a meshing frequency which varies from 1380 Hz to 1610 Hz as the engine speed increases from 1800 rpm to 2100 rpm.

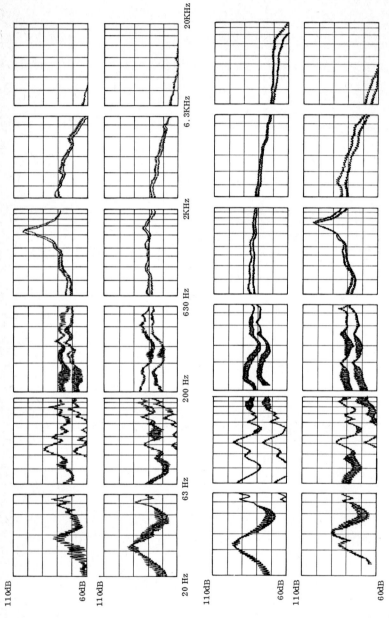

FIG. 8.8. Spectral analysis ($\frac{1}{12}$ octave) of engine and transmission noise taken at 0·3 m and 1800 rpm. The lower curves incorporate a dBA filter. (Top) Transmission nearside; (2nd) engine nearside; (3rd) engine offside; (bottom) transmission offside.

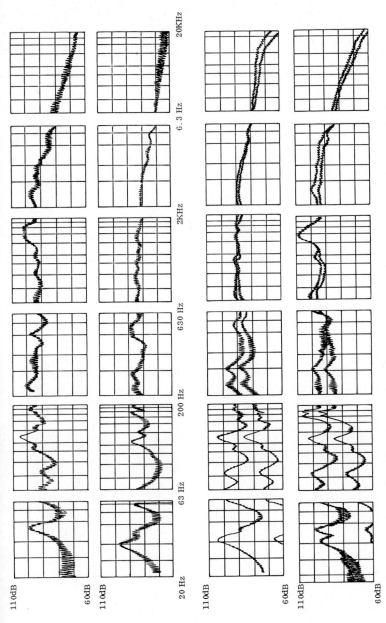

FIG. 8.9. Spectral analysis ($\frac{1}{12}$ octave) of engine and transmission noise taken at 0·3 m and 2100 rpm. The lower curve incorporates a dBA filter. (Top) Transmission nearside; (2nd) engine nearside; (3rd) engine offside; (bottom) transmission offside.

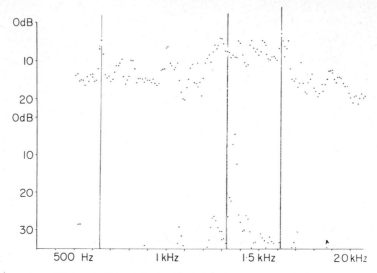

Fig. 8.10. 10 Hz bandwidth analysis. (Top) As Fig. 8.9, transmission nearside 2100 rpm; (bottom) as Fig. 8.8, transmission nearside 1800 rpm.

8.6   CONCLUSIONS

1. Adequately low cab noise levels can be achieved by using an absorbant cab lining. A further reduction in cab noise level would be welcome and could be realised by insulating the cab from the surrounding noise sources.

2. Although BS 3425 levels as low as 90 dBA have been achieved, the lower levels preferred by the CEGB for site use and night-time working cannot be reached by using exhaust silencing and simple enclosure alone. To achieve the desired levels the redesign of some components is essential and the most important of these is the transmission unit.

3. Nearly all construction vehicles of this and similar types give rise to both internal and external noise problems and the CEGB has, therefore, drawn up a standard which, as far as possible, will apply to all new vehicles. This standard will call for a BS 3425 level of 85 dBA for vehicles over 151hp on all future designs and a level of 90 dBA for existing plant. An equivalent continuous sound level of 90 dBA will be specified as the maximum cab noise level.

ACKNOWLEDGEMENTS

This work would not have been possible without the help and cooperation of Mr K. Matthews of Blackwood Hodge Ltd. I am grateful also to the CEGB and the manufacturers, Blackwood Hodge, for permission to publish.

REFERENCES

1. Aspinall, D. T. (1970). Control of road noise by vehicle design, *J. Sound Vib.*, **13** (4), 435–444.
2. Law, R. M. 'Diesel engine and highway truck noise reduction', SAE Paper No. 730240.
3. Lewis, R. P., Berry, W. C. and Spellacy, F. (1970). Practical means of implementing vehicle noise control I, II and III, *J. Sound Vib.*, **13** (4), 455–463.
4. BS 3425 (1966) 'Method for the Measurement of Noise Emitted by Motor Vehicles'.
5. Department of Employment. 'Code of Practice for the Reduction of Exposure of Employed Persons to Noise' (1972).

9

Automobile Drive-Line Vibration
and Internal Noise

D. W. PARKINS
Cranfield Institute of Technology

SUMMARY

This paper describes an experimental study of the drive-line vibration modes, and internal noise under road excitation of a conventional family car. The drive-line comprised the drive-shaft, axle, semi-elliptic multi-leaf springs and wheels. Drive-line vibration modes were identified experimentally in the laboratory by applying harmonic forces to various locations within the drive-line system. Eleven resonant modes were identified in the range 10–200 Hz. Diagrams illustrate each mode shape. Under laboratory excitation a significant internal noise was caused by the vibration mode at 23 Hz which arises from displacement within the rubber insulator separating spring and axle casing.

Axle vibration and internal noise were simultaneously recorded during road testing at 22 constant speeds covering the range 30–75 mph using fourth gear. Typical power spectra are illustrated. Excitation of the axle bending mode (67 Hz) at engine rotational frequency caused a measurable noise increase. Sub-audible noise was found to be a large component at all road speeds. At 30–40 mph, large noise contributions were due to excitation of body bending at engine rotation, and cavity acoustic resonance at twice engine rotation frequency. Engine rotation did not excite the cavity resonance at the highest road speed. Frequencies of most noise components were related to engine or wheel rotational frequencies. Important frequencies, largely independent of road speed, were 7·5, 36–39, and 73–77 Hz.

9.1   INTRODUCTION

Vibration of an automobile drive-line adversely affects the fatigue life of the components and the comfort of the passengers. If drive-line vibration creates additional contributions to the internal noise, the passenger environment is further degraded. Objectives of this work were to identify existing drive-line vibration modes and to determine their contribution to the vehicle internal noise under normal road conditions. It was necessary to establish the source of all contributions to the internal noise spectra in order to decide which could be attributed to the drive-line vibration. These objectives were attained by a program of experimental work both on the stationary vehicle in the laboratory and under normal motoring conditions.

A four-seater family saloon car was kindly made available by a major manufacturer. It had a front-mounted four-cylinder in-line engine, with a single-length drive-shaft, beam axle and semi-elliptic multi-leaf springs. Drive-line means all components between the gearbox output and the road surface. Drive-shaft comprised two full-length concentric tubes, joined at their ends by rubber bushes. This provided torsional flexibility, and allowed angular and lateral relative motion between the two tubes. The inner tube was connected to the differential pinion shaft and the outer tube to the gearbox output shaft.

In laboratory experiments, drive-line vibration modes were identified from the response to an harmonic force input to two alternative locations on the drive-line. Additionally, internal noise was measured during tests with one input location. In road testing, power spectra were obtained from the internal noise recorded at 22 different vehicle speeds. The lower frequency limit of the analyses was set at 5 Hz—well into the sub-audible range.

Gladwell [7] reviewed work on noise and vibration in motor cars published by 1964. Since that time, May [3] has calculated mode shapes and frequencies for a similar drive-line arrangement to that used for work described in this paper. He also discusses the routes by which axle vibration is transmitted to the passenger compartment. In two reports from MIRA, Mills and Dixon [5] give octave analyses of the internal noise obtained with several different cars on a noise generating surface. They also point out the importance of fore–aft vibration in addition to the vertical motion. Most recently, Priede and Jha [1] and [2] demonstrated the common features of the internal noise spectra for six different vehicles. Their analysis extended down to 2 Hz and revealed the relatively large magnitude of the sub-audible components. They indicated the various types of noise source and deal particularly with the body ring modes. References [6] and [8] give a fuller discussion of the drive-line vibration modes found in this work including those in the horizontal direction.

9.2   EXPERIMENTAL METHOD

Figure 9.1 shows the instrumentation system used in the laboratory experiments. Modal frequencies were located by response maxima to an harmonic force input of constant peak value. It was accepted that, at a

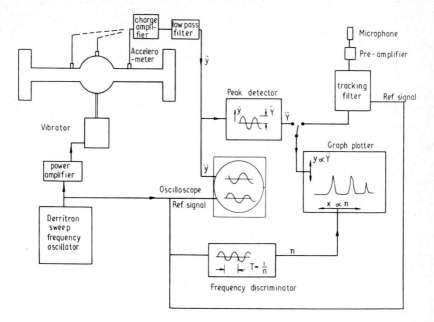

F<small>IG</small>. 9.1. Instrumentation layout.

given modal frequency, interference from adjacent modes was possible. However, previous experience suggested that modal frequencies were sufficiently separated to justify this simplification. Vibration mode shapes, illustrated in Figs. 9.2 and 9.3, were built up from the vertical response to the harmonic force input given by accelerometers located on the leaf spring, axle casing and drive-shaft outer tube. Two input locations were used: (*a*) vertical to the axle centre, and (*b*) vertical to the tyre at the road surface. The latter location was limited to a maximum frequency of 65 Hz, but excited two modes (16 and 37 Hz) which were not exhibited with the former location.

Figure 9.1 also shows the instrumentation used in laboratory testing to measure internal noise created by harmonic force input of constant peak value applied vertically to the axle centre. Figure 9.4 illustrates a typical response obtained from a microphone located at the driver's head position. A comparison of results obtained from several microphone locations showed a small shift of frequency of several noise maxima.

Battery-powered portable equipment was used in the road tests, which were conducted in fourth gear at 22 different vehicle speeds between 30

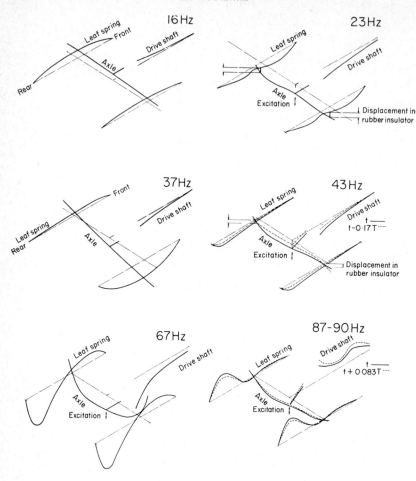

Fig. 9.2. Drive-line mode shapes 10–100 Hz.

and 75 mph. A 20-second tape recording was made of the microphone and axle-mounted accelerometer output for each constant vehicle speed setting. The microphone was located near to the driver's head, in an almost identical position to that used in the laboratory tests. A power spectral analysis was obtained from each recording. Figures 9.5 and 9.6 were constructed from the constant speed power spectra. Acoustic resonance was measured using microphone response to loudspeaker excitation within the passenger compartment.

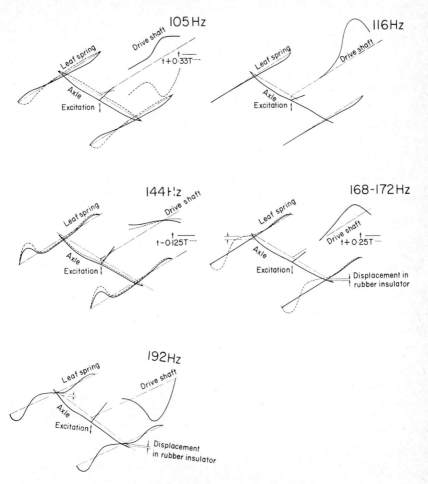

FIG. 9.3. Drive-line mode shapes 100–200 Hz.

9.3   DRIVE-LINE VIBRATION MODES

During laboratory testing with the complete vehicle, 11 drive-line vibration modes were identified within the frequency range 10–200 Hz. Figures 9.2 and 9.3 illustrate mode shapes and associated frequencies, each diagram showing acceleration response to vertical constant peak force. However, there was a relatively small excitation for the pitching mode. Each diagram

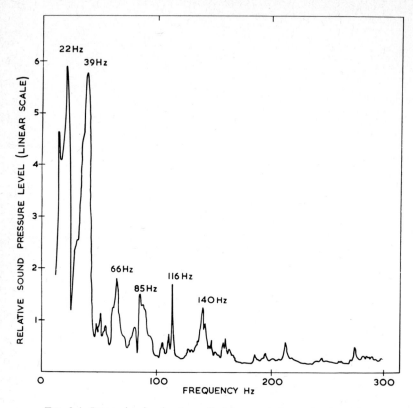

Fig. 9.4. Internal noise due to vertical harmonic force at axle centre.

shows the disturbed shape occupied by the complete system at maximum downward acceleration for the axle casing, and other parts in correct relative phase. Mode shapes which were not 'normal', i.e. elements did not occupy in-phase or anti-phase states, are indicated by dotted lines. These illustrate mode shapes at times selected to show the maximum response of a component other than the axle casing. In some cases it was observed that not all parts of the system attained a maximum response at precisely the same frequency. The extreme range of values is given. Results for drive-shaft and axle refer to the outer tubing only. A brief description of each mode shape follows. The term 'rubber insulator' refers to the rubber surrounding the spring at its junction with the axle casing. 'Torsion' means that the rubber insulator permits the axle to rotate about its own longitudinal axis relative to the spring.

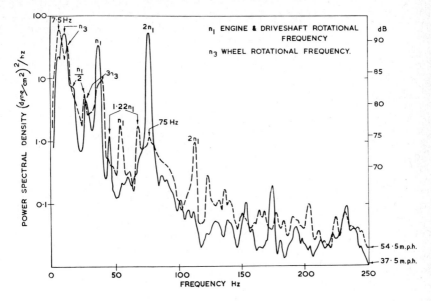

FIG. 9.5. Typical internal noise spectra—road testing.

16 Hz

A symmetrical rigid axle mode with both springs in phase in their first mode.

23 Hz

A symmetrical mode due to relatively large displacement within the rubber insulator.

37 Hz

An anti-symmetrical rigid axle mode with springs anti-phase in their first mode.

43 Hz

A combined axle-pitch and bounce mode with relatively small response. Non-alignment of drive-shaft rear and differential nose suggests motion between the drive-shaft inner and outer tubes.

67 Hz

Large axle bending characterised this symmetrical normal mode. Springs vibrate in-phase in their second mode. The junction between axle casing and spring is almost at a node for both spring and axle. There is no displacement and negligible torsion within the rubber insulator.

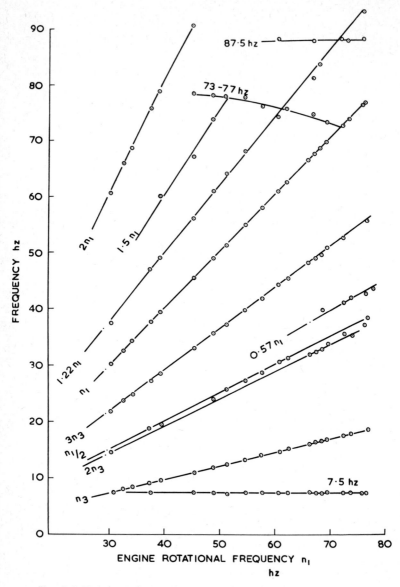

FIG. 9.6. Dominant frequency content of internal noise—road testing.

87–90 Hz

Largely an axle-pitching mode permitted by the springs.

105 Hz

An axle-pitching mode permitted by torsion in the rubber insulator.

116 Hz

Bending mode of drive-shaft.

144 Hz

A combined axle-pitch and bounce mode, permitted by spring motion and torsion in the rubber insulator.

168–172 Hz

A symmetrical axle-bounce mode with significant spring motion and displacement in the rubber insulator.

192 Hz

A normal axle-pitching mode permitted by large torsion and moderate displacement within the rubber insulator. Springs vibrate in-phase in their fourth mode.

Nodes were found at the spring ends in all modes. This finding was verified throughout the frequency range by measurement of negligible response on the bodywork adjacent to the spring attachment points. Constraints not shown on the diagrams in Figs. 9.2 and 9.3 comprise the dampers, axle-locating links, tyres and vehicle body. Table 9.1 summarises the mode shape descriptions.

9.4   INTERNAL NOISE AND ITS RELATION TO DRIVE-LINE VIBRATION

Figure 9.4 shows the sound pressure response inside the car due to harmonic excitation of the drive-line. The most significant noise peaks occurred at 22 and 39 Hz. The former frequency is coincident with that of an identified drive-line mode which was shown to be excited during the same test. The latter frequency (39 Hz) is nearly coincident with that of another identified drive-line mode at 37 Hz. However, it was shown that this mode was not excited during the laboratory tests, primarily because the input was almost at a node for that particular mode. Other noise peaks appear at 66, 85–88, 116 and 140 Hz, which are coincident with the frequencies of identified drive-line modes. There is no noise peak around 75 Hz.

TABLE 9.1
Summary of mode shape descriptions (data in boxes = largest manifestation)

Frequency	16	23	37	43	67	87–90	105	116	144	168–172	192
Axle modes											
symmetrical = S	S	S	—	—	S	—	—	S	—	S	—
roll = R	—	—	R	—	—	—	—	—	—	—	—
pitch = P	—	—	—	P	—	P	P	—	P	—	P
'Normal' mode = (N)	N	N	N	—	N	—	—	N	—	—	N
Rubber insulator											
torsion = T	—	—	—	T	—	T	T	—	T	—	[T]
displacement = D	—	[D]	—	D	—	—	—	—	—	D	D
none = 0	0	—	0	—	0	—	—	0	—	—	—
Spring mode											
1	1	1	1	—	—	—	—	—	—	—	—
2	—	—	—	—	[2]	—	2	—	—	—	—
3	—	—	—	—	—	3	—	—	3	—	—
4	—	—	—	—	—	—	—	—	—	4?	4
Axle bending											
small = S	—	S	—	S	[large]	S	S	S	S	S	S
Driveshaft outer											
bending = B	—	—	—	—	B	B	B	[large]	—	B	B
Alignment rear d/shaft to diff. nose											
alignment = A	A	A	A	—	—	A	A	—	A	A	A
not aligned = D	—	—	—	D	D	—	—	D	—	—	—

Figure 9.5 illustrates typical noise spectra obtained from road tests at two different vehicle speeds. Each dominant peak is labelled with an identifying frequency. Results for the lower vehicle speed, 37·5 mph, show three main peaks of comparable magnitude at 7·5-wheel (n_3), engine (n_1), and twice engine ($2n_1$) rotational frequencies. At the higher road speed, only the peak at 7·5-(n_3), remains at a similar magnitude to its low speed counterpart, with the other peaks, particularly that at $2n_1$, making a

markedly smaller contribution. Frequencies of main peaks in the power spectra obtained from all constant speed road tests are indicated in Fig. 9.6. This reveals frequencies of significant noise in addition to those directly related to engine and wheel rotational frequencies. Furthermore, a significant noise peak appeared at a frequency which could not be associated with either $2n_3$ or $n_1/2$.

Laboratory testing also revealed dome-shaped vibration modes of the rear window at two frequencies only: 42 and 49 Hz. Figure 9.4 shows that the internal noise incurred only minor increases at these frequencies.

Power spectra up to 500 Hz obtained from the single 70 mph road test over the M1 motorway 'tyre noise' surface, showed no significant difference to those obtained on a normal surface.

Excitation for the 23 Hz mode in the moving vehicle arises mainly from unbalanced wheel and drive-shaft rotation. During road testing, drive-shaft rotational frequencies did not reach below 30 Hz, and wheel rotational frequency did not exceed 18 Hz. Consequently, the 23 Hz mode did not receive strong excitation. However, Fig. 9.4 shows that in the laboratory, excitation of the mode produced a large increase in internal noise. Hence, if the wheel rotational frequency reached 23 Hz, then a large internal noise component could be expected. Furthermore, Fig. 9.2 shows the 23 Hz mode to be based on displacement within the rubber insulator. Therefore, a decrease in the stiffness of the insulator could bring the frequency of this mode into the range covered by wheel rotation (n_3) and thereby cause a significant internal noise increase.

Figure 9.7 illustrates the internal noise power spectra for all road speeds with curves for $n_1/2$, n_1, $2n_1$, n_3, $2n_3$ and $3n_3$. Analysis for $3n_1$ showed it to be insignificant. Whilst curves for $2n_3$ and $n_1/2$ show particular values at their respective frequency, they represent only one peak due to the small separation of their frequencies. Numbers indicate frequencies of peaks which are not related to road speeds. All the significant contributions to internal noise appear at frequencies less than 150 Hz. At low road speeds, 30–40 mph, the spectra comprised three main peaks around 7·5, 36–39 and 75 Hz. At high road speeds the third main peak (75 Hz) does not appear. Figure 9.7 shows that a large contribution to the internal noise occurs at 7·5 Hz independent of the road speed. It is attributed to bounce of the complete vehicle on its tyres. This mode was not identified in laboratory experiments because the lowest frequency used therein was 10 Hz. An alternative cause, engine vibration relative to body, was discarded because 7·5 Hz was considered too low and the frequency does not vary with engine speed. Whilst 7·5 Hz is well within the sub-audible range it was felt

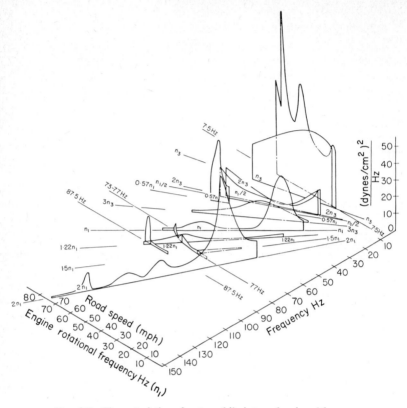

Fɪɢ. 9.7. Characteristics of automobile internal noise, 4th gear.

to be important to record this acoustic vibration because of its suggested effect on the driver fatigue. There is a large peak in the 7·5 Hz curve when n_1 equals 67 Hz. This is when the engine and drive-shaft excite the main axle-bending mode, and the two frequencies have almost an integer (9) relationship. Figure 9.7 shows that the component of internal noise at wheel rotational frequency (n_3) appears at all road speeds with almost the largest magnitude. Wheel rotational frequency is sub-audible at almost all road speeds. Similar large sub-audible noise contributions were reported by Jha and Priede [2].

The frequency band 36–39 Hz appears to be very important in terms of internal noise. Figure 9.4 shows that in the laboratory experiments a large internal noise peak was produced at 39 Hz by harmonic excitation applied vertically to the axle centre. However, during this particular laboratory experiment it was confirmed (but not illustrated) that the axle mode shown on Fig. 9.2 at 37·5 Hz was not excited. (The mode at 37·5 Hz was identified using vertical harmonic excitation to the wheel at the road surface.) It was also confirmed that the 37·5 Hz axle mode was not excited during road testing. Figure 9.7 shows that a significant noise peak occurred at this frequency at all road speeds with a particularly large response at engine and drive-shaft rotational frequency (n_1). This noise peak is attributed to the first bending mode of the vehicle body and not to the drive-line, despite the coincidence of the frequency of an identified mode. Jha and Priede [2] also report a similar significant noise contribution at all road speeds in the frequency range 35–40 Hz.

Figure 9.7 shows that 75 Hz is another frequency at which significant noise is created, especially when excited at twice engine frequency. Figure 9.2 shows that no drive-line vibration mode was identified near 75 Hz, using the central vibration. Vertical excitation to the road wheel was limited to 65 Hz. Moreover, Fig. 9.4 shows that no significant internal noise response was created in the laboratory at 75 Hz. Road testing revealed a significant internal noise component in the range 73–77 Hz at all road speeds. A very large response was shown at low speed when the engine firing frequency ($2n_1$) equalled 75 Hz. Similar findings are reported in Refs. 2 and 3. However, at high road speeds when the drive-shaft and engine frequency equals 75 Hz a peak of magnitude comparable to that of the $2n_1$ peak does not appear. This is an important difference to the findings of Ref. 2. This 75 Hz noise peak is attributed to excitation of the half-wavelength acoustic resonance of the vehicle cavity.

It receives strong excitation from the engine noise and relatively weak input from the drive-line vibration and engine fundamental, thereby accounting for the large and small response at $2n_1$ and n_1, respectively. Experiments with loudspeaker excitation within the fully trimmed passenger compartment did not clearly confirm the frequency of the half-wavelength acoustic resonance. May [3] reports a similar result and Priede and Jha [1] showed that it was necessary to resort to a solid wall cavity to enable the acoustic resonance to be identified. At 75 Hz the half-wavelength of the acoustic wave is 0·938 times the length from the rear window to the toe-board, which accords with the imaginary reflecting plane found by Priede and Jha [1] in the fully trimmed cavity.

Drive-shaft rotation provided the main excitation for the axle-bending mode identified at 67 Hz. It was confirmed that a large axle vibration peak occurred during the road tests when the drive-shaft rotational frequency equalled 67 Hz. Hence the noise peak shown around 67 Hz in the n_1 curve

(Fig. 9.7) is attributed to excitation of the drive-line vibration mode identified at that frequency. Furthermore, Fig. 9.4 shows that a small noise peak was obtained in the laboratory experiments at 67 Hz when that axle mode was known to be excited. A larger internal noise component could be expected if the frequency of the axle-bending mode coincided with that of the acoustic resonance. It appears to be advantageous to separate the two frequencies.

Figure 9.7 shows a contribution to the internal noise at $1.22n_1$ over the entire road speed range. This is attributed to the rotation of the engine fan.

A significant noise component is shown at $0.57n_1$ over a small road speed range between 70 and 75 mph. No rotating component could be identified at this frequency ratio.

Figure 9.7 shows significant noise components at 102 and 116 Hz at twice engine and drive-shaft frequencies. A twice rotational excitation is provided by the universal joints at the shaft ends. Figure 9.3 shows that an axle mounted accelerometer is insensitive to these modes and their excitation was not confirmed in road testing. It is possible that the 116 Hz peak may arise from excitation of the three-quarter-wavelength acoustic resonance—see Farnham [4]—at approximately 112 Hz, by the drive-shaft mode.

9.5 CONCLUSIONS

Eleven vertical drive-line vibration modes have been identified within the frequency range 10–200 Hz. The rubber insulator separating spring and axle casing strongly influenced several modes, particularly that at 23 Hz. This mode was not excited during road running. If, however, it were excited, by either higher road speeds or reduced rubber insulator stiffness, then a significant additional contribution to the internal noise could be expected.

The axle-bending mode at 67 Hz was excited by drive-shaft rotation and made a considerable contribution to the internal noise. This mode also caused a considerable increase in the sub-audible 7·5 Hz constant frequency component. At 30–40 mph the internal noise comprised three approximately equal dominant components, at 36–39 Hz, 75 Hz and the sub-audible n_3 to 7·5 Hz. The sub-audible contribution is dominant at all speeds but those at 36–39 and 75 Hz diminish at higher speeds. Body bending causes the 36–39 Hz noise peak, which appears at all road speeds with engine rotation causing the largest response. Half-wavelength acoustic resonance within the passenger cavity causes the 75 Hz noise peak. This appears at all road speeds with a particularly large response at twice engine rotational frequency. The vehicle used in these experiments did not exhibit a large noise component arising from excitation of the acoustic resonance by engine rotation, as reported for some other vehicles.

Drive-line vibration contributes the largest noise component at all road speeds, i.e. at 7·5 Hz, and a lesser component due to excitation of the 67 Hz mode by drive-shaft rotation. Under some circumstances a significant noise could arise from the 23 Hz mode.

ACKNOWLEDGEMENTS

The author would like to acknowledge the support of the Science Research Council and the Vehicle Manufacturers; the encouragement by Professor J. R. Ellis, Director of the School of Automotive Studies; and the assistance of colleagues at Cranfield Institute of Technology.

REFERENCES

1. Priede, T. and Jha, S. J. (1970). Low frequency noise in cars, its origins and elimination, *J. Automotive Engineering* (July).
2. Jha, S. K. and Priede, T. (1972). 'Origin of Low Frequency Noise in Motor Cars', Proc. 14th FISITA Congr., London.
3. May, B. J. 'High Frequency Noise, and Vibration of Automobile Transmission Systems', Ph.D. Thesis, University of Aston in Birmingham, 1968.
4. Farnham, J. R. 'Power Train Tuning for Quiet Cars', SAE preprint 627C.
5. Mills, C. H. G. and Dixon, J. C. 'An Investigation of the Characteristics and Causes of Road Noise in Vehicles, Mira Report Nos. 1959/9 and 1961/6.
6. Hodgetts, D. and Parkins, D. W. 'Vibration modes of an automobile drive-line', SAE Paper No. 740952, Automobile Engineering and Manufacturing Meeting, Toronto (October 1974).
7. Gladwell, G. M. L. (1964). A review of noise and vibration in motor cars, *J. Sound Vib.*, **1** (2), 202–210.
8. Hodgetts, D. and Parkins, D. W. 'Vibrations of the Drive-Line of a Motor Vehicle' Report to SRC, B/SR/6948, 1974.

10

Noise Generated at the Tyre–Road Interface

J. C. WALKER AND D. J. MAJOR
Dunlop Ltd.

SUMMARY

A review is made of recent published work on the airborne road noise produced by truck tyres including the effects of speed, tread pattern, road surface texture, tyre tread materials and load.

New results are reported of the tyre–road noise produced by car tyres; these are both in the form of frequency spectra and of sound level meter values. In the case of car tyres the measurements have again shown the advantages of certain types of road surface. The tyre variables investigated include the effect of sectional width, of sectional aspect ratio and of inflation pressure. The information obtained is sufficient to give an indication of the minimum possible tyre–road noise which, with current knowledge, would be generated by a vehicle of given weight travelling at a given speed by optimising both tyre and road texture parameters.

10.1 INTRODUCTION

It is essential that a tyre incorporates a tread pattern to provide grip under poor ground surface conditions such as in rain, mud and snow. Even 35–40 years ago car tyres had their tread segments at variable pitches to break up any dominant noise frequencies. After this problem had been solved, noise work was mainly concerned with internal vehicle noise [1]. However, since the Wilson report in 1963 [2] increasing attention has been paid to external noise [3] and with increasing traffic density and the advent of urban motorways, concern about excessive external vehicle noise has been growing [4].

Watkins [5] reports that the progress of the quiet heavy lorry project sponsored by the Transport and Road Research Laboratory (TRRL), Department of the Environment, on quietening the power train noise is encouraging; this is the noise from the engine inlet, exhaust, cooling systems and transmission, as far as the lay shaft. He also develops the case for reducing car noise, which is often dominated by tyre–road noise with current tread patterns and road textures at steady speeds above 50 km/h (32 mph). Harland [6] states that a reduction of lorry power train noise by 10 dBA is thought to be within reach of our existing technology, but the benefits of such changes will not be fully realised unless at the same time rolling noise can be brought down by about 5 dBA. Rolling noise includes that from aerodynamic sources, from the transmission beyond the lay shaft, body rattles, and tyre–road interface noise from tyre, road and vehicle.

Underwood [7] reporting on the TRRL work on the effects of tyres and surfaces on rolling noise, indicates that the tyre–road interface noise from heavy lorries could become one of the salient features of truck noise, if the target is reached on quietening power train noise.

Hence, there is a considerable amount of work being carried out around the world on this problem; the 34 references given include 10 papers published in 1974.

It is therefore necessary to investigate the nature of tyre–road noise. The approach to this is in four main parts:

1. Measure and analyse vehicle coasting noise on the road.
2. Measure and analyse tyre–surface noise on a drum in the laboratory.
3. Construct a mathematical model in the computer in order to predict results.
4. Obtain as close a correspondence as possible between the different parts of the work, and apply the knowledge gained to produce quieter tyre–road interfaces.

TABLE 10.1
Measuring equipment and procedures

Microphone or array of microphones	
Stationary	7·5 m from central line of vehicle pass-by tests, 1·2 m off ground
Travelling	Boom microphone on vehicle
Peak and time delay values	
Noise levels	
Frequency analysis	⅓ octave Narrow band and tracking filters Real time analysis
Directional effects	

10.2   EXPERIMENTAL PROCEDURES

The measuring equipment and procedures for the investigations are indicated in Table 10.1. Three microphones have been used spaced 0·5 m apart at a distance from the tyre of 0·5 m when testing in the laboratory. By combining their outputs after narrow band filtering and rectifying, any disturbing standing wave effects can be averaged out. Also, near field effects can be averaged. Using the British Standard Test for specific room suitability it was found that when the microphone to source distance was doubled there was more than 5 dB drop in sound level. Hence, the laboratory is suitable for this type of test.

The pass-by tests are to BS 3425 conditions, with the vehicle coasting past the microphone at the required speeds. The microphone is 7·5 m from the centre line of the vehicle track and 1·2 m off the ground. The impulse sound level meter, B and K Type 2209, gives very consistent readings; tape recordings are also taken. Real time narrow band analysis overcomes the problem of the Doppler effect frequency shifts as the vehicle passes. The repeatability of pass-by noise levels was investigated simultaneously with 50 repeat passes for the real time frequency analysis shown in Fig. 10.7. The standard deviation of the individual pass-by sound levels about the linear regression line with the logarithm of speed was 0·57 dBA, thus giving a standard error of the mean of 0·23 dBA for six passes and 0·18 dBA for 10 passes.

In the case of noise with a similar time and frequency spectrum character, a 3 dBA change in noise level is just perceptible to an average observer when the initial and changed levels are heard consecutively. With an interval of time occurring between them, it requires 4 or 5 dB before all observers in a group will agree a noticeable difference exists [8]. The traffic can be considered as a line source when the distance from the motorway is greater than half the average headway between the vehicles. A 3 dB reduction is a halving of sound intensity, and equivalent to doubling the distance from the motorway or to halving of traffic volume [9] or to reducing the traffic speed by 25%.

Thus, although 1 dB is fairly insignificant from a subjective point of view, it is of great importance to authorities paying compensation under the Land Compensation Act when the measured noise is close to the limit [10].

The tyre and surface variables and test conditions are shown in Table 10.2 and will be dealt with in more detail.

TABLE 10.2
Tyre and surface variables and test conditions

Tyre	Surface
Tyre Design	Road
Tread pattern	Texture
blank and plain rib	smooth
commercial $\Big\}$ variable pitch	delugrip
traction	motorway
Tread compound	macro and microtexture
hardness and resilience	road profile
Tread profile	Conditions
Tyre construction	dry
cross-ply and radial ply	wet
Tyre size	roadwear
aspect ratio	building proximity
width and diameter	ambient noise
Tyres per vehicle	Drum
Conditions	Texture
Speed, load, pressure	Acoustical environment
Wear	absorption by room
tread depth, irregular wear	ambient noise
Temperature, time	
Ageing	
Cornering and traction	
Vehicle, wheels	
alloy and steel	
Noise mechanisms	
Generation	
Impacting, stroking, air pumping	
Resonances	
contained air, tread, casing	
Other properties	
Optimise with wet grip	

10.3   TRANSPORT AND ROAD RESEARCH LABORATORY TESTS

Figure 10.1 summarises the main dBA results published in Reference 7 on the TRRL quiet lorry project. It shows the coasting noise levels in dBA at the standard distance of 7·5 m from the centre line of the vehicle for a laden truck 13·2 Mg (13 tons) travelling at 100 km/h (62 mph). There are three dry surfaces, smooth concrete, coarse quartzite and motorway surfaces, and three types of tyre pattern, blank tread, ribbed pattern and

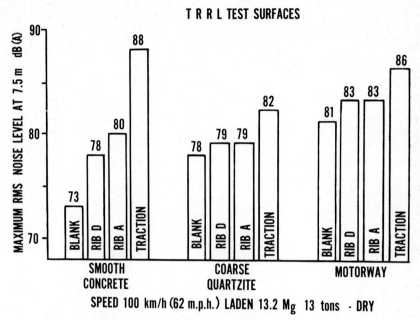

Fig. 10.1. Truck coasting noise for various tyre–road combinations.

tractive pattern, on the 10·00–20 cross-ply tyres. A blank tread is one of full tread thickness without a tread pattern.

The smooth concrete surface shows a much greater contrast in tread pattern road noise than the surfaces with the greater macrotexture—this is the large-scale texture of the road surface for water drainage. In the latter cases, ribbed tyres are 1–2 dBA noisier than smooth tyres and traction tyres are 3 dBA noisier than the ribbed tyres. Consequently any potential inprovement in dBA noise level by tread pattern changes can only be relatively small, since the total effect of any major pattern feature is of the order of 3 dBA.

The traction pattern is some 6 dBA quieter on the coarse quartzite than on the smooth concrete. It appears that the road surface texture blurs the tread bar effect on noise. The coarse quartzite surface is 3–4 dBA quieter than the motorway.

The effect of high hysteresis (H.H.) tread rubber was also measured, and as compared to natural tread rubber the average differences were less than 1–1·5 dBA. In the dry, the H.H. smooth tyre is 1 dBA noisier, the H.H. traction tyre 1 dBA quieter. In the wet, both tread patterns are 1·5 dBA noisier.

10.4   CAR AND LABORATORY TESTS

Coasting noise tests of a similar type to the TRRL tests have been carried out with a Rover 2000 on 165–14 steel breaker radial-ply tyres, and relative results are shown for tests on a smooth steel drum of 1·52 m (60 in) diameter in the laboratory (Fig. 10.2). The coasting noise levels are given for the 1·28 Mg (1·26 tons) car travelling at 64 km/h (40 mph). There are four types of tyre, blank tread, plain ribbed, ribbed and multi-slotted, and a winter tyre tractive block pattern tread; and four dry surfaces, hand laid mastic asphalt, sand carpet smooth asphalt, Delugrip* (Delugrip is a surface with textural characteristics designed for optimum performance of the tyre) [11], and Motorway BS 594.

Again the patterns are strongly contrasted on the smooth drum surface; as surface roughness is increased, the smooth tyre surface noise increases

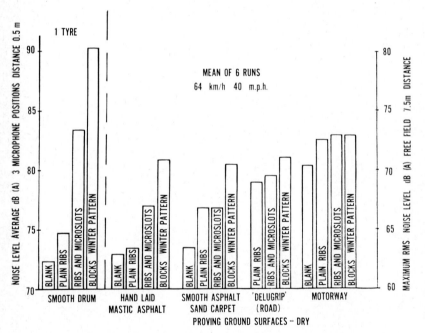

FIG. 10.2. Car coasting noise for various tyre road combinations.

* Delugrip is a registered Trade Mark of Dunlop Ltd.

and the contrast between the patterns decreases. The blank tyres were not tested on the Delugrip road since this would have been illegal. Other factors influencing matters are described below.

10.4.1   Wet Road

If bulk water does lie on the surface then the noise can be 7–11 dBA higher than in the dry with truck tyres [7]. However, if the road surface has enough drainage to drain away the surface water, such as the porous surface of friction course [12], then noise in the wet is hardly any higher than the noise in the dry. No significant difference has been found between the noise on the Delugrip and friction course surfaces in the dry with discontinuous rib pattern car tyres.

Turning now to the other variables in Table 10.2, tests were carried out to show the effect of aspect ratio and sectional width of tyres on 13 in textile breaker radial-ply tyres with serrated ribs in the dry.

10.4.2   Aspect Ratio

Figure 10.3 shows by a lattice plot, with speed on a logarithmic scale, that the low aspect ratio (low percentage sectional height divided by

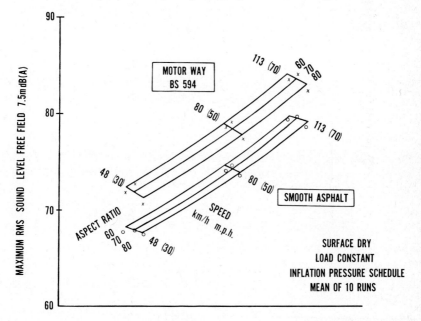

FIG. 10.3. Lattice plot effect of aspect ratio, constant sectional width, 185 series 13-in serrated rib tyre.

188   *J. C. Walker and D. J. Major*

sectional width) 60 series tyres are 0·7 dBA noisier than 80 series tyres on
the smooth asphalt and 1·2 dBA noisier on BS 594 motorway surface. This
compares with the finding of Hillquist and Carpenter [13] that 60 series
belted bias tyres are 2 dBA noisier than 78 series. With these tyres of
constant sectional width, as aspect ratio decreases tread diameter decreases,
and tread width remains constant. Thus part of the dB difference is due to
the diameter effect.

10.4.3 Sectional Width

Figure 10.4 similarly shows the effect of sectional width at constant load
on these 13 in tyres; the 145 section is 2·5 dBA quieter than the 185 section
on both surfaces. As the sectional width decreases the tread diameter also
decreases. In this case the diameter effect opposes the tread width effect.

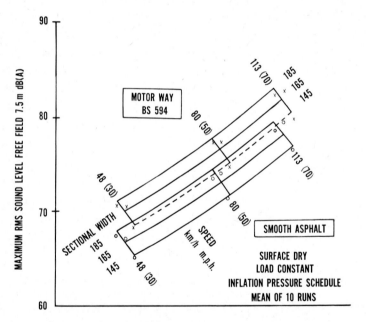

FIG. 10.4. Lattice plot effect of sectional width, constant aspect ratio, 80 series 13 in
serrated rib tyre.

10.4.4 Tyre Diameter and Wheels

In drum tests with block pattern tyres, of the same section and tread
width, 10 in tyres were 1·2 dBA noisier than 13 in tyres and a light alloy
wheel was 1·5 dBA quieter than a steel wheel.

10.4.5 Tyre Construction—Radial-Ply and Cross-Ply Car Tyres

A tyre of each construction was tested on the drum, both having basically the same winter tyre block pattern and the same tread width. The noise levels from the three microphone positions were averaged. The radial tyre was 0·7 dBA quieter than the cross ply. It is known that in the case of the radial-ply tyres there is less tread shuffle or micromovement on the road.

10.4.6 Tread Compounds

The tread compound effect was also tested in the dry; the high hysteresis serrated rib rubber tyres were 0·9 dBA quieter on smooth asphalt and 1·7 dBA quieter on BS 594 motorway.

10.4.7 Speed

The truck tyre tests previously discussed show an average 10 dBA increase with doubling of speed. This corresponds to 33 dBA per decade and 3 dBA per 25% increase in speed. The car test results in Figs. 10.3 and 10.4 show an average of 9·5 dBA increase with doubling of speed. In all the results previously discussed the differences in noise level have been fairly consistent over the speed range.

10.4.8 Load and Inflation Pressure—Cross-Ply Truck Tyres

Flanagan [14] reported that if the load is kept in the 75% to 100% range of the maximum rated load, and the scheduled pressure used, the sound level does not change appreciably. The NBS [15] showed that increasing the load per tyre from 0·69 to 2·01 Mg (1530 to 4430 lb) on cross-bar tyres gave a greater sound level increase, 6–8 dBA, than on rib tyres, 1–3 dBA. The USA Rubber Manufacturers Association [16] showed that at constant load an increase of 103 kPa (or 15 psi) gave a decrease in noise of 0·5 dBA.

10.4.9 Tyres Per Vehicle

Doubling the load and number of wheels raises the sound level by approximately 2 dBA as shown by Tetlow [17].

10.4.10 Tread Profile—Cross-Ply Cross-Bar Truck Tyres

Tetlow also showed that tyres wore to a greater tread radius than in the new state. This gave a 6 dBA noise increase. Grinding the tyre to the original smaller tread radius reduced the noise to the original value for the new tyres.

10.4.11   Tyre Wear—Cross-Ply Truck Tyres

Seldom does a tyre grow quieter at any speed as it wears out. The increase in noise level from new to half-worn treads is typically 2·5 dBA for ribbed patterns and 4·2 dBA for cross-bar patterns. The noise level then decreases as the fully worn state is approached, unless the tread pattern is such that pockets of air can be trapped at advanced stages of wear—Flanagan [14]. Irregular wear tends to occur on truck tyres, especially when the wear due to lightly laden motorway running predominates in the duty cycle. This is fairly rare in the UK because of the limited unbroken motorway mileages. Some examples of this type of wear can increase noise.

10.4.12   Temperature

Temperature causes no significant change in noise level when drum testing both rib and cross-bar cross-ply truck tyres between 25° and 125°F, according to Tetlow [17]. However, in the case of nylon car tyres which have flatted, that is, parked overnight in the cold immediately after a high speed run, the flats should be run out before testing commences—NBS [15].

10.4.13   Time-Ageing

Over a period of two years rubber will slightly harden and the noise can increase by 1–2 dBA, according to Favre and Pachiaudi [18].

10.4.14   Tread Pattern—Variable Pitch

For the last 35–40 years car tyres have had variable pitch segments in the tread pattern. Although this may not alter the overall sound level, it does break up any dominant frequencies. Empirically determined sequences have worked well over the years and now can be further refined by analysing the harmonics from the pattern sequence with a fast Fourier transform in the computer, and then optimising the sequence. This is regularly used for new snow-tyre patterns. The procedure is similar to that described by Varterasian [19]. Aural impressions of the tones were discussed by Zoeppritz [20]. Variable pitch segments are now being applied to truck tyre traction patterns. This was discussed by Thurman [21].

10.5   NOISE GENERATION MECHANISMS

Three mechanisms for tyre–road noise generation are: (*a*) impacting between the tread and road; (*b*) micromovements of rubber on the road; and (*c*) air pumping by the tread pattern.

Three resonances involved are those of the tyre, the air in the tyre and the tread elements. The impacting mechanism has been studied extensively by Richards [22]. Accelerometers inserted inside the tyre showed over 600 g change in acceleration as the tread entered and left the contact patch at a speed of 113 km/h (70 mph). Carpeting the surface to soften the impact reduced the noise level of a block pattern tyre by 8 dBA at 48 km/h (30 mph) and 3·5 dBA at 113 km/h (70 mph).

With micromovements of the tread, our glass plate studies of a blank tread, steel radial-ply tyre show up to 2·5 mm total movement of a point on the tread relative to the ground as it passes through the contact patch. It has been suggested that this is the main cause of the noise of a smooth tyre on a smooth surface [22].

The 1 kHz peak in the noise frequency spectra which is independent of speed is close to the frequency which occurs when the tyre squeals on cornering. The squeal frequency increases as tread depth decreases, as discussed by Trivisonno *et al.* [23]. This is the tread element resonance previously referred to. In the investigation to find any dominant frequency peaks, we used the averaged output from three tracking filters fed from three microphones. This is done by locking the tracking filters to a particular harmonic of wheel rotation and by varying the tyre speed on the drum between 80 and 15 km/h (50 and 9 mph). In order to determine to what extent there exist frequency peaks in the straight ahead rolling noise, corresponding to the estimated cornering squeal frequency as 0° slip angle is approached, the following test results were obtained with 8 mm and 1 mm tread depth tyres with serrated ribs and microslots.

The upper part of Fig. 10·5 shows the increase in cornering squeal frequency as slip angle is reduced. The lower part of the figure shows the frequency components of the noise tracked at the harmonics of wheel rotation for straight ahead rolling. As the speed falls, the particular harmonic passes through resonant frequencies and the level of the harmonic rises. Similar behaviour by several harmonics confirms the existence of the resonances. There is only a slight peak for both the 8 mm tread depth tyre at 1000 Hz and for the 1 mm tread depth tyre around 1900 Hz. This implies that the stroking mechanism setting up relaxation oscillations is not a dominant mechanism in tyre noise.

The third mechanism of air pumping was discussed by Hayden [24] and the theory was further developed to predict directivity patterns by Samuels and Alfredson [25]. However, as regards the noise from cavity pockets in the road, Richards [22] concluded that the impacting mechanism was dominant.

Of the other resonances, the tyre vibrations have been discussed by

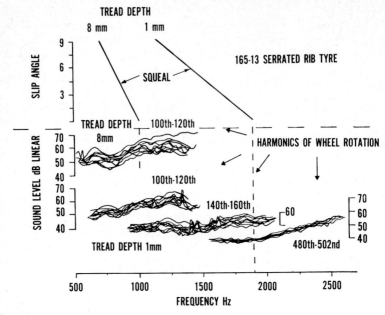

FIG. 10.5. Frequency components of noise tracked at harmonics of wheel rotation related to tread depth and cornering squeal frequency.

Leasure and Bender [26], and truck cross-ply tyre resonances below 250 Hz were investigated by Reiter [27], showing the acoustic radiation to be emanating from a region within a quarter wavelength of the tyre footprint. Figure 10.6 gives results obtained from investigating tyre resonances with a tyre having a discontinuous rib pattern. It shows frequency components of the noise due to the 40th to 65th harmonics of wheel rotation for both air and carbon dioxide inflation. The 63rd is the dominant harmonic; this corresponds to the number of pattern segments round the tyre. It can be seen that the slight resonant frequency lowering due to carbon dioxide inflation is very much less than the 24% reduction which would be expected for a resonance of the inflation medium in the tyre. The resonances are thus those of the tyre; the resonance spacing is of the same order as the vibration modes measured by Chiesa *et al.* [28] and Potts and Csora [29, 30]. The resonance of the air column at 230 Hz in a 155–15 car tyre was verified by Chiesa *et al.* [28], who obtained a frequency shift to 175 Hz on inflating the tyre with carbon dioxide. The air resonance was also noted by Gough *et al.* [31]. However, this resonance does not show any noticeable effect on the noise in Fig. 10.6.

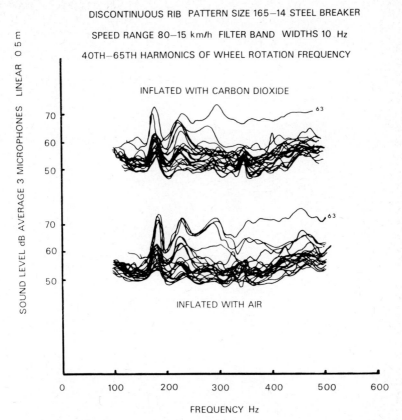

FIG. 10.6. Frequency components of noise tracked at harmonics of wheel rotation related to inflation medium—showing tyre resonances.

10.6 REAL TIME ANALYSIS

Fine frequency band analysis of pass-by noise gives a more complete description of the noise the ear hears as the vehicle passes. Analysis is needed on very short time samples of the noise to prevent Doppler effects blurring the results. However, repeated passes are needed to average out random variations occurring in such short time intervals.

The analysis is performed by feeding the tape recorded signal directly into the minicomputer/plotter system. Figure 10.7 shows such an analysis. The car travelled at 64 km/h (40 mph) on the smooth asphalt surface. It had only one block pattern tyre fitted and three plain ribbed tyres. This

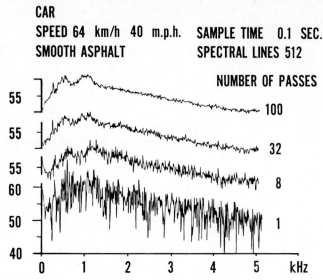

FIG. 10.7. Narrow band real time frequency analysis averaging pass-by results. (Maximum T.M.S. 10 Hz; band level free field 7·5 m dBA.)

arrangement prevents beat effects between different tyres, thus approaching the results from single tyre trailer tests that have been used for many years for car tyre tests by Pirelli (Milan) and recently for truck tyres, as described by Wilken *et al.* [32]. First, a one-tenth second sample of noise is taken at the instant the car passes the microphone. It is analysed at 10 Hz bandwidth into 512 spectral lines up to 5 kHz. The one-tenth second sample shows the random variations due to such a small bandwidth–time product (10 × $\frac{1}{10}$ = 1). As the number of passes of the same vehicle is increased to 8, 32 and finally 100 passes the random variations average out, revealing the true spectrum. The peaks are those expected from the tread pattern which rise in frequency as the speed is raised together with a broad peak at 1 kHz which is independent of speed.

To obtain a sensible answer out of narrow band real time analysis for a pass-by test requires considerable experimental effort.

10.7   NOISE DUE TO ROAD SURFACE TEXTURE AND BLOCK TREAD PATTERNS

The upper part of Fig. 10.8 shows the third octave spectrum of a plain rib steel breaker radial-ply tyre on Delugrip. A broad peak in the order of 1000 Hz which is independent of speed, together with a rapid decay rate as

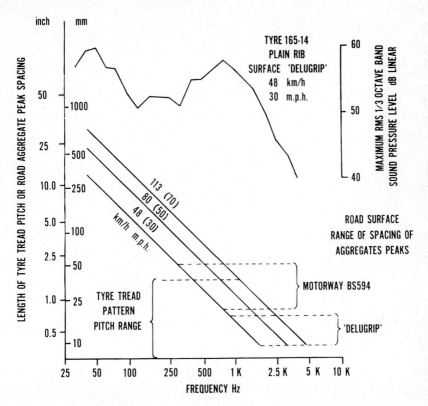

FIG. 10.8. Relationship between tyre road noise and frequency generation due to
vehicle speed, tyre tread pitch and road aggregate spacing.

the frequency rises further, is shown in this spectrum. It also occurs with
a blank tyre on a smooth tarmac surface at lower levels.

Hayden's work on vibrating a stationary car tyre [24] also shows a
falling response in this region, as does the work of Richards [22].

The lower part of Fig. 10.8 shows the relationship between length of
tyre tread pitch or mean aggregate spacing, vehicle speed, and the corresponding frequency generated. It is evident that both the road designer and
the tyre designer have to be careful in choice of aggregate size and tyre
segment pitch so that excitation is, as far as possible, in the less sensitive
higher frequency region.

As regards the amplitude of excitation from block pattern tyres,
Richards [22] points out that transverse grooves should be diagonal, that

is as 'circumferential' as possible and well staggered from rib to rib, and that blocks in shoulder ribs are quieter than blocks in central ribs.

10.8   NOISE AND WET GRIP

Figure 10.9 shows the form of the relationship between wet grip and noise in the dry for various tyre–road combinations. The truck figures are from Transport and Road Research Laboratories work [6] and the coasting noise levels are those which were shown in Fig. 10.1. The 13·2Mg (13 tons) truck at 100 km/h (62 mph) with blank tyres on smooth concrete has a low braking force coefficient of 0·03 and a low noise level of 73 dBA.

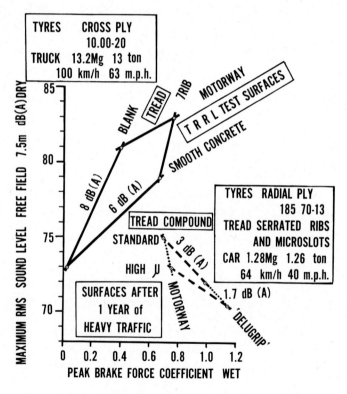

FIG. 10.9. Vehicle coasting noise related to wet grip for various tyre road combinations.

Consider the following ways of increasing grip: (*a*) with texture on the road (motorway), the noise increases 8 dBA; (*b*) with a ribbed pattern on the tyre tread and again on the smooth concrete, the noise rises 6 dBA; (*c*) with both road texture and rib pattern the noise rises 10 dBA.

However, the grip can be increased and the noise reduced. In the case of our work with a 1·28 Mg (1·26 ton) car travelling at 64 km/h (40 mph), with increasing grip, the noise level reduces by 3 dBA when changing from the BS 594 Motorway to the Delugrip, and a by further 1·7 dBA when high friction tread compound tyres are used.

It will be noted that the TRRL braking force coefficients are rather higher on their track than on the actual motorway. This is because on the track the roughening, due to weathering, dominates any traffic polishing, whereas on the motorway the reverse is true. In fact, a car has a higher grip than a lorry on the same surface.

10.9   CONCLUSIONS

The literature, to date, has shown many mechanisms for the generation and emission of tyre road noise. The work in this paper has in some measure helped to rank these in order of importance. From the literature, impacting is a very important mechanism. Air pumping is dominant in the case of treads which can trap pockets of air on smooth road surfaces. Retread truck tyres of this type have been used in some parts of the world, but in the UK, tyres are designed to avoid this throughout their wearing life. With car tyres, in the case of enclosed microslots not vented into a groove, this type of noise occurs as a 'sizzle'. However, smooth roads are now technically outdated. Micromovement of the tread and tread resonances do not generate sharply resonant noise as happens in cornering squeal. Casing resonances are sizeable especially at low frequencies. No effect of air resonance was seen on the noise.

With regard to road surfaces, increased wet grip can be obtained with less rolling noise for both cars and trucks using the Delugrip surface. In the design of this non-polishing surface we find a balance between a surface coarse enough to give adequate bulkwater drainage and fine enough to give minimum noise.

It is felt that, in the future, tyre and road surface design should be considered together, to obtain the optimum environmental conditions. This thinking is in line with that in the Noise Advisory Council Report 'Noise in the Next Ten Years' [34].

198 *J. C. Walker and D. J. Major*

ACKNOWLEDGEMENTS

The authors wish to express appreciation to Messrs M. J. Tippins, J. C. Walker Jnr and F. G. Court for their help in this work and to Dunlop Ltd for permission to publish it.

REFERENCES

1. Tomkins, E. S. (1965). 'Tyres for Modern Roads', Proc. Institute of the Rubber Industry, Vol. 12, No. 2.
2. Wilson, Sir Alan, 'Noise', Final Report of the Committee on the Problem of Noise, cmnd 2056, London, HMSO, 1963.
3. Dunlop Company Information Article, 'The Sound of Tyres' (1352H), March 1968.
4. Serendipity Inc, 'A Study of the Magnitude of Transportation Noise Generation and Potential Abatement', Report No. OST-ONA-71–1, 1970.
5. Watkins, L. H. (1974). A quiet heavy lorry, *Commercial Motor*, **139** (3539), 28–31.
6. Harland, D. G. (1974). 'Rolling Noise and Vehicle Noise', Symp. on Noise in Transportation, University of Southampton, 22 July.
7. Underwood, M. C. P. 'A Preliminary Investigation—into Lorry Tyre Noise', Transport and Road Research Laboratory Report LR 601, 1973.
8. *Engineering Equipment Users Association Hand Book No. 25*. 'Measurement and Control of Noise', 1968.
9. Millard, R. S., 'A Review of Road Traffic Noise', Transport and Road Research Laboratory Report LR 357, 1970.
10. Vulkan, G. H. (1974). 'Development in Urban Planning against Noise', Paper 10, section 3, Symp. on Noise in Transportation, University of Southampton, 22 July.
11. Bond, R., Williams, A. R. and Lees, G. (1973). 'An Approach Towards the Understanding and Design of the Pavement's Textural Characteristics Required for Optimum Performance of the Tyre', Symp. on Physics of Tire Traction, General Motors, October.
12. Martin, F. R. and Judge, R. F. A. (1966). *Civil Eng.*, 1495, December.
13. Hillquist, R. K. and Carpenter, P. C. (1974). A basic study of automobile tire noise, *J. Sound Vib.*, Feb.
14. Flanagan, W. (1972). Recent studies give unified picture of tire noise, *Automotive Engineering*, **80** (4), April.
15. Leasure, W. A., Jnr., Corley, D. M., Flynn, D. R. and Forrer, J. S. 'Truck Tire Noise I: Peak A Weighted Sound Levels due to Truck Tires', National Bureau of Standards Department of Transportation Report. OST–ONA–71–9, 1970, and Addendum Report OST–TST–72–1, 1972.

16. Rubber Manufacturers Association. 'Truck Tire Noise', Presentation of the Office of Noise Abatement and Control of the Environmental Protection Agency Hearing, Washington DC, Nov 12 and Appendix, 1971.
17. Tetlow, D. (1971), Truck tire noise, *J. Sound Vib.* 17–23, August.
18. Favre, B. and Pachiaudi, G. 'Tyre Noise, Theoretical and Experimental Aspects', Internal Report by Research Institute of Transport, Arcueil, (private communication), 1974.
19. Varterasian, J. H. 'Quieting Noise Mathematically—Its Application to Snow Tires', S.A.E. 690520, 1969.
20. Zoeppritz, H. P. (1972). Possibilities and limitations of reducing tyre rolling noise, *A.T.Z.*, **74** (1), 13–16 (MIRA Translation No. 37/72), January.
21. Thurman, G. R. 'Characteristics of Truck Tire Sound', Truck Tire Noise, SP 373, SAE Publication, 1972.
22. Richards, M. G. (1974). Automotive tire noise—a comprehensive study, *J. Sound Vib.*, May.
23. Trivisonno, N. M., Beatty, J. R. and Millar, R. F. 'The Origin of Tire Squeal', Kautschuk Und Gummi Kunststoffe, No. 5, 20 January, 1967.
24. Hayden, R. E. (1971). 'Roadside Noise from the Interaction of a Rolling Tyre with the Road Surface', Proc. of the Purdue Noise Control Conference, Purdue University, West Lafayette, Indiana.
25. Samuels, S. E. and Alfredson, R. J. (1974). 'The Effect of Tread Pattern on Tyre Noise', Noise Shock and Vibration Conf., Monash University, Melbourne.
26. Leasure, W. A., Jnr. and Bender, E. K. (1972). 'Tyre–Road Interaction Noise', 84th Meeting of Acoustical Society of America, Miami, Florida.
27. Reiter, W. F. Jnr. (1974). Resonant sound and vibration characteristics of a truck tire, *Tire Science and Technology* **2** (2) 130–141, May.
28. Chiesa, A. Oberto, L. and Tamburini, L. (1964). Transmission of tyre vibrations, *Automobile Engineer*, December.
29. Potts, G. R. (1973). Application of Holography to the study of tire vibration, *Tyre Science and Technology* **1** (3), 255–266, August.
30. Potts, G. R. and Csora, T. T. (1974). 'Tire Vibration Studies—The State of the Art', presented at Akron Rubber Group Meeting, January.
31. Gough, V. E., Barson, C. W., Hutchinson, J. C., James, D. H. (1965). Tyre and vehicle vibration, *Proc. Inst. Mech. Engrs.*, **179**, pt 2A, No. 7.
32. Wilken, I. D., Hickling, R. and Wiknich, H. V. (1974). 'A Single Wheel Trailer for Tire Noise Research', SAE 740109.
33. Siddon, T. E. (1972). Noise generation mechanism for passenger car tyres, *J. of the Acoustical Society of America*, **53** (1), 305–306 (abstract).
34. Richards, E. J. 'Noise in the Next Ten Years.' Report by the Panel on Noise in the Seventies, Noise Advisory Council, 74:7:111, HMSO, 1974.

11

Control of Noise from Conventional Diesel Engines

M. F. RUSSELL

CAV Ltd

SUMMARY

The noise from diesel engines fitted to trucks and public service vehicles may be reduced in 3 ways

1. *Control rapid rise of cylinder pressure upon combustion, plus reduction of mechanical noise.*
2. *Reduce response of engine structure to vibration exciting forces of mechanical impact and combustion.*
3. *Install engine in a soundproof box with suitable ventilation.*

A study of the vibration mode shapes of the crankcase and cylinder block castings of several in-line engines has shown that there are certain modifications which may be incorporated into conventional engine crankcases which will reduce the noise emitted by their surfaces, and yet allow these castings to be machined on the existing transfer line. Such modifications, combined with isolation and damping treatments applied to the sump, valve gear covers, crankshaft pulley and all other noise-emitting areas of the engine, have given noise reductions of 5 dBA on the four engines treated to date.

11.1 INTRODUCTION

Legislation has been introduced to limit noise from road vehicles in most European countries, and there are proposals for more stringent limits in the future, starting with a 2–4 dBA reduction, below the present levels, proposed for 1976. The present drive-by test procedures (BS 3425 and ISO R362) emphasise the noise made by the engine and those accessories, engine-driven cooling fans, etc., which rotate at speeds related to the engine speed, over noise sources such as tyres, rear axle, wind noise, etc. which are related to road speed. Any reduction in the overall vehicle noise when tested in such a way implies a similar reduction in engine noise.

The new plant and tooling required to produce a new design of engine or even a major modification to an existing design will involve very heavy

capital expenditure. It seemed to be very worth while to find how much
noise reduction could be achieved by treatments to existing engine designs
which would not require such large capital expenditure on new machinery
and which could be developed for large-scale production.

11.2   CONTROLLING NOISE RADIATED FROM ENGINE SURFACES

There are four basic approaches to controlling noise radiated by the
engine surfaces:

1. Control noise generation at source by:
   (a) smooth cylinder pressure development during combustion;
   (b) eliminate or cushion impacts between piston and cylinder wall;
   (c) eliminate or reduce impacts between timing gears;
   (d) reduce or localise impacts and high frequency components of
       torque reactions from engine accessories and other equipment
       attached to the engine.
2. Reduce transmission of vibration from sources to radiating surfaces.
3. Control vibration of external surfaces of the engine:
   (a) de-tune major resonances of external surfaces from frequencies
       where high forcing function components are present;
   (b) isolate non-load-carrying surfaces from the vibration induced in
       the crankcase and cylinder block casting by the sources;
   (c) apply efficient means of vibration damping to control resonances
       in flexible covers (e.g. sheet steel pressings and deep-drawn
       components);
   (d) develop cylinder block and crankcase casting to reduce the
       vibration level at points of attachment of noise-radiating covers,
       for example the sump flange.
4. Enclose the engine:
   (a) completely with a close-fitting shield secured to the engine itself;
   (b) as completely as possible with an absorbent lined, and ventilated,
       soundproof box secured to the vehicle chassis.

A number of engines have been measured and the relative importance of
combustion and mechanical noise generators has been ascertained, by
finding the extent of the correlation of changes in the external noise spectrum levels with changes in the cylinder pressure spectrum levels over a
wide range of injection timings. Very often what appears to the ear to be

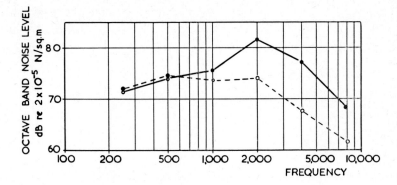

•   NOISE 3ft. IN FRONT GEARS

o   NOISE 3ft. IN FRONT CHAINS

FIG. 11.1. Effect of reducing timing drive noise. Noise at front of engine (1000 rev/min full load).

'combustion knock' turns out to be partly, and sometimes mostly, mechanical in origin. An example of an engine in which mechanical noise predominated is shown in Fig. 11.1, where the major source of noise at 1000 rev/min at full load, and also at many other conditions, was rattle of the timing gears. When a chain drive was substituted for the gear drive the noise fell dramatically, particularly at the front of the engine.

Apart from development of new timing drives and pistons to reduce mechanical noise at source, there are fundamental problems to be solved in developing a combustion chamber and the fuel injection equipment to provide an improvement in noise without adversely affecting some other important parameter such as power output, specific fuel consumption, smoke, gaseous emissions, unburned hydrocarbons, torque curve shape, etc. For a direct injection engine, simple changes to the fuel injection system, such as changing the pumping rate or even changing from an in-line pump specification to the correctly chosen distributor pump, have shown that for many engines some form of inverse proportionality exists between noise and smoke (DI engines). A series of tests with a 2×10 mm plunger distributor pump at different timings is compared with the (then) current production in-line pump and two alternative distributor pump specifications in Fig. 11.2. Only one pump seems to escape from the linear trade-off between noise and smoke ($2 \times 8\cdot5$ mm plungers timed at $21°$), and it gave 10% less power. More work is required on the effect of combustion chamber, air flow and fuel injection variables upon the noise

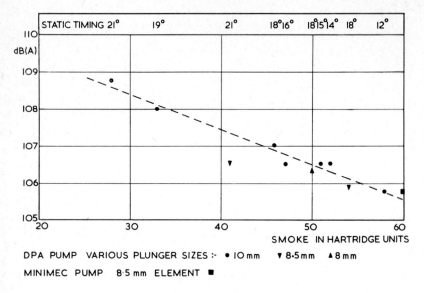

Fig. 11.2. Effect of pump and timing on noise and smoke.

pollution and performance of an engine, considered together rather than as isolated parameters to be treated individually.

When the pressure development inside the cylinder is compared to the sound pressure measured outside an engine, in which combustion is known to be the major source of noise (as in Fig. 11.3), the engine structure can be seen to have a very considerable effect, reducing the amplitude by 1 000 000 times and completely changing the character of the pulse. An examination of the effect of engine structure on several engines, by comparing the cylinder pressure spectra of Fig. 11.4 with the noise spectra of Fig. 11.5, both analysed by one-third octave band filters and plotted to the same scale, shows that there are very considerable differences between engine structures in their ability to attenuate noise. As one would expect, the surface panels and covers of engines are involved in numerous resonances and these detract from the noise-attenuating properties of the engine structure. If all the resonances of the surface structures which radiate the most noise can be found, then one of several available techniques may be applied to each, to reduce its noise emission, provided that resonances of the same surface component do not require mutually excessive treatments.

Diagnosis of the contribution to the overall noise of the engine from each

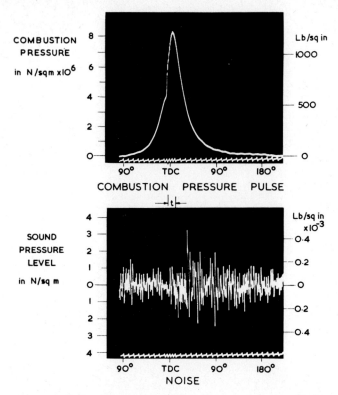

Fig. 11.3. Combustion knock (0·9 m from engine centre line).

surface area is possible by measuring the noise emitted through 'windows', which are opened over each area in turn, in an otherwise complete, absorbent-lined, lead jacket fitted closely over the whole of the engine. For the results to be meaningful, total encapsulation should reduce the engine noise by 10 dBA or more with all the 'windows' closed and sealed, and it should be possible to seal the lead jacket to the engine surface at the edges of the 'windows'. The location of the boundaries of the 'windows' requires some forethought, and misleading results have been discovered where one or more unsuspected radiators are included in a 'window' designed to open on to a single radiating surface. As an alternative it is possible to make an estimate of the sound emitted from a surface from measurements of vibration of the surface in each mode of vibration, provided that the level of vibration at the antinodes is available. The positions of the anti-nodes may be found by comparing the sound pressure equivalent of the

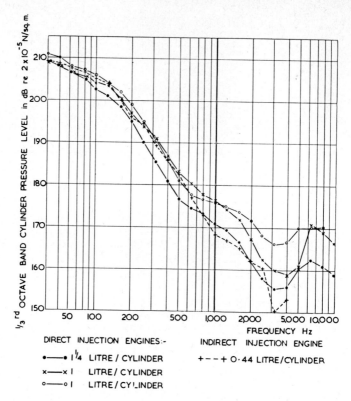

FIG. 11.4. Comparison between cylinder pressure spectra for naturally aspirated
automotive engines.

surface velocity with actual sound pressure levels measured with a microphone within $\frac{1}{2}$ in of the surface. The comparison is made in one-third
octave bands.

A comparison of the vibration velocities of various surface areas of a
small diesel engine is shown in Fig. 11.6, together with the noise measured
3 ft from the engine surface (no correction has been made for inefficient
radiation of sound at frequencies below coincidence in this comparison).
At low and medium frequencies, up to 2 kHz, the sump vibrates at high
levels, and in fact it was found essential to treat the sump to get more than
3 dBA reduction on this engine. The rocker cover and the push rod cover,
also made in sheet steel, both had large resonances in the region of 1 kHz.
Above 2 kHz the cast aluminium intake manifold and front timing gear
cover maintain high levels of vibration. The vibration of the crankcase

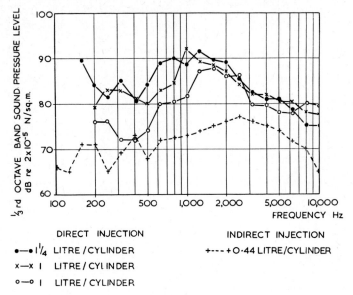

Fɪɢ. 11.5. Comparison between noise spectra for naturally aspirated automotive engines.

panels was unusually low on this engine, partly due to one $\frac{1}{2}$ in square rib cast across the middle of the panels. Unfortunately the sump flange was not similarly stiffened, which may account for the high proportion of noise radiated by the sheet steel sump.

11.3 CRANKCASE AND CYLINDER BLOCK TREATMENTS

It has been found that the most important area of the engine surface to consider, when planning surface treatments, is the crankcase/cylinder block casting, not merely because for in-line engines this area radiates an important contribution to the overall noise, but also because its vibration profoundly affects that of the valve gear covers and particularly the sump which are secured to it. The crankcase/cylinder block casting is also the area where least freedom to execute changes exists; only in exceptional circumstances is it possible to make the panels more flexible; the normal modes of this surface area are well damped in many engines; vibration isolation is difficult if not impossible to apply to crankcase and water-jacket panels. Often the only possible course of action is to make the crankcase and cylinder block stiffer.

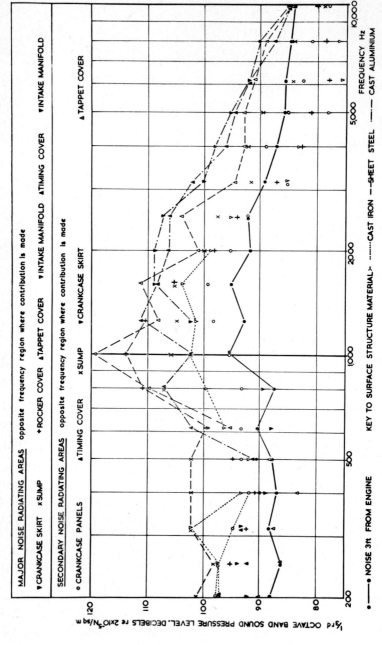

FIG. 11.6. Noise measured 3 ft from engine compared with sound pressure levels equivalent to vibration of engine surfaces.

In order to make any effective modifications to this component it is necessary to have a clear understanding of the modes of vibration which radiate significant contributions to the overall noise, and this is where the real complications start. When complete engines have been vibrated with a sinusoidal force input, the total response looked alarmingly complex, and calculation of the response of the crankcase and cylinder block structure to the high harmonics of the gas loads placed upon it, let alone 6 piston slap impacts per cycle and an unknown number of timing gear impacts, is a big operation. However, by adopting a multi-stage approach it was possible to arrive at a basis for designing modifications for an existing engine with reasonably modest resources. Most of the required results may be obtained from the one-third octave band surface vibration diagnostic technique, but the various stages will be described in sequence for clarity.

1. From the diagnosis of the areas of the surface which contribute most to the overall noise, the one-third octave bands in which the crankcase panels and water-jacket panels contribute significantly can be ascertained.

2. (Optional.) By exciting the bare crankcase/cylinder block casting (machined but with no working parts installed nor any covers attached) with a sinusoidally varying force tuned to each natural frequency in turn in these one-third octave bands, the basic mode shapes responsible for the noise may be plotted with a 'roving' accelerometer. The flexural wavelength of each mode may be compared to the wavelength of sound in air at the same frequency; if shorter (frequency higher than coincidence frequency) then a unity radiation efficiency is assumed; if longer, a 20 dB attenuation per decade decrease in frequency below coincidence is assumed for a first approximation (often this affects the fundamental mode only). More exact expressions for radiation efficiency are available from Refs. 1 and 2. The mechanisms by which these modes are damped may be found by assembling, to the bare casting, each part in turn, and measuring the logarithmic decay for each combination.

3. The actual amplitudes of vibration modes similar to those found in (2) above were plotted from measurements of vibration of a running engine, if these were not available from the initial diagnostic work. The cylinder pressure spectrum was obtained, also, particular care being taken to locate spectral troughs in this, and to check that mechanical noise did not obtrude at these frequencies when the engine was being run at high speed under full load.

4. A rib pattern may be evolved which provides sufficient extra stiffness to re-tune the major panel mode to a spectral trough, and to re-tune other noise-radiating modes to frequencies where the cylinder pressure spectrum level was (10 dB plus any radiation efficiency gain) lower. Where the ribs split panels into smaller segments, every effort was made to reduce the number of equal-sized panels to a minimum, and to couple them to vibration damping mechanisms. The sump flange should be stiffened to reduce vibration excitation of the sump, and the vibration excitation due to the increase in the natural frequency of normal modes involving the sump flange should be estimated by reference to the cylinder pressure spectrum. It is necessary to avoid interference with engine accessories such as starter motors, also to avoid decreasing the clearance around power take-off drives and anywhere else where equipment must be mounted close to the crankcase panels. It is also necessary to avoid changes to the jig pick-up points, especially those for the transfer machine.

By following this program, the vibration at the centre of the crankcase panels of one engine was reduced by 4–7 dB in one-third octave bands below the first mode, and the peak, resonant, response was reduced by 14 dB. If the response of the bare casting to sinusoidal excitation has been measured, it provides a reference for similar tests during the development of a new casting, thus obviating the need for accurate machining of early development samples and providing a worthwhile shortening of the program.

11.4 TREATMENTS FOR VALVE GEAR COVERS AND SUMP

Most covers on engines are cast in iron, or aluminium, or pressed from steel sheet. None of these materials has been found to be inherently quieter than the others (for all covers), so noise-control treatments have been devised to utilise the inherent properties of each material to some advantage.

The simplest treatment is that for stiff and heavy covers made from cast iron. Their very weight, and the stiffness of the peripheral flange, may be used to advantage by fitting a resilient gasket between the covers and the crankcase/cylinder block casting. For this to be effective, top-hat section washers should be fitted under the heads of the securing bolts, which should have shoulders turned on them, or be fitted with spacer tubes to prevent the isolation being crushed by careless maintenance. The reduction in vibration achieved by applying isolation to a front timing cover of a truck engine is shown in Fig. 11.7. The stiffness of the isolation is a compromise between the robustness of the isolating rubber, for which a higher natural frequency is desirable, and the progressively less efficient radiation of sound, for which a lower natural frequency is desirable.

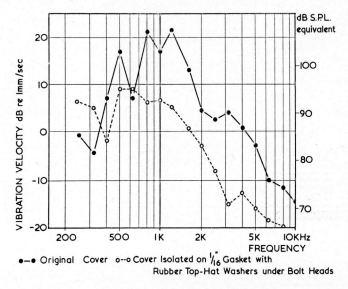

●—● Original Cover   o--o Cover Isolated on 1/16" Gasket with
Rubber Top-Hat Washers under Bolt Heads

Fig. 11.7. Isolation of cast iron timing cover.

The efficiency of radiation of sound was estimated by considering the classical results for a piston in a sphere [3] or a piston in the end of a long tube [4]. In both of these, the radiation resistance is unity at high frequencies, falling to 0·5 when the wavelength of sound $\lambda = 2\pi a/1\cdot6$, i.e. $\lambda = 4a$, where a is the piston radius. When $\lambda = 2a$, the radiation efficiency is approximately 0·16. To counteract a possible 5–10 times increase in response at the resonant frequency of the isolation system, the resonant frequency was chosen to be less than half of the frequency for which the wavelength is equal to two diameters of the circle of equivalent area to the cover (approximately 280 Hz for the timing cover in Fig. 11.7). Some care is necessary in the calculation of the thickness of the rubber, since the effective compression modulus varies with the shape. This technique has also been successfully applied to intake manifolds, cast in aluminium.

Cast aluminium covers and crankshaft pulleys are treated in a similar manner. Usually both are stiff and lend themselves to isolation by metal leaf springs incorporated into their structures. In the aluminium die-cast covers, these may be incorporated as two or more short beams joining an outer peripheral part, by which the cover is bolted to the crankcase or cylinder head, and an inner part supported from it only by the integrally cast beams. The beams are formed by casting a slit around the inner part and along the sides of the beams almost to separate it from the outer part; this slit is then filled with rubber to act as a vibration damping medium and to stop the lubricating oil from running out through the slits.

The stiffness of the beams is controlled by their length, and is chosen on the same basis as for the cast iron covers isolated on a gasket. The rubber contributes slightly to the overall stiffness, and will allow plate modes of the inner portion to be excited, unless the centre part is stiff in bending by comparison with the rubber in shear around its edges. Extra stiffening ribs have been added to some covers to improve the isolation at high frequencies—both peripheral ribs and radial ribs have been tried successfully. The vibration reduction obtained at the centre of a cast aluminium timing cover by this means is shown in Fig. 11.8. The treatment for a pulley

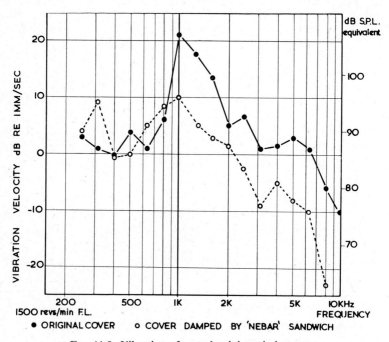

FIG. 11.8. Vibration of cast aluminium timing cover.

is similar, except that the rim is isolated from vibration excitation via the hub from crankshaft longitudinal vibration. The pulley springs are damped by laminating the spring leaves with a visco-elastic or hysteretic layer.

Sheet steel covers fall into two categories; those with many pressed-in stiffening ribs are sufficiently stiff to isolate on a thick rubber gasket, and those which are flexible may be damped by a constrained shear technique. For a viscously damped cover, the energy lost per cycle is proportional to the (velocity) coefficient of damping. The ratio that this energy lost per cycle forms with the strain energy stored per cycle decides the rate of decay of the resonant vibration. Clearly it is advantageous to increase the energy lost per cycle (always provided that the better sink does not attract more vibration energy from elsewhere in the structure); it may also be advantageous to reduce the strain energy stored per cycle by removing the pressed-in stiffeners.

Figure 11.9 shows how the most important modes of vibration were

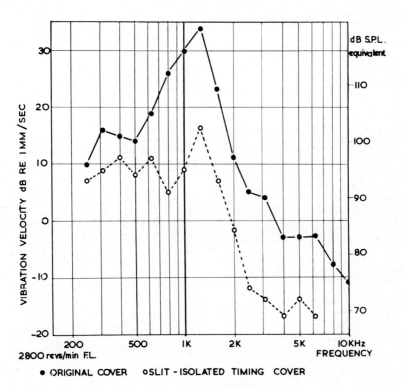

FIG. 11.9. Vibration of sheet steel rocker cover.

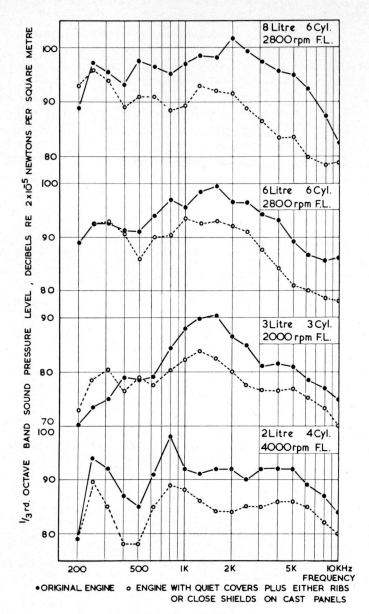

FIG. 11.10. Quieter diesel engines.

damped by attaching three 2 in wide $\frac{1}{16}$ in strips of rubber-bonded cork gasket material, covered by 18 swg steel to form a sandwich construction, along the top and sides of a rocker cover. Sheet steel sumps have been damped by this technique, but in order to reduce the strain energy stored per cycle, as well as the exciting force, a thick rubber gasket was used at the sump/crankcase-skirt joint to reduce the bending stiffness of this joint.

11.5   EFFECT OF COMBINATION OF TREATMENTS

When effective treatments have been developed for each cover, using the techniques described above, and when they are combined with suitably stiffened crankcase and cylinder block casting, then reductions of 5 dBA or more have been achieved. Where a suitably stiffened crankcase has not been available, damped sheet steel shields lined with acoustic absorbent have been bolted to the side of the engine at points where the vibration is known to be at a low level, and provided that these shields are flexible (in bending), the 5 dBA reduction can still be achieved. Figure 11.10 shows the reduction of noise spectra near rated speed at full load which has been achieved by applying these techniques to four in-line automotive diesel engines. Such modifications would appear to be quiet enough to match the requirements of the proposed noise legislation using, in the main, existing manufacturing facilities and well-known manufacturing techniques.

ACKNOWLEDGEMENTS

The author gratefully acknowledges permission to publish this paper from the Directors of CAV Ltd and Joseph Lucas Ltd, and the assistance with the experimental work rendered by Mr D. Amos and Mr C. Young. The author is grateful for the cooperation of Ricardo and Co Engineers (1927) Ltd which resulted in the data in Fig. 11.1.

REFERENCES

1. Maidenek, E. and Lyon, R. (1964). Statistical methods in vibration analysis, *AIAA Journal*, **2** (6), 1015–1024, June.
2. Wallace, C. E. (1972). Radiation resistance of a rectangular panel, *J.A.S.A.*, **51** (3), Pt 2.
3. Morse, P. M. (1948). *Vibration and Sound*, p. 324, McGraw-Hill, Ch. VII.
4. Beranek, L. L. (ed.) (1960). *Noise Reduction*, p. 426, McGraw-Hill, Ch. 16.

12

The Effect of Environmental Conditions on the Noise Level of Cooling Fans in Vehicles

J. S. B. MATHER
University of Nottingham

SUMMARY

The paper discusses origins of fan noise that pertain particularly to vehicles having confined power units. It is known that a fan running in a smooth flow and clean environment produces virtually no discrete components and a moderate level of random or broad bank noise. The environmental conditions in which many fans have to operate in practice are far from ideal and they can give rise to flow conditions through the fan which produce high levels of both discrete and random components.

Although general prediction formulae can be used to calculate the basic level of noise, there are no satisfactory ways to calculate increases caused by flow condition changes. It is necessary therefore to study the detailed flow patterns in units subjected to representative changes to determine methods of reducing the effects.

It is known that the level of random noise depends essentially on the loading on the individual blades and, in particular, on the lift fluctuations represented by the turbulent pressure fluctuations in the boundary layers on the blades. Upstream and downstream distortion in the form of water pumps, water and oil pipes, engine blocks and sumps, chassis members and radiators cause increases in blade loading and hence in the radiated noise level. If the pressure fluctuations are correlated on the blade, discrete tones may appear in the spectra. These features are discussed from a theoretical standpoint with associated experimental data.

Tip clearance between the blade tips and enclosing shrouds is a parameter that has a significant effect on the noise level. Blade and shaft vibration generate regular variations in the tip clearance and hence in the tip loading and the noise level. The paper presents theoretical calculations of this effect and early results from an experimental rig specifically designed to investigate this problem.

Finally, our recent experimental results show that the noise from a blade in a smooth flow is much lower than predicted by existing formulae, notably Sharland. With this in mind it is necessary to recalculate the penalty of having highly turbulent and badly distorted flow impinging on the fan from the radiator system.

12.1 INTRODUCTION

The noise radiated by the cooling fan of an engine installed in a vehicle has presented the designer with a number of problems. First, the contribution of the fan to the overall noise field radiating from the vehicle to an external observer is often very significant, particularly since the exhaust noise problem has received much attention in the last few years yielding a considerable success in reduction. Figure 12.1 shows typically the present contribution of a number of sources to the total level from a heavy diesel truck, when modern muffler designs are incorporated into the system [1].

Secondly, the fan noise intrudes into the interior of the vehicle, the noise being produced in the engine bay and carried as compressed waves by the air. Thirdly, the present inadequate knowledge of the mechanism of production of fan noise prevents the designer from choosing the most efficient way of alleviating the attendant noise problem should he need to increase the speed of the engine to produce more power output. Finally, the designer does not know the return on noise reduction he will achieve by sacrificing engine performance and convenience of installation in an effort to place the fan in the 'ideal' environment.

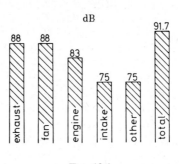

Fig. 12.1

The acoustic waves reaching the observer are carried as compressions and expansions in the air. The exhaust noise and fan noise have one feature in common, therefore, i.e. the pressure fluctuations in the exhaust pipe or the pressure forces and fluctuations on the fan blading occur in the air and readily convert directly to acoustic waves. Other sources, such as the high internal pressure fluctuations associated with the combustion process, must first pass into the metal and surrounding liquid and thence radiate into the air from the surface of the engine or from some convenient part of the vehicle structure. These processes not only reduce overall acoustic efficiency but also allow the designer to interject barriers for the sound or to divert its path to a convenient area.

The paper discusses noise sources that can be found on cooling fans, citing experimental evidence where available. A theory is presented for steady and unsteady in-flow distortions which the fan might experience in typical vehicle installations, showing that many convenient acoustic outlets are produced through which the sound can pass unattenuated to the observer. In particular, some of the study will be of direct interest to workers in the field to use as methods of acoustic diagnosis of the mechanisms of noise generation that the fan is experiencing.

Finally, a comparison is made with high performance fans and with fundamental work on blade noise which demonstrates that a reasonable target level may exist at a value considerably lower than the accepted norm of today.

12.2   SOURCES OF NOISE IN COOLING FANS

Figure 12.2 shows a simplified schematic of some of the major noise sources in a cooling fan. The sources are taken in their most generalised form, since whatever the cause of the particular aerodynamic situation it is these conditions that generate the noise at the blading. In the discussion that follows on these sources it is assumed that the fan has been designed and manufactured to modern standards of both efficiency and economy to meet the necessary conditions of (*a*) airflow; (*b*) pressure rise; (*c*) installation geometry; and (*d*) engine speed. Additionally, the discussion centres around fans with tip speeds from $30 \, \text{ms}^{-1}$ to $90 \, \text{ms}^{-1}$ and Reynolds numbers from 5×10^4 to 2×10^6 based on blade chord.

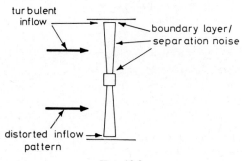

FIG. 12.2

12.2.1   Boundary Layer Noise

Any curved surface of the type used in cooling fans which provide a pressure gradient to the flow will sustain a growing boundary layer. This may be turbulent or laminar in character, depending on the Reynolds number of the flow and the conditions of the surface over which it is flowing. It was shown by Lighthill [2] and Curle [3] and, subsequently, many others that an aerodynamic pressure which fluctuates adjacent to a surface will give rise to a radiated sound wave of a dipole nature. It follows that a blade with a turbulent boundary layer or conceivably a blade with a laminar separation on the suction surface will give rise to radiated sound. The sound will be characterised by its amplitude and frequency, which will obviously depend directly on the detailed aerodynamics of the source. In general, the radiated sound is a broad band of noise with upper and lower frequency limits peaking over a range of frequencies which relate to the temporal extent of the convected pressure fluctuations.

The work of Morfey [4] and others shows that the larger the areas over which the pressure fluctuation is correlated the higher the noise level. A separated laminar boundary layer might therefore be expected to be noisier than a turbulent attached boundary layer for instance. Operating a fan over a range of speeds will alter the nature of the boundary layer flow, since the blade angles and shapes will have been designed for one operating condition. The radiated noise level and frequency distribution will simultaneously alter, and there is ample evidence of this feature in the experimental results [5].

Care should be taken therefore to minimise these pressure fluctuations at the design stage. Attention to the details of the manufacture and assembly can have a pronounced effect on the noise.

The amplitude of the noise will obviously also depend on the intensity of the pressure fluctuation. The tip flow of both a partially ducted and open rotor is known to contain high pressure fluctuations and these regions give rise to considerable contributions to the noise pattern.

The tip area also produces a second and different source from that described above. The aerodynamic conditions at the tip very often result in a scrubbing flow with radial components and in particular a bound vortex representing the lift of the blading. The passage of this vortex through the blading leads to large pressure fluctuations close to the blade surfaces and hence a high level of noise. These vortices can also be instrumental in the generation of a second source of noise described in a later section.

Equally, the hub flow conditions are poor and produce noise in precisely the same manner as the tip. However, with low flow velocities this noise source is generally lower in intensity. But should the tip conditions be improved, this second source may become more significant.

12.2.2 Rotational Noise

To a fixed observer adjacent to the fan the passage of the rotor blading represents a change in steady conditions, which is the criterion for the generation of an acoustic pressure signal. Therefore, any fan will exhibit discrete tones in the proximity of the rotor. If all the blades emit identical pressure signatures the tones are at the frequency of blade passing and its harmonics. If the conditions on the blades are not identical lower frequencies are heard at multiples of the shaft rotational speed.

Since there is obviously a degree of similarity between the conditions on each blade, the blade passing frequency, which is the blade number harmonic of the shaft frequency, would be expected to be of a high intensity. This is confirmed experimentally and Fig. 12.3 shows a typical example of an analysis of the sound from a unit with these frequencies noted on the spectrum.

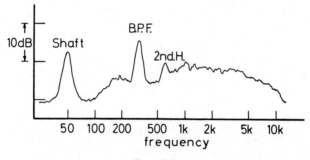

FIG. 12.3

In a ducted situation the tones from fans of low tip speed decay in level quite rapidly with distance from the unit. However, for partly ducted units, or those which are effectively open, the decay rate is somewhat different and experimental results confirm that the radiated noise patterns from these units are still dominated by tones from these sources.

The general calculation of the radiation of rotational noise from a rotor assumes that the steady lift conditions do not change as the blade rotates. The manufacture and assembly of these units and the environmental conditions in which they operate are such that it would be quite incorrect to assume that the aerodynamic situation on each blade is always the same. The acoustics are very sensitive to these minor differences, since the generation of sound depends more on the change in the level of aerodynamic pressure than on the level itself.

12.3 EFFECT OF ENVIRONMENTAL CONDITIONS
AND BLADE VIBRATION

12.3.1 Inlet Turbulence

Hanson [6] discusses in detail the effects of inlet turbulence on high
speed fans and there seems little reason to suppose that the mechanism
of generation of noise does not apply to low speed units also. Turbulence
is characterised generally by the fluctuating levels of velocity or pressure
and the correlated area over which these fluctuations act, often termed an
eddy. Intuitive arguments suggest that (see Fig. 12.4):

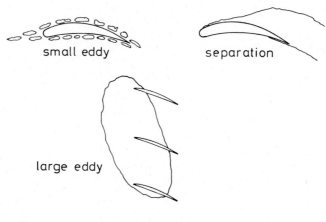

FIG. 12.4

1. If the eddy size is considerably smaller than the chord of the blade
   then the resultant total pressure change will also be small on average
   and the radiated noise level should not change significantly from the
   existing level. The argument assumes that the presence of the inlet
   turbulence causes no violent alterations to the aerodynamic situation.
2. If the eddy is large, and particularly if the fluctuating pressure is of
   high amplitude, then there may be significant changes to the aerodynamics. The individual blade angles may be transiently large
   enough to lead to the generation of a rotating stall situation which is
   discussed in more detail below. This increase in turbulent activity will
   lead to an increase in the broad band level radiated from the fan.
   Again, if the eddy size and convection speed are such that a number

of blades pass through the same eddy and therefore experience similar changes in aerodynamic behaviour, there will be an increase in discrete tone level. This is borne out experimentally and tones attributable to this mechanism are characterised by the high amplitude of fluctuations in level with time (see Fig. 12.5).

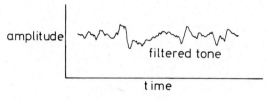

FIG. 12.5

There are a number of sources to this turbulence, some of which generate large convected eddies:

1. Radiator core flow may be at a high Reynolds number, giving rise to turbulent flow—usually a small eddy source.
2. Separated flow off large obstacles—water pipes, framework, chassis members—can give rise to large eddies convected relatively slowly.
3. Separated inlet duct flow, particularly if the inlet is not placed symmetrically in the radiator flow or if there is some obstacle generating an asymmetrical flow pattern at the inlet lip.
4. Recirculation of the flow outside the duct, carrying a discrete component reflecting the wake characteristics from the rotor blading. This may also be changed by passing water pumps, pipes, and chassis and engine members and taking on, in addition, the larger scale characteristics of these pieces.
5. Inlet guide vane wakes usually containing small scale turbulence, unless they are heavily stalled in some part by an asymmetrical inflow situation.
6. Scrubbing flow and recirculation over the tips of the blades. This flow has discrete features associated with individual blade flow and can easily result in high amplitude changes in noise.

In mitigation, however, it is not a requirement that these large pressure fluctuations must give rise to a correspondingly large increase in noise for:

1. The blading may already have poor flow conditions and may be radiating a saturated noise level from some other source. This has been experimentally observed in many instances [5].

2. The overall response function which converts the pressure fluctuation into sound waves may be small, viz. high amplitude eddies much smaller than the blade chord.
3. Cancellation effects from the adjacent blade conditions may apply.
4. The sound is unable to propagate without large decay—certainly true in many ducted and part-ducted situations.

12.3.2 Inlet/Outlet Distortion

Should the in-flow to the fan be asymmetrical in velocity or pressure profile then individual blades undergo changes to the steady forces resulting in the radiation of discrete energy at some frequency. The following theory demonstrates some parametric effects.

The acoustic pressure field generated by a rotor with unequal blading can be written as

$$p(\theta, t) = \sum_n a_n \cos(n\theta - n\Omega t + \phi_n) \qquad (12.1)$$

where θ is the circumferential angle, Ω is the shaft speed and n is the shaft harmonic number. The acoustic pressure pattern rotates at a speed of Ω, as expected. With the rotor subjected to a steady inlet distortion the amplitude coefficients a_n will depend on θ.

Let

$$a_n = \sum_p a_p \cos(p\theta + \theta_p) \qquad (12.2)$$

Thus,

$$p(\theta, t) = \sum_p \sum_n a_{np} \cos(p\theta + \phi_p) \cos(n\theta - n\Omega t + \phi_n) \qquad (12.3)$$

Rearranging,

$$p(\theta, t) = \frac{1}{2} \sum_p \sum_n a_{np} \left\{ \cos\left[(n + p)\theta - n\Omega t + \phi_1\right] \right.$$

$$\left. + \cos\left[(n - p)\theta - n\Omega t + \phi_2\right] \right\} \qquad (12.4)$$

where ϕ_1 and ϕ_2 are combinations of the original phasings.

These new acoustic pressure patterns, often called modes, are seen to be rotating at speeds Ω_s given by

$$\frac{n\Omega}{n + p} \quad \text{and} \quad \frac{n\Omega}{n - p} \qquad (12.5)$$

respectively.

Bearing in mind that the ability to propagate acoustic energy away from the fan depends on the speed of the pattern, eqn (12.5) shows that, for finite values of p, the second pattern rotates at a speed greater than Ω and the first at a speed less than Ω. The frequency is still given by $n\Omega$.

By way of explanation of the implications of these features, consider an example of a B bladed rotor. Since p represents the order of the Fourier component of the distortion entering the fan, then, excepting the case of a truly sinusoidal input, there will in general be some acoustic energy in modes related to all values of p. In particular, for each value of n, i.e. for each frequency, there will be acoustic energy at a value of p equal to n. The speed of this pattern is infinite and the acoustic energy at this frequency will be carried unattenuated from the fan. This will be true for all frequencies including blade passing where $n = B$.

The amplitude of the acoustic signal is not necessarily proportional to the amplitude of the corresponding aerodynamic Fourier component since little is known, as yet, of the response attitude of the blades to an aerodynamic change of this nature. Indeed, Peacock and Overli [7] have demonstrated experimentally that the response of the blade to inlet distortion is indeed complex, particularly if the level of the distortion is sufficient to promote angles of attack to the blade surface which exceed the steady state stall limit. Additionally, the duct or cowl imposes a further constraint on the allowable acoustic pressure patterns and the resultant amplitude will depend on the acoustic coupling between the fan and the duct. However, in a fully ducted situation for a low tip speed fan, Barry and Moore [8] have demonstrated that there is at *source* a linear relation between the amplitude of the acoustic modes caused by interaction with inflow distortion and the order of the distortion. With this in mind, Fig. 12.6, plotted from eqn (12.5), shows the optimum choice of blading numbers to be as high as possible. To propagate energy only in decaying modes the peripheral speed of the modal patterns must be less than the critical speed, which is usually slightly higher than the local sonic velocity. Thus, for a fan with a tip speed of 350 fps, the pattern ratio speed must be less than 3. If it is necessary to minimise discrete noise up to the third harmonic of blade passing frequency and only the first three orders of flow distortion need be considered, then 18 blades will be required. If the second harmonic carries the major acoustic contribution, then 12 blades will suffice.

For those involved in the testing of fans for noise, a further useful piece of information comes from this work. The radiation patterns in the far-field depend on the ratio of the actual peripheral speed of the mode to the critical speed. Tyler and Sofrin [9] and later Krishnappa and Jones [10]

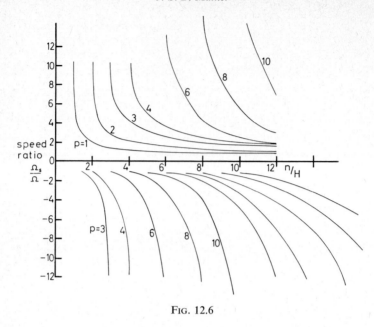

FIG. 12.6

give procedures for calculating the patterns, and many experimental examples are available in the literature. The essential features are that (see Fig. 12.7): (*a*) modes which have speeds that are slightly higher than critical radiate energy at angles greater than 60° to the axes of the fan; (*b*) modes that are well supercritical radiate energy in a series of lobular shapes, with the lobe of largest amplitude at angles less than 30° to the axis; (*c*) the plane wave modes radiate their energy along the axis of the fan—only these modes have this feature, all others giving rise to a marked dip on the axis.

For diagnostic purposes therefore, measurement of the far-field pattern can aid the researcher in determining which type of source contributes to the spectra he is measuring.

12.3.3   Unsteady Distortion or Rotating Stall

Consider a distortion which, on entering the fan, is rotating or unsteady. Then the amplitude factors for eqn (12.1) can be written as (see Ref. 11)

$$a_n = \sum_l \sum_p a_{lp} \cos{(p\theta + \phi_p)} \cos{(l\omega t + \phi_l)} \qquad (12.6)$$

where ω characterises the rotation or unsteadiness of the pattern.

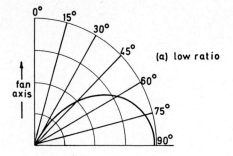

(a) low ratio

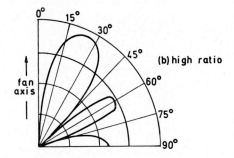

(b) high ratio

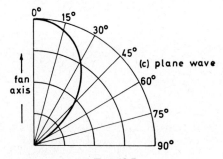

(c) plane wave

Fig. 12.7

Substituting and rearranging the terms gives

$$p(\theta, t) = \frac{1}{4} \sum_l \sum_p \sum_n a_{nlp} \bigg\{ \cos \left[(n + p)\theta - (n\Omega - l\omega)t + \phi_1\right]$$
$$+ \cos \left[(n - p)\theta - (n\Omega + l\omega)t + \phi_2\right]$$
$$+ \cos \left[(n + p)\theta - (n\Omega + l\omega)t + \phi_3\right]$$
$$+ \cos \left[(n - p)\theta - (n\Omega - l\omega)t + \phi_4\right] \bigg\} \quad (12.7)$$

where ϕ_i are combinations of $\phi_l \pm \phi_p \pm \phi_n$.

Aerodynamic considerations of rotating stall suggest that the distortion is rotating in the same direction as the rotor and at some fraction of the speed of the rotor. With this assumption, terms 1 and 2 in the square brackets can be eliminated.

The speeds of the two remaining acoustic patterns are given by

$$\Omega_1 = \frac{n\Omega + l\omega}{n + p}$$

$$\Omega_2 = \frac{n\Omega + l\omega}{n - p}$$

Now, $l\omega/p = \Omega_s$, the speed of rotation of the distortion.

Thus the two speeds can be written more conveniently as

$$\Omega_1 = \frac{n + p(\Omega_s/\Omega)}{n + p} \cdot \Omega$$

$$\Omega_2 = \frac{n - p(\Omega_s/\Omega)}{n - p} \cdot \Omega$$

The acoustic frequencies associated with these two modes are

$$f_1 = n\Omega + p\Omega_s$$

and

$$f_2 = n\Omega - p\Omega_s$$

which can be roughly classed as sum and difference frequencies from the basic frequency $n\Omega$.

Now, if the rotating stall pattern spins at a speed less than that of the rotor

$$\frac{\Omega_s}{\Omega} < 1$$

which implies that

$$\Omega_2 > \Omega > \Omega_1$$

For the unattenuated propagation of acoustic energy at these frequencies, the modes must be supercritical, i.e. their rotational tip speed must be higher than their critical value. Since the tip speed of the rotors in this discussion are well subsonic then the sum tone contribution will be small and only the acoustic energy at the difference tone frequency will be significant.

Experimental verification of this theory is given in Figs. 12.8 and 12.9, taken from data of Refs. 12 and 13. The fan has the following specification: 19 in diameter; 3000 rpm; 6 rotor blades. Blade passing frequency is

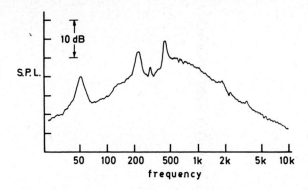

FIG. 12.8

therefore at 300 Hz and is visible as a small peak on the spectrum in Fig. 12.8. However, large peaks appear at 215 Hz and 430 Hz, which form the major contribution to the overall noise level. Since the aerodynamic performance shows no violent changes from the expected characteristics, when these noise features appear, then it seems that the fan is undergoing the early stages of the stall phenomenon. In these circumstances, the value of p, which reflects the number of cells or cellular distribution in the distortion (although does not necessarily equal the cell number), is likely to be equal or nearly equal to the number of blades.

Considering an interaction forming sum and difference tones with the blade passing frequency for the above fan then

$$\Omega_2 = \frac{6 - p\Omega_s/\Omega}{6 - p}$$

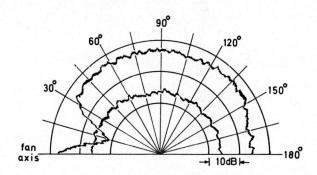

FIG. 12.9

Now, to form a difference tone at 215 Hz,

$$p\Omega_s = 300 - 215 = 85 \text{ Hz}$$

and thus

$$\frac{p\Omega_s}{\Omega} = 1.7$$

giving

$$\Omega_2 = \frac{4.3}{6 - p}$$

If $p = 5$, $\Omega_2 = 4.3$.

For the tip speed of 250 fps, the mode speed is approximately 1100 fps, which is below the minimum initial value for this mode of 2000 fps. The acoustic energy, therefore, will appear in the far-field at large angles to the fan axis. For $p = 6$, however, $\Omega_2 = \infty$ and the propagating acoustic energy will appear on the axis. The aerodynamic pattern speed ratio $\Omega_s/\Omega = 0.28$. Equally, an interaction with the second harmonic to produce a tone at 430 Hz will have an infinite rotational speed. The acoustic energy should again appear on the axis and Fig. 12.9 shows the field shapes for these tones. There are a number of examples of this phenomenon with other types of fan including some of the high speed precision units.

Figure 12.10 shows the effect of blade number on the speed of the modes

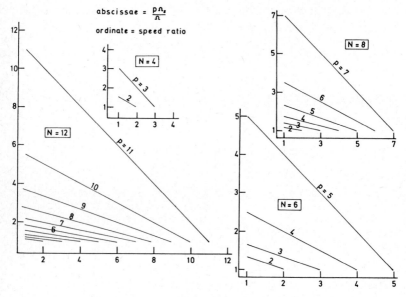

Fig. 12.10

generated in interactions between rotating distortions and fans for various values of the parameter p. The critical values for the speed ratio, calculated for a tip speed of 330 fps, are shown in Table 12.1. The plots in Fig. 12.10, show, therefore, that to reduce the possibility of noise from this type of source, fewer blades should be chosen.

TABLE 12.1

	B = 4	B = 6	B = 8	B = 12
$p = 1$	4·07	4.27	4·1	3·9
$p = 2$	5·09	4·43	4·12	3·92
$p = 3$	6·13	4·67	4·27	3·97
$p = 4$	—	5·09	4·43	4·0
$p = 5$	—	6·13	4·67	4·1
$p = 6$	—	—	5·09	4·12
$p = 7$	—	—	6·13	4·27
$p = 8$	—	—	—	4·43
$p = 9$	—	—	—	4·67
$p = 10$	—	—	—	5·09
$p = 11$	—	—	—	6·13

12.3.4 Blade Vibration

For a set of non-identical rotor blades the pressure fluctuations seen by an observer on one of the blades is given by

$$p(\theta, t) = \sum_m \sum_n a_{nm} \cos (n\Omega t + \phi_n) \cos (m\theta + \phi_m)$$

If the blade is vibrating then, relative to a fixed observer, the apparent frequency with which blades pass is given by (Ref. 14) $n\Omega \pm (l\omega)$, where ω is the frequency of vibration of the blades. The peripheral speeds of the modal patterns generated in the duct or cowling and thence in free air is given by

$$\frac{n\Omega \pm l\omega}{m}$$

and thus can be considerably higher than the speed of the rotor. In these cases some of the energy which was originally carried in decaying patterns may be transferred to propagating modes and thereby the far-field noise levels may be increased. The spectrum in Fig. 12.11, taken from a vibrating fan, shows these sum and difference tones either side of the main tone.

It is common in highly loaded fans and compressors to find that there is a definite pattern to the vibration, in that a fixed phase relationship exists

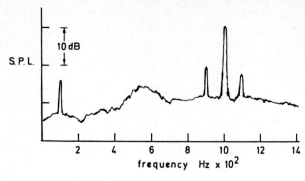

S.P.L.

10 dB

frequency　Hz x 10²

F<small>IG</small>. 12.11

between blades. The vibration of one blade generates force fluctuations via the airflow on the adjacent blades, to trigger the mechanism. This ordered system may produce significant acoustic energy.

Where the blade loading is light, this relationship does not exist and the level of the acoustic signal depends more on the coupling of the modal patterns generated by the fan and the cowling or duct.

The vibrating blades will also affect the turbulent boundary layer on the blades, giving rise to a general increase in the broad-band noise level when the correlation areas are insufficient to generate discrete energy.

12.3.5　Tip Clearance Effects

The results from many experiments on fan rigs show that the flow at the tip has a marked effect on the noise level radiated by the unit. There appear to be two mechanisms by which a change to the tip may reduce the noise:

1. The poor aerodynamic flow at the tip, with large vortex filaments adjacent to surfaces and areas of stalled flow near the trailing edge, generates broad-band acoustic energy in itself and contributes to the discrete component by virtue of its rotation with the fan. Lower tip clearances and better designs of tip with a number of ingenious devices can reduce this component.
2. Being in a high velocity region the tip flow situation greatly determines the performance of the fan. By improving the flow, the same overall performance can be achieved at lower speeds, giving a significant reduction of the discrete component.

Current research work at Nottingham is investigating the effect of shaft vibration on the noise from a fan. When the fan is mounted on the engine and the cowl on the chassis, there will be periodic oscillations of the tip clearance as the fan moves inside the cowl. In themselves these vibrations will give rise to modulations of the basic fan signal but in addition the force fluctuations, as the tip is alternately loaded and unloaded, will generate discrete modes of acoustic energy. Finally, for severe oscillations the fan blades will be easily forced into sympathetic and possibly resonant vibrations. As for the cases of blade stall, inlet flow distortion and blade vibration the fluctuations in loading will also give rise to higher broad band levels.

All these additional mechanisms generate a multiplicity of acoustic outlets for the energy that is being propagated from the fan, some of which will be at frequencies that are subjectively more significant than those of the 'clean' fan.

12.4   FUTURE PREDICTIONS

All of the foregoing analysis suggests that there is a variety of sources which can generate significant contributions to the radiated noise from a fan. It would seem sensible, therefore, to assume that unless (*a*) the aerodynamic conditions over the whole blade were maximised for efficiency, (*b*) the tip flow condition is improved, (*c*) tip clearances are optimised for noise, which probably means that they are decreased from the present conditions, (*d*) surface irregularities are eliminated, (*e*) blade vibration is eliminated, and (*f*) tip clearance modulation does not exist, then the fan is *not* producing its lowest possible noise level.

In addition, as Hebard and Treeby [12] and Staadt [1] point out, if the general environmental conditions provided by the installation and the flow and pressure requirements are not optimised by the correct choice of radiator, then the noise level is higher than necessary.

Figure 12.12 demonstrates that a precision fan correctly designed can produce a higher pressure rise, a larger volume flow with a smaller fan running at similar peripheral blade speeds and yet generate similar broad band noise levels. Both tones in the spectrum of the precision unit can be eliminated by increasing the number of stators from 11 to 26. The mechanism that generates the tones in the larger fan is not yet known.

Further, there are two recent pieces of fundamental work (Refs. 15 and 16) on the noise radiated by isolated aerofoils which are immersed in smooth non-turbulent flows. These studies both show that, at supercritical Reynolds numbers where the blade boundary layers are turbulent, the

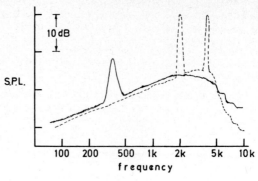

FIG. 12.12

radiated noise is considerably lower than that given by long-standing prediction formulae. The difference lies in the increased sophistication of experimentation rather than in any new features of the blades that were used. Since these existing formulae seem to agree to within a few dB with the measured results on cooling fans, the conclusion must be that at least one of the mechanisms discussed in this paper applies and retains the level of broad-band noise at a high value, and these mechanisms are primarily concerned with the environmental conditions of the unit and its response to them. The future of fan design lies in improving the detailed aerodynamic performance of the units, partly to reduce the noise levels induced by poor aerodynamics and partly to allow the peripheral speeds to be reduced.

12.5 CONCLUSIONS

A study of spectra and field shapes from a number of cooling fans placed in a variety of environments and installations shows that there are, in most cases, features of the frequency distribution that cannot be explained by the hitherto conventional arguments. These include the effects of (a) blade vibration, (b) steady inlet flow distortion, (c) spinning distortions, perhaps leading to rotating stall, and (d) shaft vibration.

The paper has described the type of spectral change to be expected from these, both as discrete energy and broad band noise.

In addition some of the installation features, allied to these effects, are listed: (a) radiator distorted flow, (b) turbulent inflow of large and small eddies, (c) flow fields caused by chassis and engine members, and (d) tip clearance, both steady and modulated.

Finally, a comparison of predicted and experimental results for isolated aerofoils suggests that the noise 'flow' for even a mass-produced fan unit is likely to be considerably lower than that generally attained at present.

REFERENCES

1. Staadt, R. L. 'Truck noise control', Twentieth L. Ray Buckendale lecture, SAE Sp-386, Jan. 1974.
2. Lighthill, M. J. (1952). On sound generated aerodynamically, *Proc. Roy. Soc.*, A211.
3. Curle, N. (1955). The influence of solid boundaries on sound, *Proc. Roy. Soc.*, A231.
4. Morfey, C. L. (1970). 'Broadband Sound Radiated from Subsonic Rotors', Int. Symp. Fluid Mechanics & Design of Turbomachinery, Penn. State.
5. Mather, J. S. B. 'On Broad Band Noise from Fans', Rolls-Royce Report INR 00087, 1971.
6. Hanson, D. B. 'Spectrum of Turbomachine Rotor Noise caused by Inlet Guide Vane Wakes and Atmospheric Turbulence', Hamilton Standard Report HSER 6191, 1973.
7. Peacock, R. E. and Overli, J. 'Rotor Dynamic Stall Observations in a Compressor with Circumferential Pressure Distortion', ARC 35260, 1974.
8. Barry, B. and Moore, C. J. (1971). Subsonic fan noise, *J. Sound Vib.* **17**, 207–220.
9. Tyler, J. M. and Sofrin, T. G. (1961). Axial flow compressor noise studies, *Trans. SAE*, **70**, 309.
10. Krishnappa, G. and Jones, L. R. 'Far-field Radiation of Rotor-Stator Interaction Tones from an Annular Duct', NRC 13260, LR–508, 1973.
11. Mather, J. S. B. and Fisher, M. J. (1974). 'Noise Generation by Steady and Unsteady Flow Distortions', 2nd Int. Symp. Air Breathing Engines.
12. Hebard, P. J. and Treeby, S. W. (1974). 'The Design and Optimisation of Engine Cooling Systems for Low Noise and Power Consumption', Paper presented at FISITA, Paris.
13. Hebard, P. J. Private communication.
14. Savidge, J. 'Blade Vibrations as a Source of Tone Noise in Gas Turbines', Rolls-Royce Report INR 00079, Dec. 1970.
15. Paterson, R. W. *et al.* (1972). 'Vortex Noise of Isolated Aerofoils', AIAA Paper No. 72–656, June.
16. Mather, J. S. B. and Davis, R. A. (1974). 'Experimental Results on the Mechanisms of Noise Generation of Blades in Smooth Flow at High Reynolds Number', Inter-Noise 74.

13

A Vibrational Analysis of a Pin–Disc System with Particular Reference to Squeal Noise in Disc-Brakes

S. W. E. Earles and G. B. Soar

Queen Mary College, London

SUMMARY

Expressions for the receptances and characteristic frequencies of a rotating disc under forced oscillations, using Bessel functions, are developed. These are combined with similar expressions, using a finite element technique, for the pin system, to give the characteristic frequencies and modal shapes of the coupled system.

The fundamental resonance frequencies of the coupled system, observed from a series of experimental results, compare favourably with theoretical predictions. Generally these coupled frequencies are at, or near to, an anti-resonance of the free disc.

An essentially torsional vibratory mode of the pin system is observed to be needed in order to generate noise producing vibratory patterns on the disc. The line of action of the resultant force on the pin, in relation to the torsional centre of the pin system, is shown to be the main criterion in determining its vibrational mode.

13.1 INTRODUCTION

For some time it was considered that brake squeal occurred as a result of a variable coefficient of friction characteristic, and in consequence it was unlikely that squeal could ever be totally eliminated. However, in 1961 Spurr [1] suggested that the component geometries of the brake were possibly of greater importance. His paper discussed in broad terms the geometric mechanism, which he termed 'sprag-slip', and although he retained flexibility solely in one component he did appreciate many of the dynamic concepts which were to be developed in later works.

Jarvis and Mills [2] presented a mathematical model of a system pertaining to a commercial disc-brake. However, their analysis fell short, in that they introduced one-mode simplifications of the dynamic elements and overlooked the 'geometric instabilities' of the system by virtue of their linearisation of the equations of motion. Consequently they derived a stability criterion, based upon a negative damping function, which lacked a meaningful correlation with their experimental results.

The audible frequency range lies between 20 Hz and 16 kHz, and for a given power dissipation the loudest apparent sounds are heard at around 3 kHz. However, the mechanism by which squeal noise is generated is independent of this audible frequency range. It is concerned only with interactive characteristics which do or do not create self-induced vibratory states.

Using a similar pin–disc system to the type described later, Earles and Soar [3] carried out a one-degree of freedom vibration analysis, assuming the pin to have (a) only a translational motion, and (b) only a torsional motion. It was concluded, theoretically, that for the system under test the former produced stable oscillations while the latter could produce unstable oscillations. Essentially these two motions were produced experimentally by varying the angle of orientation of the pin to the plane of the disc. It was found that the vibration spectrum of the disc for the translational motion had in the main a single coupled resonant peak, whereas the torsional motion produced a series of peaks, corresponding to harmonics of the fundamental, covering a wide frequency range. It was therefore concluded that pin–disc geometric configurations which induced torsional motion of the pin would give rise to squeal noise if harmonics existed within the frequency range 2–5 kHz.

Whereas the earlier work was limited to a one-degree of freedom system but allowed considerations of non-linear effects to be considered, this present work attempts to further the understanding by limiting the analysis to linear equations, while considering the system to have an infinite number of degrees of freedom.

An intermediate approach has been adopted by North [4], in which a limited number of degrees of freedom (8) has been used, including some non-linear effects. He assumed the disc to be represented by a beam having two degrees of freedom and vibrating in a particular mode. From a qualitative comparison of his theoretical and experimental results he considered it possible to examine design changes which might reduce the incidence of brake squeal. It is of interest to note that his physical explanation of the occurrence of squeal suggests the necessity of generating a torsional motion within the disc and the creation of a vibrational instability.

13.2   NOTATION

α receptance of the coupled system
β receptance of the pin subsystem
γ receptance of the disc subsystem

θ	angle of inclination of the pin to the disc
Ω	disc rotational speed
ω	excitation frequency $\times 2\pi$
p	resonant frequency $\times 2\pi$
P	excitation force amplitude
a	radius of the disc
b	radius of the pin contact
r	radius to a point on the disc
μ	coefficient of friction
t	time
(d, c)	modal form of the disc, where d is the number of modal diameters and c is the number of modal circles.

13.3 THE EXPERIMENTAL SYSTEM

Figure 13.1 shows diagrammatically the experimental system used. It was designed so that a wide variation of certain parameters would be possible, while having regard to its analytical formulation. The disc, D, is attached to the end of a horizontal shaft which is driven at a constant speed within the range ± 1000 rev/min. The discs, made from mild steel, are 203 mm in diameter and of thicknesses within the range 1·8–5·1 mm.

The pin subsystem consists of a rigid frame, f, across which is fixed a flexible beam, b. The pins, of 6 mm nominal diameter, are rigidly secured into the centre section of the beam. The frame, f, is supported at the end of a cantilever arm, A, which is pivoted at its other end on a shaft of diameter 57 mm. The shaft is supported in bearings in a large block, B. The arm can be moved vertically along the shaft, cc, and the block, B, horizontally on the surface of a heavy cast-iron table. The positioning of the block, B, in relation to the disc, D, determines the pin contact radius and the pin–disc contact angle. Loading of the pin on to the disc is achieved by a cord-spring-weight system attached to the arm, A.

Strain gauges are attached to the beam, b, to determine its translational and torsional vibration modes; these are, respectively, movement in the x-direction caused by bending of the beam, b, and rotation λ about an axis through 0 caused by twisting of the beam, b.

Sound pressure measurements are recorded using a microphone positioned near to the pin, and noise levels are displayed on a spectrum analyser.

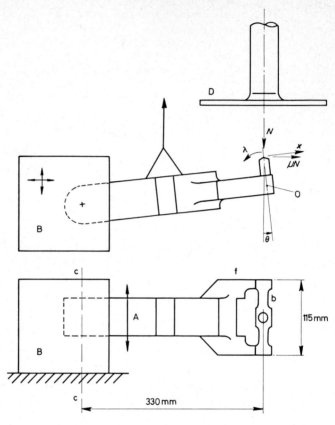

FIG. 13.1. The experimental system.

13.4 ANALYTICAL DESCRIPTION

13.4.1 The Coupled System

The pin and disc, when brought together, form a coupled system which is excited into a vibratory state by the interaction of the frictional forces generated by the external rotation of the disc. Assuming that each sub-system (pin and disc) possesses linear characteristics and that they remain in contact, then the coupled receptance of the system (normal to the disc at the pin contact point) is given by:

$$\alpha = \frac{\gamma \beta'}{\gamma + \beta'} \tag{13.1}$$

where β' is the receptance of the pin system normal to the disc and γ the corresponding receptance of the disc.

Assuming the disc to be infinitely stiff in its plane of rotation, the receptance β' is related to the 'translational' receptance, β, of the pin system, see Fig. 13.1 by

$$\beta' = \beta \sin \theta (\sin \theta - \mu \cos \theta) \tag{13.2}$$

hence

$$\alpha = \frac{\gamma \beta \sin \theta (\sin \theta - \mu \cos \theta)}{\gamma + \beta \sin \theta (\sin \theta - \mu \cos \theta)} \tag{13.3}$$

Thus the coupled resonant frequencies of the system can be found from

$$\gamma + \beta \sin\theta (\sin \theta - \mu \cos \theta) = 0 \tag{13.4}$$

13.4.2 The Disc Subsystem

In developing the equations of motion for the disc, reference was made to the works of Lamb and Southwell [5], Southwell [6], Timoshenko and Woinowsky-Krieger [7], Tobias and Arnold [8] and Bishop and McLeod [9].

Tobias and Arnold [8] developed equations for the steady-state forced vibration of a rotating imperfect disc subjected to an exciting force $P \cos \omega t$ which is stationary in space. Assuming that the preferential modes are symmetrical then two pairs of resonant conditions are found for each mode. Each pair converges to a single value, $\omega = p$, as the disc rotation, Ω, tends to zero, and the two pairs to similar values as the disc approaches a perfect disc.

Such an analysis would suffice for the present investigation if, for the self-induced excitation of the system, the preferential modes of the disc were known. However, this is not so and therefore, at least initially, a more general approach must be applied.

It is stated [8] that it can be shown experimentally for the free vibrations of a rotating disc that,

$$p^2 = p_0{}^2 + B\Omega^2$$

where p_0 is the resonant frequency of the disc when stationary and B is a constant. Now it has been found that for rotational speeds of up to 1000 rev/min the error in neglecting the term $B\Omega^2$ for the discs being considered is only of the order of 0·2%. Thus for the present investigation an analysis assuming a stationary disc would appear to suffice.

Bishop and McLeod [9] developed a receptance analysis based on a Series Bessel solution of the stationary free disc equation.

For a single point excitation force $P \sin \omega t$ applied at a radius b it is shown that the transverse deflection, y, of the disc is given by

$$\frac{y}{\sin \omega t} = R_0 + \sum_{n=1}^{\infty} R_n \cos n\phi \qquad (13.5)$$

where R_0 and R_n contain constants and Bessel functions, n is a positive integer, and ϕ is the angular coordinate to the deflection point.

Two similar expressions are used, one for the inner portion $0 < r < b$ and one for the outer portion $b < r < a$. The six constants contained in the expressions for each value of n are found from the boundary conditions at the outer edge, continuity at radius $r = b$, and applying a suitable form for the forcing function. Tables of natural frequencies and receptance functions are given in the monograph [9], from which values of the disc receptance, γ, can be calculated.

13.4.3 The Pin Subsystem

The subsystem to be examined is shown in Fig. 13.2(a). The pin-beam, b, is rigidly bolted to the end of the arm, A, which, having regard to its relative stiffness and inertia, is assumed to be stationary in space. It is further assumed that the vibrational modes and frequency range of the pin subsystem are adequately covered by considering a five-element model of the pin-beam—elements (i), (ii), (iii), (iv) and (v), Fig. 13.2(b)—being dimensionally identical.

Following the analysis given by Dawe [10] a dynamic stiffness matrix (24×24) can be developed describing in a three-coordinate form each of the eight dynamic nodes of the pin-beam.

Thus, a receptance equation may be developed [11] as:

$$\beta_{rs} = \sum_{i=1}^{n} \frac{q(s, i)q(r, i)}{\lambda_i - \omega^2} \qquad (13.6)$$

where β_{rs} is the cross-receptance between points r and s; λ_i is an eigenvalue; $q(s, i)$ and $q(r, i)$ are eigenvectors; and n is the number of eigenvalue solutions (in this case 24).

The direct pin-tip receptance was found from a linear combination of the translational and angular displacements of the four central nodal points, i.e.

$$\beta_{\text{tip}} = \frac{\beta_C + \beta_D + \beta_J + \beta_K}{4} + \frac{l}{2b'} (\beta_K + \beta_J - \beta_C - \beta_D) \qquad (13.7)$$

where β_C, etc., are the receptances at the nodal points given on Fig. 13.2(b).

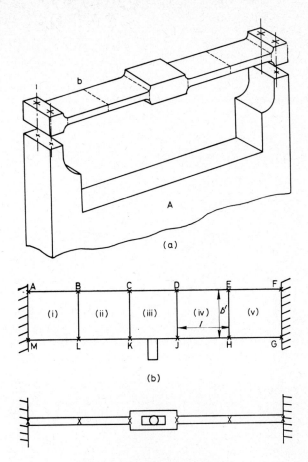

Fig. 13.2. The pin subsystem.

13.4.4 The Coupled Characteristic Frequencies

Combining the two analyses enables the characteristic frequenc es to be found and to indicate the possible corresponding modal shapes.

Two typical receptance curves are shown in Fig. 13.3. The receptance γ is for a disc of thickness 2·74 mm with the pin acting at a radius of 76·2 mm. The receptance β is for a pin-beam of thickness 0·94 mm.

The coupled resonances, given by eqn (13.4), are dependent on the pin to disc orientation angle θ. Now if θ is zero then the coupled resonances are given by $\gamma = 0$ and will correspond to the anti-resonances of the free disc.

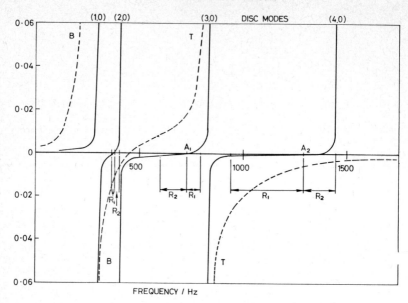

FIG. 13.3. Receptance curves; disc thickness 2·74 mm, pin-beam thickness 0·94 mm.
——— γ/(mm/N); ---- β (mm/N).

For the range of experimentally possible θ angles, i.e. $\pm 30°$, the factor $\sin \theta(\sin \theta - \mu \cos \theta)$ varies between 0·38 and $-0·21$ for a μ value of 0·29. The negative values occur for $0 < \theta < \tan^{-1} \mu$. Thus it is to be expected that the coupled resonances will not be greatly removed from the anti-resonances frequencies of the free disc for all values of θ.

For the particular example given in Fig. 13.3 the coupled frequency regions are indicated. Regions R_1 are for θ angles between 0 and $+16·2°$, and for regions R_2 between $+16·2°$ and $+30°$, and between 0 and $-30°$.

On the γ receptance curve the numbers in brackets refer to the number of nodal diameters and the number of nodal circles, respectively, and on the β receptance curve B refers to a translational (bending) mode and T to a torsional mode. Experience has shown that the (1, 0) disc mode is un-likely to be generated by the action of a single point excitation. Further, as the constraint of the disc on the pin and vice versa will effectively increase their characteristic frequencies, it may be expected that the fundamental coupled resonant frequency when the pin is essentially in a translational mode will be near to the free disc anti-resonance at A_1, and when the pin is essentially in a torsional mode near to the free disc anti-resonance at A_2.

13.5 EXPERIMENTAL RESULTS

Previously [3] the authors have described a series of experiments, using a similar pin–disc arrangement, and found that, provided surface damage was not excessive, the generation of squeal noise was substantially independent of disc rotational speed within the range 0–800 rev/min and of pin load within the range 0–60 N.

A series of tests were performed using three pin-beam thicknesses, 0·94, 1·09 and 1·17 mm, and three disc thicknesses, 2·31, 2·49 and 2·74 mm. Flat-faced pins, 6·5 mm diameter and 19 mm long, were used with a contact load of 25 N against a disc rotating at 10 rev/min in an anticlockwise direction when viewed along the pin axis. The contact angle, θ, was set at approximately 1·6° (a value which lay within the experimental squeal region) and the fundamental resonant frequencies measured for a range of contact radii between 51 and 102 mm. It was observed that the pin-beam vibrational mode was always dominantly torsional. Typical sets of results are shown in Fig. 13.4. A frequency analysis, using a 6% bandwidth frequency analyser, produced a distinctive harmonic profile, the relative dB levels of the harmonics apparently varying in some

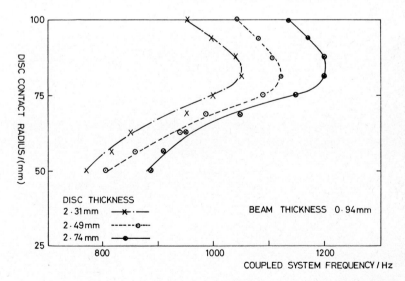

Fig. 13.4. Experimental fundamental coupled resonant frequencies. The pin-beam in a torsional mode.

undefinable manner depending on the particular configuration being used. For example, with the 1·17 mm pin-beam and the 2·74 mm disc the third harmonic at 2790 Hz had a dominant dB level.

Another series of tests used an angle of contact which lay outside the experimental squeal region. It was observed in this case that the pin-beam vibrational mode was always dominantly translational. A typical set of results is shown in Fig. 13.5(a).

Corresponding theoretical curves are shown in Figs. 13.6 and 13.5(b).

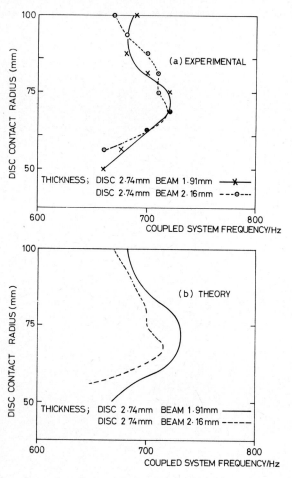

Fig. 13.5. Experimental and theoretical coupled resonant frequencies. The pin-beam in a translational mode.

For the pin-beam in a torsional mode (Fig. 13.6), the resonant frequencies plotted are those occurring near to the anti-resonance of the free disc between the (3, 0) and (4, 0) modes, typically as shown near point A_2 (Fig. 13.3), and for the pin-beam in a translational mode, Fig. 13.5(b), typically as shown near point A_1 (Fig. 13.3), i.e. near to the anti-resonance of the free beam between the (2, 0) and (3, 0) modes.

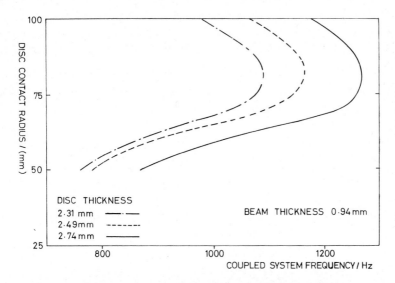

Fig. 13.6. Theoretical coupled resonant frequencies. The pin-beam in a torsional mode.

The similarity between the experimental and theoretical curves is good. The fact that the theoretical curves predict higher frequencies values is probably due to the assumption of a perfectly rigid central disc support.

In general, the correlation between the experimental and theoretical results was found to be equally good for all of the tests performed, in which the radius of contact, the angle of contact and the physical dimensions of the disc and pin were varied.

A series of tests were performed using pins tipped with brake-pad material. The composite pin was flat-faced and of length 24 mm. The contact load was 15 N and the rotation speed of the disc was 20 rev/min. Three beam–disc combinations were employed, the contact angle being set within the experimental squeal region, and results obtained for various contact radii. The graphs obtained followed essentially the same pattern as those obtained using mild steel pins. Predictably, the change in μ value altered the torsional mode region from between 0–16° to between 0–20°.

13.5.1 Generation of a Torsional Mode

It would appear, to this point, that in order to produce a squeal noise the pin system must be excited in a torsional mode, and that torsional modes are only excited when the factor $\sin \theta(\sin \theta - \mu \cos \theta)$ is negative, i.e. $0 < \theta < \tan^{-1} \mu$.

With reference to Fig. 13.7(a), the angle of inclination θ is the angle between a normal to the disc face and the line joining the point of contact P to the pivotal centre of the pin-system 0.

Figs. 13.7(b) and 13.7(c) show two pins having the same dome radius but of different lengths. This meant, as indicated, that the centres of curvature of the domes were on opposite sides of the pivotal centre 0. It was clearly

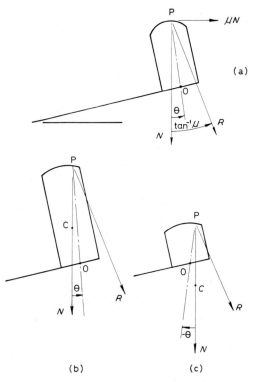

FIG. 13.7. Resultant force R in the pin in relation to the pivotal centre 0.

found experimentally that, for the orientations indicated in Fig. 13.7, (b) produced a squeal noise whereas (c) did not. Similar effects were observed using pins of the same length but having different dome radii.

Thus, as with the previous work of the authors [3], if the resultant force on the pin tends to rotate it into the disc then the pin system will have a dominantly torsional mode and squeal noise will result. Whereas if it tends to move the pin away from the disc then the pin-system will have a dominantly translational mode with no squeal noise.

Using a much thicker pin-beam (9·4 mm), it was found that the fundamental frequency of the coupled system with the pin in a torsional mode was about 7900 Hz (7600 Hz predicted from the theory). Harmonics were recorded and a faintly audible squeal noise was developed. When arranged for the pin to be in a translational mode the fundamental coupled frequency was about 2500 Hz, but even so no sound resembling a squeal was produced.

13.6 DISCUSSION

The correlation between the experimental and theoretical coupled resonant frequencies is sufficiently satisfactory to justify the theoretical approach adopted. This being so, it is of importance that the disc modal shape is shown, for the present work, to change in general from a (2, 0) form, when the pin system is in a translational mode and not producing a squeal noise, to a (3, 0) form, when the pin system is in a torsional mode and producing a squeal noise. For the thicker pin-beams the modal forms were (3, 0) and (4, 0), respectively.

The theoretical analysis here presented cannot explain why, for a torsional mode of the pin system obtained when the angle of inclination θ was in the range $0 < \theta < \tan^{-1} \mu$, a squeal noise was produced. But this is explainable from the authors' previous work [3], in which it is shown that for such a range of θ's, the self-induced vibratory state of the system is unstable, the disc becoming in practice stable by the generation of harmonics of the fundamental frequency.

From a practical point of view the present work suggests that disc-brake squeal may be eliminated (*i*) by designing for the coupled resonances to be well above the audible frequency range, or (*ii*) by designing for the resultant force on the pad system not to induce it into a torsional mode. In the former case it may be that to produce the required high frequencies the stiffnesses of the components would have to be unreasonably large, and therefore the latter case might prove more feasible. However, it should be noted that whereas a pad system may be designed such that when braking, with the vehicle in forward motion, the resultant force always passes to the desired side of the pivotal point, when braking in reverse squeal would be likely to occur.

13.7 CONCLUSIONS

A linearised analysis of a pin and disc system has been presented which predicts the coupled resonant frequencies caused by the frictional inter-action of the pin sliding on the disc. These frequencies have been found to be in good agreement with measured values.

It has been observed that for the system under consideration the coupled resonant frequencies are near to the anti-resonances of the free disc. The two pin system modes, translational and torsional, appear to excite the disc into different modal forms. In general, the translational pin mode produces a (2, 0) disc mode, and the torsional pin mode a (3, 0) disc mode.

It has been further confirmed that in order to produce a 'squeal noise' vibratory state the pin system must be excited into a torsional mode. This is obtained when the resultant force on the pin is such as to draw the pin into the disc. This is similar in its action to 'Sprag-slip', as suggested by Spurr in 1961.

ACKNOWLEDGEMENTS

The authors wish to acknowledge the support given to this research project by the Science Research Council and Ford Motor Co Ltd.

REFERENCES

1. Spurr, R. T. (1961/2). 'A Theory of Brake Squeal', I. Mech. E. Auto. Div. Proc. No. 1, pp. 33–40; discussion pp. 41–52.
2. Jarvis, R. P. and Mills, B. (1963/4). 'Vibrations Induced by Dry Friction', I. Mech. E. Proc., Vol. 178, Pt 1, No. 32, pp. 847–57.
3. Earles, S. W. E. and Soar, G. B. (1971). 'Squeal Noise in Disc Brakes', I. Mech. E. Proc. Conference on Vibration and Noise in Motor Vehicles, pp. 61–69.
4. North, M. R. (1971). 'A Mechanism of Disc Brake Squeal', 14th FISITA meeting, June.

5. Lamb, H. and Southwell, R. V. (1921). The vibrations of a spinning disc, *Proc. Roy. Soc.*, **99**, 272.

6. Southwell, R. V. (1922). On the free transverse vibrations of a uniform circular disc clamped at its centre, and on the effects of rotation, *Proc. Roy. Soc.*, **101**, 133.

7. Timoshenko, S. and Woinowsky-Krieger, S. (1959). *Theory of Plates and Shells*, 2 ed. McGraw-Hill.

8. Tobias, S. A. and Arnold, R. N. (1957). The influence of dynamical imperfection on the vibration of rotating discs, *Proc. I. Mech. E.*, **171**, 669.

9. Bishop, R. E. D. and McLeod, A. J. (1965). 'The Forced Vibrations of Circular Flat Plates', I. Mech. E. Monograph No. 1.

10. Dawe, D. J. (1965). A finite element approach to plate vibration problems, *Proc. I. Mech. E.*, **7**, No. 1.

11. Soar, G. B. 'The Dynamic Interaction in a Pin and Disc System with Special Reference to Brake Squeal', Ph.D. Thesis, London University, 1971.

14

Theoretical Analysis of an Active Suspension Fitted to a London Transport Bus

M. Cotterell

London Transport Executive

SUMMARY

For the past decade, the Automotive Products Group have been developing an active suspension system for road vehicles. Early in 1974 this system will be fitted to a London Transport Route Master bus for evaluation. This paper presents a theoretical analysis of the active suspension system and the results of tests on the bus.

The suspension system consists of gas springs in which a fluid may be pumped in or out. The movement of the fluid is controlled by a model whose purpose is to identify inertia forces acting on the vehicle. The suspension system thus has two modes of operation (a) a passive mode—in which no fluid is pumped in or out of the system; (b) an active mode—in which pumping does take place.

In the passive mode, the model does not come into play, and the system acts in a manner similar to a conventional suspension system. The passive mode governs the response of the system to variations in road surface. When inertia forces are acting on the vehicle (e.g. in cornering) they are identified by the model and bring into operation the active mode. In the active mode, hydraulic fluid can be pumped in or out of the gas springs leading to a form of integral control. The model simulates the passive response of the vehicle and discriminates between road surface variations and inertia forces acting on the vehicle.

This paper deals principally with the theoretical design and response of the active suspension system and the advantages of partial or total decoupling of the six degrees of freedom of the main vehicle body. Decoupling simplifies the task of predicting the vehicle response and hence the selection of suspension parameters. The main advantage of the active suspension system over conventional systems lies in its superior anti-roll behaviour.

14.1   INTRODUCTION

The design of a passive suspension system for a road vehicle is necessarily a compromise between two basic aims. First, the suspension must isolate vehicle occupants from road irregularities to provide a comfortable ride. Second, the suspension must prevent undue vehicle pitching or rolling in order to give good road holding. The former requirement suggests the use of soft springs, whereas the latter requires the use of hard springs. This conflict can be overcome, to a degree, by the use of anti-roll bars. If gas spring suspension units are used, they can be coupled to allow fluid transfer; this provides an anti-roll/anti-pitch capability. This latter approach is well illustrated by the Hydrogas suspension system developed by Alex Moulton, as described in Hartley [1].

An active suspension system can achieve both a comfortable ride and good road holding by separating these two functions of the suspension system. Simple mechanical sensors can be used to discriminate between road irregularities and applied forces due to either vehicle manœuvres or aerodynamics. By using the sensor outputs to control the flow of fluid in

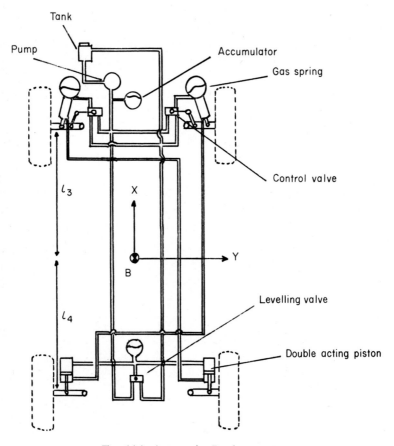

FIG. 14.1. Automotive Products system.

and out of gas springs, the suspension system can provide a soft response to road irregularities (referred to as passive mode) and a 'hard' response to vehicle manœuvres (referred to as active mode). An active suspension system has been fitted to a London Transport Route Master Bus. The system was developed by Automotive Products using practical development techniques on a Rover 3500. The system is shown schematically in Fig. 14.1 and details of the sensor/actuator valve are given in Fig. 14.2.

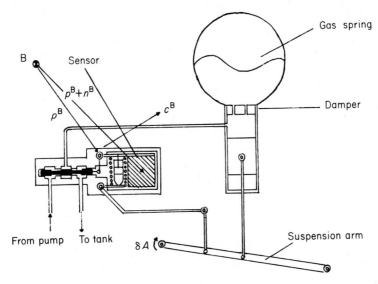

Fig. 14.2. Sensor/actuator valve.

The system provides a soft suspension coupled with a stable active roll and pitch loop on the front axles with open-loop control to the rear axles. The open-loop control is provided by coupling the front gas springs to double-acting pistons at the rear.

The work in this paper deals with the design of a fully closed-loop system which is both simple mechanically and easy to analyse. The system is shown in Fig. 14.3. It can be seen that the main difference lies in the method of controlling the rear axles; essentially, the rear suspension is a duplicate of the front suspension. The additional rear sensor allows complete closed-loop control. The structure of the sensor/actuator valve has been simplified considerably, as can be seen by comparing Figs. 14.2 and 14.4. The sensor/actuator valve (Fig. 14.4) can be made to perform in

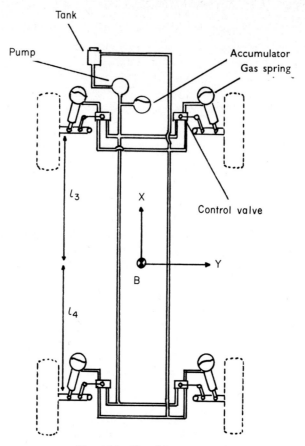

Fig. 14.3. Closed-loop system.

exactly the same manner as the Automotive Products sensor/actuator valve, by suitable choice of the angle α. This equivalence is demonstrated in Appendix 14.2.

The concept of an active suspension system is demonstrated by the analysis of a very simple system—see next section. An analysis of closed-loop control of vehicle bounce, pitch and roll is presented. This analysis is simplified by ignoring tyre flexibility and slip angle. To gain full benefit from active suspension one must fully decouple the passive response (due to road irregularities) from the active response resulting from vehicle manœuvres. Conditions for achieving this are given.

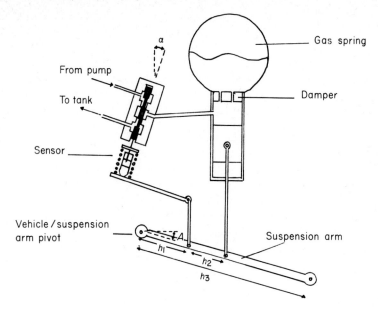

FIG. 14.4. Simplified sensor/actuator valve.

14.2   CONCEPT OF ACTIVE SUSPENSION

The basic concept which lies behind the idea of active suspension can be appreciated by analysing the system shown in Fig. 14.5. A mass M_1 is supported by a spring/damper suspension above a second mass M_2 which is in contact with a moving surface. This displacement of the surface with respect to inertial space is denoted by n. The displacement of M_1, which is denoted by z, satisfies the equation

$$M_1\ddot{z} + c(\dot{z} - \dot{n}) + k(z - n) = -W_z + H_x \tag{14.1}$$

where W_z is the external applied force and H_x the force applied by active suspension.

The active suspension system supplies a force H_x, which is a function of the relative displacement, x, of a sensor mass m with respect to M_1. The sensor mass is coupled to M_2 by a spring and damper. The external force W_z does not act directly on the sensor, whose motion is defined by the equation

$$m(\ddot{x} + \ddot{z}) = -C_m(\dot{x} + \dot{z} - \dot{n}) - K_m(x + z - n) \tag{14.2}$$

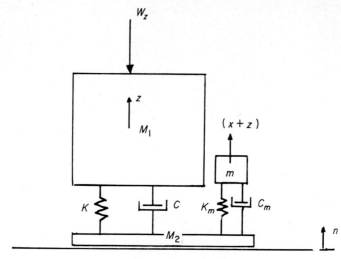

FIG. 14.5. Active suspension.

Comparing the two equations above, it can be seen that if the sensor parameters are chosen to model M_1, then the sensor output is independent of both z and n. That is, if

$$\frac{C_m}{m} = \frac{C}{M_1} \qquad (14.3)$$

$$\frac{K_m}{m} = \frac{K}{M_1} \qquad (14.4)$$

Then (14.2) becomes

$$m\ddot{x} + C_m\dot{x} + K_m x = \frac{m}{M_1}[W_z - H_x] \qquad (14.5)$$

Define ζ, w, λ by

$$2\zeta w = \frac{C}{M_1} \qquad (14.6)$$

$$w^2 = \frac{K}{M_1} \qquad (14.7)$$

$$\lambda = \frac{m}{M_1} \qquad (14.8)$$

Taking the Laplace transform, one has

$$m(s^2 + 2\zeta ws + w^2)\tilde{x} = \lambda[\tilde{W}_z - H(s)\tilde{x}] \qquad (14.9)$$

where $H(s)$ is the transfer function of the active suspension system, assumed here to be linear. Solving for $\tilde{x}$ yields

$$\tilde{x} = \frac{\lambda \tilde{W}_z}{\lambda H(s) + m(s^2 + 2\zeta ws + w^2)} \tag{14.10}$$

which, when combined with eqn (14.1), gives

$$\tilde{z} = \frac{(2\zeta ws + w^2)\tilde{n}}{s^2 + 2\zeta ws + w^2} + \frac{-\lambda \tilde{W}_z}{\lambda H(s) + m(s^2 + 2\zeta ws + w^2)} \tag{14.11}$$

From the above two terms it is clear that the system can operate in two modes:

1. *A passive mode*—In this mode the system responds only to surface irregularities n, as given by the first term of eqn (14.11). The response of the system is identical to that of a conventional passive spring/damper system.
2. *An active mode*—In this mode the vehicle responds to external applied forces W_z, as given by the second term of eqn (14.11). By suitable choice of $H(s)$ the response can be tailored to satisfy requirements placed on the system.

A particular case of interest (see Appendix 14.1) is when $H(s)$ takes the form

$$H(s) = \frac{\hat{K}M_1}{s}(2\zeta ws + w^2) \tag{14.12}$$

Then in the active mode, i.e. in response to external applied force, the motion is given by

$$\tilde{z} = \frac{-s\tilde{W}_z}{M_1[s^3 + 2\zeta ws^2 + (w^2 + 2\zeta w\hat{K})s + \hat{K}w^2]} \tag{14.13}$$

Providing $\hat{K}$ is chosen to make the system stable, it can be seen that in response to a steady applied force, the displacement tends to zero. If z is interpreted as vehicle bounce, a change in load is equivalent to an applied force acting on M_1. The vehicle will thus exhibit constant static deflection under all working conditions.

If the passive mode is stable, the active mode will be stable, for $H(s)$ of the form (14.12), if

$$\left.\begin{array}{l} \hat{K} > 0 \\ 2\zeta w > \hat{K}(1 - 4\zeta^2) \end{array}\right\} \tag{14.14}$$

For $\zeta > 0.5$, the active mode will be stable for all positive $\hat{K}$. But for $\zeta < 0.5$, $\hat{K}$ must be chosen to satisfy

$$0 < \hat{K} < \frac{2\zeta w}{1 - 4\zeta^2} \tag{14.15}$$

Define μ, Ω, α by

$$(s^2 + 2\mu\Omega s + \Omega^2)(s + \alpha) = s^3 + 2\zeta w s^2 + (w^2 + 2\zeta wK)s + Kw^2 \tag{14.16}$$

For large $\hat{K}$, and $\zeta > 0.5$,

$$\alpha \doteq \frac{w}{2\zeta} \tag{14.17}$$

$$\Omega \doteq (2\zeta w\hat{K})^{1/2} \tag{14.18}$$

$$\mu \doteq \left(\frac{\zeta w}{2\hat{K}}\right)^{1/2}\left(1 - \frac{1}{4\zeta^2}\right) \tag{14.19}$$

The natural frequency Ω becomes large for large $\hat{K}$. The natural frequency of the passive mode w is generally chosen to be small to provide narrow bandwidth to surface irregularities, and hence a comfortable ride. If the active mode were to respond to surface irregularities, the wide bandwidth provided by a large Ω would degrade the ride comfort. For this reason it is desirable to decouple the active and passive modes of operation.

14.3   VEHICLE DYNAMICS

14.3.1   Axes Systems

A set of body-fixed axes are defined by the right-handed triad $BX_BY_BZ_B$, such that B is the mass centre of vehicle; BX_B the principal axis of roll inertia, positive towards front of vehicle; BY_B the principal axis of pitch inertia, positive in offside lateral direction; and BZ_B the principal axis of yaw inertia, positive vertically downwards.

A vector, whose components are specified with respect to body-fixed axes, is denoted by a superscript B.

A set of inertial axes is defined by a right-handed triad $IX_IY_IZ_I$, nominally coincident with the body-fixed triad $BX_BY_BZ_B$. A vector, whose components are specified with respect to inertial axes, is denoted by a superscript I. If $\mathbf{U}$ is an arbitrary vector then the following transformation law is satisfied:

$$\mathbf{U}^I = Q^{IB}\mathbf{U}^B \tag{14.20}$$

where Q^{IB} is the rotation matrix specifying the attitude of the vehicle with respect to inertial axes.

The attitude of the vehicle, with respect to inertial axes, is defined by three Euler angles ϕ, θ, ψ (roll, pitch and yaw, respectively). Small angles are assumed for roll and pitch but not for yaw (since during cornering ψ is certainly not small). The order of the rotations in going from inertial axes to body-fixed axes is taken to be yaw, pitch, roll.

Thus, Q^{IB} can be expressed as

$$Q^{IB} = \begin{bmatrix} \cos\psi & -\sin\psi & (\theta\cos\psi + \phi\sin\psi) \\ \sin\psi & \cos\psi & (\theta\sin\psi - \phi\cos\psi) \\ -\theta & \phi & 1 \end{bmatrix} \quad (14.21)$$

14.3.2 Euler's Equations of Motion

The motion of the vehicle can be described by Euler's equations of motion as

$$\frac{d}{dt}(\mathscr{I}^{BB}\mathbf{w}^B) + \mathbf{w}^B \wedge (\mathscr{I}^{BB} \wedge \mathbf{w}^B) = \mathbf{T}^B \quad (14.22)$$

where $\mathscr{I}^{BB}$ is the inertial tensor of vehicle in body-fixed axes; $\mathbf{w}^B$ the angular velocity of the vehicle; and $\mathbf{T}^B$ the applied torques acting on the vehicle.

Since the body-fixed axes have been defined to be coincident with the principal axes of inertia, the inertial tensor can be written in the simple form

$$\mathscr{I}^{BB} = \begin{bmatrix} I_1 & 0 & 0 \\ 0 & I_2 & 0 \\ 0 & 0 & I_3 \end{bmatrix} \quad (14.23)$$

The angular velocity $\mathbf{w}^B$ is defined such that

$$Q^{BI\cdot}Q^{IB} = \mathbf{w}^B \wedge \quad (14.24)$$

That is,

$$\mathbf{w}^B = \begin{bmatrix} \dot{\phi} - \dot{\psi}\theta \\ \dot{\theta} + \dot{\psi}\phi \\ \dot{\psi} \end{bmatrix} \quad (14.25)$$

Equation (14.22) can be written as

$$I_1\dot{w}_1{}^B + (I_3 - I_2)w_3{}^B w_2{}^B = T_1{}^B \quad (14.26)$$

$$I_2\dot{w}_2{}^B + (I_1 - I_3)w_1{}^B w_3{}^B = T_2{}^B \quad (14.27)$$

$$I_3\dot{w}_3{}^B + (I_2 - I_1)w_2{}^B w_1{}^B = T_3{}^B \quad (14.28)$$

14.3.3   Applied Torques

The main torques acting on the vehicle are: (*a*) torques produced by the suspension units; (*b*) torques produced by the traction forces, and (*c*) aerodynamic torques.

The following assumptions are made:

1. The vehicle possesses a sufficient degree of mass symmetry, such that the triad of principal axes of inertia coincide with the axes of vertical, lateral and forward 'symmetry' of the vehicle.
2. The suspension arms and wheels have zero mass.
3. The changes in mass centre and moments of inertia due to changes in the distribution of the actuator fluid are negligible.
4. The wheels/tyres are assumed to be perfectly rigid and wheelslip is neglected.
5. The suspension is rigid laterally and in yaw.

The vehicle is attached to four identical (massless) suspension arms, one of which is shown in Fig. 14.6. Suspension units are attached between the

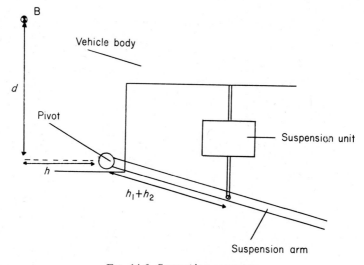

FIG. 14.6. Suspension geometry.

vehicle and the suspension arm. To distinguish between the four suspension arms, the following indices are used:

1. Front nearside.
2. Front offside.

3. Rear nearside.
4. Rear offside.

In body-fixed axes, the forces produced by the suspension units are

$$
F(1)\begin{bmatrix} 0 \\ 0 \\ -1 \end{bmatrix}, \quad F(2)\begin{bmatrix} 0 \\ 0 \\ -1 \end{bmatrix}, \quad F(3)\begin{bmatrix} 0 \\ 0 \\ -1 \end{bmatrix}, \quad F(4)\begin{bmatrix} 0 \\ 0 \\ -1 \end{bmatrix}
$$

with corresponding moment arms of

$$
\begin{bmatrix} l_3 \\ -d - (h_1 + h_2)\cos A \\ 0 \end{bmatrix}, \quad \begin{bmatrix} l_3 \\ d + (h_1 + h_2)\cos A \\ 0 \end{bmatrix},
$$

$$
\begin{bmatrix} -l_4 \\ -d - (h_1 + h_2)\cos A \\ 0 \end{bmatrix}, \quad \begin{bmatrix} -l_4 \\ d + (h_1 + h_2)\cos A \\ 0 \end{bmatrix}
$$

The contribution to the applied torque (in body-fixed axes) is

$$
\begin{bmatrix} [d + (h_1 + h_2)\cos A][F(1) + F(3) - F(2) - F(4)] \\ l_3[F(1) + F(2)] - l_4[F(3) + F(4)] \\ 0 \end{bmatrix}
$$

The suspension arms are pivoted at their interfaces with the vehicle body. At these pivots there are constraint forces

$$
\begin{bmatrix} C_1(1) \\ C_2(1) \\ C_3(1) \end{bmatrix}, \quad \begin{bmatrix} C_1(2) \\ C_2(2) \\ C_3(2) \end{bmatrix}, \quad \begin{bmatrix} C_1(3) \\ C_2(3) \\ C_3(3) \end{bmatrix}, \quad \begin{bmatrix} C_1(4) \\ C_2(4) \\ C_3(4) \end{bmatrix}
$$

with corresponding moment arms

$$
\begin{bmatrix} l_3 \\ -d \\ h \end{bmatrix}, \quad \begin{bmatrix} l_3 \\ d \\ h \end{bmatrix}, \quad \begin{bmatrix} -l_4 \\ -d \\ h \end{bmatrix}, \quad \begin{bmatrix} -l_4 \\ d \\ h \end{bmatrix}
$$

The above give rise to an applied torque:

$$
\begin{bmatrix} d[-C_3(1) + C_3(2) - C_3(3) + C_3(4)] - h[C_2(1) + C_2(2) + C_2(3) + C_2(4)] \\ -l_3[C_3(1) + C_3(2)] + l_4[C_3(3) + C_3(4)] + h[C_1(1) + C_1(2) + C_1(3) + C_1(4)] \\ l_3[C_2(1) + C_2(2)] - l_4[C_2(3) + C_2(4)] + d[C_1(1) - C_1(2) + C_1(3) - C_1(4)] \end{bmatrix}
$$

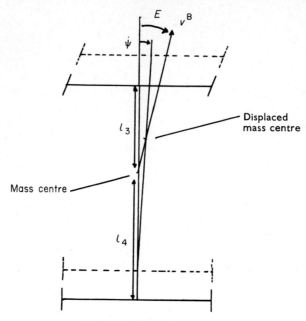

FIG. 14.7. Cornering geometry.

Consider Fig. 14.7: if the suspension is rigid both laterally and in yaw, the velocity of the vehicle mass centre is given by

$$\mathbf{V}^B = V \begin{bmatrix} \cos E \\ \sin E \\ (\theta - \alpha) \cos E - \phi \sin E \end{bmatrix} \qquad (14.29)$$

where

$$\tan E = \frac{l_4 \dot{\psi}}{V} \qquad (14.30)$$

and α is the local road gradient relative to the inertial triad. Road cant is neglected. In an inertial frame I' instantaneously coincident with body-fixed axes, the acceleration $\mathbf{a}^{I'}$ of the vehicle mass-centre is given by

$$\mathbf{a}^{I'} = {}^B\dot{\mathbf{v}} + \mathbf{w}^B \wedge \mathbf{v}^B \qquad (14.31)$$

i.e. ignoring second-order terms:

$$\mathbf{a}^{I'} = \begin{bmatrix} \dot{v} - l_4 \dot{\psi}^2 \\ v\dot{\psi} + l_4 \ddot{\psi} \\ -\dot{v}\alpha - v\dot{\alpha} \end{bmatrix} = \mathbf{a}^B \qquad (14.32)$$

The BX_B and BY_B components of this acceleration are provided by the joint action of the constraint forces and aerodynamic forces. Thus

$$M(\dot{v} - l_4\dot{\psi}^2) = C_1(1) + C_1(2) + C_1(3) + C_1(4) + W_x \quad (14.33)$$

$$M(v\dot{\psi} + l_4\ddot{\psi}) = C_2(1) + C_2(2) + C_2(3) + C_2(4) + W_y \quad (14.34)$$

where M denotes mass of vehicle, and W_x, W_y denote aerodynamic forces.

Taking moments about the junction of the suspension arms and their respective wheels leads to

$$C_3(1) = \left[1 - \frac{h_1 + h_2}{h_3}\right]F(i) \quad i = 1, 2, 3, 4, \ldots \quad (14.35)$$

Combining the above enables the roll/pitch components of $\mathbf{T}^B$ to be expressed as

Roll: $T_1^{\,B} = (h_1 + h_2)\left(\cos A + \dfrac{d}{h_3}\right)[F(1) + F(3) - F(2) - F(4)]$

$$- Mh(l_4\ddot{\psi} + v\dot{\psi}) + W_y h + \mathscr{F}_1 \quad (14.36)$$

Pitch: $T_2^{\,B} = \dfrac{(h_1 + h_2)}{h_3}\{l_3[F(1) + F(2)] - l_4[F(3) + F(4)]\}$

$$+ Mh(\dot{v} - l_4\dot{\psi}^2) - W_x h + \mathscr{F}_2 \quad (14.37)$$

where $\mathscr{F}_1$, $\mathscr{F}_2$ are the roll/pitch components of aerodynamic torque.

In addition, the vertical applied force, F_z, acting on the body can be expressed as

$$F_z = \frac{(h_1 + h_2)}{h_3}[F(1) + F(2) + F(3) + F(4)] + Mg + W_z \quad (14.38)$$

14.3.4 Vehicle Equations of Motion

The motion of the vehicle body can be described by six degrees of freedom. However, three degrees of freedom, namely, forward, lateral and yaw, are to a large extent under the direct influence of the driver of the vehicle. In this paper the three remaining degrees of freedom are analysed, i.e. roll, pitch, vertical. Combining Sections 14.3.2 and 14.3.3, the equations of motion describing the vehicle in roll, pitch and vertical can be written as

Roll: $I_1\dot{w}_1^{\,B} + (I_3 - I_2)\dot{\psi}w_2^{\,B}$

$$= (h_1 + h_2)\left(\cos A + \frac{d}{h_3}\right)[F(1) + F(3) - F(2) - F(4)]$$

$$- Mh(l_4\ddot{\psi} + V\dot{\psi}) + W_y h + \mathscr{F}_1 \quad (14.39)$$

Pitch: $I_2 \dot{w}_2{}^B + (I_1 - I_3)\dot{\psi}w_1{}^B$

$$= \frac{(h_1 + h_2)}{h_3} \{l_3[F(1) + F(2)] - l_4[F(3) + F(4)]\}$$

$$+ Mh(\dot{v} - l_4\dot{\psi}^2) - W_x h + \mathscr{F}_2 \qquad (14.40)$$

Vertical: $M\ddot{z} = \dfrac{-(h_1 + h_2)}{h_3} [F(1) + F(2) + F(3) + F(4)]$

$$+ Mg + W_z \qquad (14.41)$$

14.4 PASSIVE MODE

14.4.1 Suspension Arm Movement

The vertical displacement of the junction of the suspension arm and wheel in inertial space is given by

$$\begin{bmatrix} x \\ y \\ z \end{bmatrix} + Q^{IB} \begin{bmatrix} l_3 \\ -d - h_3 \cos [A + \delta A(1)] \\ h + h_3 \sin [A + \delta A(1)] \end{bmatrix}$$

for the front nearside suspension arm. x, y, z are the displacements of the wheel mass centre. Expanding the above vertical displacement gives

$$-l_3\theta - \phi(d + h_3 \cos A) + h + h_3 \sin A + z + h_3 \cos A\, \delta A(1)$$

Assuming a rigid wheel, the change in vertical displacement irom static equilibrium can be equated to the road surface displacement $n(1)$ to yield

$$n(1) = -\theta l_3 - \phi(d + h_3 \cos A) + Z + h_3 \cos A\, \delta A(1) \qquad (14.42)$$

That is,

$$\delta A(1) = \frac{n(1) + l_3\theta - \phi(d + h_3 \cos A) - Z}{h_3 \cos A} \qquad (14.43)$$

For the other three suspension arms, the relevant expressions are

$$\delta A(2) = \frac{n(2) + l_3\theta - \phi(d + h_3 \cos A) - Z}{h_3 \cos A} \qquad (14.44)$$

$$\delta A(3) = \frac{n(3) - l_4\theta + \phi(d + h_3 \cos A) - Z}{h_3 \cos A} \qquad (14.45)$$

$$\delta A(4) = \frac{n(4) - l_4\theta - \phi(d + h_3 \cos A) - Z}{h_3 \cos A} \qquad (14.46)$$

14.4.2 Passive Response

If the vehicle is subject only to variations in the road surface, the sensor/actuators produce no net effect on the motion of the vehicle. The vehicle is then said to be operating in its passive mode. The manner in which the passive mode is decoupled from the action of the sensor/actuators is discussed later in this paper.

Ignoring kinematic and dynamic cross-coupling of roll and pitch (which vanishes during non-cornering motion), the dynamics of the vehicle can be expressed as

$$I_1\ddot{\phi} = (h_1 + h_2)\left(\cos A + \frac{d}{h_3}\right)[Fp(1) + Fp(3) - Fp(2) - Fp(4)] \qquad (14.47)$$

$$I_2\ddot{\theta} = \frac{(h_1 + h_2)}{h_3}\{l_3[Fp(1) + Fp(2)] - l_4[Fp(3) + Fp(4)]\} \qquad (14.48)$$

$$M\ddot{z} = \frac{-(h_1 + h_2)}{h_3}[Fp(1) + Fp(2) + Fp(3) + Fp(4)] \qquad (14.49)$$

From Appendix 14.1, $Fp(i)$ takes the form

$$Fp(i) = \frac{-128\eta LC(i)^2(h_1 + h_2)}{n\pi\tau d^4}[\delta A(i) + \tau \dot{A}(i)] \qquad (14.50)$$

If the area of the pistons are chosen such that

$$C(1) = C(2) = C \qquad (14.51)$$

$$C(3) = C(4) = \left(\frac{l_3}{l_4}\right)^{1/2} C \qquad (14.52)$$

then, in the passive mode, the vehicle dynamics in roll, pitch and bounce are decoupled. Using the results of the previous section, the vehicle dynamics are governed by the equations (for passive mode)

Roll:
$$I_1\ddot{\phi} = \frac{-256\,\eta L(l_3 + l_4)}{n\pi\tau l_4 \cos A}\left[\frac{(h_1 + h_2)(h_3 \cos A + d)\,C}{h_3 d^2}\right]^2$$
$$\times (\tau\dot{\phi} + \phi - \tau\dot{u}_\phi - u_\phi) \qquad (14.53)$$

Pitch:
$$I_2\ddot{\theta} = \frac{-256\,\eta L(l_3 + l_4)l_3}{n\pi\tau \cos A}\left[\frac{(h_1 + h_2)C}{h_3 d^2}\right]^2 (\tau\dot{\theta} + \theta - \tau\dot{u}_\theta - u_\theta) \qquad (14.54)$$

Vertical:
$$M\ddot{z} = \frac{-256\,\eta L(l_3 + l_4)}{nl_4\pi\tau \cos A}\left[\frac{(h_1 + h_2)\,C}{h_3 d^2}\right]^2$$
$$\times (\tau\dot{z} + z - \tau\dot{u}_z - u_z) \qquad (14.55)$$

where

$$u_\phi = \frac{-\{l_4[n(1) - n(2)] + l_3[n(3) - n(4)]\}}{2(l_3 + l_4)(d + h_3 \cos A)} \qquad (14.56)$$

$$u_\theta = \frac{-[n(1) + n(2) - n(3) - n(4)]}{2(l_3 + l_4)} \qquad (14.57)$$

$$u_z = \frac{\{l_4[n(1) + n(2)] + l_3[n(3) + n(4)]\}}{2(l_3 + l_4)} \qquad (14.58)$$

The inputs u_ϕ, u_θ, u_z define a pseudo-road surface plane. If the road surface were indeed planar it would coincide with this pseudo-road surface. In steady state, in response to road surface irregularities, the vehicle takes up an attitude parallel to the pseudo-road surface.

Equations (14.53)–(14.55) can be written more simply, using the Laplace transform as,

$$\tilde{\phi} = \frac{(2\xi_\phi w_\phi s + w_\phi{}^2)\tilde{u}_\phi}{s^2 + 2\xi_\phi w_\phi s + w_\phi{}^2} \qquad (14.59)$$

$$\tilde{\theta} = \frac{(2\xi_\theta w_\theta s + w_\theta{}^2)\tilde{u}_\theta}{s^2 + 2\xi_\theta w_\theta s + w_\theta{}^2} \qquad (14.60)$$

$$\tilde{z} = \frac{(2\xi_z w_z s + w_z{}^2)\tilde{u}_z}{s^2 + 2\xi_z w_z s + w_z{}^2} \qquad (14.61)$$

The bounce, natural frequency and damping factor are given by

$$w_z = \frac{(h_1 + h_2)CP_0}{h_3}\left[\frac{2\gamma(l_3 + l_4)}{l_4 M\beta RT_0 \cos A}\right]^{1/2} \qquad (14.62)$$

$$\xi_z = \frac{64CL\eta(h_1 + h_2)}{\pi n d^4 P_0 h_3}\left[\frac{2\beta RT_0(l_3 + l_4)}{\gamma l_4 M \cos A}\right]^{1/2} \qquad (14.63)$$

The roll, pitch natural frequencies and damping factors are related to w_z, ξ_z by

$$w_\phi = (d + h_3 \cos A)\left(\frac{M}{I_1}\right)^{1/2} w_z \qquad (14.64)$$

$$\xi_\phi = \left(\frac{I_1}{M}\right)^{1/2}\frac{\xi_z}{(d + h_3 \cos A)} \qquad (14.65)$$

$$w_\theta = \left(\frac{Ml_3l_4}{I_2}\right)^{1/2} w_z \qquad (14.66)$$

$$\xi_\theta = \left(\frac{I_2}{Ml_3l_4}\right)^{1/2} \xi_z \qquad (14.67)$$

Because the passive mode responds only to road surface irregularities, one can choose the parameters to give a soft suspension and hence a comfortable ride. The passive mode response is similar to that of a conventional soft passive suspension to road surface irregularities.

14.5 ACTIVE MODE

14.5.1 Decoupling of Active/Passive Modes

Neglecting kinematic and dynamic cross-coupling of pitch and roll, the dynamics of the vehicle in roll, pitch, and bounce become, using the Laplace transform,

Roll: $(s^2 + 2\xi_\phi w_\phi s + w_\phi^2)\tilde{\phi} - (2\xi_\phi w_\phi s + w_\phi^2)\tilde{u}_\phi$

$$= \frac{\tilde{T}_1^B}{I_1} + \frac{(h_1 + h_2)}{I_1 h_3}(d + h_3 \cos A)$$

$$\times [\tilde{F}_A(1) + \tilde{F}_A(3) - \tilde{F}_A(2) - \tilde{F}_A(4)] \tag{14.68}$$

Pitch: $(s^2 + 2\xi_\theta w_\theta s + w_\theta^2)\tilde{\theta} - (2\xi_\theta w_\theta s + w_\theta^2)\tilde{u}_\theta$

$$= \frac{\tilde{T}_2^B}{I_2} + \frac{(h_1 + h_2)}{I_2 h_3}$$

$$\times \{l_3[\tilde{F}_A(1) + \tilde{F}_A(2)] - l_4[\tilde{F}_A(3) + \tilde{F}_A(4)]\} \tag{14.69}$$

Vertical: $(s^2 + 2\xi_z w_z s + w_z^2)\tilde{z} - (2\xi_z w_z s + w_z^2)\tilde{u}_z$

$$= \frac{\tilde{W}_z}{M} - \frac{(h_1 + h_2)}{M h_3}[\tilde{F}_A(1) + \tilde{F}_A(2) + \tilde{F}_A(3) + \tilde{F}_A(4)]$$

$$\tag{14.70}$$

The M_g term goes out with the $F_{st}(i)$ terms.

From Appendix 14.1, one has

Roll: $\tilde{F}_A(1) + \tilde{F}_A(3) - \tilde{F}_A(2) - \tilde{F}_A(4)$

$$= \frac{-128\eta LDC(1 + \tau s)}{n\pi d^4 \sigma \tau s}\left\{\tilde{x}(1) - \tilde{x}(2) + \left(\frac{l_3}{l_4}\right)^{1/2}[\tilde{x}(3) - \tilde{x}(4)]\right\}$$

$$\tag{14.71}$$

Pitch: $l_3[\tilde{F}_A(1) + \tilde{F}_A(2)] - l_4[\tilde{F}_A(3) + \tilde{F}_A(4)]$

$$= \frac{-128\eta LDC(1 + \tau s)}{n\pi d^4 \sigma \tau s}$$

$$\times \{l_3[\tilde{x}(1) + \tilde{x}(2)] - (l_3 l_4)^{1/2}[\tilde{x}(3) + \tilde{x}(4)]\} \tag{14.72}$$

Vertical: $\quad F_A(1) + F_A(2) + F_A(3) + F_A(4)$

$$= \frac{-128\eta LDC(1 + \tau s)}{n\pi d^4 \sigma \tau s}$$

$$\times \left\{ x(1) + x(2) + \left(\frac{l_3}{l_4}\right)^{1/2} [x(3) + x(4)] \right\} \qquad (14.73)$$

Define q_ϕ, q_θ, q_z by

$$q_\phi = x(1) - x(2) + \left(\frac{l_3}{l_4}\right)^{1/2} [x(3) - x(4)] \qquad (14.74)$$

$$q_\theta = l_3[x(1) + x(2)] - (l_3 l_4)^{1/2} [x(3) + x(4)] \qquad (14.75)$$

$$q_z = x(1) + x(2) + \left(\frac{l_3}{l_4}\right)^{1/2} [x(3) + x(4)] \qquad (14.76)$$

It is now assumed that m, C_m, K_m are the same for all four models but μ, r_2, r_1 may be different. Then using Appendix 14.1, and guided by Section 14.4,

$$m\ddot{q}_\phi + C_m \dot{q}_\phi + K_m q_\phi = -m\ddot{\phi}\left\{ r_2(1) - r_2(2) + \left(\frac{l_3}{l_4}\right)^{1/2} [r_2(3) - r_2(4)] \right\}$$

$$+ \frac{2K_m \Lambda (l_3 + l_4)}{l_4 h_3 \cos A} (d + h_3 \cos A)(\phi - u_\phi)$$

$$+ \frac{2C_m \Lambda (l_3 + l_4)}{l_4 h_3 \cos A} (d + h_3 \cos A)(\dot{\phi} - \dot{u}_\phi) \quad (14.77)$$

$$m\ddot{q}_\theta + C_m \dot{q}_\theta + K_m q_\theta = m\ddot{\theta}\{ l_3[r_1(1) + r_1(2)] - (l_3 l_4)^{1/2} [r_1(3) + r_1(4)] \}$$

$$+ \frac{2K_m \Lambda l_3}{h_3 \cos A} (l_3 + l_4)(\theta - u_\theta)$$

$$+ \frac{2C_m \Lambda l_3}{h_3 \cos A} (l_3 + l_4)(\dot{\theta} - \dot{u}_\theta) \qquad (14.78)$$

$$m\ddot{q}_z + C_m \dot{q}_z + K_m q_z = -2m\left[1 + \left(\frac{l_3}{l_4}\right)^{1/2} \right] \ddot{z}$$

$$- \frac{2K_m \Lambda (l_3 + l_4)}{h_3 l_4 \cos A} (z - u_z)$$

$$- \frac{2C_m \Lambda (l_3 + l_4)}{h_3 l_4 \cos A} (\dot{z} - \dot{u}_z) \qquad (14.79)$$

Providing the following constraints are satisfied,

$$\mu(1) = \mu(2) = \Lambda \qquad (14.80)$$

$$\mu(3) = \mu(4) = \left(\frac{l_3}{l_4}\right)^{1/2} \Lambda \qquad (14.81)$$

$$r_1(1) - r_1(2) + \left(\frac{l_3}{l_4}\right)^{1/2} [r_1(3) - r_1(4)] = 0 \tag{14.82}$$

$$l_3[r_2(1) + r_2(2)] - (l_3l_4)^{1/2}[r_2(3) + r_2(4)] = 0 \tag{14.83}$$

$$r_1(1) + r_1(2) + \left(\frac{l_3}{l_4}\right)^{1/2} [r_1(3) + r_1(4)] = 0 \tag{14.84}$$

$$r_2(1) + r_2(2) + \left(\frac{l_3}{l_4}\right)^{1/2} [r_2(3) + r_2(4)] = 0 \tag{14.85}$$

The constraints (14.82)–(14.85) are satisfied if and only if

$$r_2(1) = -r_2(2) \tag{14.86}$$

$$r_2(3) = -r_2(4) \tag{14.87}$$

$$r_1(1) = -\left(\frac{l_3}{l_4}\right)^{1/2} r_1(3) \tag{14.88}$$

$$r_1(2) = -\left(\frac{l_3}{l_4}\right)^{1/2} r_1(4) \tag{14.89}$$

Comparing the above equations for q_ϕ, q_θ, q_z with Section 14.4, it can be seen that for complete decoupling of active and passive modes one requires

$$\frac{C_m}{K_m} = \tau \tag{14.90}$$

$$-mw_\phi^2 \left[r_2(1) + \left(\frac{l_3}{l_4}\right)^{1/2} r_2(3)\right] = \frac{K_m \Lambda(l_3 + l_4)}{h_3 l_4 \cos A} (d + h_3 \cos A) \tag{14.91}$$

$$mw_\phi^2 l_3[r_1(1) + r_1(2)] = \frac{K_m l_3 (l_3 + l_4)\Lambda}{h_3 \cos A} \tag{14.92}$$

$$mw_z^2 \left[1 + \left(\frac{l_3}{l_4}\right)^{1/2}\right] = \frac{K_m \Lambda(l_3 + l_4)}{h_3 l_4 \cos A} \tag{14.93}$$

From which,

$$K_m \Lambda = \frac{mw_z^2 [1 + (l_3/l_4)^{1/2}]}{(l_3 + l_4)} l_4 h_3 \cos A \tag{14.94}$$

$$r_1(1) + r_1(2) = l_4 \left(\frac{w_z}{w_\theta}\right)^2 \left[1 + \left(\frac{l_3}{l_4}\right)^{1/2}\right] \tag{14.95}$$

$$r_2(1) + \left(\frac{l_3}{l_4}\right)^{1/2} r_2(3) = -(d + h_3 \cos A)\left(\frac{w_z}{w_\phi}\right)^2 \left[1 + \left(\frac{l_3}{l_4}\right)^{1/2}\right] \tag{14.96}$$

Now, using the Laplace transform and substituting into (14.68)–(14.70), one has

Roll:
$$\tilde{\phi} = \frac{(2\xi_\phi w_\phi s + w_\phi{}^2)\tilde{u}_\phi}{(s^2 + 2\xi_\phi w_\phi s + w_\phi{}^2)}$$

$$+ \frac{s\tilde{T}_1 F(ms^2 + C_m s + K_m)}{I_1(s^2 + 2\xi_\phi w_\phi s + w_\phi{}^2\{ms^3 + C_m s^2 + K_m s} + (2\gamma P_0 m DC/MV_0 h_3 \sigma)[1 + (l_3/l_4)^{1/2}](h_1 + h_2)(1 + \tau s)\}}$$

(14.97)

Pitch:
$$\tilde{\theta} = \frac{(2\xi_\theta w_\theta s + w_\theta{}^2)\tilde{u}_\theta}{(s^2 + 2\xi_\theta w_\theta s + w_{\theta 2})}$$

$$+ \frac{s\tilde{T}_2{}^B(ms^2 + C_m s + K_m)}{I_2(s^2 + 2\xi_\theta w_\theta s + w_\theta{}^2)\{ms^3 + C_m s^2 + K_m s} + (2\gamma P_0 m DC/MV_0 h_3 \sigma)[1 + (l_3/l_4)^{1/2}](h_1 + h_2((1 + \tau s)\}}$$

(14.98)

Vertical:

$$\tilde{z} = \frac{(2\xi_z w_z s + w_z{}^2)\tilde{u}_z}{(s^2 + 2\xi_z w_z s + w_z{}^2)}$$

$$+ \frac{s\tilde{w}_z(ms^2 + C_m s + K_m)}{M(s^2 + 2\xi_z w_z \xi s + w_z{}^2)\{ms^3 + C_m s^2 + K_m s} + (2\gamma P_0 m DC/MV_0 h_3 \sigma)[1 + (l_3/l_4)^{1/2}](h_1 + h_2)(1 + \tau s)\}}$$

(14.99)

From the above equations it can be seen that, in the active mode, the response is, in general, given by five poles in the s-plane. Two of these poles are connected with the corresponding passive mode. For one of the above, the passive mode poles can be removed from the active mode by suitable choice of the sensor parameters. An obvious choice is roll. If K_m is chosen such that

$$K_m = mw_\phi{}^2 \tag{14.100}$$

Then, eqn (14.97) becomes

$$\tilde{\phi} = \frac{(2\xi_\phi w_\phi s + w_\phi{}^2)\tilde{u}_\phi}{(s^2 + 2\xi_\phi w_\phi s + w_\phi{}^2)}$$

$$+ \frac{s\tilde{T}_1{}^B}{I_1\{s^3 + 2\xi_\phi w_\phi s^2 + w_\phi{}^2 s} + (2\gamma P_0 DC/MV_0 h_3 \sigma)[1 + (l_3/l_4)^{1/2}](h_1 + h_2)(1 + \tau s)\}}$$

(14.101)

which is of the same form as the system considered in Section 15.4.2. The simple nature of the sensors precludes the possibility of achieving the same for pitch and vertical.

14.5.2   Self-Levelling Capability

Consider the effects of a change in load. The F_{st} components of the forces produced by the suspension units no longer completely counteract the load. Two effects occur:

1. Due to the load dependence of the gas spring time constant, the change in load will result in some coupling between active and passive modes.
2. The sensor/actuator valve will pump fluid in or out of the gas springs to counteract the change in load. The integral control action of F_A will mean that, in steady state, x tends to zero. Hence, the system will accommodate the change in load with zero steady state offset. That is, the system is self-levelling.

It is clear that the load, for which decoupling of the active and passive modes is designed, should be selected to minimise the degradation in the ride comfort due to coupling induced by changes in load. This problem could be overcome if, instead of gas springs, pneumatically damped air-springs are employed.

14.6   APPLICATION TO ROUTE MASTER BUSES

To illustrate the anti-roll behaviour of active suspension, a design is generated for a Route Master bus, taking as a baseline the following parameters:

$$M = \ \ 6\,870 \text{ kg}$$
$$I_1 = \ \ 5720 \text{ kg m}^2 \ \Big\} \text{tare}$$
$$I_2 = 42\,400 \text{ kg m}^2$$
$$h = 1 \cdot 2 \text{ m}$$
$$l_3 = 2 \cdot 79 \text{ m}$$
$$l_4 = 2 \cdot 35 \text{ m}$$
$$d = 0 \cdot 48 \text{ m}$$
$$h_1 + h_2 = 0 \cdot 145 \text{ m}$$
$$h_3 = 0 \cdot 516 \text{ m}$$
$$A = 3^\circ$$

In bounce, a Route Master bus with its usual suspension has a natural frequency of 1·9 Hz and a damping factor of 0.45. Here the decoupling of passive/active modes is taken advantage of to reduce the natural frequency to 1 Hz. Taking a damping factor of 0·60, it follows from Section 14.4.2 that

$$w_z = 1 \text{ Hz}$$
$$\xi_z = 0\cdot60$$
$$w_\phi = 1\cdot095 \text{ Hz}$$
$$\xi_\phi = 0\cdot548$$
$$w_\theta = 1\cdot031 \text{ Hz}$$
$$\xi_\theta = 0\cdot582$$

In response to road irregularities the active suspension system will provide a better ride due to the lowered natural frequencies. For the active mode D is selected such that,

$$\frac{2\gamma P_0 DC(h_1 + h_2)[1 + (l_3/l_4)^{1/2}]}{MV_0 h_3 \sigma} = 1000 \tag{14.102}$$

The remaining poles of the system are given by the roots of

$$s^3 + 2\xi_\phi w_\phi s^2 + w_\phi^2 s + 1000(1 + \tau s) = 0 \tag{14.103}$$

i.e.

$$s = -1\cdot197\ 143 \pm 13\cdot888\ 150\text{j}, \quad -5\cdot146\ 314$$

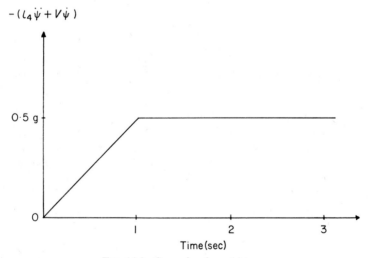

FIG. 14.8. Cornering force history.

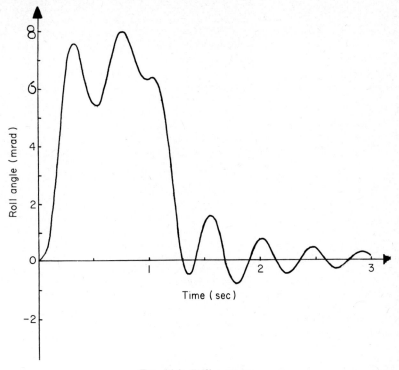

Fig. 14.9. Roll response.

The cornering response of the vehicle in roll is shown in Fig. 14.9. The input $-(l_4\ddot{\psi} + V\dot{\psi})$ ramps up from zero to a limiting value of 0·5 g in 1 sec., as shown in Fig. 14.8. This constant force is roughly equivalent to describing a circle of 30 ft radius at 15 mph. During the resulting roll transient, the peak excursion is 0·455°. In steady state, the roll angle settles down to a zero offset.

14.7. ADVANTAGES OF ACTIVE SUSPENSION

The main advantages of the use of an active suspension as indicated by the analysis in this paper are:

1. One can employ the equivalent of a soft passive suspension, to give a comfortable ride in response to road surface irregularities.

2. In response to constant external forces (e.g. steady state cornering *or* cross wind) the active suspension gives zero steady state offset. The fast transient response limits the vehicle excursions to a low value.

3. Related to the above, the active suspension has a self-levelling capability in response to changes in load. This eliminates the large static deflections which occur with conventional soft suspensions. In addition, the self-levelling capability has obvious advantages for passenger-carrying vehicles.

4. The active suspension tends to keep the wheels normal to the road surface. This allows corners to be taken at higher speeds before the wheels break away. In addition, it also increases tyre life.

14.8.   CONCLUSIONS

A theoretical analysis of a closed-loop active suspension system, based loosely on a system developed by Automotive Products, has been presented in this paper. An indication of the anti-roll behaviour of the system has been given by applying the results to a London Transport Route Master bus.

ACKNOWLEDGEMENT

The author would like to thank Mr S. F. Smith, Chief Mechanical Engineer, London Transport Executive, for permission to present this paper.

REFERENCE

1. Hartley, J. (1973). Design evaluation of the Moulton hydrogas suspension, *Engineering Materials and Design*, pp. 23–28, June.

APPENDIX 14.1 GAS SPRING DYNAMICS

A14.1.1   Gas Spring Time Constant

The suspension unit consists of a gas spring shown schematically in Fig. 14.4. The volume of the gas spring above the capillaries contains both fluid and gas separated by a flexible membrane. Below the capillaries the fluid can enter through a pipe connected to the actuator valve. The volume of the fluid below the capillaries is determined by the action of a piston connected directly to the suspension arm. The gas spring itself is rigidly attached to the vehicle. The pressure acting on the piston provides a control action.

The gas spring behaviour is analysed using the following assumptions:

1. The actuator valve is so shaped that the mass flow rate through it is a linear function of the valve displacement.
2. Changes in the pressure, volume and density of the gas are small compared to their equilibrium values.
3. The fluid is incompressible.
4. The gas in the system can be treated as an ideal gas.
5. During operation the gas undergoes adiabatic compression and expansion.
6. The fluid flow in the capillaries is laminar.
7. The capillaries are smooth.

Consider the volume of the gas spring above the capillaries. Assuming laminar flow through a smooth pipe, the rate $\dot{m}$, at which mass enters the system is given by

$$\dot{m} = \frac{n\pi\sigma d^4}{128\eta L}(\rho_2 - \rho_1) \qquad \text{(A14.1.1)}$$

where n is the number of capillaries; d the diameter of capillary; L the length of capillary; η the kinematic viscosity; ρ_1 the reduced pressure above capillaries; ρ_2 the reduced pressure below capillaries; and σ the density of fluid.

The reduced pressure is the actual pressure less that pressure necessary to support the static load.

If V is the volume of gas, then

$$\dot{V} = -\frac{1}{\sigma}\dot{m} \qquad \text{(A14.1.2)}$$

Taking the equilibrium pressure to be P_0, the behaviour of the gas is given by

$$(P_0 + \rho_1)V^\gamma = \text{constant, } Q \text{ say} \qquad \text{(A14.1.3)}$$

where γ is the adiabatic gas constant. Differentiating, yields

$$\dot{\rho}_1 = \frac{-\gamma(P_0 + \rho_1)^{1+1/\gamma}\dot{V}}{Q^{1/\gamma}} \qquad \text{(A14.1.4)}$$

Combining (A14.1.4) and (A14.1.2), and taking $\rho_1 \ll P_0$, gives

$$\dot{\rho}_1 = \frac{\gamma P_0^{1+1/\gamma}}{Q^{1/\gamma}} \frac{n\pi d^4}{128\eta L} (\rho_2 - \rho_1) \qquad (A14.1.5)$$

From the ideal gas law, for β gram mols of gas per gas spring,

$$P_0 V_0 = \beta R T_0 \qquad (A14.1.6)$$

i.e.

$$Q = P_0 \left[\frac{\beta R T_0}{P_0}\right]^{\gamma} \qquad (A14.1.7)$$

T_0, V_0 being the equilibrium temperature and volume of the gas, respectively.

Thus (A14.1.5) becomes

$$\dot{\rho}_1 = \frac{n\gamma P_0^2 \pi d^4}{128\eta L \beta R T_0} (\rho_2 - \rho_1) \qquad (A14.1.8)$$

Defining the gas spring time constant τ by

$$\tau = \frac{128\eta L \beta R T_0}{n\gamma P_0^2 \pi d^4} \qquad (A14.1.9)$$

(A14.1.8) can be written, using the Laplace transform, as

$$\bar{\rho}_1 = \frac{\bar{\rho}_2}{1 + \tau s} \qquad (14.1.10)$$

One consequence of (14.1.9) is that the time constant of the gas spring is temperature dependent. The time constant is linearly proportional to ηT_0 and hence the fluid should be chosen such that this parameter is insensitive to temperature over the operating range of the vehicle.

A14.1.2   Control Forces

The mass flow rate $\dot{m}'$ into the gas spring from the actuator valve is given by

$$\dot{m}' = D\tilde{x} \qquad (A14.1.11)$$

where $\tilde{x}$ is the displacement of the valve and D is the gain. Applying conservation of mass to the volume of the gas spring below the capillaries, yields the equation

$$D\tilde{x} + (h_1 + h_2)C\sigma\, \delta\dot{A} + \frac{n\pi d^4 \sigma}{128\eta L} (\rho_1 - \rho_2) = 0 \qquad (A14.1.12)$$

where C is the area of piston and δA is the deflection angle of suspension arm in body-fixed axes (measured vertically downwards).

Combining (A14.1.12) and (A14.1.10) and solving for ρ_2 yields,

$$\tilde{\rho}_2 = \frac{128\eta L}{n\pi d^4 \sigma}\frac{(1 + \tau s)}{\tau s}[D\tilde{x} + (h_1 + h_2)C\sigma\,\delta\tilde{A}] \quad (A14.1.13)$$

Thus, the force F produced by the gas spring can be expressed as

$$\tilde{F} = \tilde{F}_{st} - \frac{128\eta LC}{n\pi d^4 \sigma}\frac{(1 + \tau s)}{\tau s}[D\tilde{x} + (h_1 + h_2)\sigma C s\,\delta\tilde{A}] \quad (A14.1.14)$$

F_{st} is the static force developed to counteract the load.

It is useful to define an active and passive component of the force, F_A and F_p, respectively, by

$$\tilde{F}_A = \frac{-128\eta LCD(1 + \tau s)\tilde{x}}{n\pi d^4 \sigma\tau s} \quad (A14.1.15)$$

$$\tilde{F}_p = \frac{-128\eta LC^2(h_1 + h_2)(1 + \tau s)}{n\pi d^4 \tau}\delta\tilde{A} \quad (A14.1.16)$$

such that (A14.1.4) can be written as

$$F = F_{st} + F_A + F_p \quad (A14.1.17)$$

APPENDIX 14.2 SENSOR/ACTUATOR VALVE DYNAMICS

A14.2.1 Sensor Dynamics

From Fig. 14.4, the acceleration of the sensor mass m, in body-fixed axes, is given by

$$\begin{bmatrix} \alpha_x^B \\ \alpha_y^B - \ddot{x}\sin\alpha \\ \alpha_z^B + \ddot{x}\cos\alpha \end{bmatrix} + \begin{bmatrix} \dot{w}_1^B \\ \dot{w}_2^B \\ \dot{w}_3^B \end{bmatrix} \wedge \begin{bmatrix} r_1 \\ r_2 - x\sin\alpha \\ r_3 + x\cos\alpha \end{bmatrix} + \begin{bmatrix} w_1^B \\ w_2^B \\ w_3^B \end{bmatrix}$$

$$\wedge \left\{ \begin{bmatrix} w_1^B \\ w_2^B \\ w_3^B \end{bmatrix} \wedge \begin{bmatrix} r_1 \\ r_2 - x\sin\alpha \\ r_3 + x\cos\alpha \end{bmatrix} + 2\begin{bmatrix} 0 \\ -\dot{x}\sin\alpha \\ \dot{x}\cos\alpha \end{bmatrix} \right\}$$

where α_x^B, α_y^B, α_z^B denote components of vehicle mass-centre acceleration, and r_1, r_2, r_3 denote location of sensor mass in body-fixed axes.

The sensor mass is constrained to move in the direction $(0 - \sin \alpha \cos \alpha)^T$. Thus, the motion of the sensor mass is given by the equation,

$$m[\ddot{x} + \alpha_z{}^B \cos \alpha - \alpha_y{}^B \sin \alpha + \dot{w}_1{}^B(r_2 \cos \alpha + r_3 \sin \alpha) - \dot{w}_2{}^B r_1 \cos \alpha$$
$$- \dot{w}_3{}^B r_1 \sin \alpha - \sin \alpha(w_1{}^B w_2{}^B r_1 + w_2{}^B w_3{}^B r_3 - (w_1{}^{B2} + w_3{}^{B2})r_2)$$
$$- x w_2{}^B w_3{}^B \sin 2\alpha - w_1{}^{B2} x + \cos \alpha(w_1{}^B w_3{}^B r_1 + w_2{}^B w_3{}^B r_2$$
$$- (w_1{}^{B2} + w_2{}^{B2})r_3) - w_3{}^{B2} x \sin^2 \alpha - w_2{}^{B2} x \cos^2 \alpha]$$
$$+ Km(x - \mu\, \delta A) + Cm(\dot{x} - \mu\, \delta \dot{A}) = 0 \qquad \text{(A14.2.1)}$$

In the special case when α is zero, and ignoring second-order terms, the above reduces to

$$m\ddot{x} + C_m \dot{x} + K_m x = \mu(C_m\, \delta\dot{A} + K_m\, \delta A) + m[-\alpha_2{}^B - r_2 \dot{w}_1{}^B + r_1 \dot{w}_2{}^B] \qquad \text{(A14.2.2)}$$

A14.2.2   Equivalence of Sensor/Actuator Values

The Automotive Products sensor/actuator value is shown schematically in Fig. 14.2, where $\mathbf{P}^B$ is the position of pivot point P; $\mathbf{n}^B$ the position of pendulous mass with respect to pivot point P; $\mathbf{c}^B$ the axis of rotation of sensor (unit vector); and Ω the output angle of sensor (clockwise looking in direction of $\mathbf{c}^B$).

In an inertial frame of reference instanteously coincident with body-fixed axes, the acceleration of the pendulous mass is

$$\ddot{\mathbf{B}}^{I\prime} + \ddot{\Omega}(\mathbf{c}^B \wedge \mathbf{n}^B) + 2\mathbf{w}^B \wedge (\mathbf{c}^B \wedge \mathbf{n}^B)\dot{\Omega}$$
$$+ \dot{\mathbf{w}}^B \wedge [\mathbf{P}^B + \Omega(\mathbf{c}^B \wedge \mathbf{n}^B) + \mathbf{n}^B]$$
$$+ \mathbf{w}^B \wedge [\mathbf{w}^B \wedge [\mathbf{P}^B + \Omega(\mathbf{c}^B \wedge \mathbf{n}^B) + \mathbf{n}^B]]$$

The spring/damper system attached to the sensor produces a force given by

$$[K_m{}'(a\Omega - \mu'\, \delta A) + C_m{}'(a\dot{\Omega} - \mu'\, \delta\dot{A})]\mathbf{n}'^B$$

Taking moments about the pivot point P:

$$m(\mathbf{c}^B \wedge \mathbf{n}^B)[\ddot{\mathbf{B}}^{I\prime} + \ddot{\Omega}(\mathbf{c}^B \wedge \mathbf{n}^B) + 2\mathbf{w}^B \wedge (\mathbf{c}^B \wedge \mathbf{n}^B)\dot{\Omega}$$
$$+ \dot{\mathbf{w}}^B \wedge [\mathbf{P}^B + \Omega(\mathbf{c}^B \wedge \mathbf{n}^B) + \mathbf{n}^B]$$
$$+ \mathbf{w}^B \wedge [\mathbf{w}^B \wedge [\mathbf{P}^B + \Omega(\mathbf{c}^B \wedge \mathbf{n}^B) + \mathbf{n}^B]]]$$
$$= \mathbf{c}^B \cdot \mathbf{n}^{11B} \wedge \mathbf{n}^{1B}[K_m{}'(a\Omega - \mu'\, \delta A) + C_m{}'(a\dot{\Omega} - \mu'\, \delta\dot{A})] \qquad \text{(A14.2.3)}$$

where, $\mathbf{n}^{11B}$ is the position at which spring/damper force is applied relative to point P and $\mathbf{n}^{11B}$ is the direction of spring/damper force (unit vector).

Define N by

$$N = |\mathbf{n}^B| = (n_1{}^2 + n_2{}^2)^{1/2} \tag{A14.2.4}$$

Thus, $\mathbf{c}^B \wedge \mathbf{n}^B$ can be written as

$$\mathbf{c}^B \wedge \mathbf{n}^B = N\mathbf{e}^B \tag{A14.2.5}$$

where $\mathbf{e}^B$ is a unit vector, since $\mathbf{c}^B$, $\mathbf{n}^B$ are orthogonal.

Defining x by

$$x = -N\Omega \tag{A14.2.6}$$

(A14.2.3) can be written as

$$
m\mathbf{e}^B[\ddot{\mathbf{B}}^{I\prime} + \ddot{x}\mathbf{e}^B + 2\dot{x}\mathbf{w}^B \wedge \mathbf{e}^B + \dot{\mathbf{w}}^B \wedge (\mathbf{P}^B + x\mathbf{w}^B \wedge \mathbf{e}^B + \mathbf{n}^B)
$$
$$
+ \mathbf{w}^B \wedge [\mathbf{w}^B \wedge [\mathbf{P}^B + x\mathbf{w}^B \wedge \mathbf{e}^B + \mathbf{n}^B]]]
$$
$$
= -\frac{G}{N}\left[K_m{}' \left(\frac{ax}{N} - \mu' \,\delta A \right) + C_m{}' \left(\frac{a\dot{x}}{N} - \mu' \,\delta \dot{A} \right) \right] \tag{A14.2.7}
$$

where G is given by the triple scalar product.

$$G = \mathbf{c}^B \cdot \mathbf{n}^{11B} \wedge \mathbf{n}^{1B} \tag{A14.2.8}$$

Equation (A14.2.7) is directly equivalent to (A14.2.1) if

$$
\mathbf{P}^B + \mathbf{n}^B = \begin{bmatrix} r_1 \\ r_2 \\ r_3 \end{bmatrix} \tag{A14.2.9}
$$

$$
\mathbf{e}^B = \begin{bmatrix} 0 \\ -\sin \alpha \\ \cos \alpha \end{bmatrix} \tag{A14.2.10}
$$

$$
K_m = \frac{aGK_m{}'}{N^2} \tag{A14.2.11}
$$

$$
C_m = \frac{aGC_m{}'}{N^2} \tag{A14.2.12}
$$

$$
\mu = \frac{N\mu'}{a} \tag{A14.2.13}
$$

The above analysis demonstrates the equivalence of the simplified sensor/actuator (as shown in Fig. 14.4) and the Automotive Products design (shown in Fig. 14.2). The effective non-zero α, for the latter system, introduces a forcing function $w_3{}^{B2}r^2 \sin \alpha$ (i.e. a centripetal force) which is used to provide open-loop control of the rear axles.

15

Static and Dynamic Analysis of a Light Van Body Using the Finite Element Method

B. Mills and J. Sayer

University of Birmingham and London Transport Executive

SUMMARY

An integral construction, light van body was analysed statically and dynamically using the finite element method. Static tests included bending and torsion and used a special rig test to support the van without imposing statically indeterminate constraints. Measured deflections were compared with those predicted by two half-structure idealisations, the second, more refined idealisation giving better agreement. Dynamic tests, using the MAMA excitation system, over the frequency range 5–60 Hz, exposed ten natural frequencies, six of them being symmetric and four of them anti-symmetric. Measured natural frequencies and mode shapes were compared with those predicted by each idealisation and again the second idealisation gave the better results.

15.1 INTRODUCTION

Most of the literature on vehicle structural analysis has been devoted to chassis frames and passenger cars. Integral construction vans, consisting of side and roof panelling superimposed on a load-bearing platform, may be regarded as hybrid structures, with the load being taken by both the underfloor beams and the beams and panels of the bodywork.

Literature related to the structural analysis of integral construction vehicles can be considered in two parts; the first being without finite elements and the second with finite elements. In the former area, Garrett [1] examined an imaginary vehicle structure by first defining bending moment and shear force diagrams for the complete structure and then separately analysing individual components. Panels were neglected in order to simplify the analysis, but because they contribute significantly to the strength and stiffness of the structure accurate design information would not be provided by this method. Cooke [2] considered that designers were suspicious of computer-based analysis methods and describes a method for assessing the torsional stiffness of saloon cars. Only the passenger compartment was considered, manual computation was used and the approximation in the method led to a conservative estimate of stiffness. Myers [3] discussed practical design considerations arising from techniques similar to those due to Garrett [1] and recognised the importance of accurate estimates of structural behaviour at the design stage. Shigeta *et al.* [4] considered the effect of joint factors in an analysis of a vehicle sideframe. They showed that variation in joint flexibility could considerably alter the predicted stiffness of the sideframe. However, in the absence of the remainder of the structure, the analysis of a sub-structure can give misleading results.

In the field of finite element analysis McKenna [5] idealised an integral construction vehicle using only beam elements, representing panels by diagonal and peripheral booms. Significant alterations to the panel approximations were made before good correlation between predicted and experimental results was obtained. Kirioka [6] produced a very simple idealisation using beams and shear panels. The force method was used because, for small problems, this makes more efficient use of computer storage than does the displacement method. Good correlation was obtained with stresses measured on a specially made model but it was concluded that more detailed idealisations were necessary for more complex body structures. Allwood and Norville [7] analysed a vehicle underbody using the displacement method with beam and panel elements and obtained a slightly over-stiff model in bending, but their predictions for torsional loads showed poor agreement with experiment. Kirioka *et al.* [8] produced a more sophisticated analysis than that in Ref. 6 using a symmetric half of the vehicle with about 600 nodes. Beams and panel elements were used with the displacement method of analysis and predictions in bending and torsion were about 10% stiffer than the experimental values, displacement patterns showing good agreement. Petersen [9] initially analysed a vehicle side structure using beams and triangular panel elements and concluded that to represent the joints correctly the beams should be replaced by panel elements. The resulting idealisation for one symmetric half of the body used more than 1700 nodes and 3000 elements. Predicted displacements in bending were smaller than experimental values but there was good agreement between the shapes of the deflection curves. Norville and Mills [10] analysed a Land-Rover type bodyshell, using the finite element displacement method, producing idealisations varying between 8 and 60% over-stiff, and concluded that elements with compatible in-plane displacements should be used to preclude the production of unpredictably flexible idealisations.

15.2 COMPUTER PROGRAMS

15.2.1 Static Analysis

The program used for static analysis and its mode of operation were essentially similar to those described in Mills and Johnson [11]. The elements used included a general beam element, triangular and rectangular panel elements and a general quadrilateral panel element. The displacement functions used for the beam, triangular and rectangular elements were those used in Ref. 11. The quadrilateral element was limited to in-plane displacements based on linear functions along a set of non-orthogonal axes—see Taig [12].

15.2.2 Dynamic Analysis

Inertia matrices for dynamic analysis may be formed either on the distributed mass or lumped mass principle. In the former approach the matrices contain both diagonal and off-diagonal terms, while in the latter they contain only diagonal terms and this can simplify the solution process. Although the use of distributed mass is more realistic than lumped mass, several authors, such as Craig and Bampton [13] and Anderson and Mills [14], have used lumped mass with satisfactory results.

In the present work the static analysis program was used to formulate the 'free-in-space' structure stiffness matrix for each problem, while the lumped mass matrix was formed using a separate program. A reduction technique was then applied to the matrices so that the solution could be carried out in the core of the computer. A further program was then used to calculate natural frequencies and mode shapes within a specified frequency range. The reduction process consisted of choosing a number of master degrees of freedom and expressing the structure stiffness and inertia matrices in terms of them, allowing for the kinetic energy of the remaining, slave, degrees of freedom.

15.3 EXPERIMENTAL APPARATUS AND TEST PROGRAM

15.3.1 Static Tests

The van was mounted, using stiff springs to replace the road springs, on a testing frame which applied no statically indeterminate restraints. All displacements were measured by clock gauges relative to a reference frame suspended from the van. The mounting details are similar to those given in Mills and Johnson [11] and the constraints applied by the rig are shown in Fig. 3.7 of that paper.

In the bending test, loads of 250 kg each were applied to the van floor at four points, in the region of stations 15, 18, 35 and 38 shown in Fig. 15.1. Also shown in this figure are the positions of points of measurement and support dimensioned with reference to an origin at the intersection of the centrelines of the front axle and the body. For the torsion test, a load of 250 kg was applied in opposite directions at each of the two front mounting points (stations 11 and 31 of Fig. 15.1), giving a torque of 225 kg m. In both static tests, deflections were recorded as the loads were applied incrementally to the maximum value and removed in a similar fashion. This enables the linearity of the results to be checked, and hysteresis effects to be eliminated from the results.

15.3.2   Dynamic Tests

The van structure was symmetrically supported by four elastic ropes so that the natural frequency of each of the rigid body modes was less than 2 Hz. Multi-point excitation was used to determine the natural frequencies and mode shapes of the structure. The equipment, which has the acronym of MAMA (Manual-Automatic Multi-point Apparatus), was developed by RAE at Farnborough. A brief description of its mode of operation is given in Appendix 15.1 and its application to dynamic tests on a chassis frame is given in Anderson and Mills [15].

Initially, all the natural frequencies in the range 5–60 Hz were determined using the method suggested by Kennedy and Pancu [16]. Two vibrators were used, attached in turn to each of the four symmetrically disposed pairs of spring mounting brackets (the stiff springs used in the static tests having been removed) and driven both in phase and in antiphase for each pair. Piezoelectric accelerometers were used to detect motion on the structure and their outputs were fed via charge amplifiers and the resolved components indicator to an X–Y plotter. For each accelerometer station a frequency sweep was carried out producing polar plots (see Fig. 15.21). Each natural frequency was located at a frequency for which the rate of change of phase of the response vector with frequency was a maximum (for a pure mode, 90° out of phase with the exciting force).

The second part of the dynamic test programme was the measurement of the mode shape at each natural frequency. It was found that using two vibrators in positions chosen individually for each natural frequency produced reasonably pure mode shapes. For each mode a reference response was chosen at a point with a large dynamic deflection and an

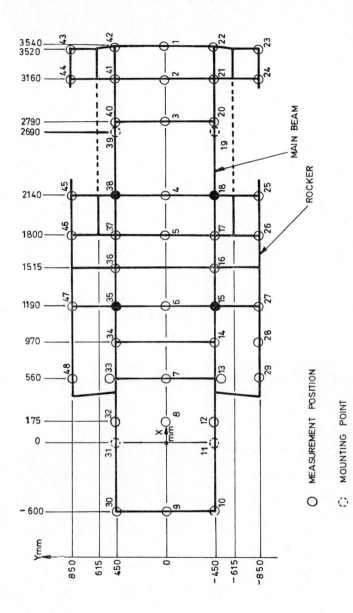

Fig. 15.1. Van floor—measurement positions.

accelerometer was attached at that point. A second, roving accelerometer was used to plot the mode shape. For plotting the mode shape a paper carrying line drawings of the floor, side and roof of the van was placed on the X–Y plotter. The plotter was zeroed over the point on the appropriate line drawing that represented the measurement point to which the roving accelerometer was attached, and the tip of the response vector was plotted. This method gave a visual display of the magnitude and phase of the response at each measurement point from which nodal lines and nor-malised mode shapes could be determined.

15.4   VAN BODY IDEALISATIONS

The representation of beam-to-beam and beam-to-panel connections presents difficulties. The typical beam joint shown in Fig. 15.2(a) may be represented without a finite size joint, as in Fig. 15.2(b) or with a finite size joint, as in Fig. 15.2(c). In joints between beams and panels the latter are often attached to the faces of the beams, as shown in Fig. 15.3(a). This may be modelled as in Fig. 15.3(b) using finite size joints, preserving geometric similarity with the original structure, or without finite size joints as in Fig. 15.3(c), at the cost of geometrical inaccuracy which would have implications for the idealisation of adjacent parts of the structure. For dynamic analysis, geometrical similarity between the model and the real structure can be more important than for static analysis because the geometric disposition of the structure then defines the mass distribution, and hence the dynamic load distribution.

The two idealisations used are shown in Figs. 15.4 and 15.5. To reduce the size of the problem only one-half of the van was modelled, taking advantage of the high degree of symmetry about the vertical plane through the longitudinal centrelines. Idealisation 1, shown in Fig. 15.4, was a relatively coarse model which incorporated the following characteristics:

1. Underfloor stiffeners of stiffness an order of magnitude less than the major floor beams were combined with other members.
2. Areas of local stiffening, such as round the edges of the wheel arch, were omitted.
3. Areas of shallow curved panelling, such as the roof, were considered flat.
4. Non-prismatic beams were modelled as prismatic beams with average section properties.
5. Where a minor beam, such as a roof bow, was attached to one or

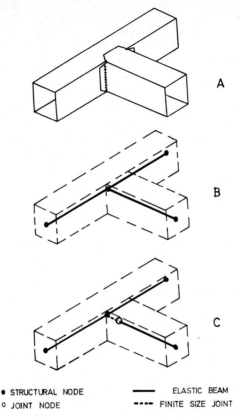

<table>
<tr><td>● STRUCTURAL NODE</td><td>——— ELASTIC BEAM</td></tr>
<tr><td>○ JOINT NODE</td><td>---- FINITE SIZE JOINT</td></tr>
</table>

FIG. 15.2. Beam joint idealisations.

more panels the element was assumed to lie in the plane of the intersection of the panels—as shown in Fig. 15.3(c).

6. Finite size joints—as shown in Fig. 15.2(c)—were used for the underfloor beam assembly.

Thus, in idealisation 1, coarseness existed mainly in the areas of the roof and side panels and the front fender–dash assembly. In idealisation 2, these areas of panelling were refined and underfloor stiffeners, previously omitted, were included leading to an improvement in the structural and geometrical accuracies and mass distribution of the model. The statistics of the two idealisations are summarised in Table 15.1.

Two sets of constraints were prepared for each idealisation to suppress mechanisms and rigid body motion and to constrain the plane of symmetry so that symmetric and anti-symmetric loading could be simulated.

TABLE 15.1

Idealisation number	1	2
Structural nodes	99	162
Finite size joint nodes	25	29
Beam elements	83	112
Triangular panels	19	31
Quadrilateral panels	64	111
Bending test, 250 kg at nodes	39 and 59	71 and 104
Torsion test, 250 kg at nodes	21	29

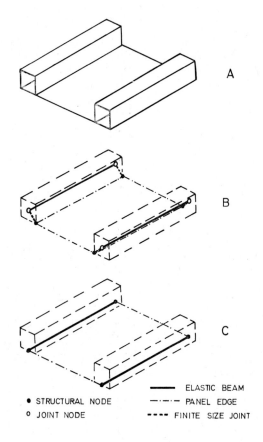

• STRUCTURAL NODE   ——— ELASTIC BEAM
○ JOINT NODE   —·—·— PANEL EDGE
                       ---- FINITE SIZE JOINT

FIG. 15.3. Beam–panel idealisations.

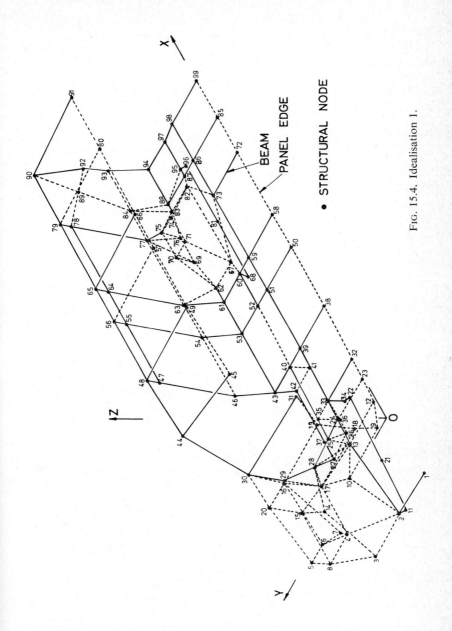

BEAM

PANEL EDGE

● STRUCTURAL NODE

Fig. 15.4. Idealisation 1.

B. Mills and J. Sayer

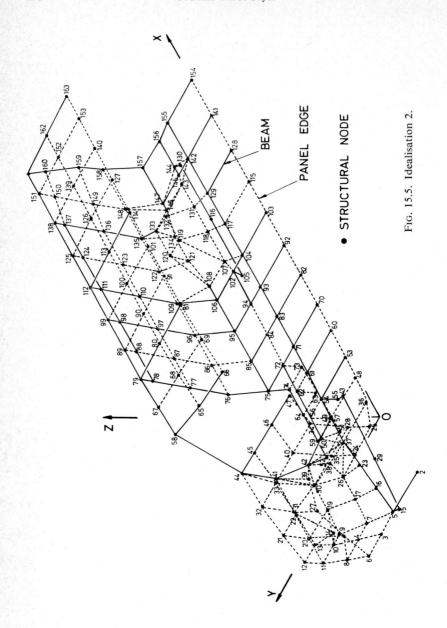

• STRUCTURAL NODE

PANEL EDGE

BEAM

Fig. 15.5. Idealisation 2.

15.5 DISCUSSION OF EXPERIMENTAL RESULTS AND COMPUTER PREDICTIONS

15.5.1 Static Tests

For the bending test, displacements measured along the centreline, main beam and rocker are compared with predicted values in Figs. 15.6, 15.7 and 15.8, respectively. It can be seen that both idealisations gave similar predictions, and that these predictions were slightly over-stiff, especially at the front and rear of the van. An upward 'kink' in the measured centreline displacement pattern (Fig. 15.6) is apparent. The transverse member at this point was a thin Z-shaped floor stiffener, whose effective bending stiffness was less than that implied by its second moments of area; no allowance was made for this in the idealised models, thus the predicted curves do not exhibit the 'kink'.

Measured and predicted displacements for the torsion test are compared for the main beam and rocker in Fig. 15.9 and 15.10, respectively. The predicted values along the centrelines were all zero, and the corresponding measured values insignificant. Both idealisations were over-stiff, but idealisation 2 was less stiff, showing that the finer idealisation of the

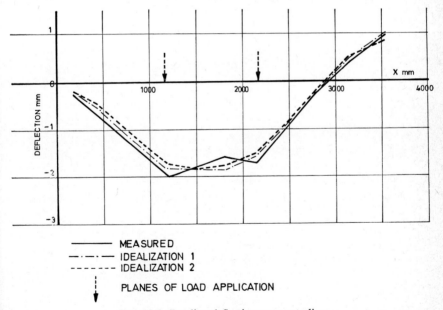

———— MEASURED
—·—·— IDEALIZATION 1
- - - - - - IDEALIZATION 2

PLANES OF LOAD APPLICATION

FIG. 15.6. Bending deflections on centreline.

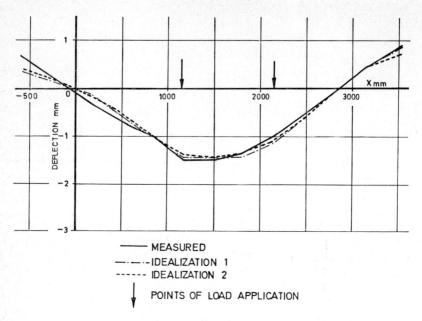

—— MEASURED
—·—·— IDEALIZATION 1
------ IDEALIZATION 2

↓   POINTS OF LOAD APPLICATION

FIG. 15.7. Bending deflections on main beam.

panelling gave improved results for torsion, where a high proportion of the load is taken by the panels in shear. Even in idealisation 2, however, the complex construction of the front of the van was only approximately represented, and this may account for the over-stiff prediction in this area.

15.5.2 Dynamic Tests

Natural frequencies and mode shapes were measured as described in Section 15.3.2. Mode shapes were taken as acceptably pure if the phase difference between any major response vector and the reference response vector was not more than 10°. Non-linearity in the structure was very low and the change in natural frequency of each mode was not more that 0·1% for a change in amplitude from just detectable to the highest possible without causing intermittent contact between adjacent parts of the structure. The ten measured natural frequencies and descriptions of mode shapes are summarised in Tables 15.2 and 15.3. The MAMA system used for the tests enabled modes with close natural frequencies to be readily distinguished and excited independently (e.g. symmetric modes 4 and 5).

It will be seen that the symmetric modes were not simply bending modes of increasing order but combinations of different types of motion.

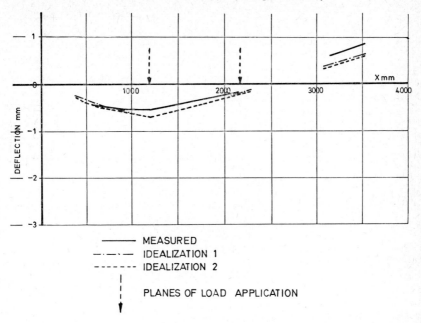

FIG. 15.8. Bending deflections on rocker.

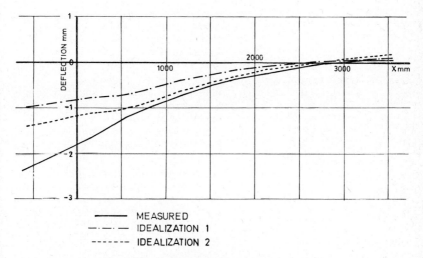

FIG. 15.9. Torsion deflections on main beam.

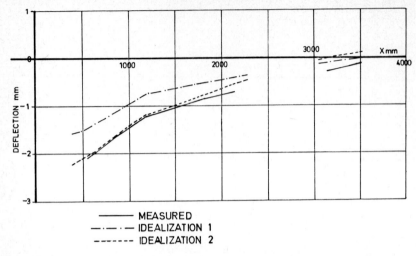

FIG. 15.10. Torsion deflections on rocker.

TABLE 15.2
Measured symmetric modes

Mode no.	Natural frequency (Hz)	Figure number	Description
1	24·90	15.11	Breathing mode, floor and roof in antiphase, sides in antiphase moving together while roof and floor move apart. Longitudinal bending of the floor.
2	32·56	15.12	Same as mode 1 but with greater motion of sides and front of roof.
3	38·03	15.13	Combination of longitudinal and transverse bending in both floor and roof with their motion in phase.
4	46·87	15.14	Same as mode 3 but the longitudinal and transverse motions are combined in a different sense.
5	47·55	15.15	Transverse bending of the roof and rear floor together with longitudinal bending of the front.
6	52·16	15.16	Same as mode 5 but with a reversed phase relationship between the transverse bending of the rear floor and the longitudinal bending of the front.

TABLE 15.3
Measured anti-symmetric modes

Mode no.	Natural frequency (Hz)	Figure number	Description
1	20·54	15.17	Primary lozenging of the open-ended load-carrying area with the magnitude increasing towards the rear. Floor and roof moving laterally in antiphase, sides moving vertically in antiphase.
2	27·12	15.18	Torsion of the floor and roof with secondary lozenging of the load-carrying area so that the front and rear lozenge in antiphase. Lateral bending about the door opening was also present.
3	39·60	15.19	Secondary torsion of the floor but not the roof together with tertiary lozenging of the load-carrying area so the centre of the van was lozenging in antiphase with the front and rear.
4	49·36	15.20	Secondary torsion of both floor and roof with vertical bending of the sides giving a form of secondary lozenging across the load-carrying area.

This is due to the disparity between the stiffnesses of different parts of the van and to the nature of its construction with large cut-outs and fairly flexible connections between various parts of the shell.

In the anti-symmetric modes, the presence of large cut-outs and flexible connections in the structure prevented the appearance of pure torsional modes. The preferred motion was a combination of lozenging of the load-carrying area with torsion or bending of the floor, roof and sides.

The use of half-idealisations under symmetric or anti-symmetric constraints was considered justified because all the measured modes in the test frequency range were found to be either symmetric or anti-symmetric. Both idealisations were used to predict the natural frequencies and mode shapes and the results are summarised in Table 15.4, together with the figure numbers in which the mode shapes predicted by idealisation 2 are compared with the corresponding experimentally measured modes. The idealisation 1 predicted mode shapes are not presented, since the idealisation 2 results were generally superior.

TABLE 15.4

Comparison of predicted and measured natural frequencies and mode shapes

Mode number	Measured natural frequency (Hz)	Idealisation 1 Natural frequency (Hz)	Idealisation 2 Natural frequency (Hz)	Figure number
Symmetric				
1	24·90	22·44	20·17	15.11
1M	—	—	26·20	—
2	32·56	25·89	32·42	15.12
3	38·03	36·81	37·04	15.13
4	46·87	39·78	41·01	15.14
4M	—	—	41·66	—
5	47·55	46·41	44·74	15.15
6	52·16	49·19	45·93	15.16
6M	—	—	48·21	—
Anti-symmetric				
1	20·54	18·89	13·12	15.17
2	27·12	36·19	33·76	15.18
2M	—	—	31·38	—
3	39·60	50·84	46·38	15.19
4	49·36	44·70	39·55	15.20
4M	—	—	40·51	—

All the experimentally measured modes were predicted by both idealisations, but the first, fourth and sixth symmetric modes, and the second and fourth anti-symmetric modes, were also predicted in modified form by idealisation 2. These modified modes (1M, 4M and 6M symmetric and 2M and 4M anti-symmetric) differed from the unmodified versions by exhibiting phase reversal of the motion of part of the van structure. This emphasises the importance of the comment about the construction of the van, namely the flexible connections between various parts. Attempts to excite the modified modes were unsuccessful, implying that the curvature of the roof and side panels created preferential displacement patterns and inhibited the reverse-phase motion. Large predicted displacements should be discounted because the solution process assumed zero damping, but it should be remembered that their presence can lead to a shift in the positions of nodal lines. Apart from 1M, all the predicted natural frequencies were lower than the measured values, suggesting that in contrast to the static tests the model stiffness was too low.

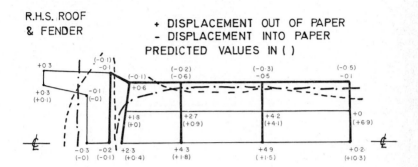

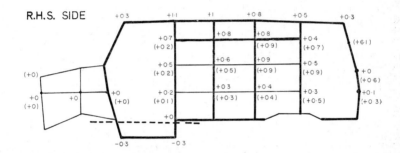

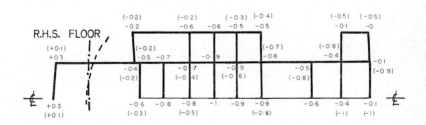

FIG. 15.11. Symmetric mode 1. ----- nodal line measured: frequency 24·90 Hz; —·— nodal line idealisation 2: frequency 20·17 Hz.

B. Mills and J. Sayer

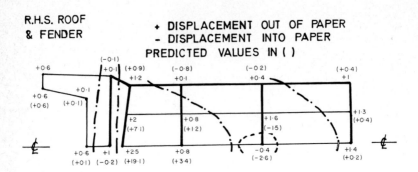

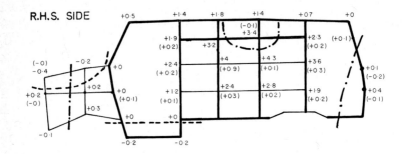

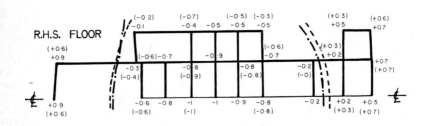

FIG. 15.12. Symmetric mode 2. ----- nodal line measured: frequency 32·56 Hz; —·— nodal line idealisation 2: frequency 32·42 Hz.

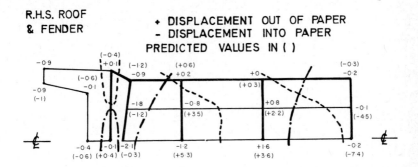

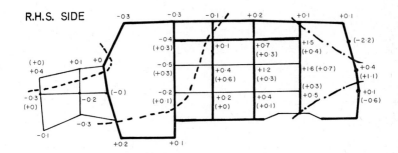

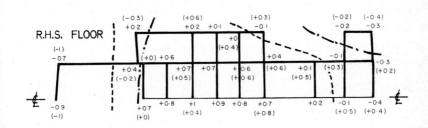

Fig. 15.13. Symmetric mode 3. ――――― nodal line measured: frequency 38·03 Hz;
―――·― nodal line idealisation 2: frequency 37·04 Hz.

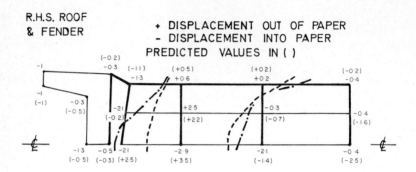

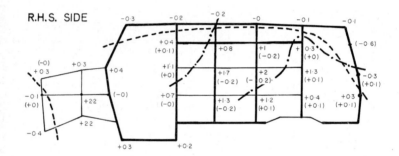

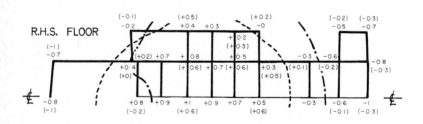

FIG. 15.14. Symmetric mode 4. ----- nodal line measured: frequency 46·87 Hz;
———· nodal line idealisation 2: frequency 41·01 Hz.

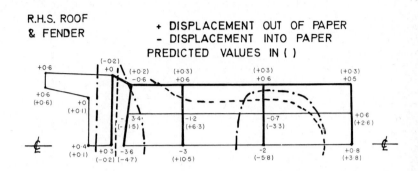

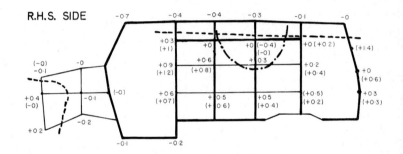

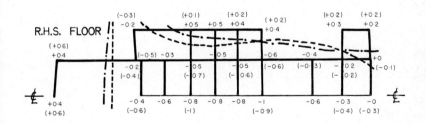

Fig. 15.15. Symmetric mode 5. ----- nodal line measured: frequency 47·55 Hz; ⌐·⌐·⌐ nodal line idealisation 2: frequency 44·74 Hz.

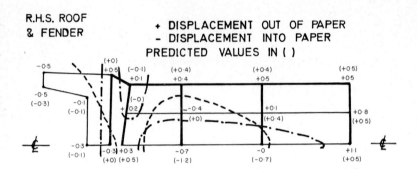

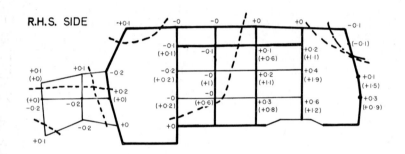

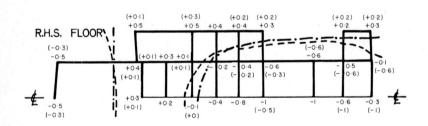

Fig. 15.16. Symmetric mode 6. ----- nodal line measured; frequency 52·16 Hz; —·— nodal line idealisation 2: frequency 45·93 Hz.

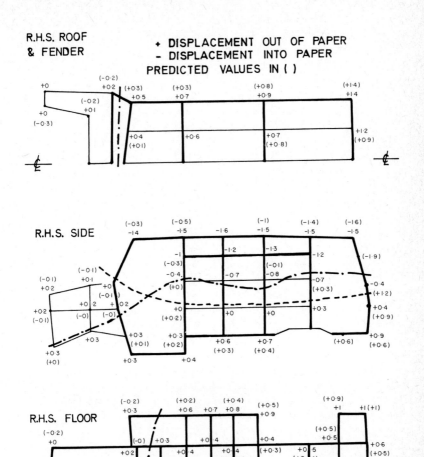

FIG. 15.17. Anti-symmetric mode 1. −−−−− nodal line measured: frequency 20·54 Hz;
—·—· nodal line idealisation 2: frequency 13·12 Hz.

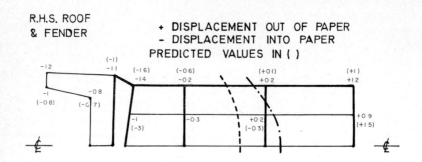

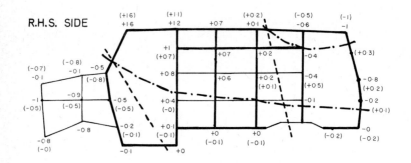

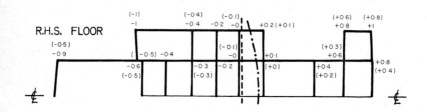

FIG. 15.18. Anti-symmetric mode 2. ----- nodal line measured: frequency 27·12·Hz; —·— nodal line idealisation 2: frequency 33·76 Hz.

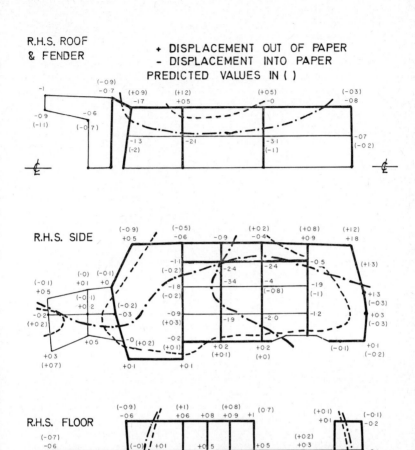

FIG. 15.19. Anti-symmetric mode 3. ----- nodal line measured: frequency 39·60 Hz; —·—· nodal line idealisation 2: frequency 46·38 Hz.

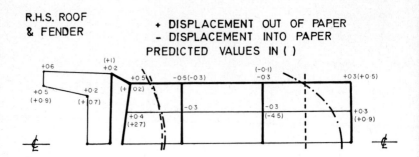

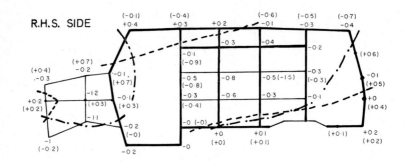

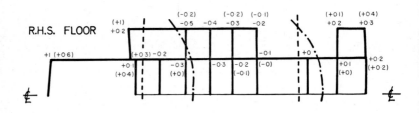

FIG. 15.20. Anti-symmetric mode 4. – – – – – nodal line measured: frequency 49·36 Hz; —·—·— nodal line idealisation 2: frequency 39·55 Hz.

15.6 CONCLUSIONS

For the box van structure tested statically and dynamically and analysed using the finite element method, it is concluded that:

1. The static loading and measurement systems performed satisfactorily and gave repeatable results.
2. Both idealisations gave generally good but slightly over-stiff predictions for the bending test.
3. The second idealisation was demonstrably superior to the first in the torsion test, although both were over-stiff; further refinement in the areas of panelling having rapid changes in contour should predict results closer to those measured experimentally.
4. The dynamic excitation equipment and method of measurement performed satisfactorily, allowing the measurement of modes with close natural frequencies and giving repeatable results.
5. The second, finer idealisation gave, overall, the better prediction of natural frequencies and mode shapes.
6. Idealisation criteria for dynamic predictions include:
   - (*a*) careful selection of master degrees of freedom when using the mass condensation technique, taking the symmetry conditions into account;
   - (*b*) fine mesh representation of areas where there are curved panels and rapid changes in contour;
   - (*c*) realistic representations of beam–beam and beam–panel joints.
7. Allowing for the relative coarseness of the idealisation of some parts of the structure, the finite element method proved to be a powerful technique for the prediction of the static and dynamic characteristics of the van body.

ACKNOWLEDGEMENTS

The authors wish to thank Professor S. A. Tobias for the provision of laboratory facilities in the Department of Mechanical Engineering at the University of Birmingham; the Ford Motor Company Ltd for the provision of the van body and the Science Research Council for financial support during the computer program development.

REFERENCES

1. Garrett, T. K. (1953). Structure design, *Automobile Engineer*, March/April.
2. Cooke, C. J. (1965/66). 'Torsional Stiffness Analysis of Car Bodies', I. Mech. E. Proc. Vol. 180, Pt 2A, No. 1.
3. Myers, R. A. 'Body Stress Analysis', SAE Paper No. 660005, 1966.
4. Shigeta, K., Nakajima, K. and Tanabe, M. (1966). An analysis of a car body side structure with elastic joints, *J. Soc. Auto. Engrs., Japan*, **20** (2).
5. McKenna, E. R. (1961). 'Computer Evaluation of Automobile Body Structures'. Am. Soc. of Body Engrs. 16th Annual Convention, Oct. (MIRA Ref. 62/4/6).
6. Kirioka, K. 'An Analysis of Body Structures', SAE 979A, Jan. 1965.
7. Allwood, R. J. and Norville, C. C. (1965/66). 'The Analysis by Computer of a Motor Car Underbody Structure,' I. Mech. E. Proc. (Auto. Div.). Vol. 180, Pt 2A, No. 7.
8. Kirioka, K., Ohkobuo, Y. and Hotta, Y. (1971). 'An Analysis of Body Structures', Part II, SAE No. 710157, Jan.
9. Petersen, W. (1971). 'An Application of the Finite Element Method to Predict the Static Response of Automotive Body Structures.' SAE No. 710263, Jan.
10. Norville, C. C. and Mills, B. (1972). An applied finite element displacement analysis of a simple integral construction vehicle body shell, *Int. J. Mech. Sci.* **14**, Pergamon.
11. Mills, B. and Johnson, P. J. (1974). 'Static Analysis of a Light Truck Frame using the Finite Element Method', Conf. Stress, Vibration and Noise Analysis in Vehicles, University of Aston in Birmingham, September.
12. Taig, I. C. 'Structural Analysis by the Matrix Displacement Method', English Electric Aviation Report No. SO 17, 1961.
13. Craig, R. R. and Bampton, M. C. (1968). Coupling of substructures for dynamic analysis. *AIAA Journal*, **3** (7) July.
14. Anderson, D. T. and Mills, B. (1972). Dynamic analysis of a car chassis frame using the finite element method, *Int. J. Mech. Sci.*, **14**, Pergamon.
15. Anderson, D. T. and Mills, B. (1971). Multi-point excitation techniques, *Environmental Engineering*, No. 51, Dec.
16. Kennedy, C. C. and Pancu, C. D. P. (1947). Use of vectors in vibration measurement and analysis, *J. Aero. Soc.*, Nov.

APPENDIX 15.1   THE MAMA SYSTEM

In the MAMA (Manual-Automatic Multipoint Apparatus) system, shown in Fig. 15.21, the excitation signal is provided by a wide range, continuously variable voltage tuned oscillator. The oscillator may be tuned either manually or automatically. Automatic tuning is achieved by comparing the

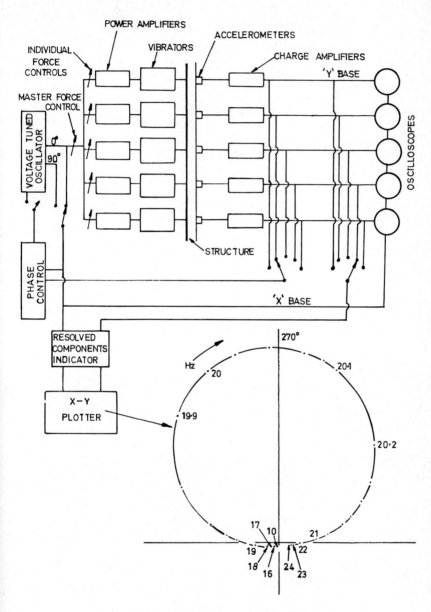

FIG. 15.21. MAMA system and polar plot.

phase angle between the input force and a chosen response signal with a demanded phase angle, and using the error in a servo-loop to control the oscillator frequency. The demanded phase angle is continuously variable between 0° and 270° to permit the use of displacement, velocity or acceleration response signals and to allow for variation in the theoretical phase relationships when impure mode shapes are being excited. The same oscillator signal is used for all the electromagnetic exciters (up to a maximum of five). Each channel has an independent continuously variable level control, permitting signals either in phase or 180° out of phase with the oscillator output, as well as being controlled by an overall level control. The force provided by the exciters is maintained in phase (or 180° out of phase) with the oscillator output by means of power amplifiers with negligible phase difference between input voltage and output current, and high output impedance, and the use of coils wound on non-inductive cores in the exciters to minimise the phase difference between input current and force. Such an arrangement permits the use of the oscillator output as a reference force signal.

Although the system can work with displacement or velocity response signals, in this work it was used with piezoelectric accelerometers, whose output signals were fed to charge amplifiers. The output from each charge amplifier was fed to the Y-base of an oscilloscope, the X-base being fed from the oscillator output, producing Lissajous figures of acceleration against force. The use of the oscillator signal, rather than a measured force signal, is advantageous because the cleaner waveform effectively filters the output of the resolved components indicator. The charge amplifier output can be fed to a resolved components indicator whose output is two dc voltages; one proportional to the component of response in phase with the force and the other proportional to the component of response at 90° to the force. The resolved components thus obtained may then be either measured and processed manually, or fed to an X–Y plotter to give a visual display, as shown in Fig. 15.21.

16

A Preliminary Investigation into the Structural Behaviour of an Underground Railway Coach

A. L. Yettram and D. J. Smith

Brunel University and London Transport Executive

SUMMARY

The specialised function of urban underground railways, that of providing a frequent-stop, mass transportation facility catering for a very high volume of passengers with a large amount of changing at stations, sets an 'architectural' form on underground rolling stock, which is much more prescribed than that possible for main-line railways. Thus, not only is the exterior geometry largely decided by loading gauge, tunnel height, platform curvature, etc. when an existing network is being used but the internal layout is also closely defined. In particular, the number of doorways, their position, size and type, along with the need for large windows, dominates the form of the structure of the coach sides. Furthermore, freedom of circulation internally inhibits the over-use of structural bulkheads and pillars. Thus, the structural designer is confined to a large extent as to the geometrical parameters which he can vary.

An underground railcar conventionally has a very heavy chassis or underframe which includes two main longitudinals, the solebars. These alone constitute a large proportion of the structural cost of the entire car. Much of the work done in the project described in this paper was concerned with examining the effects of alternative sizing of the main structure, the solebars, doors and window pillars and roof, in an endeavour to make the coach body work more efficiently overall. The loading case mainly considered was the dead-weight plus 'super-crush' passenger load.

The analyses were carried out by the finite element method. This was the first time, as far as is known, that this method had been used on underground rolling stock in this country. The computer program used was the NEWPAC package, developed by the Engineering Research Division of British Rail at Derby, and the computation was performed on the ICL 1903A computer at Brunel University.

The paper describes the idealisations used for the analyses, the main results, with comparisons with existing data available from other methods, and general conclusions concerning the structural behaviour and design of railcars for the loading case considered.

16.1 INTRODUCTION

The world's first public passenger-carrying underground railway, the Metropolitan, opened in London on 10 January 1863, running from Bishop's Road, Paddington to Farringdon St. in the City. Steam locomotives operated this 3¾-mile route and it was not until 1890 that electrification came to the Underground. The system, which developed from the original Metropolitan and which now incorporates the District and Circle lines, is essentially a 'surface' system with shallow underground parts constructed by cut-and-cover methods. The cross-sectional profile of surface stock can therefore be relatively 'tall' and 'square'.

The present stock for the Metropolitan line, (see Figs. 16.1 and 16.2), known as the 'A60' stock, was ordered from Messrs Cravens Ltd, of

FIG. 16.1. 'A60' Metropolitan Line stock—exterior. (Photograph by courtesy of London Transport Executive.)

Sheffield, in 1959, with a further batch, 'A62', ordered subsequently in 1962. Both of these types are virtually identical, the bodies being constructed of light alloy but with the bolsters of fabricated welded steel. Light alloy castings were used for the doorways and corner pillars, which also formed part of the exterior finish of the cars; external panelling was of unpainted aluminium alloy sheet. Two pairs of double sliding doors were provided down the side of each motor car, plus a single sliding door, at the trailing end, whilst the trailer cars had three pairs of double sliding doors. The width of the cars was 9 ft 8 in and the length 53 ft.

In 1968, an order for 212 cars for the Circle line was placed with Messrs Metropolitan-Cammell Ltd, which became known as the 'C69' stock

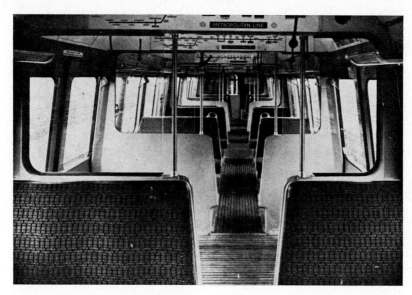

Fig. 16.2. 'A60' Metropolitan Line stock—interior. (Photograph by courtesy of London Transport Executive.)

(Figs. 16.3 and 16.4). Its appearance is similar to the 'A' stock, it being of unpainted aluminium alloy, although the 'C' stock motor cars are 3 ft 7 in longer than the trailer cars, since although both types have the same seating layout, the motor cars have, in addition, a driving cab. Thus, in order to reduce the body overhang, the bogie centres of the two cars are

Fig. 16.3. 'C69' Circle Line stock—exterior. (Photograph by courtesy of London Transport Executive.)

FIG. 16.4. 'C69' Circle Line stock—interior. (Photograph by courtesy of London Transport Executive.)

different. Each car is provided with four pairs of double sliding doors down each side, which are top-hung with an open-type sill plate. The driver's cab contains an air-operated sliding door for the first time, and the ventilation of the carbody is provided by fixed openings above the cantrail level. Additionally, because of the presence of four double doorways per car side, a much deeper section solebar is employed, and this also serves to carry many of the cables throughout the car.

Electrification came to the London Underground with the first tube railway, the City and South London, opened on 18 December 1890, running from Stockwell to King William Street. In contrast to the 'surface' system the tube lines were constructed by bored tunnels at large depth and, as the cost of tunnelling is roughly proportional to the square of the diameter, the cross-section profiles of tube stock are of necessity tending towards being circular. Thus, from the very first began the development of the shape of the underground car in the distinctive form that we know today.

The first tube stock built since World War II were experimental sets constructed by Messrs Metropolitan-Cammell Ltd, in 1956. The carbodies had external panelling of unpainted aluminium alloy and rubber suspension was provided on the bogies. This stock formed the basis for the 1959 and 1962 tube stocks.

A small number of experimental cars were built in 1960 by Messrs Cravens Ltd. The layout of doors and the seating arrangement was similar to that provided in the 1959 tube stock, but was modified to allow more space at the double-door draught screen. Also double-width, effectively double-glazed windows were fitted. The exterior finish consisted of aluminium alloy sheets riveted to a steel frame and interior painting was reduced to a minimum by the use of melamine-faced plastic panelling, with the grab poles provided in either satin finish aluminium or stainless steel. The ceiling was of painted peg-board in an attempt to improve sound absorption.

The rolling stock for the Victoria line, built by Messrs Metropolitan-Cammell Ltd and known as the 1967 tube stock, '67T', was based on the designs of the 1960 stock (Figs. 16.5 and 16.6). The cars have wrap-around

Fig. 16.5. '67T' Victoria line stock—exterior. (Photograph by courtesy of London Transport Executive.)

front windows to the driving cab, and the glass in the air-operated doors is taken up into the curved part of the door. The glazed door screens have been set back nearly nine inches to give more room and to provide easier access. The main window and ventilator design gives a double-glazed effect. The exterior of the cars is finished in unpainted aluminium alloy, and the interiors have plastic panelling with stainless steel or anodised aluminium grab-rails and other fittings.

London Transport Executive have published various books and

Fig. 16.6. '67T' Victoria Line stock—interior. (Photograph by courtesy of London Transport Executive.)

booklets giving a detailed account of the development of the rolling stock used on the Underground [1–3].

The specialised function of urban underground railways, that of providing a frequent-stop, mass transportation facilitity catering for a very high volume of passengers with a large inflow and outflow at stations, sets an 'architectural' or 'functional' form on underground stock which is much more prescribed than that for main-line railways. The general overall design problem and the main criteria which have to be met have been well described by Mr S. A. Driver, Chief Draughtsman, London Transport Executive in a paper to the Institution of Mechanical Engineers in 1970 [4].

It is useful here to recapitulate some of the main points made by Driver as far as the structural design is concerned. Fitting a stock to an existing network of track, stations and tunnel bore determines the loading gauge for the design. Thus there is very little latitude available for deciding on the outside cross-sectional profile, and also not a great deal for altering bogie-centre distance and car overhang. The need to cater for increasing passenger densities demands that the interior of a car be as unobstructed as possible to allow for reasonable passenger circulation and comfort. Furthermore, the increased passenger inflow and outflow at stations forces the designer to give the maximum consideration to door space, and the trend to more and/or larger doors per car is very noticeable in the recent development of London Transport stock, both surface and tube. Likewise, but from the point of view of passenger psychology, the designer is loth to reduce the window area.

Faced with the constraints just mentioned the designer must then endeavour to produce a structure which works as efficiently as possible with regard to both strength and stiffness, under the design loads. Weight saving is important with regard to improving the performance of a vehicle which provides a frequent stopping service with a correspondingly high ratio of acceleration to constant-speed running times. The percentage of the total weight of typical tube stock, say the 67T Victoria line trailer car, which is due to the body structure, is in the order of 27%, of which 15% is underframe and 12% body shell.

Apart from the obvious requirement of design for strength, local and overall stiffness is an important requirement. The latter is significant in deciding the overall dynamic characteristics and this is discussed further in the next chapter. But local static deflection under working load must also be kept to a minimum, as should this be excessive door opening and closing could be affected.

Essentially the conventional coach structure has developed as a heavy, stiff underframe (consisting of a solebar on each side with other longitudinal members, and transverse beams) above which there is a relatively light semi-monoque shell in which are very large door and window cutouts. Apart from having to carry the passenger, seating and equipment loads to the bogies, with the aid possibly of the body shell, the underframe has to be able to transmit the normal buffing loads when the conventional buffing and drawing gear is incorporated into the design. It has long been suspected that, because of the relatively high ratio of underframe to body shell stiffness, the shell made little contribution to the overall structural performance of the car.

The investigation to be described here was begun in early 1971 with the intention of gaining some insight into the overall structural behaviour and to explore some alternative ways the body shell might be proportioned to increase its structural contribution.

16.2   STRUCTURAL IDEALISATION AND ANALYSIS

Prior to beginning the present investigation the most sophisticated analysis carried out had concerned the design of the '67T' Victoria line stock. This had been done by Messrs Metropolitan-Cammell Ltd and

used the moment-distribution method [5]. The idealisation was two dimensional, one-half of the car being considered just as a plane framework,
in effect a Vierendeel girder with the upper chord at approximately
cantrail level and the lower chord at solebar level. The vertical members
were located at the door and window pillar locations. Little is known as
to how account was taken of the roof and side panel stiffness but it appears
that some values of cross-sectional area and second moment of area
were rather arbitrarily lumped with those of the skeletal frame. Certainly,
no attempt appears to have been made to cater for them by a proper
equivalent framework idealisation [6,7].

In deciding on the programme of work to be carried out for the present
investigation various alternatives were considered. The analyses were to
be done on the Brunel University ICL 1903A machine, which at that time
had only 32K of store. The software library for the machine included both
planeframe and spaceframe packages [8,9]. However both of these
seemed to allow for only a relatively small size of structure. In particular,
and rather surprisingly, the number of members which could be dealt with
was rather limited. This is a severe restriction when a proper equivalent
framework model is to be used, as each rectangular framework cell
requires the presence of two diagonals.

In considering the use of the finite element method two packages were
examined—PAFEC 70 [10] produced by the University of Nottingham
and NEWPAC [11] developed by British Rail at Derby. Jobs of various
complexity were run on both of these programs and, for the work in hand,
NEWPAC was selected. The choice was mainly based on the ease by which
data could be prepared for NEWPAC and then run directly. PAFEC, on
the other hand essentially consisted of a library of subroutines which
required a master segment, and input/output routines to knit them together. Although somewhat less efficient than PAFEC as regards computer
time, NEWPAC seemed that much more ready for immediate use and
was therefore purchased by the university from British Rail. It also had
within its menu of elements the referred beam, which appeared to be
necessary for the structural idealisation of the railcar.

Mainly due to the limited size of computer available at the time, the
only loading cases dealt with throughout the investigation were those due
to vertical loading, i.e. bending of the carbody between supports representing the bogie centres. Thus the two-way symmetry of the structure
in plan-view could be utilised and only one-quarter of the car needed to
be analysed. The actual values of the loads represented conditions from
tare weight through to what is known in London Transport as 'super-

crush', i.e. a factored value considering maximum number of passengers, both seated and standing. All the results given here are for 'super-crush' loading. The computer runs carried out can be summarised into five separate sections. These will be outlined in the chronological order in which they were undertaken, and will be called Test Series I to V.

16.2.1 Test Series I

As was noted earlier, prior to the start of this investigation the standard method of analysis was to idealise one-half a car into a Vierendeel type of framework and analyse this by the moment distribution method. One such analysis was done by Messrs Cravens Ltd for the 'A60' stock [12]. It was decided to reanalyse their plane-framework idealisation using the computer and then to re-idealise the stock for a three-dimensional finite element analysis using NEWPAC.

The framework model for this stock is shown in Fig. 16.7. This consists of merely 19 nodes of three degrees-of-freedom each and 22 beam elements. The loads are applied vertically downwards at the nodes of the bottom edge.

The idealisation for a proper finite element analysis is far more sophisticated. The basic mesh is shown in Fig. 16.8. There are 95 active nodes of six degrees-of-freedom each, giving 570 degrees-of-freedom in all. The number of elements is 245 of which there are four different types. These are: 'BM2' of which there are 63, which are straightforward beam elements; 'RB4' of which there are 86, which are 'referred beams', i.e. beams whose flexural axes are offset a known distance from the line of the structural nodes; 'MQ4' of which there are 48, which take into account the membrane stiffness of the skin panels; and 'BQ4' of which there are also 48, which account for their flexural stiffness.

With regard to this idealisation certain points should be noted. The version of NEWPAC which was used did not have in its library curved shell elements, and thus the curved roof of the car was considered to be made up of four flat panels over the half-width. The end-pillar of the car, being remote from the area of interest, was simply considered as a beam element spanning from node 2 to node 9. This was done to keep down the number of nodes in the structure. The beam elements were considered where there were obvious beam or stiffening members in the structure. Typical cross-sections (to various scales) are shown in Figs. 16.9 and 16.10.

The second moments of area of these sections had to be calculated relative to their principal axes, u, v, for input to the program, as had the angle θ, shown diagrammatically on the figures, which located these axes

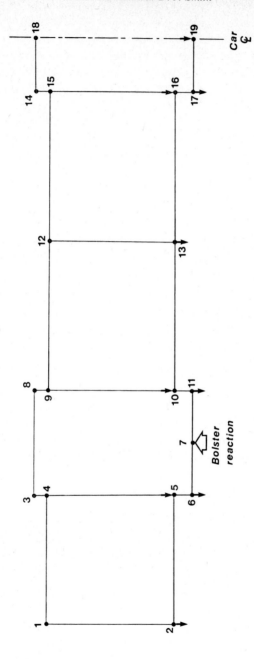

Fig. 16.7. Framework mesh for analysis of 'A60' three-door car.

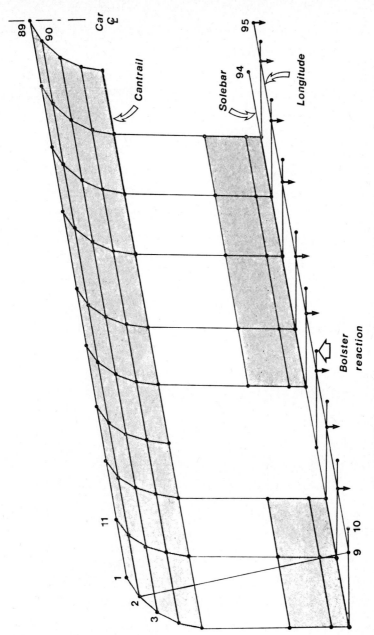

Fig. 16.8. Finite element mesh for analysis of 'A60' three-door car.

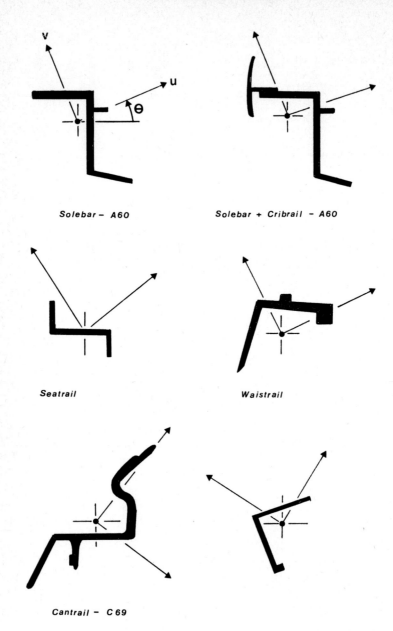

Solebar – A60

Solebar + Cribrail – A60

Seatrail

Waistrail

Cantrail – C 69

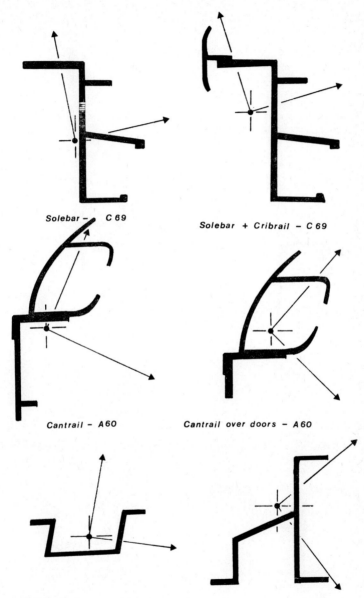

FIG. 16.9. Cross-section shapes for members in 'A60' stock structure.

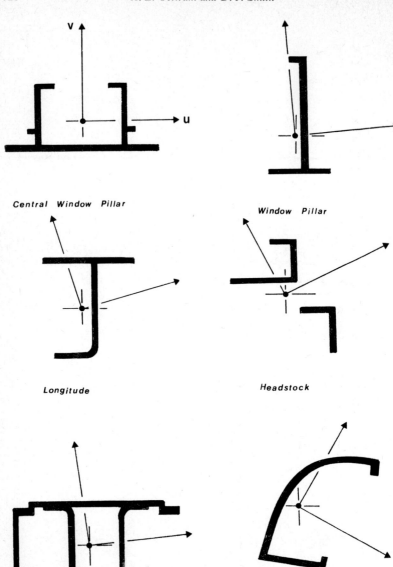

Central Window Pillar

Window Pillar

Longitude

Headstock

Bolster mid-section

Corner Pillar

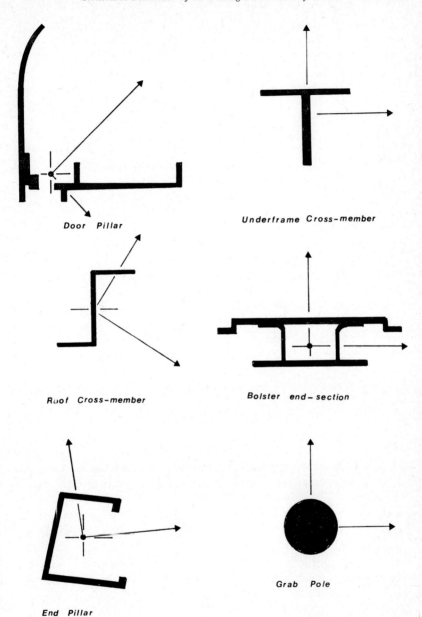

Door   Pillar

Underframe Cross-member

Roof Cross-member

Bolster end - section

End Pillar

Grab   Pole

FIG. 16.10. Cross-section shapes for members in 'A60' stock structure.

relative to the overall structural Cartesian axes. The structural nodes shown in the earlier figure were taken at the notional connecting points between the beam and panel members and thus the offset distances between these points and the axes of the beams had to be calculated. These are nodes 96 to 208 which are shown in Fig. 16.11.

These nodes do not have, of course, any effective degrees-of-freedom and hence do not contribute to the overall size of the set of equilibrium equations which is being solved.

The vertical deflection profiles are shown in Fig. 16.12. The centre-line deflection of the bottom chord by the framework idealisation is 0·671 in which falls between that of the solebar, at 0·325 in and the inner longitudinal member of the underframe, at 0·988 in, by the finite element analysis; the profiles are similar for the two methods. For the upper part of the carbody there is a distinct difference between the deflections by both methods. The framework analysis predicts a vertical deflection of 0·660 in for the upper chord at the centre-line, whereas the finite element analysis predicts 0·398 in at that position, while the centre-line of the roof actually deflects upwards over most of its length, with a value of 0·339 in at the mid-plane. For example, the change in cross-sectional profile at the position of the centre-door pillar is shown in Fig. 16.13. The profile tends to 'oval' as part of the load is transmitted upwards through the flexure of the pillars. The distortion of the shape of the door openings is similar from both analyses. These are shown to an exaggerated scale in Fig. 16.14.

In considering the stress-resultants, the bending moment distribution in the bottom chord for the framework analysis is shown with the sum of the bending moments in the solebar and longitude from the finite element analysis (Fig. 16.15). Also shown is that calculated by Cravens. The three plots follow a similar pattern (that given by Cravens did not cover the region of support at the bolster). However the large bending moments predicted by the framework idealisation half-way between the bolster and the car centre-line is not apparent in the NEWPAC distribution which shows the rather more uniform variation which would be expected from a more refined model. It is worth noting, however, that the finite element analysis shows up larger thrusts in the underframe, solebar plus longitudinal, than is given by the framework analysis, Fig. 16.16.

16.2.2   Test Series II

The 'A60' Metropolitan line car dealt with in the first tests was a three-door trailer car. The new stock for the Circle line, the 'C69', followed a

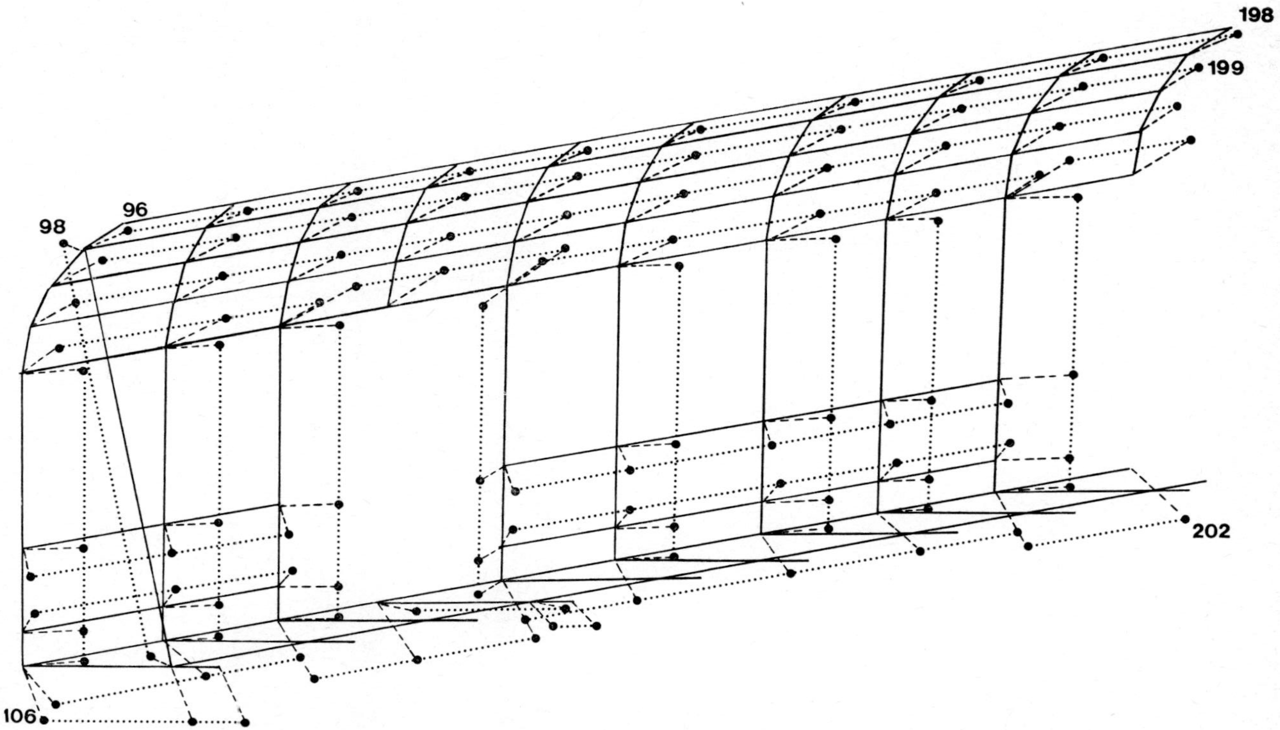

FIG. 16.11. Mesh for referred beams in finite element analysis of 'A60' three-door car.

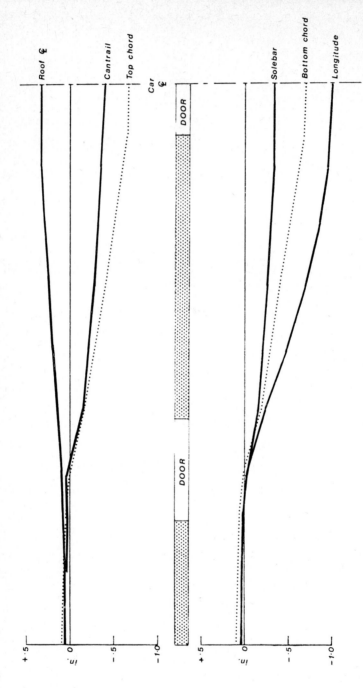

FIG. 16.12. Longitudinal deflection profiles, 'A60' three-door car. ····· framework (computer); ——— finite element.

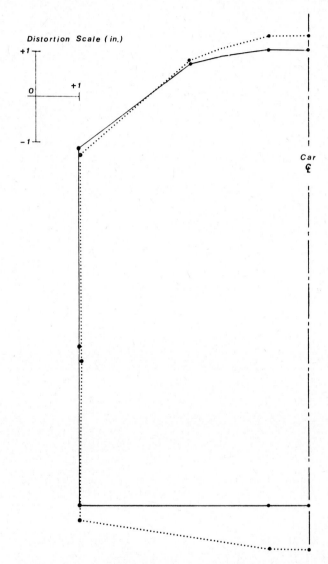

Fig. 16.13. Distortion of cross-section at centre door pillar; 'A60' three-door car.

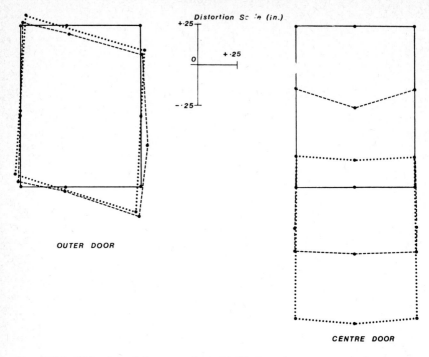

FIG. 16.14. Distortion of door openings; 'A60' three-door car. ····· framework
(computer); ——— finite element.

similar configuration, the main difference being that the latter has four-
door trailers. In order to gain some appreciation of the effect of the fourth
door opening, rather than attempt to model the 'C69' as closely as
possible, the basic 'A60' idealisation was revised to incorporate the extra
door. The section properties and overall dimensions of the structure were
kept the same wherever possible. This hypothetical design, which might
be denoted by 'A60/4', was then analysed under the same 'super-crush'
loading, and constraint conditions, as had the basic 'A60'. The mesh of
83 structural nodes is shown in Fig. 16.17, extra to which were a further
101 offset nodes for the referred beams.

The deflection profiles of the solebars, longitudes, cantrails and roof
centre-lines for the three-door and four-door 'A60' stock, with the three-
door structural properties, are shown in Fig. 16.18.

The presence of the extra door does not change the maximum centre-car
deflections inordinately. The solebar deflections are increased by 20·4%
at the centre-line, and are higher over the mid-car region, but lower

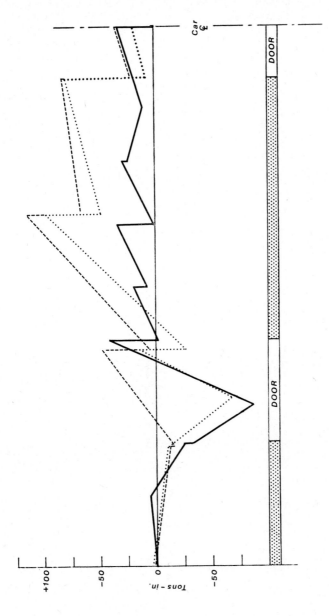

Fig. 16.15. Underframe bending moment distribution; 'A60' three-door car. ----- framework (Cravens); ····· framework (computer); ⸻ finite element.

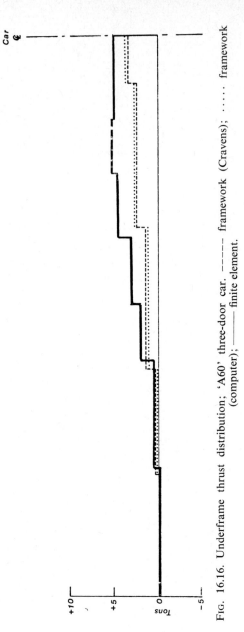

Fig. 16.16. Underframe thrust distribution; 'A60' three-door car. ----- framework (Cravens); ····· framework (computer); ——— finite element.

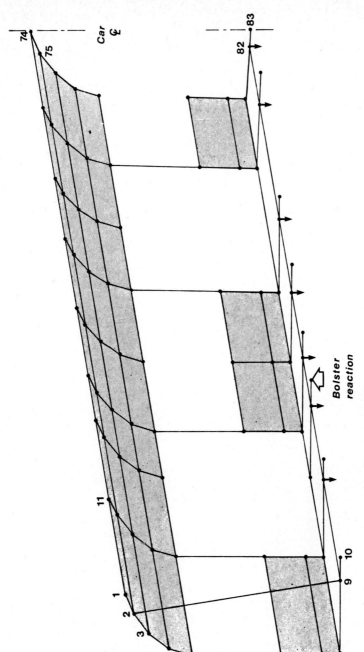

Fig. 16.17. Finite element mesh for analysis of 'A60/4' four-door car.

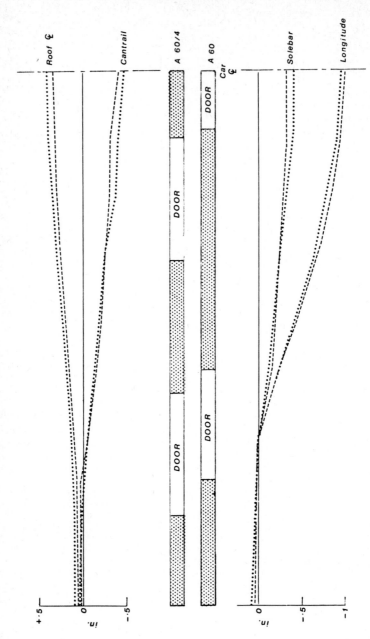

Fig. 16.18. Longitudinal deflection profiles; 'A60' and 'A60/4' cars. –––– A60; ⋯⋯ A60/4.

nearer the bolster, while the longitude deflections are generally less in the four-door case. The cantrail deflection at the centre-line is 14·4% greater but shows a reverse curve in its profile; the roof centre-line deflects generally more in the four-door than in the three-door car.

The bending moment distributions in the solebar follow similar patterns in both cases (Fig. 16.19), and as one would expect there are higher values of positive bending in the mid-car region for the four-door car, although even this is numerically lower than the larger negative bending for the three-door solebar at the bolster.

16.2.3   Test Series III

The four-door stock for the Circle line, the 'C69', was an actual development from the three-door 'A60'. The structure sizing was generally the same, except for two definite changes. In anticipation of the higher positive bending moments in the mid-car region and the higher deflection there, due to the fourth door, the solebar was increased in depth. It also transpired that, due to a change from natural to forced ventilation of the car, the cantrail had to be reduced in section.

The 'A60/4' finite element model was therefore modified according to these changes to produce a reasonable representation of a 'C69' trailer car, which will be denoted by 'A60/4C'.

Comprehensive static testing of a prototype 'C69' motor-car was carried out by Messrs Metropolitan-Cammell Ltd in 1969 [13] for various loading cases and the results from deflection and strain gauges showed that the structural performance was within the London Transport specification. Because this test was of a motor-car, and not a trailer car, i.e. it was of slightly differing dimensions and included at one end the extra door to the driver's cab, comparison of their experimental results with the 'A60/4C' finite element model must be qualified. The relevant solebar and longitude deflection profiles are shown in Fig. 16.20.

The net effect of solebar increase and cantrail reduction is generally to decrease the deflection profiles. The far greater influence of the solebar on the distortion was confirmed from analyses which treated each of these modifications separately. The average values of some of the experimental deflections are also shown on the figure. Bearing in mind the differences between the trailer-car structures as analysed and the motor-car actually tested, and also that the experimental behaviour as reported was distinctly non-symmetrical with regard to the longitudinal centre-line, there is a reasonable correlation, at least as far as order of magnitude is concerned, between the experimental and analytical results.

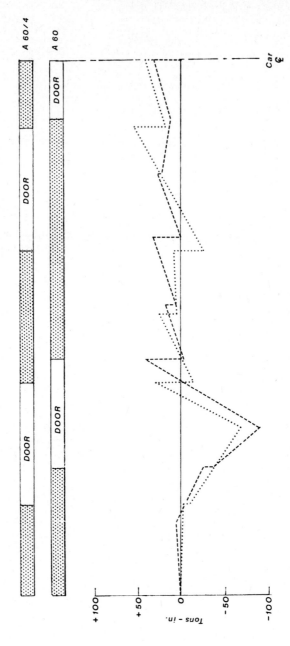

Fig. 16.19. Underframe bending moment distribution; 'A60' and 'A60/4' cars. ——— A60; ······ A60/4.

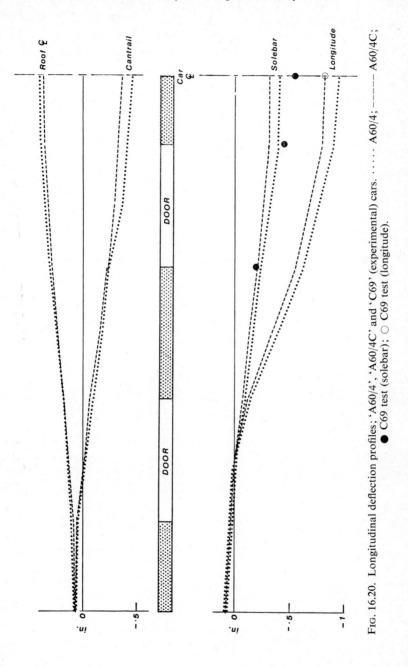

FIG. 16.20. Longitudinal deflection profiles; 'A60/4', 'A60/4C' and 'C69' (experimental) cars. ······ A60/4; ——— A60/4C; ● C69 test (solebar); ○ C69 test (longitude).

That the 'A60/4C' model is over-stiff compared with the tested 'C69' motor-car is also evident from a comparison of the distortion of the door openings (Fig. 16.21). The amount of shortening of one diagonal compares closely with the average values from the experimental tests. On the other hand, the lengthening of the other diagonals is predicted to be merely a third of the averaged test values.

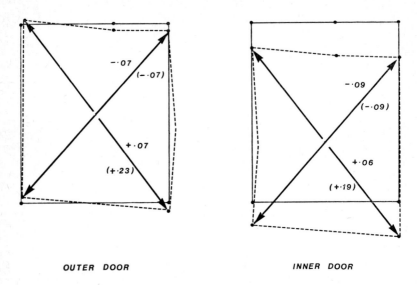

OUTER DOOR   INNER DOOR

FIG. 16.21. Distortion of door openings; 'A60/4C' car. Units, inches; test values in brackets.

The effect of increasing the solebar size has a marked effect upon the amount of bending moment which it carries. As one would expect, stiffening up this member causes the maximum bending moments, both positive and negative, to increase, in effect to double, in value (Fig. 16.22). However, the shapes of the bending moment diagrams are similar.

It is interesting that the stiffening of the solebar has not had much effect on the bending moments in the longitude, practically all the extra load which the underframe now carries being taken by the solebar itself.

16.2.4   Test Series IV

The composite action of the complete trailer car depends to a large extent on the stiffness of the structure between the roof and the underframe. This is provided by the door pillars, window pillars and end panels, as well as by any internal structure, such as vertical grab-poles, where this is

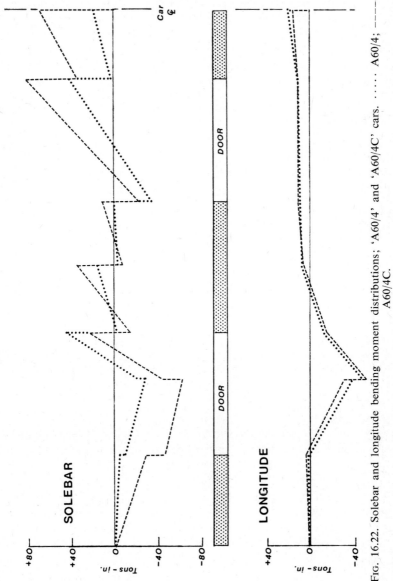

Fig. 16.22. Solebar and longitude bending moment distributions; 'A60/4' and 'A60/4C' cars. ‥‥‥ A60/4; ———— A60/4C.

present. Due to the doors being of the sliding type in all current London Transport stock, the door pillars are, in effect, split.

In the previous finite element models the pillars were treated as a composite section, with the result that the structure as a whole appeared to be somewhat over-stiff, at least as measured by the solebar deflection at mid-car. To investigate the effect of the split-door pillar, the 'A60/4C' model was modified to incorporate separate inner and outer door pillars, each as separate 'referred beam' elements, as shown diagrammatically in Fig. 16.23. This model is denoted here as 'A60/4C/D'.

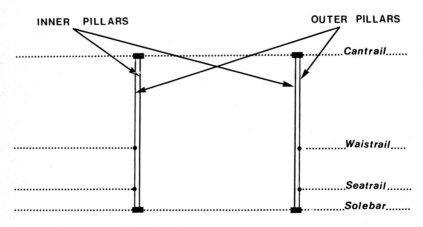

FIG. 16.23. Arrangement for separate door pillars.

The effect of this modification is marked with regard to both the deflections and the stress-resultants. From a plot of the deflection profiles (Fig. 16.24) it can be seen that the deflections are generally increased by a factor of around two, for the solebar, longitude and cantrail. The roof centre-line upward deflection is however decreased by this factor over the length of the car between the bogie centres

The plots of bending moment in the underframe (Fig. 16.25) show quite dramatically the effect of making the vertical members more flexible. The solebar bending moments in particular show a significant increase.

It might be noted here that in all of the analyses of the various models, i.e. whether three-door or four-door, larger or smaller solebar, stiffer or more flexible pillars, the end loads carried by the longitudinal members did not change significantly. This was so for both shape of distribution as well as for magnitude.

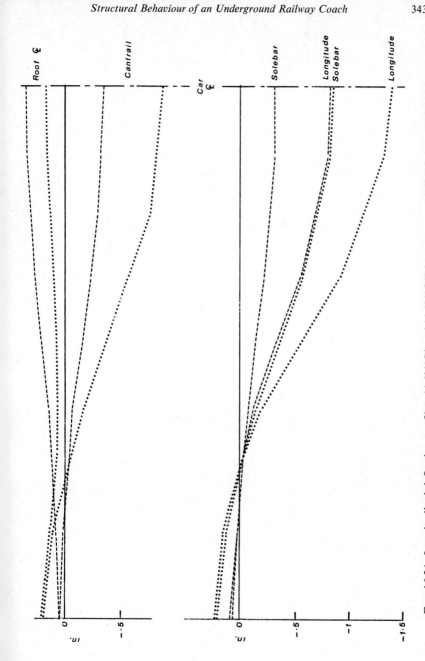

FIG. 16.24. Longitudinal deflection profiles; 'A60/4C' and 'A60/4C/D' cars. ————— A60/4C; ····· A60/4C/D.

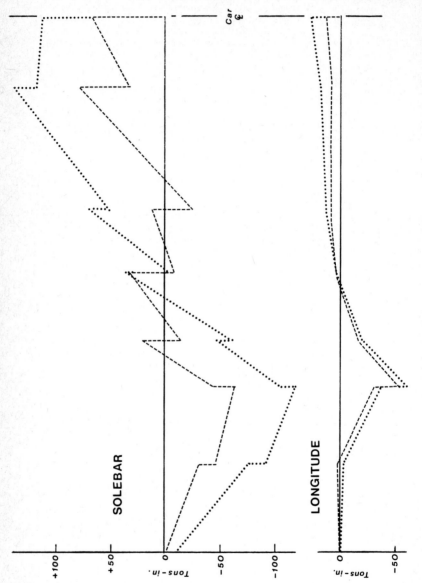

Fig. 16.25. Solebar longitude bending moment distributions; 'A60/4C' and 'A60/4C/D' cars. —— A60/4C; ······· A60/4C/D.

16.2.5 Test Series V

It became apparent that if the intention is to make the carbody work more effectively, i.e. to enable the superstructure to carry a higher proportion of the load, then, bearing in mind the 'architectural' constraints, the only possibility is to vary the member section properties and then to examine the overall effect. As a final exercise, a basic model was chosen and analysed and various quite arbitrary changes to section properties made. The datum chosen was the four-door car with original 'A60' solebar, but with the double-door pillars, denoted by 'A60/4/D'. A large number of separate variations were made and just the results of a few of these are given here. Again, the solebar deflection and bending moment curves are presented, as these are sufficient to show the trends in the overall behaviour. The notation for the various models, and the differences between them, are shown in Table 16.1.

TABLE 16.1

Model	Details
A60/4/D	A60, 4-door, A60 properties, double-door pillar
A60/4/D1	as A60/4/D except C69 (larger) solebar
A60/4C/D	as A60/4/D except C69 (larger) solebar + C69 (smaller) cantrail
A60/4/D2	as A60/4/D except double-thickness roof panels
A60/4/D3	as A60/4/D except door pillar increase (area × 4, I × 16)
A60/4/D4	as A60/4/D except door pillar further increase (area × $4\sqrt{(2)}$, I × 32)
A60/4/D5	as A60/4/D except 1 in dia grab-poles added

It must be borne in mind that the changes which were made to the basic model were quite arbitrary, in the sense that none of the practical ramifications of increasing section sizes, such as cost or practicality, were considered. One can only therefore draw generalised, qualitative conclusions from the plots of solebar deflection profile (Fig. 16.26).

It can be seen that the overall deflection can be reduced by increasing the solebar size itself, which was in fact done in developing the 'C69' from the 'A60' stock. But the same effect can be achieved, and for the sizes chosen here even more so, by stiffening the door pillars. It appears that altering the size of the roof structure, either through the cantrails or the roof panel thickness, has little effect on the deflection of the car. The addition of grab-poles into the active structure will stiffen it overall in the

A. L. Yettram and D. J. Smith

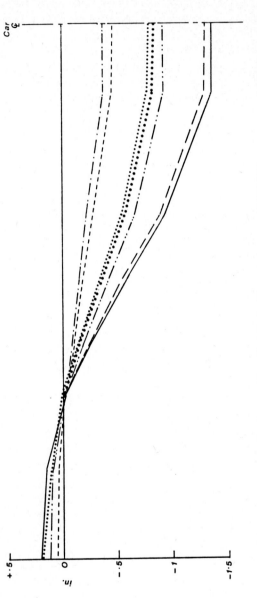

Fig. 16.26. Longitudinal deflection profiles; Test Series V, variations on 'A60/4/D' car. ——— A60/4/D; ·······
A60/4C/D; ······ A60/4/D1; ——— A60/4/D2; ——— A60/4/D3; ——— A60/4/D4; ——·— A60/4/D5.

manner of increasing pillar size, and in particular helps to stabilise the tendency of the car roof centre-line to deflect upwards.

The plots of solebar bending moment (Fig. 16.27) show the advantages of concentrating upon the door pillar sizes, if the structural designer wishes to make the best use of the carbody as a whole.

Most dramatically it can be seen that the increase in solebar size merely attracts more load to the underframe. The door pillar increase on the other hand, as well as having the desired effect in reducing deflection, as was seen in the previous figure, keeps control of the bending moments in the solebar by providing extra shear carrying capacity for the loads to be transferred to the upper parts of the structure.

16.3. GENERAL CONCLUSIONS

The structure of an underground railcar is a most complex assemblage of framework and panel members, the configuration of which is controlled by functional rather than structural considerations. As such, the finite element method is ideal for its analysis. The investigation described here was very limited in its scope. Only a very conventional current design was examined and then only statically and for one loading case. Nevertheless the analyses of the many variations of structure which were carried out, produced an enormous amount of output. Only very little of this, and for only a selection of cases, has been reported here. In summing up, however, it is perhaps possible to come to some general conclusions.

First, with regard to the finite element method itself and in particular the NEWPAC program used, the work was carried out on a machine which, at the time, had 32K of store and used four magnetic tapes as scratch files. Each of the major runs required over two hours of computer time (50 min of mill time). The package is now available on both the British Rail and the Atlas Computer Laboratory IBM computers. Also, at Brunel University work is currently going on to implement it on the ULCC CDC 7600 computer. On these newer, more advanced machines run times are dramatically less and the use of the package in a design/analyse/re-design/reanalyse context is very much more practical. Furthermore, finer meshes will be able to be used and analyses carried out which cannot take advantage of carbody symmetry. It is felt that the mesh used for the analyses described above, which simply fitted along the main skeletal components of the structure, was the minimum from which one could expect reasonable results. With regard to the idealisation, the use of the

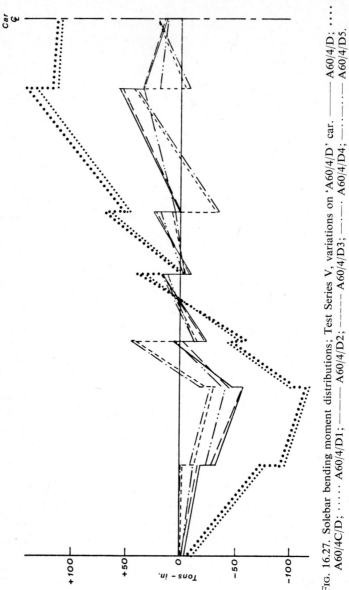

Fig. 16.27. Solebar bending moment distributions; Test Series V, variations on 'A60/4/D' car. ——— A60/4/D; · · · ·
A60/4C/D; · · · · · A60/4/D1; ——— A60/4/D2; ——— A60/4/D3; ——— A60/4/D4; · · —· · —· A60/4/D5.

referred beam element, proved to be essential for the type of structure being treated.

As far as the structural behaviour of a car is concerned, certain generalised conclusions may be made. If the ideal in railway car design is to approach the state of composite stressed-skin semi-monocoque construction, of the aircraft type, then it must always be borne in mind that certain functional factors place barriers in the way. Many of these are associated with mass-transportation stock such as that for an underground or urban system, e.g. the amount and location of doorway space, and are not met, or can be avoided, in the design of main-line stock. This is clearly seen in the advanced passenger train designed by British Rail.

Nevertheless there may well be scope in attempting to produce a design with that goal in mind. However it would of necessity require fairly radical departures from current practice. This would apply both with regard to detail (for example the use of 'plug' rather than 'sliding' doors in order that more structural use can be made of integral door pillars, or a change of design of internal screens so that they can have a structural role to play), as well as more general concepts (such as a complete change of the buffing and drawing gear so that inter-car buffing loads are carried around the car profile and hence avoid, at least for that reason, the need for the heavy underframe).

That the need for continuing research and development work in the field of underground train carbody design is fully appreciated by London Transport Executive, is perhaps best expressed by their having recently set up the new Dynamics Section within the Design Division of the Chief Mechanical Engineers Department. Some of the work of the section is described in the next chapter.

ACKNOWLEDGEMENTS

The authors would like to thank Mr Bingham, former Chief Mechanical Engineer, and Mr S. A. Driver, Chief Draughtsman for London Transport Executive, for their assistance and encouragement.

REFERENCES

1. Day, J. R. (1963). *The Story of London's Underground*, London Transport Executive.
2. Bruce, J. G. (1970). *Steam to Silver*, London Transport Executive.

3. Bruce, J. G. (1968). *Tube Trains Under London*, London Transport Executive.
4. Driver, S. A. (1970). 'Design of Railway Rolling Stock for Heavy Urban Service', Proc. Conf. on Rapid Transit Vehicles for City Services (Paris, November 1970), Inst. of Mech. Engrs, London.
5. Metropolitan-Cammell Ltd. 'Design Study for Railway Rolling Stock for Victoria Line' (Sept. 1963), private communication to London Transport Board.
6. Yettram, A. L. and Husain, H. M. (1965). Grid-framework method for plates in flexure, *J. Eng. Mechs Divn*, ASCE, June.
7. Yettram, A. L. and Husain, H. M. (1966). Plane-framework methods for plates in extension, *J. Eng. Mechs Divn*, ASCE, Feb.
8. ICL. 'Analysis of Plane Frames and Grids', User Manual No. TP4178.
9. ICL. 'Analysis of Space Frames', User Manual No. TP4220.
10. Henshell, R. D., 'Pafec 70', Dept. of Mechanical Engineering, University of Nottingham.
11. Lythgoe, W. F. *et al.*, 'NEWPAC—Mark I, A Guide to the Newpac Program for Structural Analysis using the Finite Element Method', British Rail, Engineering Research Divn, Derby.
12. Cravens Ltd. 'Analysis of A60 Stock', private communication to London Transport Board.
13. Metropolitan-Cammell Ltd. 'LTT.B. C69 Surface Stock. Structural Testing of Prototype, Motor Car,' Report T33, October 1969, private communication to London Transport Board.

17

Application of the Finite Element Technique to the Structural Analysis of Road and Rail Vehicles at London Transport

H. HILLEL, J. SAYER AND R. A. PHIPPS
London Transport Executive

SUMMARY

The structures of road and rail vehicles being used by London Transport are of conventional design. Road vehicles consist of a separate body and chassis, the main structural members being steel and the skin panels being aluminium. Underground rolling stock, because of the constraints imposed on shape, size and interior layout, are of 'tubular construction' and in most stocks consist of an aluminium roof and bodyside, with large openings for windows and doors, mounted on a heavy steel underframe.

The structural design of these vehicles has been the responsibility of the carbuilders and has been based on traditional stress analysis techniques consisting, in the main, of equivalent framework type analyses and relying heavily on past experience. Recently, however, London Transport has been taking a greater involvement in the design of these vehicles and there has been a departure from the conventional designs.

An emphasis on light weight has meant the use of aluminium throughout the vehicles and there is a tendency towards a more integral type of structure (as opposed to separate body and chassis) in the case of road vehicles. This departure from conventionality has led to the need for a more refined stress analysis technique. An investigation into the structural behaviour of an underground railway coach (Chapter 16) has shown that the finite element technique is superior to the other techniques in predicting stresses and deflections.

The Dynamics Section which has recently been set up within the Design Division of the Chief Mechanical Engineer's Department at London Transport, has been applying the finite element technique to analysing bus and railway coach structures (including wheels) and to the calculation of the natural frequencies of these structures. The computer program used is the NEWPAC package developed by the engineering Research Division of British Rail at Derby, the computation being performed at Derby on the IBM 370 computer. The computation facilities include an input/output graphical display which enables data checking and presentation.

This paper describes the analyses of an underground structure (including natural frequencies) and a bus structure for various load cases, and is intended as a sequel to Chapter 16.

17.1   INTRODUCTION

The structures of London Transport's road and rail vehicles employ various types of construction and materials. Road vehicles (buses) in the

1950s employed an integral type of construction consisting of a steel front suspension unit (carrying the engine) and a steel rear suspension unit (carrying the final drive assembly), with both units connected to the aluminium body structure (Fig. 17.1). The later 'grant standard' buses have a chassis with a separate body. (Fig. 17.2).

Fig. 17.1. Routemaster bus.

Underground railway rolling stock comprises two basic types, known as surface stock (Fig. 17.3) and tube stock (Fig. 17.4). Both stocks consist of an underframe connected to a body framework to which is riveted the exterior body panelling. Large openings for doorways and windows are present. On surface stock, the larger of the two types of vehicles, aluminium has been employed throughout since the early 1950s, with the exception of certain underframe members. On tube stock, the underframe is in steel and since the mid-1950s the body panelling has been in aluminium with either a steel, or more recently, aluminium, body framework.

The structural analysis of these vehicles has been the responsibility of the carbuilders and has been based on traditional stress analysis techniques consisting, in the main, of equivalent framework-type analyses and relying heavily on past experience. Recently, however, London Transport

FIG. 17.2. DMS bus.

has been taking a greater involvement in the analysis of these vehicles and more advanced methods of analysis are being used to examine the effects of departures from existing designs.

This is of extreme importance if weight reductions are being sought in the structure design and it is important that the structure is correctly optimised for weight and stress before any fatigue testing is undertaken. An investigation into the structural behaviour of an underground railway

FIG. 17.3. A60 surface stock.

FIG. 17.4. 1959 tube stock.

coach has shown that the finite element technique is superior to the other techniques in predicting stresses and deflections.

The Dynamics Group, which has recently been set up within the Design Division of the Chief Mechanical Engineer's Department at London Transport, has been applying the finite element technique to analyse bus and railway coach structures and to calculate the natural frequencies of these structures. The computer program used is the NEWPAC package [1], developed by the Engineering Research Division of British Rail at Derby, the computation being performed at Derby on an IBM 370 computer.

A number of bus and railway coach structures have been analysed to date, but to present them all is outside the scope of this paper. In Chapter 16, Yettram and Smith describe the analysis of a surface stock carbody under static vertical load. This paper presents the analysis of a tube stock carbody under vertical load and under buffing load, and the calculation of its natural frequencies. In order to highlight the versatility of the finite element technique in dealing with large problems, the paper also presents the analysis of a proposed double-deck bus under static vertical load.

17.2. BRIEF DESCRIPTION OF THE ANALYSIS PROCEDURE USED IN NEWPAC

Reference 1 describes a user's guide to NEWPAC. Briefly the analysis procedure involves the following steps:

1. The idealisation of structure under consideration as a number of elements (members), connected at nodes (joints). The movements of

each node are defined in terms of displacements (both linear and rotational).

2. The specification of this idealisation (as nodal coordinates and element properties) and also of the loading and constraints imposed on the structure in a form suitable to the computer. This is done on specially designed 'input' data sheets.

3. The computer analysis itself. The input information is used to calculate the relationships between the forces on each element and the displacements of its connecting nodes. These relationships are called 'element stiffness matrices' and are used for setting up simultaneous equations which, in matrix notation, can be represented as

$$\{P\} = [K]\{d\} \tag{17.1}$$

where $\{d\}$ is the vector (set) of the unknown nodal displacements and $\{P\}$ the vector of the loads applied at the nodes. The matrix $[K]$ is referred to as the 'assembled stiffness matrix' since all the forces on all the elements as assembled into the complete structure are taken into account. The stress/displacement characteristics of each element are also generated in the computer. This may be expressed in matrix form as

$$\{S\} = [F]\{d\} \tag{17.2}$$

where $\{S\}$ is the vector of stresses and $[F]$ the 'stress matrix'. The loads $\{P\}$ are given and the computer determines the displacements from eqn (17.1) and then calculates the stresses for each element from eqn (17.2).

4. A reappraisal stage, which, when applied to design, should be the assessment of the computer output to see whether any changes in the elements are required.

The elements available in the NEWPAC library include a variety of beam and panel elements. A description of some of the elements is given in Table 17.1. The program allows a variety of loading inputs, which include point loads, uniformly distributed loads (on beams) and pressure loads (on panels). The program provides a facility for constraining displacements, which in addition to allowing rigid constraints also permits the displacement of a degree of freedom to be constrained, so that it is a linear function of the displacements of other degrees of freedom. If requested the program will calculate fibre stresses for beam elements and if the relevant data is supplied it will calculate the natural frequencies of the structure.

TABLE 17.1

Some of the elements from NEWPAC

Code	Description	Displacement variation	Stiffness terms/node
Beam elements			
EL2	End-load element	Linear	1 translation
BM2	Bending beam with shear, torsion and end-load	Cubic bending, linear torsion and end-load	3 translation, 3 rotation
RB4	Referred beam (2 active nodes)	BM2 with offsets	3 translation, 3 rotation
BM4	Four mode beam (4 active nodes) neutral axis bisects each pair of nodes	Derived from BM2	2 translation
Panel elements (*in-plane stiffness only*)			
WR4	Web rectangle	Quadratic	2 translation
MT3	Membrane triangle	Linear (uniform strain)	2 translation
MQ4	Membrane quadrilateral	Derived from MT3	2 translation
Bending panel elements			
BR4	Bending rectangle	Cubic	1 translation, 2 rotation
BT3	Bending triangle	Quadratic	1 translation, 2 rotation
BQ4	Bending quadrilateral	Derived from BT3	1 translation, 2 rotation

Limitations on problem size are determined by the maximum displacement number difference (semi-bandwidth) of the assembled stiffness matrix. The semi-bandwidth determines the partition size required on the IBM 370 computer and the computation time, and by judicious numbering of the active nodes of the structure these can be minimised.

The computation facilities at Derby include an interactive graphics unit which facilitates data preparation and checking. Results can also be saved and retrieved at a later date so that combinations of load cases can be taken. If required, a graph plotter is available to obtain a graphical output to the results.

17.3   ANALYSIS OF A TUBE STOCK CARBODY

This chapter describes the static and dynamic analysis of a tube stock car which was a design proposed by Metro Cammell Ltd, for the Fleet line. Load gauge constraints, i.e. tunnel size, impose severe restrictions on the size and shape of the car and these have a significant influence on the design of the structure [2]. A brief description of the structure is given in Section 17.3.1.

17.3.1   Static Analysis

(a) Brief description of the structure

Figure 17.5 and 17.6 show the basic structure of a tube stock carbody, comprising bodyside, roof and underframe. The bodyside consists of a framework of vertical members (pillars) at various positions along the length of the car, which run from the underframe to the roof, and longitudinal members (crib rail, waist rail, cantrail and header rail) at various heights. The crib rail connects the bodyside to the underframe, whilst

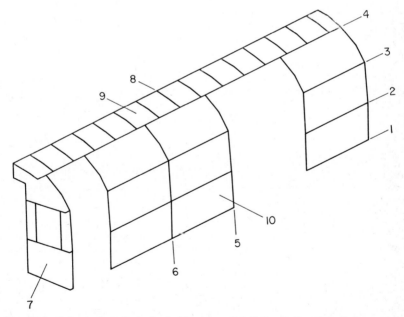

FIG. 17.5. Tube stock carbody, bodyside and roof. 1, Crib rail; 2, waist rail; 3, cantrail; 4, header rail; 5, door pillar; 6, body pillar; 7, end face; 8, carline; 9, roof panel; 10, body panel.

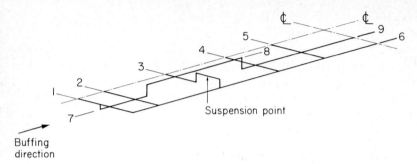

Fig. 17.6. Tube stock carbody underframe. 1, Headstock; 2, buffing beam; 3, bolster; 4, crossbar; 5, crossbar; 6, solebar; 7, buffing longitude; 8, seat riser; 9, centre longitude.

the waist rail and cantrail run below and above the windows, respectively; all three of these being absent in the doorway regions. The header rail connects the bodyside to the roof and runs the length of the car. Large cut-outs for doorways and windows are present in the bodyside, the remaining area being filled in with body skin panelling. The roof consists of skin panelling with transverse stiffeners (carlines) at various positions along the car length.

Because of the low height and curved profile of the cars (which is dictated by load gauge constraints), the pillars and the doorway openings curve into the roof with the result that the roof/bodyside connection (header rail) lies out of the main vertical plane of the bodyside. This, together with the large doorway and window openings, diminishes the structural effectiveness of the bodyside in vertical bending. (The bodyside does, however, provide shear stiffness.) Thus the underframe must provide the stiffness in vertical bending and as a result is very heavy.

The underframe consists of four main longitudinal members which run the entire length of the car and are connected at various positions along the car length by a number of crossmembers, comprising the headstocks (at the car ends), buffing beams, bolsters (above the bogies) and crossbars. The two outer longitudes are called solebars and are connected to the bodyside via the crib rail. The two inner longitudes are of varying section and height and consist of a buffing longitude (between the headstock and buffing beam) below floor level which then rises via a suitable transition piece to form the seat riser (which supports the longitudinal seats) above floor level to clear the bogie; the level then drops (before the centre doorway) via a suitable transition piece to form the centre longitude which is again below floor level.

This particular stock was designed with the emphasis on lightweight carbodies. Thus, the entire carbody was to be made from aluminium with the underframe being of all welded construction and body and roof framing being of riveted construction. This is a departure from existing designs where the body framing is made from aluminium and the underframe is made of steel.

The idealisation is described below. Three load cases are considered: two vertical load cases and a buffing load case. Since the underframe is the main departure from existing designs and since it is the main load-bearing part of the structure for the above load cases, the emphasis in the idealisation and discussion of results is on the underframe, particularly the solebars and centre longitudes.

(b) Idealisation

Figure 17.7 shows the idealised grid for the structure. The structure is symmetrical about its longitudinal and transverse centrelines so that only a quarter of the car was considered (this has the advantage of reducing the size and cost of the analysis). The other three-quarters of the car was represented by suitable symmetry constraints in the planes of symmetry (these constraints could be symmetric or anti-symmetric depending on the load case in question). For the load cases considered here, only the symmetric/symmetric constraints in the planes of symmetry were required, i.e. the translation degree of freedom normal to the plane of symmetry and the two rotational degrees of freedom about the axes parallel to the plane of symmetry. In addition to the above constraints the vertical degree of freedom at the suspension point (at the bolster between solebar and seat riser) was constrained so as to prevent rigid body motion.

In the idealisation (Fig. 17.7), the basic framework of the structure was represented by beam elements whilst the body and roof skin was represented by panel elements. Thus the entire underframe (consisting of solebar and crib rail, inner longitude, headstock, buffing beam, bolster and crossbars), the body framework (consisting of waist rail, cantrail, header rail, door pillars and body pillars), and roof framework (consisting of carlines and longitudinal panel stiffeners) were represented as beams. The RB4 beam element was used for the representations; this element has the facility that the nodes on the beam neutral axis (beam nodes) need not be coincident with the structure nodes but are connected to them via rigid offsets. This facility was particularly useful at junctions between beams whose neutral axes did not intersect (e.g. bolster to solebar or inner longitude connection and pillar to solebar connection) or connections

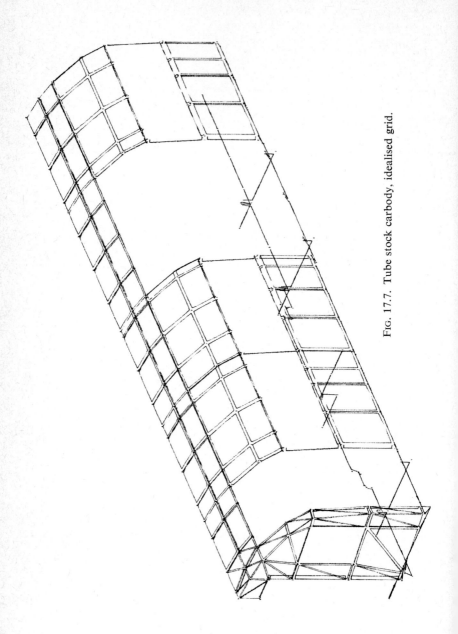

FIG. 17.7. Tube stock carbody, idealised grid.

between beams and panel edges (e.g. solebar to body skin panel connection), where the structure nodes (of necessity) were at the panel edges but the neutral axes of the beams were not.

Membrane elements (elements possessing in-plane stiffness only) were used to represent the skin panelling. Wherever possible, WR4 elements were used (i.e. where the geometry of the idealisation permitted the use of rectangular elements), otherwise MT3 (triangular) elements were used. Thus the complete bodyside panelling and roof panelling were represented by WR4 elements, whereas the panelling on the end face was represented by MT3 elements. Since the flexural stiffness of the skin was small this was not represented in the idealisation.

As an indication of the size of the problem, the idealisation used here consisted of approximately 180 active nodes, together with 200 RB4 elements, 72 WR4 elements and 24 MT3 elements. The semi-bandwidth in this case was 78.

As previously mentioned, three load cases were considered: two vertical load cases and a buffing load case. These cases are the most important as regards the structure as a whole and are consistent with the symmetric/symmetric constraints for the quarter-car idealisation. The two vertical load cases considered were the tare case, consisting of structure plus equipment weight, and the crush load case consisting of structure plus equipment plus full passenger load. The total vertical load in the crush load case was 6.71×10^4 N for the quarter-car. This is equivalent to 26.84×10^4 N for the whole car and includes 12×10^4 N of passenger weight. Point loading was used, all the load being applied to the underframe nodes; i.e. the bodyside and roof framework and panelling weight was applied to the solebar nodes, whilst the underframe weight was apportioned appropriately to the relevant nodes. The equipment weight was apportioned to the nodes encompassing the equipment bays, whilst passenger loading was apportioned to the relevant nodes to account for seated and standing passengers.

The buffing load was applied mainly to the headstock at the buffer position, with the small remainder being applied to the buffing longitude at the drawgear connection. The magnitudes of the loads for the quarter-car were 21×10^4 N at the buffer/headstock connection and 4×10^4 N, plus an appropriate moment (since the drawgear axis is offset from the longitude axis), at the drawgear/buffing longitude connection. This is equivalent to a buffing load of 50×10^4 N for the whole car and represents a compression of the carbody under a severe buff.

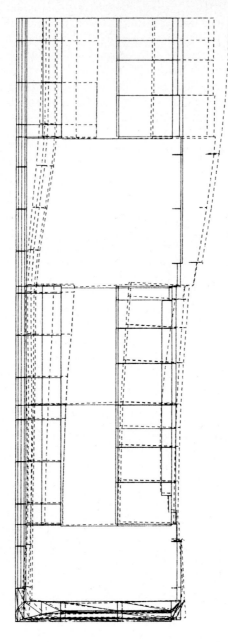

FIG. 17.8. Tube stock carbody, deflection for crush load.

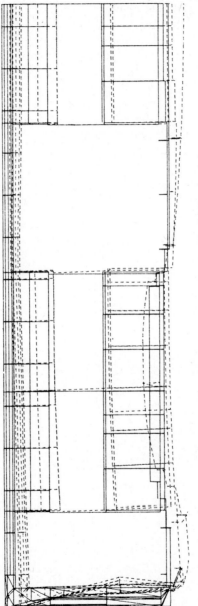

FIG. 17.9. Tube stock carbody, deflection for buffing load.

(c) Results

This section presents the results of the static analysis, the emphasis being on the underframe, particularly the deflections of the solebar and the centre longitude. Two computer runs were performed. For the first run, large displacements (particularly for the centre longitude) and as a result large stresses were predicted, which suggested that the flexural stiffness of the underframe should be increased. A proposed modification to the underframe increased substantially the flexural stiffness of the centre longitude. Only the results for the second configuration are presented.

Figures 17.8 and 17.9 show the deflected shape of the bodyside and solebar for the crush load and buffing load cases, respectively. These were produced by the British Rail graph plotter. The vertical deflections of the solebar and inner longitude for the three load cases are shown in Figs. 17.10 and 17.11. These show that the greatest change in deflection occurs

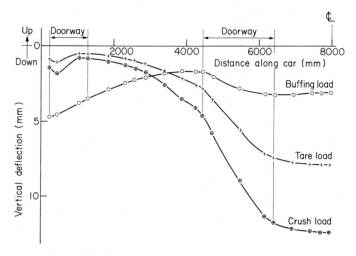

FIG. 17.10. Tube stock carbody, deflection of solebar.

across the doorway regions. The numerical values of the deflections for vertical load compare well with measured values (obtained by Metro Cammell Ltd) on other tube stocks which have steel underframes. These are presented in Table 17.2.

Predicted stress levels throughout the structure were acceptable. The allowable fatigue stress level of 45 N/mm² was not exceeded, except in a few localised areas, for the crush load case. A factor of 1·3 was imposed on stress results to cater for dynamic overloads. Stresses in the skin were

TABLE 17.2

Comparison of vertical deflections for various tube stocks

	Vertical deflections (mm)								
	Solebar at centre			Centre longitude at centre			Solebar across middle door		
	Tare	Crush load	Tare to crush load	Tare	Crush load	Tare to crush load	Tare	Crush load	Tare to crush load
Proposed tube stock aluminium underframe[a]	7·9	12·3	4·4	9·7	15·8	6·1	4·59	7·26	2·67
1973 tube stock[a]	8·6	13·5	4·9	7·8	13·2	5·4	4·07	6·09	2·02
steel underframe[b]	8·6	12·5	3·9						
1967 tube stock steel underframe[b]	4·9	10·3	5·4						

[a] Predicted values by finite element method.
[b] Measured values.

generally low, being of the order of 20 N/mm² for direct stress and 12 N/mm² for shear stress. Stress levels for the buffing load case (which is an ultimate load case) were well within the allowable ultimate tensile stress for the grade of material being considered.

(d) Comments on the static analysis

The fineness of the idealisation was consistent with the available data on the structure at that stage of the design. The analysis helped to highlight necessary changes in the initial design and subsequently verify that the modified design was of adequate strength. The stiffness of the structure, as evidenced by the vertical deflection of the solebar and inner longitude, was comparable to that of existing tube stock structures with steel underframes. The stiffness affects the natural frequencies and mode shapes of the structure and the calculation of these is described in Section 17.3.2.

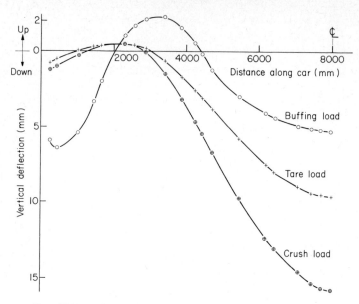

FIG. 17.11. Tube stock carbody, deflection of inner longitude.

17.3.2 Dynamic Analysis

(a) Introduction

This section is concerned with the prediction of the natural frequencies and mode shapes of the structure whose static analysis is described in Section 17.3.1. These data are required for incorporation in a dynamic model, including both suspension and carbody parameters, for the determination of ride characteristics of the car.

(b) The analysis method

The program used was the dynamics version of NEWPAC, the statics version of which was used for the static analyses presented in this paper. The structure stiffness matrix for a dynamic analysis is formed in the same way as that for a static analysis, but a lumped mass matrix is also formed, After constraining the idealisation to account for symmetry conditions, etc., mass condensation is carried out to reduce the size of the resulting eigen solution problem. The primary degrees of freedom, which are those remaining after condensation, are specified by the user; degrees of freedom exhibiting high kinetic energies should be chosen. All the eigenvalues and eigenvectors for the reduced system are found; these correspond to the natural frequencies and normalised mode shapes, respectively. The complete normalised mode shapes, including the displacements of all the original degrees of freedom, may be found by back substitution. Graph plots of the mode shapes may be produced if required.

(c) Idealisation

The idealisation used for the dynamic analysis was basically similar to that for which the static results were presented (see Section 17.3.1), but minor modifications were made to take account of the different conditions obtaining dynamically. One modification comprised the addition of elements to model stiffnesses which would be of little significance under static load, but which would restrain certain deflection patterns which might otherwise be expected to occur dynamically, e.g. the grab poles in the passenger compartment. Another modification was the replacement of rigid constraints at the support points by low stiffness elements to model the suspension springs.

In addition to the modifications to the modelling of the stiffness of the structure, a model of the inertia of the structure was prepared. This model consisted of point masses at all the structure nodes, representing the distribution of mass of the structure and its attached equipment. Passenger mass was not included, since it was considered that the passengers would be effectively isolated, dynamically, from the structure.

Only one-quarter of the car was idealised, thus symmetry constraints were required. With both symmetric and anti-symmetric constraints possible in each of the two planes of symmetry, the longitudinal and transverse planes through the centroid of the car, four symmetry conditions were possible. All four conditions were analysed dynamically, whereas only the symmetric/symmetric condition was considered in the static analysis.

The use of symmetric or anti-symmetric constraints affects the expected pattern of distribution of kinetic energy in a structure, and hence affects the choice of primary degrees of freedom for mass condensation; thus separate choices were made for the different symmetry conditions. For conditions symmetric about the longitudinal plane of symmetry, 49 primary freedoms were chosen; these consisted of vertical freedoms in the solebar, floor longitude and header rail, and transverse freedoms in the cantrail and waist rail. The positions of the various longitudinal members are illustrated in Figs. 17.5 and 17.6. For conditions anti-symmetric about the longitudinal plane of symmetry, 58 primary freedoms were chosen, consisting of vertical freedoms in the solebar and cantrail, and transverse freedoms in the solebar, floor longitude, header rail and waist rail. The total number of unconstrained freedoms in the structure was 875 for conditions symmetric about the longitudinal plane of symmetry, and 870 for the anti-symmetric conditions. The degree of condensation was thus very severe, to 5·6% and 6·7% of total unconstrained freedoms, respectively, for conditions symmetric and anti-symmetric about the longitudinal plane.

(d) Results

Table 17.3 gives the predicted free–free flexural natural frequencies of the car up to 20 Hz, together with brief descriptions of the corresponding mode shapes. Figures 17.12–17.17 show the deflected shape for each predicted natural frequency up to 15 Hz, superimposed on isometric plots of the structure grid; the appropriate figure numbers for the modes are given in Table 17.3.

The predicted flexural modes include those involving motion of the car structure as a composite beam, for example longitudinal and lateral bending, and torsion, and those involving distortion of the cross-section, for example transverse bending, breathing and lozenging. (Breathing modes occur when the floor and roof move towards each other while the two sides move apart; lozenging modes occur when one solebar and the cantrail on the opposite side of the car move towards each other, while the other solebar and cantrail move apart.)

TABLE 17.3

Proposed tube stock carbody with aluminium underframe predicted free–free flexural vibration modes

Frequency (Hz)	Mode shape description	Figure no.
6·93	2nd lateral bending	17.12
7·56	1st lateral bending	17.13
9·07	1st longitudinal vertical bending	17.14
10·76	1st torsion	17.15
13·31	1st lozenging	17.16
14·91	2nd longitudinal vertical bending	17.17
16·73	3rd lateral bending	—
18·45	3rd longitudinal vertical bending	—
18·48	2nd lozenging	—
18·81	3rd lateral bending + local lateral breathing (at car centre)	—

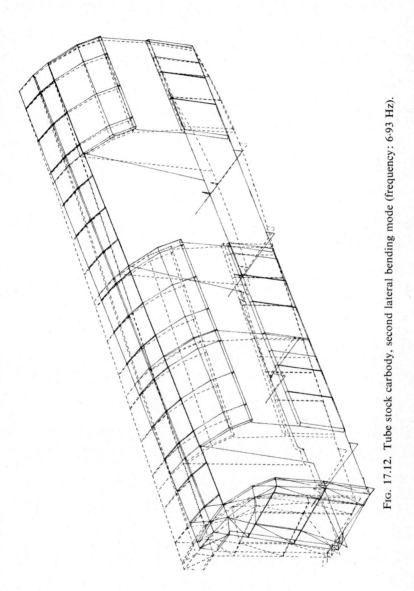

FIG. 17.12. Tube stock carbody, second lateral bending mode (frequency: 6·93 Hz).

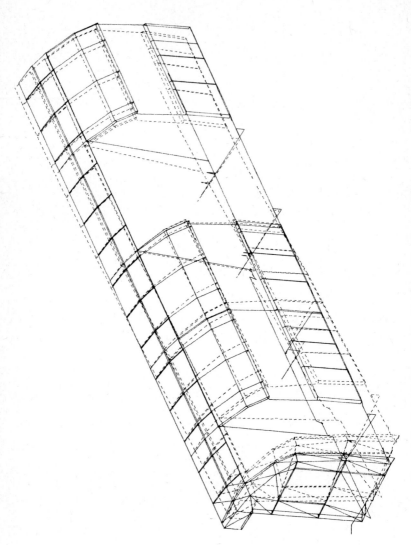

Fig. 17.13. Tube stock carbody, first lateral bending mode (frequency: 7·56 Hz.)

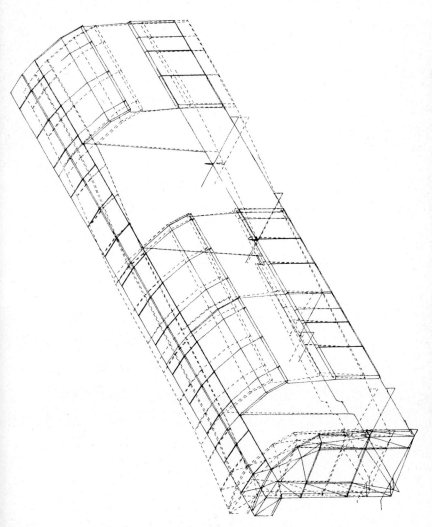

FIG. 17.14. Tube stock carbody, first vertical bending mode (frequency: 9·07 Hz).

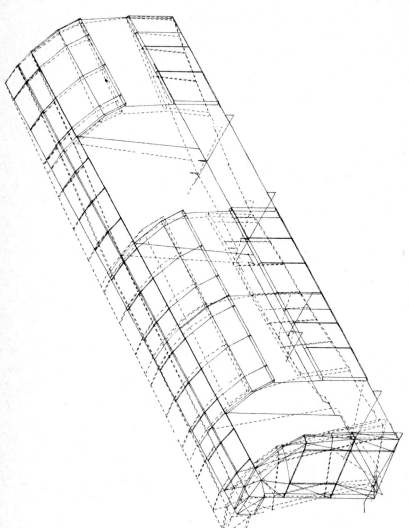

Fig. 17.15. Tube stock carbody, first torsion mode (frequency: 10·76 Hz).

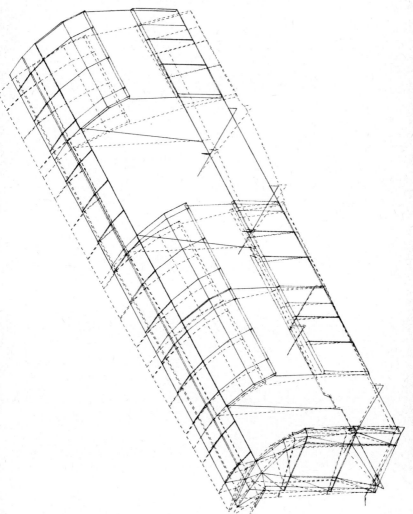

FIG. 17.16. Tube stock carbody, first lozenging mode (frequency: 13·31 Hz).

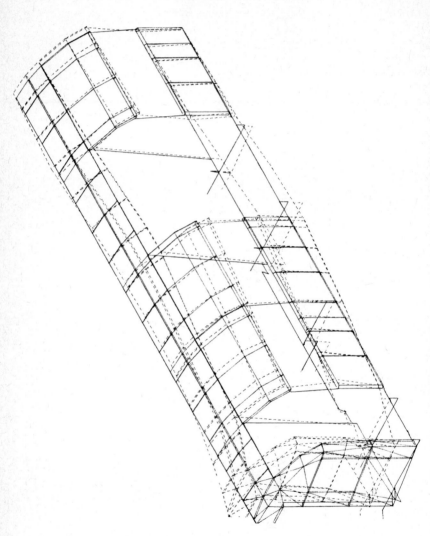

Fig. 17.17. Tube stock carbody, second vertical bending mode (frequency 14·91 Hz).

Neither the stiffness distribution nor the mass distribution along the length of a tube car is uniform, thus the positions of the nodes of the bending modes do not correspond with positions calculated assuming uniform beam bending; a comparison illustrating the differences for the first three vertical and lateral bending modes is given in Table 17.4. The differences are significant, for example the finite element prediction puts the nodes of the first vertical bending mode 1·70 m from the bogie centres, compared to 0·71 m predicted by uniform beam bending. The coupling between bogie bounce and primary vertical bending of the carbody will therefore be very much greater if the finite element prediction is taken than if the uniform beam theory prediction is taken.

It should also be noted that the ratios between the predicted frequencies of bending modes of increasing order do not correspond with the values

TABLE 17.4

Proposed tube stock carbody with aluminium underframe predicted nodal positions

Mode	Nodal positions distance from car end (m)		Distance between finite element and uniform beam nodal positions (m)
	Finite element predictions	Uniform beam predictions	
1st longitudinal	4·57	3·58	0·99
vertical bending	11·42	12·41	−0·99
2nd longitudinal	1·87	2·11	−0·24
vertical bending	7·995	7·995	0·000
	14·12	13·88	0·24
3rd longitudinal	1·49	1·51	−0·02
vertical bending	6·97	5·69	1·28
	9·02	10·30	−1·28
	14·50	14·48	0·02
1st lateral bending	4·25	3·58	0·67
	11·74	12·41	−0·67
2nd lateral bending	1·90	2·11	−0·21
	7·995	7·995	0·000
	14·09	13·88	0·21
3rd lateral bending	1·67	1·51	0·16
	6·44	5·69	0·75
	9·55	10·30	−0·75
	14·32	14·48	−0·16

for free–free vibration of a uniform beam; the frequencies are very much less widely spaced. Indeed, the frequencies of the first and second lateral bending modes are reversed (i.e. the second has the lower frequency), although very close in value. This apparent anomaly arises because the high lateral bending stiffness of the roof is dominant in the primary mode, and the lower lateral bending stiffness of the floor is dominant in the secondary mode.

(e) Comments on the dynamic analysis

The condensation employed in the solution was very severe; this will have implications for the accuracy of the predictions of both the mode shapes and the corresponding natural frequencies. The better the chosen primary freedoms are capable of describing the mode shape, the more accurate the results for that mode can be expected to be. Thus the accuracy of the higher order modes, or of local modes, may be less than that of the low order modes involving the whole structure.

Zero damping was assumed in the solution. Although the damping inherent in the structure would be low, the damping due to trim and equipment mountings could be significant. One effect of such damping could be to modify the mode shapes by limiting high amplitudes, especially in low stiffness regions.

Composite beam modes and cross-section distortion modes were both predicted in the low frequency range, which is of interest as regards track inputs, with the frequencies closely spaced over much of the range. Thus a number of modes of structural vibration may be excited by track inputs and, in this connection, modes in addition to the primary longitudinal vertical bending, primary lateral bending and primary torsion modes may be significant.

17.4. STATIC ANALYSIS OF A PROPOSED DOUBLE-DECKER BUS

17.4.1 The Design

This bus is a double-deck eight-wheeled bus currently being designed by London Transport. The structure is fundamentally different from that of any previous LT bus and for this reason it is inadvisable to rely heavily on past practice in estimating stresses. Thus finite element analysis can be used with advantage.

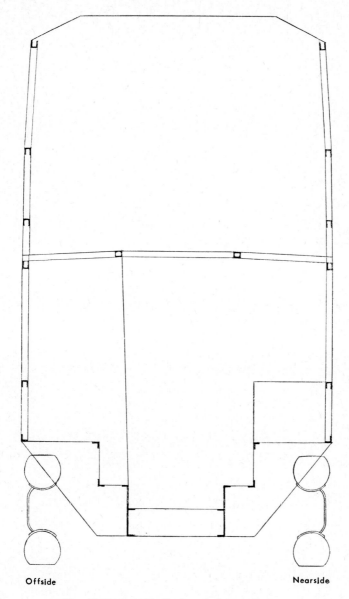

Offside   Nearside

FIG. 17.18. Bus: idealised typical cross-section.

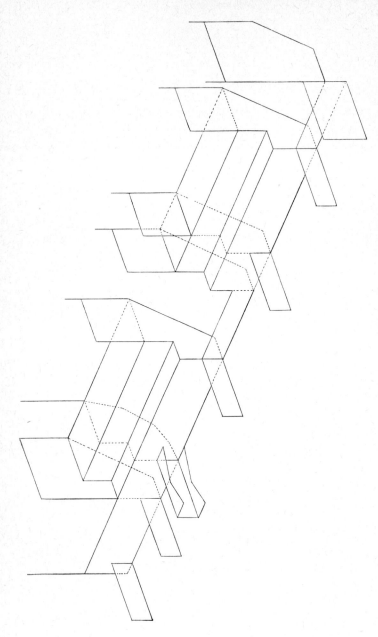

Fig. 17.19. Bus: idealised nearside lower structure.

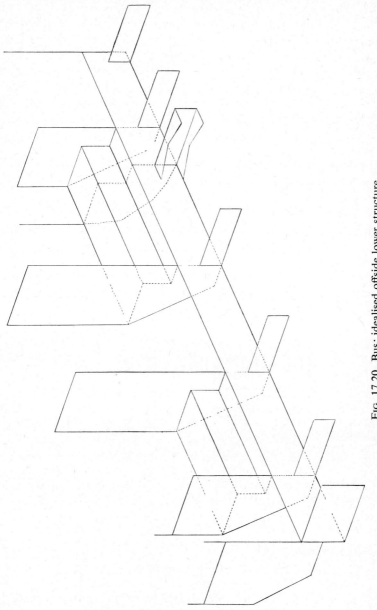

FIG. 17.20. Bus: idealised offside lower structure.

The bus has a front entrance door and middle exit door; the stairs are opposite the exit door. This is the same layout as on existing DMS buses (Fig. 17.2) but the similarity goes no further. The engine is sited under the stairs, causing a large offset load. The lower deck seating is mainly longitudinal and the upper deck has conventional transverse seating.

Unitary construction is used, and the structure is entirely of aluminium alloy—including the main underframe. The cross-section of the bus is shown in Fig. 17.18. Being of light alloy, the two main longitudes naturally have to be deeper than equivalent steel ones would be, while at the same time an important feature of this bus is its low step and lower deck gangway height. The lower deck gangway is consequently sunk between the main longitudes, reminiscent of tube train practice. The crossmembers of the main underframe must pass beneath the sunken gangway, so are of approximately half the height of the main longitudes, and most importantly the nearside main longitude itself is down to about half its normal height (but reinforced) in the vicinity of the doorways. Either side of the main underframe the body underside rises in a series of steps conforming to the underside of the longitudinal seating, to meet the bodysides at a line about 1 m above road level; the part of the sides below this line is not structural, it being the policy to minimise structural damage in a crash.

The bodysides themselves are conventional, being unstressed panels on a framework of pillars and longitudes. Most of the upper deck load is transmitted down these pillars, and it can be seen from Figure 17.18 that it is impossible to provide simple crossmembers to support the lower ends of these side pillars, as would be normal practice. Support is instead provided by means of a series of bulkheads inside the bus, positioned as convenient around the doorways and engine compartment. These bulkheads transfer load from the bodyside pillars to the main underframe. They are of particular interest and concern due to the possibility of their buckling, and their method of attachment to the chassis could also be a problem. Figure 17.19 shows the structure around the nearside main longitude, as viewed from the offside ahead. The load-bearing bulkheads may be seen, as well as the cut-down regions of the main longitude. Figure 17.20 shows the equivalent offside, and emphasises the asymmetry.

17.4.2   The Idealisation

The geometric idealisation, as plotted, is shown in Figs. 17.21–17.23. A bus structure is more demanding of machine core size than a train structure modelled to a similar degree of detail. A bus structure has no symmetry at all so must be modelled whole, and in this case it is double

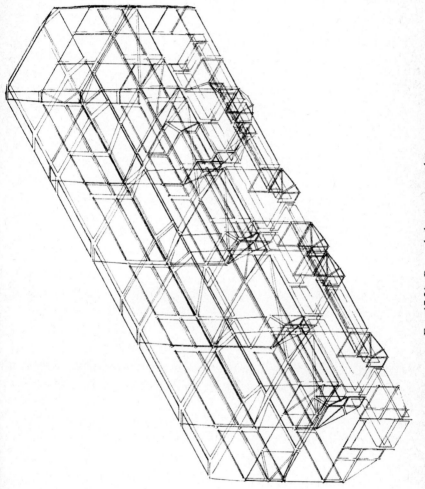

Fig. 17.21. Bus: whole structure plot.

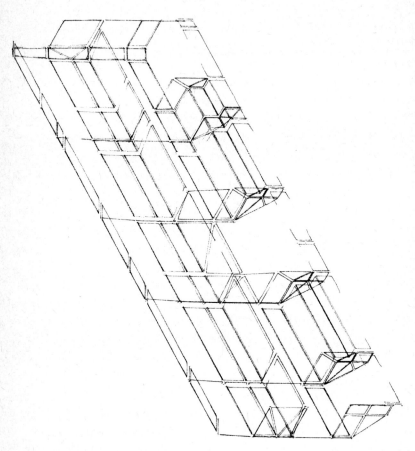

FIG. 17.22. Bus: nearside structure plot.

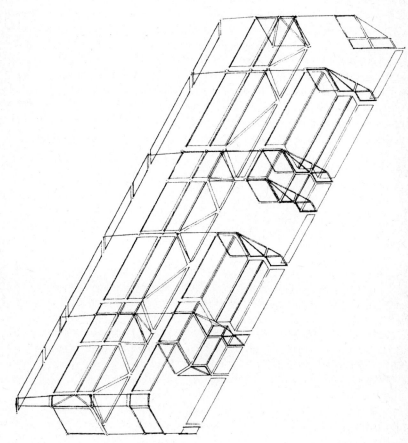

FIG. 17.23. Bus: offside structure plot.

celled in cross-section, being a double decker. In fact this job was near to filling the maximum partition size of the BR computer at Derby. The job statistics are: semi-bandwidth, 209; active nodes, 340 approximately; elements, 766.

The two main longitudes posed a slightly unusual problem in that, although they were obviously beam-like in their properties, their height is important from the geometric point of view so they could not be represented by normal line beam elements. The four-node beam element was therefore chosen. This is basically a conventional line beam with the addition of rigid crosspieces at both ends, enabling it to span four points. This element does, however, have drawbacks in use, such as the lack of any stiffness out of its own plane, and must be compounded with other elements, geometric constraints, or both. The idealisation of the ladder-like main underframe as an assembly of four node beams, with the necessary superpositions and geometric constraints, was the most difficult part of the whole work.

The remainder of the structure idealisation was fairly straightforward, following the same practice as that described for trains. The load-bearing bulkheads were represented by panel elements with in-plane stiffness superimposed upon ones with bending stiffness; because these bulkheads are constructed either from honeycomb sandwich panels or from sheets on battens, and because NEWPAC assumes all elements to be homogeneous, it was necessary to work out the equivalent homogeneous thicknesses, separately of course, for bending stiffness and direct stiffness.

In reality, the bus is supported at the eight wheels, but this would have been wasteful in the idealisation, requiring an extra four node hoops. Instead, the underframe was supported by eight point stiffnesses (six in the first run, with only two at the rear) at the nearest available nodes, and at the same time couples were applied at these points to account for the transfer of position. The magnitudes of these couples were based on pre-estimates of the vertical wheel loads. Inaccuracies introduced by this considerable simplification are small and local only.

The discrete loads of mechanical equipment were applied by distributing them between nearby nodes in appropriate portions. The distributed loads of the passengers and structure weight were applied using a facility which has recently become available in NEWPAC. This facility allows a hydro-static load to be applied to a panel or group of panels, and though called hydrostatic it can, if required, be directed parallel to any of the coordinate axes rather than normal to the panel. This is obviously ideal for applying a passenger load to a deck. In using it to apply the self-weight of the structure, this weight was divided by the total panel area of the bus to give a hydrostatic pressure to be applied downwards to all panelling. Because panelling is spread fairly evenly over the bus, this automatically gives an even weight distribution. After the first run the roof was excluded from this procedure, as, having a very large area, it took an unfair portion of the total load and being a comparatively flimsy structure it distorted badly as a result.

17.4.3   Results

The results of the first run showed unacceptably high stresses in the underframe in the region of the rear wheels. This is shown in Figs. 17.24 and 17.25. Remarkably, the cut-down nearside longitude by the exit doors did not show any high stresses, presumably because the engine is cantilevered off the opposite side of the underframe there, applying an upward load to the nearside longitude. There were high stresses in the roof and local to it, due to the previously mentioned overloading of the roof.

It was concluded that the high underframe stresses at the rear were due to a lack of effective connection between body pillars and chassis in the region. Due to window and seating arrangements, one bulkhead (the

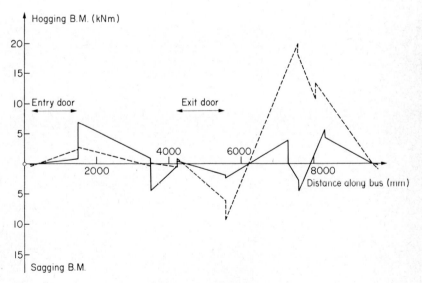

FIG. 17.24. Bus: bending moments in nearside main longitude. ----- first run; ——— second run.

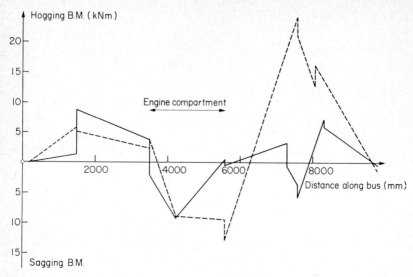

FIG. 17.25. Bus: bending moments in offside main longitude. ----- first run;
———— second run.

rearmost) was not aligned with any side pillar with the result that upper
deck loads were taking a path down the rear of the bus and in consequence
had a large moment arm about the rear suspension points. Finite element
analysis allows such load paths to be traced.

The Bus Drawing Office therefore produced a modification consisting
of a pair of extra bulkheads in line with the existing pillars between the
rear wheels. The bulkhead needed careful design to confine it below the
seating and also to clear the rear suspension. It may be seen in Figs. 17.24
and 17.25 by the flanged crossmember. For the second run this was the
main modification made. In addition, all four rear suspension points were
now represented as they had been seen to lie in a critical area. The results
show a great improvement in the underframe stresses, shown in Figs.
17.24 and 17.25, leaving it comfortably understressed throughout its
length. Bulkhead stresses appear acceptable but must be investigated more
deeply for any possibility of buckling. The most highly stressed bulkheads
are those adjacent to the exit door, and one is shown in Fig. 17.26. Any
bulkhead modifications found necessary would not cause further major
design changes.

Thus the finite element analysis highlighted a problem area, allayed
fears in other areas, and after modification has verified that the structure
is sound.

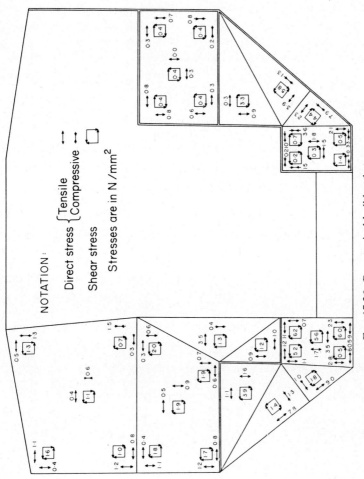

Fig. 17.26. Bus: typical bulkhead stress.

17.5 CONCLUDING REMARKS

The analyses of an underground railway coach (tube stock) and a double-deck bus, by the finite element method, have been described. In both cases the analysis helped to highlight necessary changes in the initial designs and subsequently verify the soundness of the modified designs. A number of other vehicle structures have been analysed; these include a single-deck bus and another underground railway coach. Work is currently proceeding on the analysis of a surface-stock carbody and its bogie which is to be the replacement stock for the District line. The analysis of a disc railway wheel by the finite element method is also planned.

The use of the finite element method has provided the Design Division at London Transport with a powerful analysis tool which, in addition to confirming the adequacy of completed designs, has proved extremely useful in the initial design stages of new vehicle structures.

ACKNOWLEDGEMENT

The authors would like to thank Mr S. F. Smith, Chief Mechanical Engineer, London Transport Executive for permission to present this paper.

REFERENCES

1. Patel, N. L., Agyeman-Prempeh, E. O. and Scholes, A. 'NEWPAC—A User's Guide to the Newpac Program for Structural Analysis Using the Finite Element Method', EMMA 15 ISSUE 3, British Railways Research and Development Division, February, 1974.
2. Driver, S. A. (1970). 'Design of Railway Rolling Stock for Heavy Urban Service.' Proc. Conf. on Rapid Transit Vehicles for City Services (Paris, November 1970), Inst. Mech. Engrs, London.

18

The Optimisation of Undercarriage Characteristics in Transport Aeroplanes Using a Hybrid Computation Technique

M. R. WHITEHEAD
Loughborough University of Technology

SUMMARY

A hybrid computer technique is described, with which optimisation of undercarriage parameters is attempted in order to create an improved vibration environment in an airframe. The airframe/undercarriage model is represented in two dimensions and a measure of performance postulated. The limitations of the system are discussed and an alternative use for the hybrid model is considered.

18.1   INTRODUCTION

During recent years it has become apparent that the world-wide intensification of the air transportation system has caused a number of socio-economic and technological problems. There are factors which have prompted the aircraft industry to introduce larger, faster and quieter transport aeroplanes, and with each innovation, design philosophy has, of necessity, been revised. A common feature of aeroplane operation which has been largely ignored by designers in the past is the effect on the airframe of runway-induced vibrations; it has been accepted generally that undercarriages were designed to meet loads incurred during landing, and such ground manœuvres as turning and braking. It is relevant to note that undercarriage loads can contribute to the design of up to 40% of an airframe by weight; therefore, as aeroplanes become more flexible due to their size and configuration, the effect of taxiing loads on the airframe may be a significant cause of fatigue damage, as well as creating crew and passenger discomfort, and possibly overstressing of some components. The particular aircraft configuration for which these problems are likely to be most acute is the long and slender shape associated with supersonic transport aeroplanes. This is not to say that these effects are less important in other designs; a large part of the aircraft market today is concerned with the quick turnround 'bus stop' variety of operation and inherently these aircraft spend a significant proportion of their life in taxiing manœuvres.

18.2 NOTATION

$(a\ b\ c)_i$	coordinates of $(u\ v\ w)$ axes of the ith undercarriage relative to the wheel hub centre
A_{e1}	aerodynamic lift force
A_{e2}	aerodynamic pitching moment
A_{e3}	aerodynamic damping force
$\mathbf{B}$	diagonal matrix of aerodynamic damping
C_L	coefficient of lift
C_m	coefficient of pitching moment
$D_{u_{zir}}$	matrix of aircraft vertical modal displacements in the rth mode at the base of the ith undercarriage in its mean position
F_D	damping force
F_F	friction force
$\mathbf{F}_{ni}$	vector of forces at the ith undercarriage hub centre
$F_{q_{wi}}$	shock absorber force ith undercarriage
$F(q_w)_i$	spring force characteristic ith undercarriage
g	acceleration due to gravity
h_{TL}	height of torque link centre from v axis
I	aircraft pitch inertia
J_{uu}	undercarriage sliding member inertia about u axis
k_0	constant friction
k_1	friction coefficient proportional to vertical load
m	distance between bearings when undercarriage is fully extended
M_A	mass of aircraft
$\mathbf{M}_D$	diagonal matrix of generalised masses
M_{sc_i}	mass of the ith undercarriage sliding member
p	distance of upper bearing from the sliding member reference axis, undercarriage fully extended
q_r	generalised coordinate in the rth mode
q_w	sliding member axial displacement along axis w
T_i	constraint forces, ith undercarriage

T_L	constraint force, lower bearing
T_T	constraint force, upper bearing
$(u \, v \, w)$	sliding member reference axis
$(x \, y \, z)$	aircraft rigid body axes
$(X \, Y Z)$	earth axes
$(X_0 \, Y_0 \, Z_0)$	coordinates of the aircraft rigid body axes relative to earth axes
$(X_{hc} \, Y_{hc} \, Z_{hc})$	axes at the hub centre of ith wheel
$(x_u \, y_u \, z_u)$	coordinates of the sliding member reference relative to rigid body axes, ith undercarriage in its mean position
$\ddot{Z}_p$	acceleration at the cockpit
$\ddot{Z}_T$	human acceleration tolerance criterion
$\ddot{Z}_z$	normalised acceleration at cockpit
$(\alpha \, \beta \, \gamma)$	aircraft rigid body rotations
$\delta(\,)$	perturbed variable
η	elevator angle
λ_{i1}	linear damping coefficient, ith undercarriage
λ_{i2}	non-linear damping coefficient, ith undercarriage
λ_c	damping coefficient in compression
λ_r	damping coefficient in recoil
μ	coefficient of friction
μ_s	coefficient of stiction
σ	stress
θ	angle of attack
ω	circular frequency

18.3   METHOD OF ANALYSIS

There are two principal methods of analysis which have found favour with authors in the past, a statistical analysis [1–4] and a deterministic analysis [5–7].

The biggest problem associated with the statistical analysis is the non-linearities inherent in an undercarriage telescopic member. Their inclusion in the analysis is usually achieved by linear approximation methods, and as airframe response has been found to be strongly influenced by under-carriage non-linearities [6] the statistical approach has not been used.

The method chosen for this study is deterministic, with a view to pro-ducing an analysis which will provide an engineering solution to aircraft taxiing problems, and thence to investigate the feasibility of optimising

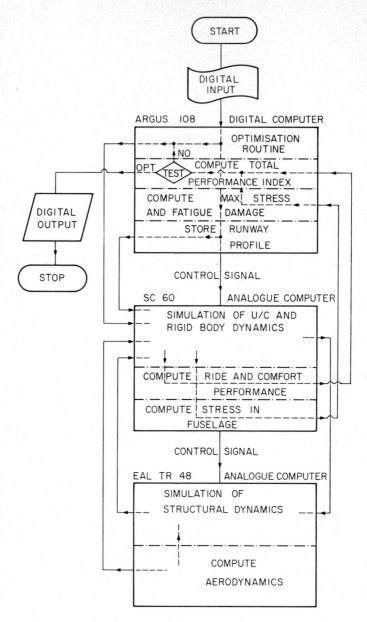

FIG. 18.1. Hybrid computer layout.

undercarriage parameters to create a better vibration environment in an airframe.

Obviously an analysis including an optimisation routine will involve a large number of traverses of at least one runway and preferably as many runways as possible. Hence the use of a digital computer to solve the dynamic equations would be very time consuming, even in two dimensions. Consequently the analysis has been designed for solution using a hybrid computer facility where the analogue complement simulates the dynamic equations of motion and the digital complement provides the control logic, processes the optimisation routines and stores the runway profile data, as shown in Fig. 18.1. By this method, solution of the dynamic equations is in real time, one runway traverse taking in the order of a half-minute plus a small allowance for optimisation at the end of each traverse.

18.4   DETERMINISTIC MATHEMATICAL MODEL

The mathematical model given below was originally suggested by Reynolds *et al.* [7], and is seen to be two dimensional in the vertical and longitudinal plane (Fig. 18.2). The model was derived in a most general form by the method of Lagrange, and then simplified to a size compatible with an existing hybrid computing facility. It should be stressed that the ultimate size and complexity of the model is limited by the available computer hardware. In this case the hybrid facility consisted of two independent analogue computers and a small digital computer, all interfaced to provide the following total complement:

Digital computer store	8096	words
Analogue computer operational amplifiers	120	total
Digital to analogue channels	10	
Analogue to digital channels	24	

In its final simplified form the mathematical model contains two airframe rigid body freedoms—pitch and bounce. The elastic characteristics of the airframe are represented by the first five symmetric modes of vibration, and there is provision for two undercarriages. The usual pair of main undercarriages are represented by a single equivalent unit positioned on the aircraft centre-line, but their symmetric modal displacements are those according to their true location in the airframe. The telescopic undercarriage members are assumed to be rigid and constrained to a single degree of freedom along the line of action of the shock absorber.

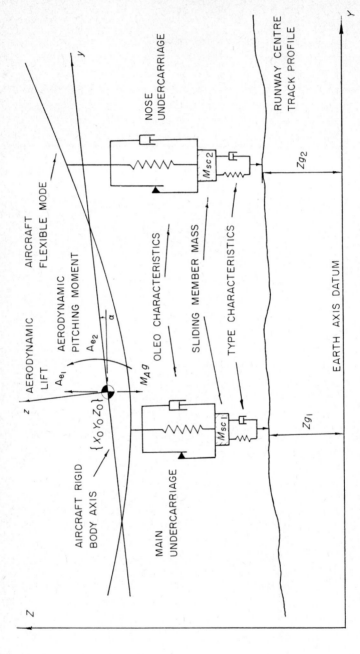

FIG. 18.2. General arrangement of mathematical model.

Within this single degree of freedom there are included three non-linear characteristics associated with the shock absorber, spring force, friction at the bearings, and hydraulic damping.

The tyre is assumed to be a linear spring and damper having point contact with the runway surface.

Actual measured runway profiles are used and the model may be run across the surface with velocity as a constant or as a function of time; the ground inputs are thus partially dissipated in the shock absorber and partially transmitted through the undercarriages to the airframe.

Secondary inputs to the airframe are provided by aerodynamic forces and moments which are functions of (forward velocity)^2, angle of attack and elevator angle.

18.5   AIRFRAME STRUCTURAL MODES OF VIBRATION

Structural flexibility is represented in terms of the first five symmetric modes of vibration. The airframe is assumed to be a 'free–free' structure and is excited by the generalised undercarriage forces, which are computed by multiplying the total undercarriage internal force by the modal displacement at the attachment point. Hence the generalised coordinates q_r and their derivatives will define the motion in each mode according to the equations:

$$\mathbf{M}_D \cdot \ddot{\mathbf{q}}_r + \cdot 04 \mathbf{M}_D \omega \dot{\mathbf{q}}_r + \mathbf{M}_D \omega^2 \cdot \mathbf{q}_r$$
$$= \mathbf{B} \cdot \mathbf{v} \cdot \dot{\mathbf{q}}_r + \mathbf{F}_{q_w 1} \cdot \mathbf{D}_{u_z 1_r} + \mathbf{F}_{q_w 2} \cdot \mathbf{D}_{u_z 2_r} \qquad (r = 1, 2, \ldots, 5) \quad (18.1)$$

18.6   UNDERCARRIAGE NON-LINEARITIES

Most commonly, undercarriage springs have either a single-stage or a two-stage characteristic, as shown in Fig. 18.3. Both characteristics are non-linear with respect to closure and are derived from the volumetric compression of gas or oil.

The single-stage spring is preferred in a main undercarriage design as it allows a minimum weight design and produces an adequate landing performance. Nose undercarriages, however, very often employ the two-stage design because they tend to experience a wider range of operating loads than the main undercarriage, say 10% all-up-weight at static equilibrium increasing to two or three times this figure under dynamic

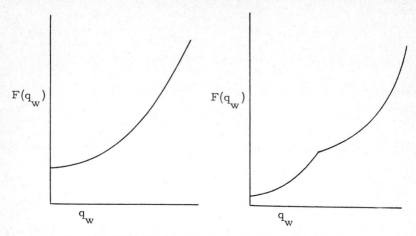

Fig. 18.3. (left) Single-stage spring. (right) Two-stage spring.

loading. Hence the two-stage design provides a more equitable characteristic and the extra weight is minimised as there is, in general, only a
single nose undercarriage and this is much lighter than the main gear.

Damping in an undercarriage shock absorber has to fulfil several
functions in both the landing and taxiing phases of operation, and unfortunately the damping requirements for each phase are different. It is
common for a shock absorber to have a significantly greater damping
effect during the expansion stroke than that experienced in compression,
in order to allow maximum energy absorption during high vertical velocity
landing (compression) cases, and maximum energy dissipation during the
lower velocity recoil (expansion) stroke. Hence the aircraft vertical motion
is controlled and the possibility of bouncing back into the air reduced.
Taxiing conditions produce velocities within the moving parts of the
shock absorber much lower than landing velocities, typically 0·5 ft/sec
during taxiing and 5–10 ft/sec during design landing cases; therefore,
although recoil damping has provided adequate damping during the taxi
phase in many cases in the past, it may become desirable to introduce
damping specifically for taxiing if ground-induced vibrations in the airframe become too severe. A typical damping characteristic is shown in
Fig. 18.4; thus, in compression,

$$F_{D_c} = \lambda_c \cdot \dot{q}_w |\dot{q}_w| \qquad (18.2)$$

and in recoil

$$F_{D_r} = \lambda_r \cdot \dot{q}_w |\dot{q}_w| \qquad (18.3)$$

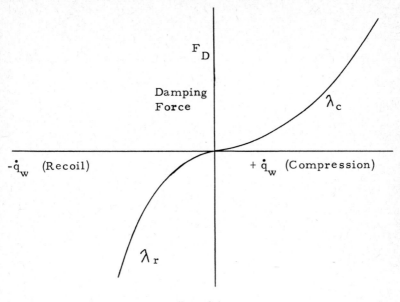

FIG. 18.4

The friction forces in an undercarriage strut exist at points of contact between the sliding assembly and the fixed leg structure. For axial motion, the sliding assembly is constrained by high-quality journal bearings, designed in materials giving a compromise between minimum coefficient of friction at the rubbing surfaces and an acceptable operational life.

Consider friction to have two component parts—stiction and coulomb friction—where stiction is that property of friction occurring when there is no relative motion between two bodies in contact, and coulomb friction exists when there is relative motion, i.e. as shown diagrammatically in Fig. 18.5.

Referring to Fig. 18.6, the resultant bearing force normal to the telescopic axis is:

$$T_i = (T_{L_u}^2 + T_{L_v}^2)_i^{1/2} + (T_{T_u}^2 + T_{T_v}^2)_i^{1/2} \qquad (18.4)$$

and

$$F_{F_i} = \mu \cdot |T_i| \frac{\dot{q}_{wi}}{|\dot{q}_{wi}|} \quad \text{when} \quad \dot{q}_{wi} \neq 0 \qquad (18.5)$$

or

$$F_{F_i} = \mu_s |T_i| \quad \text{when} \quad \dot{q}_{wi} = 0 \qquad (18.6)$$

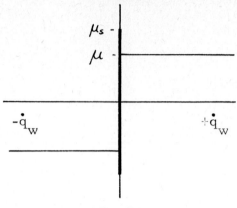

$$\text{Fig. 18.5}$$

18.7   GROUND REACTION FORCES

In this two-dimensional model, which is not designed to experience input forces and moments due to yawing and rolling, the following additional assumptions are made:

1. Drag forces, typically assumed to be 2% vertical tyre force acting in the fore-aft direction, are not included.
2. Ground forces due to modal rotations at tyre–ground interface of undercarriages have been assumed to be zero.
3. Forces and moments due to braking effects are not included.

These assumptions have been introduced into this study to maintain the model within the limiting size of the computer hardware.

Therefore, referring to Fig. 18.7, the vector of external forces acting at the hub centre is

$$\mathbf{F}_{ni} = \begin{bmatrix} F_{nx} \\ F_{ny} \\ F_{nz} \end{bmatrix}_i = \begin{bmatrix} 0 \\ 0 \\ F_{nzi} \end{bmatrix} \tag{18.7}$$

18.8   DYNAMIC EQUATIONS REPRESENTING THE MATHEMATICAL MODEL

The following equations of motion define the mathematical model which is assumed to be perturbed about a mean equilibrium level:

$$M_A \cdot \delta \ddot{Z}_0 = A_{e1} + F_{q_{w1}} + F_{q_{w2}} \tag{18.8}$$

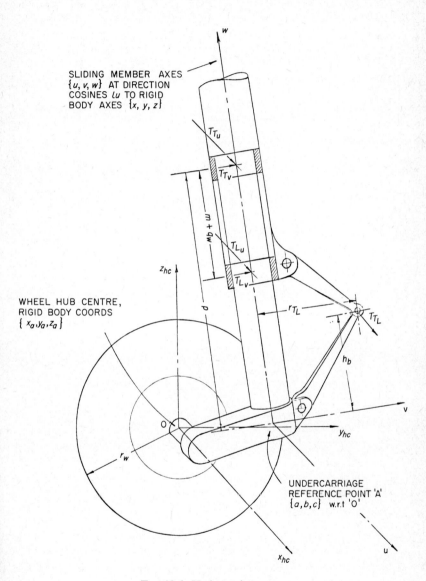

FIG. 18.6. Undercarriage axes.

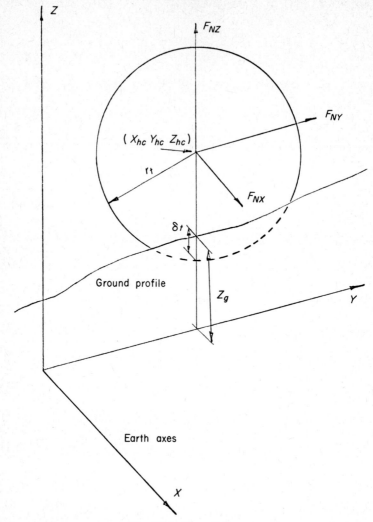

FIG. 18.7. Ground forces.

$$I \cdot \delta \ddot{\alpha} = A_{e2} + F_{q_{w1}} \cdot y_{u1} + F_{q_{w2}} \cdot y_{u2} \tag{18.9}$$

$$\mathbf{M}_D \delta \ddot{\mathbf{q}}_r = \mathbf{A}_{e3} - 0 \cdot 04 \, \mathbf{M}_D \omega \delta \dot{\mathbf{q}}_r - \mathbf{M}_D \omega^2 \delta \mathbf{q}_r$$
$$+ \mathbf{F}_{q_{w1}} \cdot \mathbf{D}_{u_{z1r}} + \mathbf{F}_{q_{w2}} \cdot \mathbf{D}_{u_{z2r}} \quad (r = 1, 2, \ldots, 5) \tag{18.10}$$

$$M_{sc_1} \cdot \delta \ddot{Z}_{hc_1} = \delta F_{nz1} - F_{q_{w1}} \tag{18.11}$$

$$M_{sc_2} \cdot \delta \ddot{Z}_{hc_2} = \delta F_{nz2} - F_{q_{w2}} \tag{18.12}$$

$$A_{e1} = \tfrac{1}{2}\rho S v^2 \left\{ C_{L0} + \frac{\partial C_L}{\partial \theta} \left\{ \delta\alpha - \frac{\delta\dot{Z}_0}{v} \right\} + \frac{\partial C_L}{\partial \eta} \cdot \delta\eta \right\} \qquad (18.13)$$

$$A_{e2} = \tfrac{1}{2}\rho S \dot{c} v^2 \left\{ C_{m0} + \frac{\partial C_m}{\partial \theta} \left\{ \delta\alpha - \frac{\delta\dot{Z}_0}{v} \right\} + \frac{\partial C_m}{\partial \eta} \cdot \delta\eta \right\} \qquad (18.14)$$

$$A_{e3} = \mathbf{B}_r v \cdot \delta\dot{q}_r \qquad (r = 1, 2, \ldots, 5) \qquad (18.15)$$

$$F_{q_{wi}} = F(\delta q_w)_i + \lambda_{i1} \cdot \delta\dot{q}_{wi} + \lambda_{i2} \cdot \delta\dot{q}_{wi} |\delta\dot{q}_{wi}| + \delta F_{F_i} \qquad (i = 1, 2)$$
$$(18.16)$$

$$\delta F_{F_i} = \mu\{k_0 + k_1 F_{nz} + |T_{Lv}| + |T_{Tv}|\}_i \frac{\delta\dot{q}_{wi}}{|\delta\dot{q}_{wi}|} \quad \text{if} \quad \delta\dot{q}_{wi} \neq 0$$
$$(i = 1, 2) \quad (18.17)$$

or

$$\delta F_{F_i} = \mu_s\{k_0 + k_1 F_{nz} + |T_{Lv}| + |T_{Tv}|\}_i \quad \text{if } \delta\dot{q}_{wi} = 0 \; (i = 1, 2) \qquad (18.18)$$

$$T_{Lvi} = \frac{1}{m + \bar{q}_w} (J_{uu} - M_{sc_i} \cdot p \cdot z_u)\delta\ddot{\alpha}$$

$$- \frac{p}{m + \bar{q}_w} (\bar{\alpha} \cdot \bar{F}_{nz} + \bar{\alpha} \cdot \delta F_{nz} + \bar{F}_{nz} \cdot \delta\alpha)_i + \frac{b}{m + \bar{q}_w} (\bar{F}_{nz} + \delta F_{nz})_i$$
$$(18.19)$$

$$T_{Tvi} = - \frac{1}{m + \bar{q}_w} (J_{uu} + M_{sc_i} \cdot z_u\{m + \bar{q}_w - p\}) \cdot \delta\ddot{\alpha}$$

$$- \frac{(m + \bar{q}_w - p)}{m + \bar{q}_w} \{\bar{\alpha} \cdot \bar{F}_{nz} + \bar{\alpha} \cdot \delta F_{nz} + \bar{F}_{nz} \cdot \delta\alpha\}$$

$$- \frac{b}{m + \bar{q}_w} \cdot (\bar{F}_{nz} + \delta F_{nz}) \qquad (18.20)$$

18.9   OPTIMISATION

In order to optimise the system, a measure of behaviour must be introduced such that a change in any of the system variables may be judged to cause an improvement or deterioration in response. This measure of behaviour will be known as the performance index.

18.10   PERFORMANCE INDEX

The performance index is related to the function of an aeroplane; hence it is unlikely that a single definitive performance index can be found which will be suitable for all aeroplanes. Much of the content of the overall

performance index postulated below remains subjective but is derived
with a civil passenger aeroplane in mind.

Three important aspects will be considered as being component parts
of a practical performance index: (a) ride comfort; (b) maximum stress in
the airframe; (c) airframe fatigue.

18.10.1 Ride Comfort

Riding comfort of the crew and passengers is the subjective constituent
part of this performance index, as much of it depends on psychological
factors surrounding human beings. For instance, a seated human being
within a vibration environment will recognise at least three thresholds—
perception of vibration; discomfort; limit of tolerance—none of which
has an absolute definition. However, it is recognised that human reaction
to vibration is a function of the amplitude and frequency of acceleration
applied to the body and contours of tolerance have been suggested by
several authors, as shown in Fig. 18.8.

It is shown in Figs. 18.9–18.11 that the vertical accelerations experienced
in the cockpit of a typical slender aeroplane are substantially greater than
those occurring at the centre of gravity. If the centre of gravity is chosen
to represent a point in the passenger cabin, then it can be said that by
ensuring that the pilot has an acceptable standard of ride comfort, the
passengers should be even more comfortable. Alternatively, it would be
necessary to develop a weighting function along the length of the fuselage,
considering such factors as the working environment of the pilot and the
status of the passengers, e.g. first class or economy class.

From Fig. 18.8 a first-order approximation may be obtained for tolerance contour IV, i.e.

$$\ddot{Z}_T = \frac{0\cdot934\,(1 + 0\cdot0265S)(1 + 0\cdot008S)\,\text{ft/s}^2}{0\cdot0265S} \qquad (18.21)$$

where $S = j\omega$.

Hence, normalising the applied acceleration at the cockpit

$$|\ddot{Z}_z| = \left|\frac{\ddot{Z}_p}{\ddot{Z}_T}\right| \qquad (18.22)$$

The performance index is then written according to the integral of error
squared, where the error is defined as any acceleration about a '1 g'
datum, i.e.

$$I_{rc} = \frac{1}{T}\int_0^T \ddot{Z}_z{}^2\,\mathrm{d}t \qquad (18.23)$$

where T is the time of runway traverse.

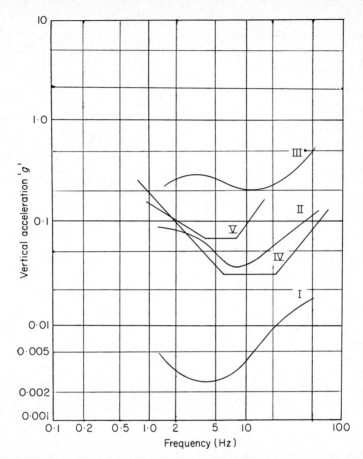

FIG. 18.8. Contours of vibration tolerance. I, Threshold of perception, ref. 10; II unpleasant, ref. 10; III, intolerable, ref. 10; IV, recommended vibration limit, ref. 8, V, reduced comfort boundary, ref. 9.

18.10.2 Maximum Stress in the Airframe

In this two-dimensional model we are restricted to the consideration of stresses along the fuselage centre-line. Assuming bending stresses predominate, there will be bending flexure in the fuselage due to ground inputs through the undercarriages. Hence it is necessary to find the most critical section *j* of the fuselage and ensure that the material proof stresses

COCKPIT VERTICAL ACCELERATION

CG VERTICAL ACCELERATION

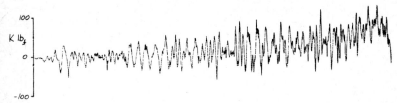

MAIN U/C VERTICAL REACTION (2 GEARS)

MAIN OLEO DEFLECTION

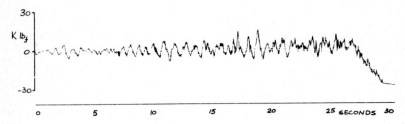

FIG. 18.9. Nose u/c vertical reaction.

COCKPIT VERTICAL ACCELERATION

CG VERTICAL ACCELERATION

MAIN U/C VERTICAL REACTION (2 GEARS)

MAIN OLEO DEFLECTION

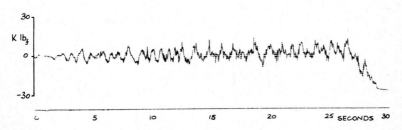

FIG. 18.10. Nose u/c vertical reaction.

405

AEROPLANE RESPONSE TO RUNWAY C

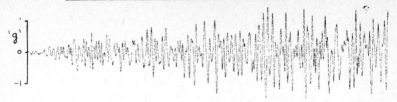

COCKPIT VERTICAL ACCELERATION

C G VERTICAL ACCELERATION

MAIN u/c VERTICAL REACTION (2 GEARS)

MAIN OLEO DEFLECTION

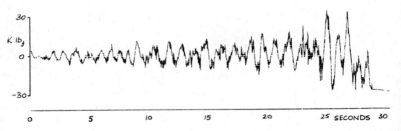

FIG. 18.11. Nose u/c vertical reaction.

406

are not exceeded in that section. This may be included in the performance index in the form of a penalty function, viz.

$$I_{ms} = \left(\frac{\sigma_j \text{ max.}}{\sigma \text{ proof}}\right)^{2m} \tag{18.24}$$

where m is some large positive integer.

18.10.3 Fatigue Damage

Using Miner's cumulative damage hypothesis, the total fatigue damage at j is given by

$$d_j = \sum_{\sigma_i} \frac{n_i}{N_i} \tag{18.25}$$

where n_i is the number of stress reversals at a level of alternating stress σ_i. N_i is the number of stress reversals to failure at a level of alternating stress σ_i.

According to Miner's hypothesis, failure occurs when

$$\sum_{\sigma_i} \frac{n_i}{N_i} = 1 \tag{18.26}$$

Therefore, a penalty function can be incorporated into the performance index, similar to that used above for I_{ms}, should the value exceed unity, i.e.

$$I_F = \left\{ N_T \sum_{\sigma_i} \frac{n_i}{N_i} \right\}_T^{2m} \tag{18.27}$$

where suffix T implies summation over time T. N_T is the number of traverses of time T.

Each constituent part of the total performance index can be weighted according to its relative importance. Hence

$$I = w_1 \cdot I_{rc} + w_2 I_{ms} + w_3 I_F \tag{18.28}$$

18.11   OPTIMISATION ROUTINES

In the absence of a universally accepted 'best' optimisation method, it is necessary to consider several alternatives and find the most suitable for a given measure of performance. Gradient methods require that the function gradient can be analytically defined and hence are not appropriate in this work. The direct search methods appear to offer a solution, as they only require a knowledge of the value of the performance index at each stage;

such methods, developed by Rosenbrock [11], Hooke and Jeeves [12] and
Nelder and Mead [13], are chosen and their performance will be judged
in terms of speed and accuracy when used in conjunction with the previously described model and performance measure.

Each of the routines has been written in, or translated into the auto-
code language suitable for use in a Ferranti Argus digital computer. The
Rosenbrock routine has been tested using a test function introduced by
Rosenbrock, which is a banana-shaped valley described in Ref. 14. The
test was conducted entirely within the digital computer and confirmed that
the translated routine worked correctly. In order to test that the routine
would be similarly effective within the hybrid facility, the same test function was set up on the analogue computer and the optimisation routine in
the digital. Operating the analogue computer manually showed that the
test function was correct and that the true extremum could be resolved.
However, when the optimisation routine in the digital computer was
asked to find the extremum of the test function on the analogue computer,
it failed. Step-by-step check showed that the procedure began to optimise
in a similar manner to the 'all-digital' test and then foundered, indicating
that an optimum had been found at some intermediate point. It was found
that the fault lay in the interface system between the two computers. The
interface was unable to resolve small voltages, less than 400 mV, to allow
the routine to converge on to the extremum. It is essential, therefore, that
the interface is able to resolve to the same degree as the analogue computer, i.e. 0·01% or 1 mV.

18.12 HYBRID COMPUTER SIMULATION OF A TAXIING AEROPLANE

The hybrid computer simulation has been proved, however, as a feasible
tool of analysis for an aircraft in the taxi mode.

Real time simulation of an aircraft taxiing over three different runways
is shown in Figs. 8.9–8.11. The runways are designated A, B and C, where
A and B are typically good runway profiles and C is abnormally rough.
High levels of acceleration response in the airframe are attributed to
friction in the main undercarriage, evidenced by the stick/slip motion of the
oleos. As the shock absorber can only do useful work when the oleos are
in motion, then it follows that whilst the oleos are 'stuck' all the energy
is transmitted through the undercarriages into the flexible airframe
structure, instead of being partially absorbed or dissipated through the

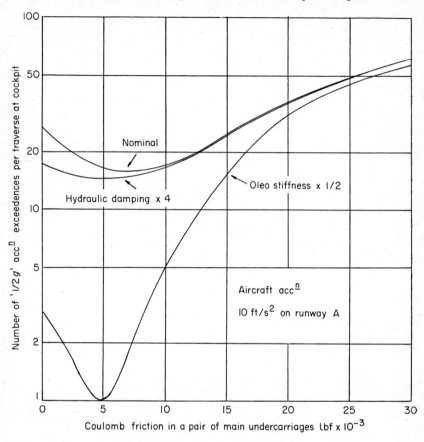

FIG. 18.12. Coulomb friction in a pair of main undercarriages (lbf $\times$ 10^{-3}).

shock absorbers. The effect that various parameters have on airframe response is shown as an example in Fig. 18.12, where values of under-carriage friction, stiffness and damping are adjusted manually. It might be that this feature is a more appropriate result than the complete opti-misation program, as it offers a simple 'hands on' analysis tool for the designer, without the added complication of a full optimisation which would involve very severe constraints imposed to meet the landing conditions.

The conclusions of Fig. 18.12 imply that there is a value of friction which would cause minimum airframe response to a ground input, which can be interpreted to mean that bearing friction should be low enough to prevent the oleos from locking, thus allowing maximum dissipation of energy through the shock absorber.

The optimum solution is not zero friction, since a small value of friction is beneficial as an auxiliary damping device during axial motion of the undercarriage. Hydraulic damping is shown to have negligible effect on the response when friction is high, due to the limited motion available for energy dissipation. However, at low values of friction, hydraulic damping becomes more effective but hardly significant even when the damping coefficient is increased by a factor of four. It may be beneficial, therefore, to consider different damping coefficients for different flow velocities. For example, a flow-controlled valve within the undercarriage could be used to provide a high damping coefficient at the low stroking velocities consistent with taxiing, and a lower damping coefficient at the high stroking velocities associated with landing.

Spring stiffness is obviously a significant parameter and should be as soft as is practicable, without creating extra weight and complexity and increasing the shock absorber stroke excessively.

It would seem that unless greater attention is given to ground-induced vibrations at the preliminary design stage, then the improved constraints from the design landing cases will not allow undercarriage parameter optimisation to proceed successfully.

ACKNOWLEDGEMENT

This work was carried out with the support of the Procurement Executive of the Ministry of Defence, whose cooperation is hereby acknowledged.

REFERENCES

1. Kirk, C. L. and Perry, P. J. (1971). Analysis of taxying induced vibrations in aircraft by the P.S.D. method, *The Aeronautical Journal*, **75** (723), March.
2. Kirk, C. L. (1971). The random heave-pitch response of aircraft to runway roughness, *The Aeronautical Journal*, **75**, July.
3. Silsby, N. S. 'An Analytical Study of Effects of some Landing Gear Factors on the Response to Runway Roughness with Application to Supersonic Transports', NASA TN-1492, 1962.
4. Corsetti, C. D. 'A Study of the Practicality of Active Vibration Isolation Applied to Aircraft during the Taxi Conditions', AFIT Thesis, GGC/EE/71-6, Wright Patterson AFB.

5. Tung, C. C., Penzien, J. and Horonjeff, R. 'The Effect of Runway Unevenness on the Dynamic Response of Supersonic Transports', NASA CR-119, 1964.
6. Mitchell, C. G. B. 'A Theoretical Analysis of Undercarriage Loads and Taxi Vibration on a Supersonic Transport Aircraft', RAE TR 70173, 1970.
7. Reynolds, J., Johns, D. J. and Aird, R. J. (1972). 'The Optimisation of Undercarriage Suspension Characteristics by a Deterministic Method', Symposium on Non-Linear Dynamics; Loughborough University of Technology (March), Paper C-1.
8. Janeway, R. N. 'Ride and Vibration Data' (Riding Comfort Committee), SAE, June 1950.
9. Janeway, R. N. 'Guide for the Evaluation of Human Exposure to Whole-body Vibration', ISO/DIS 2631.
10. Harris, C.M. and Crede, C.E. (1961). *Shock and Vibration Handbook*, Vol. 3, McGraw-Hill.
11. Rosenbrock, H. H. (1960). An automatic method for finding the greatest or least value of a function, *Computer Journal*, **3**, 175–184.
12. Hooke, R. and Jeeves, T. A. (1961). Direct search solution of numerical and statistical problems, *J. Assoc. Computer Machines*, **8**, 2123–2229.
13. Nelder, J. A. and Mead, R. (1964). A simplex method for function minimisation, *Computer Journal*, **7**, 308–313.
14. Pierre, D. (1969). *Optimization Theory with Applications*, Wiley.

19

A Theoretical and Practical
Examination of Engine Shake

A. Eames-Jones and C. Ashley
Dunlop Ltd and U O P Bostrom Ltd

SUMMARY

Although the problem of engine shake has received considerable attention, theoretical analyses have tended to over-simplify the situation by assuming planes of symmetry in the engine, and ignoring the dynamic characteristics of the engine mounts.

The object of the present work was to put engine shake on a firmer theoretical basis. The engine was considered as a rigid mass with three translational and three rotational degrees of freedom. The analysis was not confined to simply predicting the resonant frequencies of the system but also to the complete frequency response. Inputs to the engine were taken to be via the engine mounts.

To cater for a fully general case typical of actual conditions the inputs at each engine mount were taken as three independent sine wave displacements of equal frequency. The amplitudes and phase relationships could be made equal to any real measurements. A computer program was developed to predict the response of the engine at its centre of gravity and at the engine mounting points.

The computer program was validated by practical work on a vehicle. The inertia tensor of the engine relative to a convenient axis system was measured using a pendulum technique. The dynamic properties of the engine mounts were measured relative to the same axis system using a purpose-built rig based on an electrohydraulic vibrator. A frequency range of 5–50Hz and a variety of different preloads and applied strains were examined. The results were consistent with the complex modulus model of rubber, and the frequency dependence of this modulus was included in the theoretical analysis.

Inputs to the engine were measured by placing the vehicle on a four-station electrohydraulic vibrator, one ram under each wheel. The acceleration in the three coordinate directions on the body side of each mount was measured for a constant velocity sinusoidal input at the wheels, and hence displacement inputs to the engine could be calculated.

The computer program was supplied with the various data and produced the frequency response of the engine. This was compared with the measured frequency response and reasonable agreement was obtained.

Having validated the method the effects of varying the mount stiffness and positions were examined, and in particular a mounting system based on the concept of the centre of percussion was examined. Some improvement over the existing system was observed.

The technique developed could be used to optimise a mounting system, and to help towards minimising the effects of engine shake on the occupants of a vehicle.

19.1   INTRODUCTION

In the very early days of automobile design, it was accepted practice to utilise the engine as a structural member in the construction of a vehicle. It was securely bolted to the chassis, and acted as a cross-member, thus taking advantage of its high rigidity. This method of mounting the engine provided a suitably stiff chassis, but it meant that any vibration generated by the engine passed through the chassis to the passengers in the vehicle.

Gradually, the passenger came to expect more comfort from his automobile and, as roads and suspension systems improved, the engine vibration became more apparent. It was realised that it would be desirable to isolate the engine from the remainder of the vehicle, so that the effect of the troublesome engine vibration could be minimised. Considerable theoretical work—see for example Iliffe [1], Harrison [2], The Automobile Engineer [3], Horovitz [4]—was carried out on predicting the nature of the forces generated by the engine, and on the most effective methods of isolating the rest of the vehicle from the effects of these forces.

As the vibration caused by the engine became less of a problem, due to improved balancing of rotating and reciprocating parts, and also due to the improved mounting systems adopted, another engine-mounting problem became apparent. This problem was that of engine 'shake'. The system comprising the engine and its mounts, together with the rest of the vehicle, has certain preferred frequencies of vibration, called frequency eigenvalues. If the forces generated by road inputs, out of balance and out of round of the road wheels and tyres are at frequencies close to the eigenvalues, then resonance of the engine on its mounts will occur. The resulting vibrations of the engine may be of considerable amplitude and can affect passenger comfort to a marked degree, and in extreme cases they may cause problems in the handling of the vehicle. The problem of engine shake has been the subject of much work, and is the centre of interest of the present work.

Previous theoretical work on this topic seemed, in general, to be directed towards finding the eigenvalues of the engine on its mounts. It also seemed to be usual to simplify the analysis considerably by assuming planes of symmetry in the engine and neglecting any damping present in the mounts. It was felt that a need existed for a more rigorous theoretical approach to the problem, which made as few simplifying assumptions as possible.

A theory was developed which treated the dynamic system of the engine and its mounts connected to the body in a completely general way. A computer program based on this theory gives a complete description of the engine motion when it is subjected to excitation from the vehicle body, as happens in engine shake.

Such a theory is only useful if it can be shown adequately to describe the phenomenon under consideration. With this in mind, it is necessary to examine an existing engine-mounting system, in order that the methods developed may be validated. Only if they are validated in such a manner may they be used to examine new mounting systems.

The work reported here falls naturally into three parts. First, the theory is developed, and an outline is given in this paper. Secondly, the methods are validated by examining an existing system, and a description of the way in which this was done is given below. Finally, some modified mounting systems are examined using the methods developed.

19.2   AN OUTLINE OF THE THEORY

The engine–gearbox assembly was idealised as a rigid mass attached to a movable foundation by viscoelastic springs. Preliminary work showed that measurements of engine shake made in the laboratory with the engine running were very similar indeed, within the frequency range examined (0–50 Hz), to measurements made without the engine running.

The engine was allowed six degrees of freedom, these being translation along and rotation about three mutually perpendicular axes. The axes were chosen in a convenient manner, with their origin at the centre of gravity of the engine.

A total of six equations may be derived which completely describe the dynamic behaviour of the engine. Three equations similar to

$$M\ddot{x} = \sum_i F_{ix}$$

describe motion along the coordinate directions, and three similar to the following describe the rotation

$$I_{XX}\ddot{\alpha} - I_{XY}\ddot{\beta} - I_{ZX}\ddot{\gamma} = \sum_i Y_i \Gamma_{iz} - \sum_i Z_i F_{iy}$$

where M is the engine mass; x, α, β, γ the coordinates of the c.g.; F_{ix} the force applied to the engine by the ith mount in the x direction; I_{XX}, I_{XY}, I_{YZ} the moments and products of inertia; Y_i, Z_i the coordinates of the ith mount.

Similar formulations of the problem have been made by Grootenhuis and Ewins [5] and Andrews [6].

It is clear that the force produced by a mount is a function only of the relative displacement of its two sides. The displacement of the engine side of a mount can be expressed in terms of the coordinates of the system, and so, by suitable substitution, all the unknowns can be moved to the left-hand sides of the equations, and the right-hand sides become functions of the displacements on the body sides of the mounts. Using this formulation of the equations, it is not necessary to know any force inputs to the system, which considerably simplifies experimental verification.

The theory assumes that the input excitation to the mounts is sinusoidal, and by using straightforward methods of solution it is possible to solve the equations for a specified set of displacement inputs at a discrete frequency. By repeating this process at a number of frequencies, the frequency response of the engine can be obtained.

19.3   EXPERIMENTAL VERIFICATION

The parameters involved in the formulation of the equations are the mass and inertia of the engine, the mount positions and stiffnesses, and the input excitation. These parameters had to be measured before proceeding with any analysis. The engine mass and mount positions are very easily established, but the other items are worthy of more detailed discussion.

19.4   ENGINE INERTIA

It was not sufficient to measure only the moments of inertia of the engine about the coordinate axes, as the products of inertia also were required by the equations.

The radii of gyration of a solid, about all directions through its centre of gravity, map out an ellipsoid in space, known as the inertia ellipsoid. The coefficients of the equation of this ellipsoid are the moments and products of inertia. The problem of defining the rotational inertia of a solid reduces to that of finding sufficient radii of gyration about a number of axes through its c.g. to adequately define its ellipsoid of inertia. In theory, six suitably chosen radii of gyration are sufficient, but to minimise the effect of experimental error, a total of 15 measurements were made on the engine.

The engine was supported in a purpose-built frame and this attached by four light strings to a crossbar some 4 m above ground level. The inertias of the frame itself were established by calculation.

The cooling system of the engine was filled with water, and the oil normally present was replaced by paraffin wax, this substance has approximately the same density as engine oil, but has the advantage of being solid at room temperature. Liquid oil would have spilt out of the engine during the measurements, and would not have remained in the position it normally adopts in the engine in service. Replacing a liquid by a solid will obviously have some effect on the accuracy of the results, but the effect is unlikely to be large.

One of the best methods of measuring the moments of inertia of a large cumbersome object such as an engine is to use an extension of the simple bifilar suspension technique, in which the mass is suspended by a number of strings of equal length and oscillated about a vertical axis. The principal disadvantage of this technique in the present context was that the strings would have had to be extremely long to achieve measurable periodic times. Further, there was no suitable point of attachment available in the laboratory for such strings, and so an alternative approach had to be found.

The method decided upon uses an extension of simple pendulum theory. In a simple pendulum, the bob is considered as a point mass, with no rotational inertia of its own. If the bob has inertia, then this affects the periodic time of the pendulum, and this effect can be used to measure the moment of inertia of the bob.

The necessary equation is

$$T = 2\pi \sqrt{\left[\frac{l}{g} (1 + r^2/l^2) \right]}$$

where T is the periodic time; l the string length; and r the radius of gyration of the bob.

As can be seen, the alteration in periodic time from the simple pendulum case is a second-order effect, and if r is small compared with l, then the change will be difficult to detect.

In order to minimise the errors introduced by a method which is in itself not capable of great precision, measurements of a single inertia were made for ten different string lengths, and the radius of gyration of the engine obtained from these results using regression techniques.

As mentioned above, a total of 15 radii of gyration were measured, and these were fitted to an ellipsoid, making use once again of regression techniques. Due to experimental error, the fit was not good, and there was considerable uncertainty in the values assigned to the moments and products of inertia of the engine.

19.5 MOUNT STIFFNESSES

Each engine mount was modelled as three independent, mutually per-pendicular, viscoelastic springs. The direction of action of these springs was taken to be coincident with the coordinate axes.

Each spring was allocated a complex stiffness, where the real, or elastic, part of the stiffness acted in phase with the driving force and the imaginary, or loss, part was 90° out of phase. Both the real and imaginary parts of the stiffness were made frequency dependent. Expressed mathematically we have

$$G^* = G(\omega)\{1 + j\delta(\omega)\}$$

where G^* is the complex stiffness; G the elastic stiffness; and δ the loss factor.

This complex model of rubber behaviour is well reported in the litera-ture—see, for example, Buswell *et al.* [7], Payne and Scott [8], Edwards and Farrand [9], Davey and Payne [10] and Snowden [11]. The mount stiffnesses were measured using a purpose-built rig. The mounts were located in pairs between an inertial mass and a rigid foundation, and arranged such that the axis of interest was vertical. An electrohydraulic vibrator was coupled to the inertial mass through a load cell. The feedback signal from the vibrator provided displacement information and the load cell the force information required to analyse the system.

Sinusoidal displacement was used at a large number of frequencies between 5 and 50 Hz, and the resulting force and its phase angle relative to the displacement were measured, and values of G and δ found at the various frequencies.

There were six stiffnesses to be measured in all. The engine was supported on three mounts but the front mounts were identical, and so the necessary measurements were of the rear mount in each coordinate direction and similarly for the front mount.

From an examination of the mounts it was clear that the front mounts in the vertical and longitudinal directions and the rear mount in the transverse direction acted principally in shear, and the other three stiffnesses were mainly compressive.

A problem encountered using the test method described was in deciding the value of the inertial mass. Apart from the mass deliberately introduced into the system, the metal bonded to the mounts, and the various nuts and bolts holding the system together also contributed mass. The mass of rubber in the mounts themselves was also significant and of course, at the higher end of the frequency range considered, the acceleration applied to the inertial mass absorbed most of the force applied to the system.

It was finally decided to include all the mass of the rubber in the calculations, although this is somewhat of an overestimate. Having made this compromise, the inertial mass of the system was simply found by unbolting the mounts from the rigid foundations and measuring the force required at various frequencies. The resulting force–frequency curve was of the form

$$F = m\omega^2$$

and a regression method was used to find m.

The test procedure allowed measurements to be made over a wide range of applied force and preload. An estimate of the order of force and preload met in service was made, and a full frequency analysis of the mount stiffnesses was made at these values. The effect of varying force and preload over wide ranges was also examined.

Some of the results obtained from the frequency analysis are shown in Figs. 19.1–19.3. The elastic modulus shows the anticipated rise with frequency, and the compressive stiffnesses are higher than the shear stiffnesses, also as expected. The rise in stiffnesses with frequency is characteristic of rubber, and has been well reported elsewhere—Snowden [11], Payne and Scott [8], Davey and Payne [10] and Hall [12]. The loss factor also increased with frequency, and here the two shear cases at the front mount gave similar results, as did the two compressive cases at the rear mount. It has been expected that the loss factor would be approximately constant for each mount, as it is principally a function of the material, but it also proved to be sensitive to the mode of deformation of the mount. The composition of the mounts was found by chemical and microscopic analysis, and the front mount proved to be the more heavily loaded with carbon black, which implies a larger loss factor. This was consistent with the observed results.

In view of the results obtained, it was considered acceptable to model the frequency dependence of the complex stiffnesses by fitting the results obtained to straight lines. The complex modulus then becomes

$$G^* = (G_1 f + G_2)\{1 + j[\delta_1 f + \delta_2]\}$$

Using this model it was possible to obtain a reasonable fit to the experimental data.

The examination of the effects produced by varying applied force and

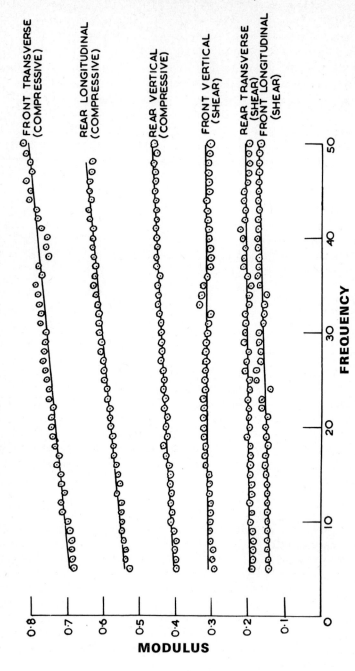

FRONT TRANSVERSE (COMPRESSIVE)

REAR LONGITUDINAL (COMPRESSIVE)

REAR VERTICAL (COMPRESSIVE)

FRONT VERTICAL (SHEAR)

REAR TRANSVERSE (SHEAR)
FRONT LONGITUDINAL (SHEAR)

FREQUENCY

MODULUS

Fig. 19.1. Elastic modulus (MN m^{-2}) vs. frequency (Hz).

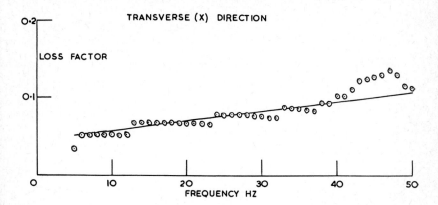

FIG. 19.2. Loss factor vs. frequency. Front mount in compression.

preload showed that there was very little variation in either elastic stiffness or loss factor with preload.

The elastic modulus showed a slight decrease and the loss factor an increase with increasing applied force. These results were as expected, because increasing the force level is equivalent to increasing the strain at which the results were measured, and similar results have been published by other workers investigating strain dependence of dynamic moduli—Payne *et al.* [13], Smith and Sumner [14], Ferry and Ninomiya [15].

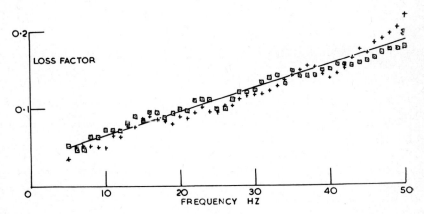

FIG. 19.3. Loss factor vs. frequency. Front mount in shear. ×, vertical (Z) direction; ⊡, longitudinal (Y) direction.

19.6   INPUT EXCITATION

The final parameter to be measured was the input excitation applied by the body to the mounts. It was considered necessary to use actual measurements as input data to the theoretical considerations, as only in this way could the relative magnitudes and phase angles of the nine different input excitations be correct.

The inputs were measured by placing the vehicle on a four-station electrohydraulic rig, with a vibrator under each wheel. The vehicle was then subjected to sinusoidal displacement at a total of 96 frequencies between 5 and 50 Hz.

The input amplitude was passed through a filter which arranged that amplitude was inversely proportional to frequency. This meant that the peak velocity of the input was constant throughout the frequency range, and this type of spectrum is similar to that generated by a typical road surface.

Having removed the propeller shaft, which was not modelled in the theory, an accelerometer was attached in turn to the body side of each mount in each of the three coordinate directions, and the acceleration measured over the frequency range. The measuring equipment used dealt with fundamentals only, and so the accelerations were readily converted into amplitudes. The phase angle between the response and the driving signal was also measured.

Similar measurements were made on the engine side of each mount to serve as a check on the theoretical predictions. In this way, a total of nine sine wave inputs, expressed in terms of amplitude and phase angle, were obtained at each frequency.

These amplitude and phase angles were used as input data to the theoretical work.

19.7   RESULTS

A computer program based on the theory was supplied with the various measured parameters and produced amplitude–frequency curves at each mount in each of the three directions. A second program predicted the six frequency eigenvalues of the system. Although the principal objective of the work was to predict the frequency response of the engine, it was felt that a knowledge of the eigenvalues would be useful for two purposes.

First, it would serve as an approximate check on the accuracy of the measured inertias and spring rates and, secondly, it would establish which peaks in the engine response were due to the dynamics of the engine mounting system itself, and which were due to resonances in other parts of the vehicle. The longitudinal acceleration measured at the nearside front mount is shown in Fig. 19.4. Peaks are evident at the eigenvalues

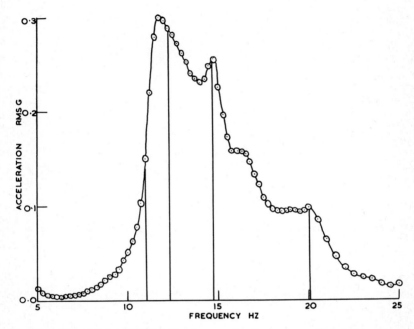

FIG. 19.4. Mount 2, longitudinal direction acceleration. —— predicted eigenvalues.

12·3, 15·7 and 20·1 Hz. The vertical acceleration at the offside mount (Fig. 19.5) shows peaks at the eigenvalues 12·3 and 14·7 Hz, and peaks at 11·0, 12·3 and 20·1 Hz can be seen in the vertical acceleration at the rear mount (Fig. 19.6). The eigenvalue predicted at 23·8 Hz can be seen in Fig. 19.7, which shows the transverse acceleration at the front mount. There is no experimental evidence to support a predicted eigenvalue at 9·8 Hz.

Figure 19.8–19.10 compare the predicted and measured frequency response curves. Agreement between the two sets of curves was disappointing, particularly at the low end of the frequency scale. The predicted curve has, in general, more peaks than the measured curves, these peaks usually being coincident with the predicted eigenvalues.

The reasons for the disagreement are difficult to establish. The fact

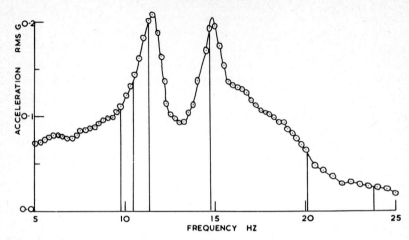

FIG. 19.5. Mount 1, vertical acceleration. ——— predicted eigenvalues.

that there was agreement to a reasonable extent between the predicted eigenvalues and the observed resonances would tend to imply that the values used for the mount stiffnesses were correct. It should be pointed out, however, that the mount stiffnesses were measured uniaxially, whereas in service they are subjected to simultaneous displacement in a number of directions. It is probable that, due to the near incompressibility of rubber, the three mount stiffnesses measured are interdependent, and this effect was not allowed for. Further, it is most probable that the mount stiffnesses

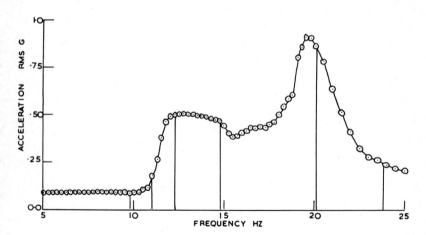

FIG. 19.6. Rear mount, vertical acceleration. ——— predicted eigenvalues.

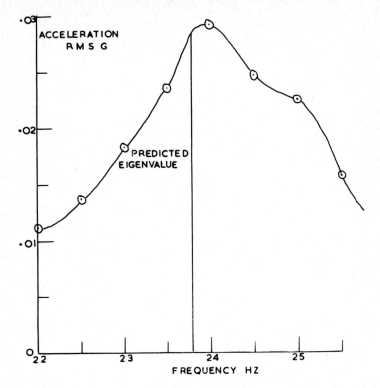

Fig. 19.7. Mount 1, transverse acceleration.

are amplitude dependent, and this effect was also ignored in the analysis.

A further source of error lies in the relative uncertainty in the values used for the moments and products of inertia, which no doubt had a contributory effect to the poor agreement.

19.8 APPLICATIONS

Although agreement between theory and practice was not ideal, it was felt to be sufficiently good to justify the use of the analysis to examine different mounting systems.

In the limited time available, only two types of analysis were attempted. In one, the mount stiffnesses were systematically varied over a wide range, and in the other, the stiffnesses remained unaltered, but the mount positions were chosen to form a centre of percussion system.

A. Eames-Jones and C. Ashley

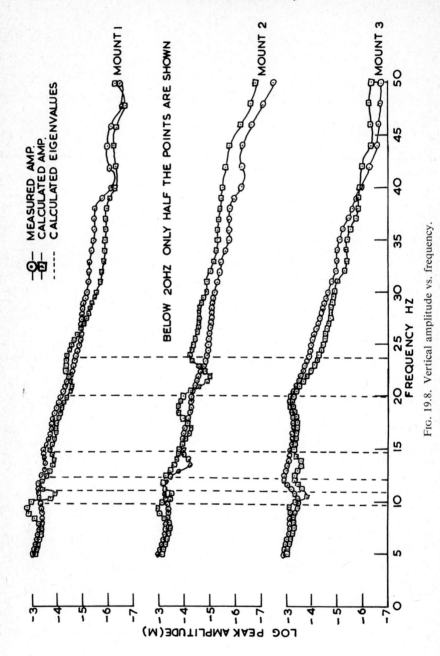

Fig. 19.8. Vertical amplitude vs. frequency.

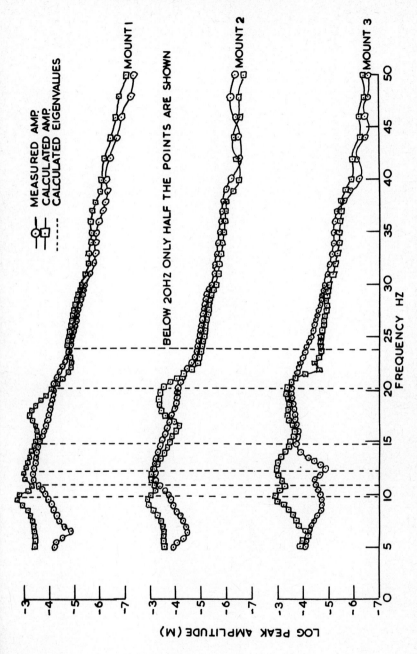

FIG. 19.9. Longitudinal amplitude vs. frequency.

A. Eames-Jones and C. Ashley

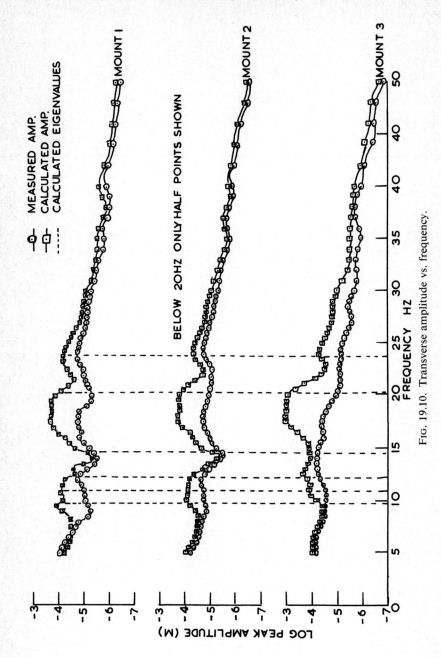

Fig. 19.10. Transverse amplitude vs. frequency.

19.9   STIFFNESS VARIATION

The program was run with all the complex stiffnesses first decreased by 25% and 50%, and then increased by 25%, 50%, 75% and 100%.

The direction of main interest is the vertical, as the majority of the engine motion was in this direction. Transmissibility curves at the front nearside mount and the rear mount are shown in Fig. 19.11 and 19.12. All seven conditions are shown in each set so that they may be compared.

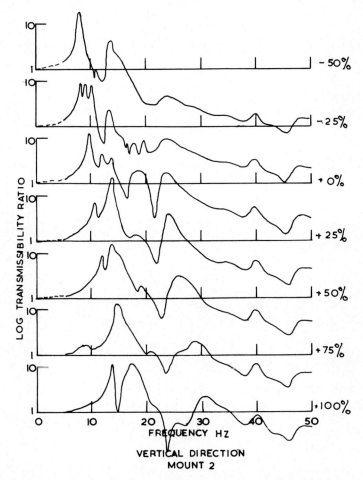

FIG. 19.11. Transmissibility variation (vertical direction, rear mount).

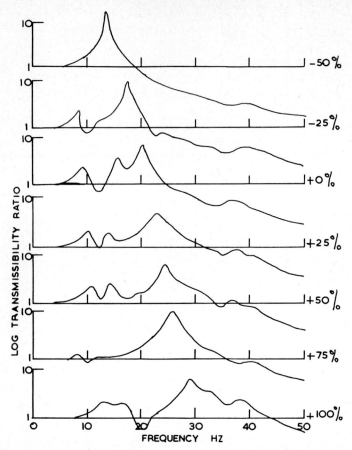

Fig. 19.12. Transmissibility variation (vertical direction, Mount 3).

The curves are difficult to analyse with any precision because of their complex nature. Some peaks in the curves seem to be dependent on the changes and some independent of them.

In the vertical direction at the rear mount (Fig. 19.11), there is a stationary peak around 38 Hz. The peak at 14 Hz moves progressively up the frequency scale as the mount rates are increased, as does the peak at 8 Hz in the −25% case. As would be expected, when the mounts are soft the high frequency transmissibility is much reduced, but the low frequency performance is less good.

At the front mount in the vertical direction (Fig. 19.12), there is a static peak around 42 Hz. The peak at 25 Hz in the −50% case moves up the scale to 30 Hz in the $+100\%$ case. There is a considerable peak at 8 Hz in the -50% case which separates into three peaks at -25%. As the mounts become stiffer the peaks move up the scale, gradually separating as they do so.

To summarise, there are some frequencies at which peaks occur irrespective of mount stiffness, and others which move up the frequency scale as the mounts are made stiffer.

The static peaks may be attributed to resonances in other parts of the vehicle, and demonstrate convincingly the importance of using realistic input data. The behaviour of the moving peaks was largely as expected.

Curves of transmissibility variation across the engine mounts allow the dynamic behaviour of the engine to be studied, but of greater interest is the effect of these variations on passengers in the vehicle.

The measurements of engine inertia, and mount stiffnesses, together with other suitable data were used in a second computer model—this time a simple idealisation of the entire vehicle. This model had ten degrees of freedom, but now the engine was allowed only two degrees of freedom. A description of this model is outside the scope of the present paper, but suffice to say that it was shown to give not unreasonable results. Similar models of varying complexity have been examined by Clarke [16], Mitschke [17] and Wyman [18].

One use to which the model was put was an examination of the effects of stiffening and softening the mount stiffnesses, as was done with the engine in isolation. The results are shown in Figs. 19.13 and 19.14. Three distinct resonance peaks are apparent: the lowest peak is the body and engine moving together on the suspension; the middle peak may be attributed to wheel hop, which is a resonance of the unsprung mass; and the highest peak is due to engine shake.

Predictably, the worst level of vibration from the point of view of the passenger occurs when the engine shake resonance coincides with the wheel hop resonance, which happens when the mount stiffnesses are halved (shown as -50% in the figure).

19.10 CENTRE OF PERCUSSION SYSTEM

It was decided to arrange the mounts symmetrically about the principal axes of inertia of the engine, which has the effect of eliminating the coupling between the modes of vibration which is introduced by the products of inertia terms. Further, the mounts were arranged in such a way as to form a centre of percussion (COP) system. This means that a vertical

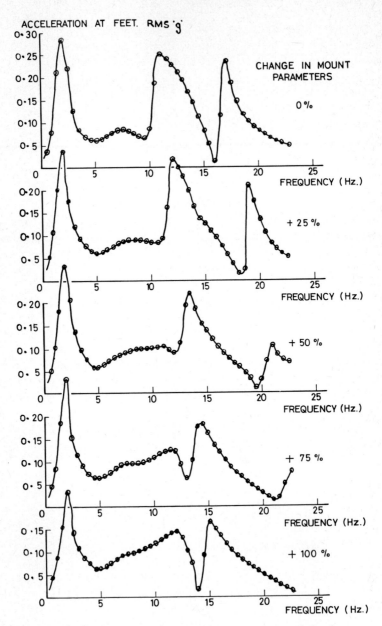

FIG. 19.13. Response at feet as engine mounts are made harder.

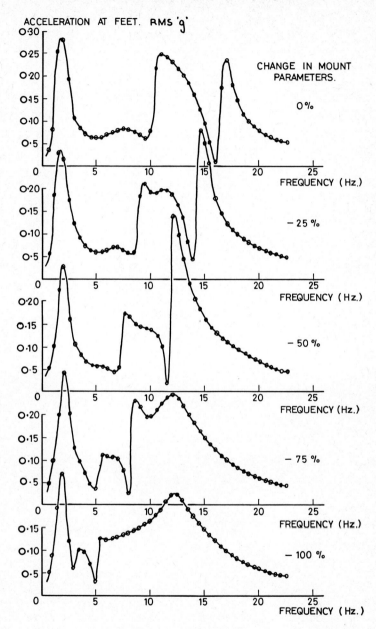

FIG. 19.14. Response at feet as engine mounts are made softer.

force input at the front mounts causes no reaction at the rear mount. The COP effect was extended by using two mounts at the rear of the engine, and arranging the mounts so that there was also a COP effect from side to side; that is, a vertical force at the mounts on one side of the engine caused no reaction at the mounts on the other side.

As no clear preference has emerged from the previous series of tests, the existing mount rates were used in the COP system, save that the rates at the rear mount were of course halved, there now being two mounts.

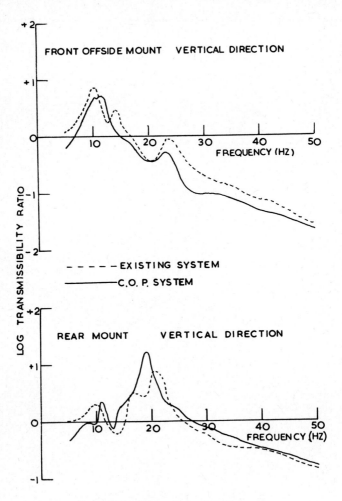

FIG. 19.15. Comparison of COP system.

The curves obtained in the vertical direction at a front mount and a rear mount are shown in Fig. 19.15, together with the curves for the original system. The level at the front is slightly lower with the COP system, with the exception of the peak at 12 Hz. The level at the rear mount is, in general, worse for the COP system, particularly around 20 Hz.

The longitudinal direction curves for the same two mounts are shown in Fig. 19.16. The COP system shows an improvement over the existing system, particularly around 15 Hz at the rear mount. The results indicate

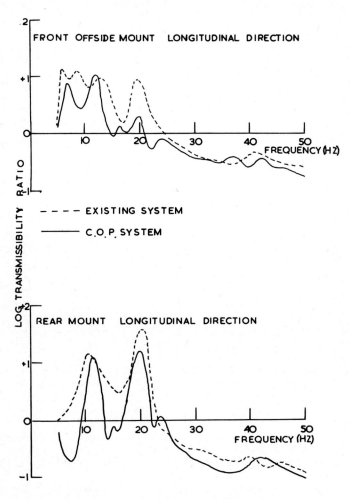

FIG. 19.16. Comparison of COP system.

that the COP system used offers slight advantages over the existing system, particularly in the longitudinal direction at the rear mount.

The system, as programmed, is only one of a great number of possible COP systems, and for each of these systems the mount rates may be varied at will. One of the possible combinations could well result in a significant improvement on the existing system, but there would seem to be no systematic method of arriving at the optimum arrangement of mount positions and rates.

19.11   CONCLUSION

The objective of the work was to establish a method of predicting, realistically, the frequency response of an engine on its mounting system. To a limited extent this objective was achieved, and it is felt that a more accurate method of measuring the engine inertias and possibly a more sophisticated model of the mounts would improve the method sufficiently for its use as a design aid.

REFERENCES

1. Iliffe, C. (1939/40). The theory of flexible mountings for internal combustion engines, *Proc. Inst. Auto. Eng.*, **34**, p. 77.
2. Harrison, H. C. (1956). Engine installation, *The Automobile Engineer*, **46**, 380, Oct.
3. Anon. (1953). Engine mounting, *The Automobile Engineer*, **43**, 87, March.
4. Horovitz, M. (1956/57). The suspension of the internal combustion engine in vehicles, *Proc. Instn. Mech. Eng., Auto. Div.*, p. 17.
5. Grootenhuis, P. and Ewins, D. J. (1965). Vibration of a spring supported body, *J. Mech. Eng. Science*, **7**, (2), 185–192.
6. Andrews, G. J. (1968). Vibration isolation of rigid bodies on resilient supports, *J. Account. Soc. America*, **32**, (8), 995–1001, Aug.
7. Buswell, A. G. *et al.* (1967). Dynamic testing and interpretation of results, *J. IRI*, **1**, 43, Jan./Feb.
8. Payne, A. R. and Scott, J. R. (1969). *Engineering Design with Rubber*, Maclaren, Chap. 2, p. 18.
9. Edwards, A. C. and Farrand, G. N. S. (1961). *The Applied Science of Rubber* (Ed. W. J. S. Naunton), Edward Arnold, London, Ch. VIII, Pt 1, p. 517.
10. Davey, A. B. and Payne, A. R. (1964). *Rubber in Engineering Practice*, Maclaren, Ch. 13, pp. 369–376.
11. Snowden, J. S. (1968). *Vibration and Shock in Damped Mechanical Systems*, Wiley, Ch. 1, p. 3.

12. Hall, M. M. (1972). Dynamic testing of rubber, *RAPRA Bulletin*, pp. 325–331, Nov.
13. Payne, A. R. *et al.* (1972). Effect of vulcanisation on the low strain dynamic properties of filled rubbers, *J. Appl. Poly. Sci.*, **16**, 1191–1212.
14. Smith, J. E. and Sumner, E. C. (1972). 'An automatic Dynamic Response Apparatus', Proc. International Rubber Conference, Brighton, May.
15. Ferry, J. D. and Ninomiya, K. (1960). 'Comparisons of viscoelastic behaviour in seven typical polymer systems', in *Viscoelasticity—Phenomenological Aspects* (Ed. J. T. Bergen), pp. 55–63, Academic Press, London.
16. Clarke, D. C. (1962). A preliminary investigation into the dynamic behaviour of vehicles and highways, *Trans. SAE, NY*, **70**, 447.
17. Mitschke, E. M. (1962). Influence of road and vehicle dimensions on the amplitude of body motions and dynamic loads, *Trans. SAE NY*, **70**, 434–446.
18. Wyman, W. (1971). 'The Use of Digital Computer Models in Solving Vibration Problems in the Motor Industry', Proc. SEE Symp. on Dynamic Testing, London, Jan.

20

Application of the WKBJ Approximation Processes for the Analysis of the Torsional Vibrations of Diesel Engine Systems

M. S. PASRICHA AND W. D. CARNEGIE

Banares Hindu University and University of Surrey

SUMMARY

For many years the effects of the variable inertia characteristics of reciprocating engines on the accuracy of torsional vibration calculations were considered to be negligible. But in recent years some cases of crankshaft failures in large slow-speed marine engines could not be explained by neglecting the variation in inertia torques of the system arising from the motion of the reciprocating parts. When the variable inertia effect is allowed for, the equations of motion taking into account the effect are non-linear. Assuming small displacements, the equations can be linearised to predict important characteristics of the motion.

Such an equation, when solved by numerical methods using a digital computer, predicts the manner in which the amplitude and frequency vary with the speed of rotation of the engine. The solutions of equations of motion obtained by use of numerical processes may sometimes be misleading. Hence it is thought to be desirable to obtain time responses from some analytical process as an independent verification of the numerical methods. Therefore, the solutions are determined by use of the method given by Wentzel, Kramers, Brillouin and Jeffreys, generally known as the WKBJ approximation and the process of variation of parameters. The results are compared with solutions of the equation obtained from numerical analysis techniques.

The present analysis suggests a reason as to how dangerous vibrations are evoked due to secondary resonance in certain cases of marine diesel engines.

20.1 INTRODUCTION

In recent years, several cases of marine crankshaft failures have been attributed to the phenomenon of secondary resonance, whereby an otherwise innocuous critical in the region of the service speed can be magnified by interaction with powerful but non-resonant excitations of order $(n - 2)$ and $(n + 2)$. The simplified theory, neglecting the effect of variable inertia, is not adequate to explain the existence of the secondary resonance phenomenon in torsional vibrations, since such a simplified system does not reproduce the exact dynamic characteristics of the actual system.

In the past, engineers had a tendency to dismiss the associated secondary resonances as interesting mathematical curiosities. In view of the importance of the torsional vibrations in engineering practice, Goldsbrough [1,2] carried out a theoretical and experimental study to examine the effect of the reciprocating parts in producing or modifying the vibrations. Draminsky [3] indicated that secondary resonance effects could have contributed to a number of otherwise inexplicable crankshaft failures in large slow-speed marine engines.

Archer [4] published examples of crankshaft failures in large 10-cylinder and 12-cylinder engines from service, which demonstrated the existence of a secondary resonance phenomenon. Carnegie and Pasricha [5,6] for the first time made an attempt to provide a systematic and fundamental appraisal of the problem by use of numerical analysis techniques. After developing the investigatory tools by use of numerical processes, the authors have felt it essential to confirm their results by analytical methods so that the solutions obtained are more convincing.

The results of the present paper predict, in a limited range of the shaft speeds, the variation of amplitudes, frequencies and the shapes of the complex waveforms for the linear motion of a single-cylinder engine.

20.2 NOTATION

$A_{\max}$ maximum amplitude of γ

a crank radius

I moment of inertia of the rotating parts

I_m $I + \frac{1}{2}Ma^2$

M mass of reciprocating parts

r ratio of the angular velocity ω of crankshaft to the natural frequency ω/n of the system neglecting variable inertia effects

ε $\dfrac{\frac{1}{2}Ma^2}{I + \frac{1}{2}Ma^2}$

μ torsional stiffness of crankshaft

γ displacement of torsional motion

ω angular velocity of crankshaft

ω_n natural frequency of the system neglecting variable inertia effects,

$$= \left[\frac{\mu}{I + \frac{1}{2}Ma^2}\right]^{1/2}$$

20.3   EQUATION OF MOTION

With the symbols defined in the notation, the basic equation which takes into account the second-order variation in inertia and governs the vibratory motion in a single-cylinder engine, the gas pressure in the cylinder being omitted, is

$$I_m(1 - \varepsilon \cos 2\omega t)\frac{d_\gamma^2}{dt^2} + (2I_m\omega\varepsilon \sin 2\omega t)\frac{d\gamma}{dt}$$

$$+ \left(\frac{\omega^2}{r^2} + 2\omega^2\varepsilon \cos 2\omega t\right)I_m\gamma = -\tfrac{1}{2}Ma^2\omega^2 \sin 2\omega t \quad (20.1)$$

Equation (20.1) can be simplified by dividing it throughout by $\omega^2 I_m$ and changing the independent variable to $\tau = \omega t$,

$$(1 - \varepsilon \cos 2\tau)\gamma'' + (2\varepsilon \sin 2\tau)\gamma' + \left(\frac{1}{r^2} + 2\varepsilon \cos 2\tau\right)\gamma = -\varepsilon \sin 2\tau \quad (20.2)$$

where primes represent differentiation with respect to τ.

The solutions of the equation of motion (20.2), at definite rotational speeds, determined by use of numerical methods, are discussed in another paper [5]. In view of the practical importance of the subject it was considered necessary to confirm the numerical analysis by alternative methods. The results of the investigations based on the WKBJ approximation and the method of variation of parameters are given in the present paper.

20.4   SOLUTION OF THE EQUATION OF MOTION BY THE WKBJ APPROXIMATION AND THE PROCESS OF VARIATION OF PARAMETERS [7]

Rewriting equation (20.2) in the form

$$\gamma'' + 2\left[\frac{\varepsilon \sin 2\tau}{1 - \varepsilon \cos 2\tau}\right]\gamma' + \left[\frac{\lambda + 2\varepsilon \cos 2\tau}{1 - \varepsilon \cos 2\tau}\right]\gamma = \frac{-\varepsilon \sin 2\tau}{1 - \varepsilon \cos 2\tau}$$

$$(20.3)$$

where $\lambda = 1/r^2$, let

$$U(\tau) = \frac{\varepsilon \sin 2\tau}{1 - \varepsilon \cos 2\tau}, \qquad V^2(\tau) = \frac{\lambda + 2\varepsilon \cos 2\tau}{1 - \varepsilon \cos 2\tau}$$

and

$$F(\tau) = \frac{-\varepsilon \sin 2\tau}{1 - \varepsilon \cos 2\tau}$$

Equation (20.3) then reduces to

$$\gamma'' + 2U(\tau)\gamma' + V^2(\tau)\gamma = F(\tau) \tag{20.4}$$

Changing the dependent variable from γ to y through the relationship

$$\gamma = y \exp\left(-\int U(\tau)\,d\,\tau\right)$$

it becomes

$$y'' + [V^2(\tau) - U^2(\tau) - U'(\tau)]y = F(\tau)\exp\left[\int U(\tau)\,d\tau\right] \tag{20.5}$$

or

$$y'' + \left[\frac{\lambda + 2\varepsilon\cos 2\tau}{1 - \varepsilon\cos 2\tau} - \left(\frac{\varepsilon\sin 2\tau}{1 - \varepsilon\cos 2\tau}\right)^2 - \frac{(2\varepsilon\cos 2\tau - 2\varepsilon^2)}{(1 - \varepsilon\cos 2\tau)^2}\right]y$$
$$= F(\tau)\exp\left[\tfrac{1}{2}(\log_e(1 - \varepsilon\cos 2\tau)\right] \tag{20.6}$$

since

$$U'(\tau) = \frac{(2\varepsilon\cos 2\tau - 2\varepsilon^2)}{(1 - \varepsilon\cos 2\tau)}$$

and

$$\int U(\tau)\,d\tau = \tfrac{1}{2}\log_e(1 - \varepsilon\cos 2\tau)$$

Equation (20.6), on simplification, reduces to,

$$y'' + \left[\frac{\lambda - \lambda\varepsilon\cos 2\tau + \varepsilon^2\sin^2 2\tau}{(1 - \varepsilon\cos 2\tau)^2}\right]y = F(\tau)\exp\left[\tfrac{1}{2}\log_e(1 - \varepsilon\cos 2\tau)\right] \tag{20.7}$$

Substituting

$$\frac{\lambda - \lambda\varepsilon\cos 2\tau + \varepsilon^2\sin^2 2\tau}{(1 - \varepsilon\cos 2\tau)^2} = G^2(\tau)$$

eqn (20.7) can be expressed as

$$y'' + G^2(\tau)\,y = F(\tau)\exp\left[\tfrac{1}{2}\log_e(1 - \varepsilon\cos 2\tau)\right] \tag{20.8}$$

For the complementary function, eqn (20.8) is written in the form

$$y'' + G^2(\tau)y = 0 \tag{20.9}$$

If the condition

$$|G^2| \gg \left|\frac{G''}{2G} - \frac{3}{4}\left(\frac{G'}{G}\right)^2\right| \tag{20.10}$$

is satisfied, so that $G(\tau)$ and $\phi(\tau)$ are both real, then the complementary function for eqn (20.9) from the WKBJ approximation is

$$y = [G(\tau)]^{-1/2}[A \cos \phi(\tau) + B \sin \phi(\tau)] \qquad (20.11)$$

where $\phi(\tau) = \int G(\tau) \, d\tau$. Therefore,

$$\gamma = [G(\tau)]^{-1/2}[A \cos \phi(\tau) + B \sin \phi(\tau)] \exp \left[-\tfrac{1}{2} \log_e (1 - \varepsilon \cos 2\tau) \right. \tag{20.12}$$

A computer program in Algol language is written for the expression (20.10) to determine the range of r in which the above method is applicable for the specific value of $\varepsilon = 0\cdot544$. It is found that the condition (20.10) is satisfied for low values of $r \leqslant 0\cdot08$, which fully serves the purpose of illustrating the existence of secondary resonance phenomenon and that of providing a comparison of results obtained from analytical methods and the numerical analysis.

Writing the complementary solution (20.12) in the form

$$\gamma = A\gamma_1 + B\gamma_2 \qquad (20.13)$$

where

$$\gamma_1 = G^{-1/2}[\cos \phi \exp \{-\tfrac{1}{2} \log_e (1 - \varepsilon \cos 2\tau)\}] \qquad (20.14)$$

and

$$\gamma_2 = G^{-1/2}[\sin \phi \exp \{-\tfrac{1}{2} \log_e (1 - \varepsilon \cos 2\tau)\}] \qquad (20.15)$$

the method of variation of parameters can be applied by allowing the quantities A and B to vary with τ.

20.5   METHOD OF VARIATION OF PARAMETERS FOR DETERMINATION OF PARTICULAR INTEGRAL

Equation (20.4) can be reduced into two simultaneous first-order equations through the substitution $\gamma' = x$, so as to give

$$\left. \begin{array}{l} \gamma' = x \\ x' = -2U(\tau)x - V^2(\tau)\gamma + F(\tau) \end{array} \right\} \qquad (20.16)$$

The complementary function, as given in eqn (20.13), is

$$\gamma = A\gamma_1 + B\gamma_2$$

and

$$x = A\gamma_1' + B\gamma_2'$$

where A and B are arbitrary constants. Now, allowing the quantities A and B to vary with respect to τ and making use of these relationships, the first of the eqns (20.16) gives

$$A'\gamma_1 + B'\gamma_2 = 0 \qquad (20.17)$$

The second part of the relations (20.16) yields

$$A'\gamma_1' + B'\gamma_2' = F(\tau) \qquad (20.18)$$

By solving eqns (20.17) and (20.18) as simultaneous algebraic equations, the expressions for A' and B' are

$$\left.\begin{aligned} A' &= \frac{-F\gamma_2}{\gamma_1\gamma_2' - \gamma_1'\gamma_2} \\ B' &= \frac{F\gamma_1}{\gamma_1\gamma_2' - \gamma_1'\gamma_2} \end{aligned}\right\} \qquad (20.19)$$

These relations may be integrated to give values for $A(\tau)$ and $B(\tau)$, and substitution of the expressions thus obtained in eqn (20.13) would give the solution of eqn (20.2) that

$$\gamma = \left(-\int \frac{F\gamma_2}{\gamma_1\gamma_2' - \gamma_1'\gamma_2}\, d\tau + C_1\right)\gamma_1 + \left(\int \frac{F\gamma_1}{\gamma_1\gamma_2' - \gamma_1'\gamma_2}\, d\tau + C_2\right)\gamma_2$$

$$(20.20)$$

where C_1 and C_2 are arbitrary constants which are determined from the initial conditions $\gamma = 1$, when $\tau = 0$; $\gamma' = 0$, when $\tau = 0$. Thus,

$$C_1 = \left(\frac{\lambda}{1 - \varepsilon}\right)^{1/4} \exp\{\tfrac{1}{2}\log_e (1 - \varepsilon)\}$$

and

$$C_2 = 0$$

γ_1' and γ_2' are obtained by differentiating eqns (20.14) and (20.15), so as to give

$$\gamma_1' = -G^{-1/2}\left[\frac{\varepsilon \sin 2\tau \cos \phi}{(1 - \varepsilon \cos 2\tau)} + \phi' \sin \phi + \frac{(G^2)'}{4G^2} \cos \phi\right]$$
$$\exp\{-\tfrac{1}{2}\log_e (1 - \varepsilon \cos 2\tau)\} \qquad (20.21)$$

$$\gamma_2' = -G^{-1/2}\left[\frac{\varepsilon \sin 2\tau \sin \phi}{(1 - \varepsilon \cos 2\tau)} - \phi' \cos \phi + \frac{(G^2)'}{4G^2} \sin \phi\right]$$
$$\exp\{-\tfrac{1}{2}\log_e (1 - \varepsilon \cos 2\tau)\} \qquad (20.22)$$

Therefore, the complete solution of eqn (20.2) is

$$\gamma = \left[-\int \frac{F\gamma_2}{\gamma_1\gamma_2' - \gamma_1'\gamma_2}\, d\tau + \left(\frac{\lambda}{1-\varepsilon}\right)^{1/4} \exp\left\{\tfrac{1}{2}\log_e(1-\varepsilon)\right\} \right]\gamma_1$$
$$+ \left[\int \frac{F\gamma_1}{\gamma_1\gamma_2' - \gamma_1'\gamma_2}\, d\tau \right]\gamma_2 \tag{20.23}$$

Making use of Simpson's rule for integration, eqn (20.23) is programmed in Algol language for the solution of eqn (20.2) on a digital computer.

Using the WKBJ approximation and the method of variation of parameters, the time responses of the system for ratios of the angular velocity of the shaft to the natural frequency of the system $r = 1/16$ and $r = 1/12$ are given in Figs. 20.1 and 20.2, when $\varepsilon = 0\cdot544$. In Figs. 20.3 and 20.4 are given the corresponding waveform relationships of $\gamma \sim t$, determined

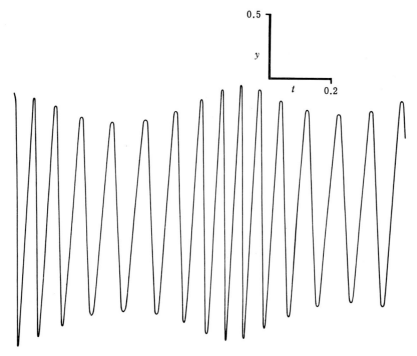

FIG. 20.1. Theoretical waveform relationship of $y \sim t$ for $r = \tfrac{1}{16}$ and $\varepsilon = 0\cdot544$ determined by use of the method of variation of parameters and the WKBJ approximation.

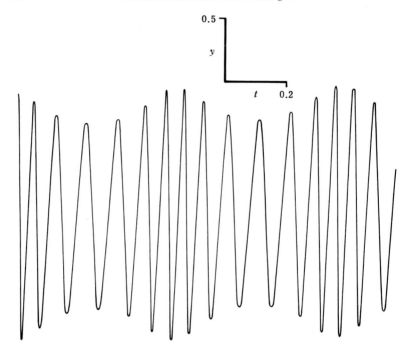

FIG. 20.2. Theoretical waveform relationship of $y \sim t$ for $r = \frac{1}{12}$ and $\varepsilon = 0.544$ determined by use of the method of variation of parameters and the WKBJ approximation.

by the use of the modified Euler's method. Comparing Fig. 20.1 with Fig. 20.3 and Fig. 20.2 with Fig. 20.4, it can be seen that the solutions determined from analytical methods are in close agreement with those found from the numerical analysis techniques.

The waveform solutions of Figs. 20.1 and 20.2 show the occurrence of a modulation of both amplitude and frequency conforming to the form of beats. The harmonic analysis of the waveform in Fig. 20.1 suggests that it is composed of a principal component of order 16 and the secondary components of order 12, 14, 18, 20, 22, 24, etc. A similar analysis of the waveform solution of Fig. 20.2, for the speed of the engine for $r = 1/12$ and $\varepsilon = 0.544$, shows that the waveform contains a principal component of order 12 and secondary components of order 10, 14, 16, 18, 20, etc. Such an analysis gives the order of the principal component at a specific speed of the engine, which can be excited to increased amplitudes by the exciting torques of the same orders as those of secondary components.

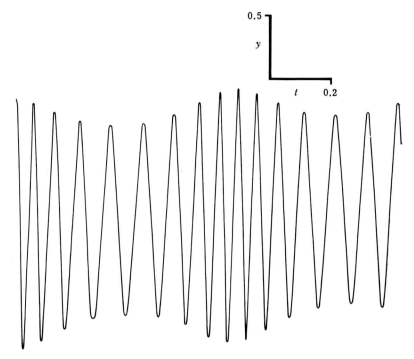

FIG. 20.3. Theoretical waveform relationship of $y \sim t$ for $r = \frac{1}{16}$ and $\varepsilon = 0.544$.

20.6   CONCLUSIONS

The results presented in this paper predict the time responses of a single-cylinder engine system in the limited range of engine speed $r \leqslant 0.08$, for specific value of $\varepsilon = 0.544$. The solutions obtained by use of WKBJ approximation and the process of variation of parameters are in close agreement with those determined from the numerical analysis techniques. The waveform solutions show a modulation of amplitude and instantaneous frequency and the maximum amplitude and maximum apparent frequency of one oscillation of the solution occur together, as do the minimum values of these same quantities. It is also shown that there are two beats in one revolution of the shaft.

The orders of the harmonic components of motion through which the energy can be transferred to the system from external excitations of the same orders can be determined from the harmonic analysis of the waveform solutions at the specific speed of rotation.

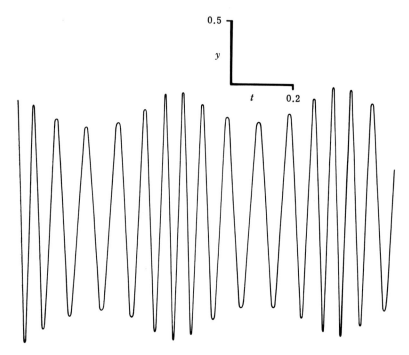

FIG. 20.4. Theoretical waveform relationship of $y \sim t$ for $r = \frac{1}{12}$ and $\varepsilon = 0\cdot544$.

This explains the possibility of an otherwise harmless principal component being magnified by the interaction with powerful secondary excitations. Thus, dangerous vibrations may be evoked due to a secondary resonance phenomenon in marine diesel engines.

REFERENCES

1. Goldsbrough, G. R. (1925). Torsional vibrations in reciprocating engine shafts, *Proc. Roy. Soc.*, **109**, 99.
2. Goldsbrough, G. R. (1926). The properties of torsional vibration in reciprocating engine shafts, *Proc. Roy. Soc.*, **113**, 259.
3. Draminsky, P. (1961). Secondary resonance and subharmonics in torsional vibration, *Acta Polytechnica, Scandinavica* (me 10), Copenhagen.
4. Archer, S. (1964). Some factors influencing the life of marine crankshafts, *Trans. Inst. Marine Engrs*, **76**, 73–134.
5. Carnegie, W. and Pasricha, M. S. (1971). An examination of the effects

of variable inertia on the torsional vibrations of marine engine systems, *Trans. Inst. Marine Engrs,* **84**, 160–167.

6. Carnegie, W. and Pasricha, M. S. (1973). Secondary resonance in marine engine systems, *Shipbuilding and Marine Engineering International*, **96**, (1168), 583–584.

7. Cunningham, W. J. (1958). *Introduction to Non-Linear Analysis*, McGraw-Hill, Inc., New York, Toronto, London.

8. Draminsky, P. (1965). Extended treatment of secondary resonance, *Marine Engineer and Naval Architect*, **88**, 180–186, April.

21

Simplified Modelling of High Order Linear Systems

M. COTTERELL

London Transport Executive

SUMMARY

Investigations of the response of railway vehicles frequently lead to high order linear systems. Such systems can be solved digitally to any required accuracy but this approach is often time-consuming and does not yield much information on how the response depends on vehicle parameters. In many cases the system can be adequately represented by a low order model.

A very simple method of producing such models has been developed by London Transport and forms the basis of this paper. The method, based on the Schwarz inequality, is relatively easy to apply and ideally suited to systems with an associated quadratic cost function. As well as the theory the paper also presents a practical application to the response of a railway vehicle to random vertical track irregularities.

21.1   INTRODUCTION

The response of a linear system to stochastic inputs is usually measured in terms of the statistics of the system outputs. These statistics can be formulated in terms of a quadratic cost function, which for example might take the form of the expected mean square value of a linear combination of the system outputs. In general, the quadratic cost function can be expressed in terms of the system impulse response function. For low order systems, an analytic solution is feasible, but for high order systems one often has to resort to numerical methods such as, for instance, the fast Fourier transform. An alternative approach is to replace the system by a simple model, whose response, in some chosen sense, approximates that of the original system.

For systems described by a set of time-invariant linear ordinary differential equations, Mitra [1] has shown that the best model of a given order is associated with the eigenvectors of the W-matrix. The W-matrix is obtained by integrating a weighted square of the impulse response matrix of the system. The weighting matrix used reflects the sense in which approximation error of the model is measured. By appropriate weighting (which can be time-dependent), the W-matrix for a system subject to stochastic inputs can be equated to the covariance matrix of the system outputs. Then, if the W-matrix is known, there is no need to produce a model of the system. For an Nth order system subject to white noise inputs, the W-matrix can be found algebraically by solving $\frac{1}{2}N(N-1)$ linear simultaneous equations. For high order systems, the number of operations involved in evaluating the W-matrix increases in proportion to N^6 making it somewhat unattractive. For low order systems, the W-matrix is easy to use, as is demonstrated by Hedrick [2] for a simple monocycle suspension system.

A simpler approach is to replace the Laplace transform of the system response by a modified Padé approximation, using the technique described by Chuang [3]. In this paper, an approach via the Laplace transform is also used to generate models of the system. The poles of the model can be selected freely, providing the resultant model is stable. The model generated provides a strict lower bound to the quadratic cost function. The accuracy of the model depends on the choice of the poles used, but provided one has some physical insight into the nature of the system, it is usually possible to select the poles to give reasonable accuracy. The technique is illustrated by application to the bounce dynamics of a railway vehicle subject to track irregularities.

21.2   THEORETICAL APPROACH

Let H be a Hilbert space with inner product (f, g) and norm $\|f\|$ for f, $g \in H$. Here the elements of H are taken to be vector functions $f(\tau) \in C^N$ defined for all $\tau \in V \subseteq C^n$. Consider the problem of approximating an element $u \in H$ by an element f of some subspace $F \subset H$, in order to provide an estimate of (u, u). It is assumed that u is known only as the solution of the equation

$$Lu(\tau) = q(\tau) \qquad (21.1)$$

Subject to conditions specified on the boundary ∂V. $q(\tau)$ is a known element of H and $L: H \to H$ is a linear operator.

From Plesner [4] there exists a subspace $F^* \subset H$, such that F, F^* are orthogonal and H can be written as the direct sum:

$$H = F \oplus F^* \qquad (21.2)$$

It follows that u has a unique representation

$$u = B + g \tag{21.3}$$

where $B \in F$, $g \in F^*$ and

$$(B, g) = 0 \tag{21.4}$$

The best approximation to u from the subspace F is defined as the element $f \in F$ which minimises $(u - f, u - f)$. But

$$(u - f, u - f) = (B - f, B - f) + (g, g) \tag{21.5}$$

from which it can be seen that the best approximation is simply the element B, which is referred to as the projection of u on to the subspace F. Further,

$$(u, u) = (B, B) + (g, g) \tag{21.6}$$

Hence, the inner product (B, B) provides a strict lower bound to (u, u).

Returning to eqn (21.1), the inner product (Lu, f) can be expressed in the form

$$(Lu, f) = (u, L^*f) + S(u, f) \tag{21.7}$$

where L^* is the adjoint of L and $S(u, f)$, known as the conjunct of u and f, is dependent only on boundary values. If the subspace F is invariant under L^* then,

$$(u, L^*f) = (B, L^*f) \qquad \forall f \in F \tag{21.8}$$

Thus,

$$(Lu - q, f) = (LB - q, f) + S(u - B, f) = 0 \qquad \forall f \in F \tag{21.9}$$

Let F possess a basis $f_1, \ldots, f_m$, then B can be expressed as the linear combination,

$$B = \sum_{i=1}^{m} C_i f_i \qquad C_i \in C \tag{21.10}$$

The coefficients c_i can be found by solving the m equations

$$\left[L\left(\sum_{i=1}^{m} c_i f_i \right) - q, f_j \right] = -S\left(u - \sum_{i=1}^{m} c_i f_i, f_j \right) \qquad j = 1, \ldots, m \tag{21.11}$$

In order to be able to solve the above, a necessary condition is that the boundary conditions imposed on u are compatible with evaluation of the conjunct. In the special case, when the boundary conditions on u and the f_i's cause the conjunct in (21.11) to vanish, the above approach reduces to a Galerkin scheme.

Now let H be the space $L_2(0, \infty)$ of all complex-valued square-integrable scalar functions $f(t)$ defined everywhere on the real interval $0 \leqslant t < \infty$. The inner product (f, g) is defined by

$$(f, g) = \int_0^\infty f(t)\bar{g}(t)\, dt \tag{21.12}$$

and the norm $\|f\|$ by

$$\|f\|^2 = (f, f) \tag{21.13}$$

Let L represent an ordinary time-invariant Hurwitzian differential operator. Note that L is constrained to be Hurwitzian, so that the solution u of (21.1) lies in $L_2(0, \infty)$. If F possesses a basis of the form

$$f_i = e^{-p_i t}, \qquad Re(p_i) > 0 \qquad i = 1, \ldots, m \tag{21.14}$$

the set F is clearly invariant under L^*. Thus, the best approximation B to u from the set F can be found from (21.11) provided the initial values of u and its derivatives are given at time $t = 0$. However, the inner product (u, f_i) represents a Laplace transform. Denoting the Laplace transform of u by $\tilde{u}(s)$ and of B by $\tilde{B}(s)$, eqn (21.11) is equivalent to saying

$$\tilde{B}(\bar{p}_i) = \tilde{u}(\bar{p}_i) \qquad i = 1, \ldots, m \tag{21.15}$$

Thus, from (21.10), B is the element whose Laplace transform

$$\tilde{B}(S) = \sum_{i=1}^{m} \frac{c_i}{S + P_i} \tag{21.16}$$

takes the same values as the Laplace transform of u at the points $s = \bar{p}_1, \ldots, \bar{p}_m$.

For any choice of $p_1, \ldots, p_m$, subject to $Re(p_i) > 0$, one can generate a model $\tilde{B}(s)$ of the system response $\tilde{u}(s)$. For a given m, an infinite number of models can be generated; clearly the optimum choice of $p_1, \ldots, p_m$ will be the same as that given by Mitra's approach. In general, one will use a non-optimal choice for the poles of the model. A fairly simple way of generating a set of poles is to set all but m of the system state variables to zero and to use the poles of the resulting system. Physical insight into the behaviour of the system can be employed to select which state variables are important. It may happen that one knows little about the probable behaviour of the system. In this case, one can make hypotheses about the relative importance of the system variables—different hypotheses will lead to different models of the system. Here the property of strict lower boundness for the estimate of the quadratic cost function can be used to select the best of these different models.

21.3 BOUNCE DYNAMICS OF A RAILWAY VEHICLE

Figure 21.1 is a schematic of the suspension system proposed for a railway vehicle known as 'D' Stock currently under design at London Transport. The vehicle has conventional primary suspension, but the secondary suspension between the carbody and bogies incorporates a pneumatically damped airspring. To ensure that the vehicle does not foul the loading gauge, i.e. excursions of the vehicle relative to the track do not exceed a given threshold, it was necessary to calculate the mean square displacement of the vehicle, σ_d^2 at its foremost point, relative to the track when subject to vertical track irregularities.

The spectrum of the track irregularities was based on a British Rail measured track spectrum—Pollard [5]—and assumed the form

$$S_z(\omega) = \frac{F^2}{\omega^2(\omega^2 + \tau^2)} \text{ m}^2/\text{Hz} \tag{21.17}$$

where z is the vertical displacement of the track, and the parameters F^2, τ are given by

$$F^2 = 3 \cdot 373\,47 \times 10^{0.5} V^3 \tag{21.18}$$

$$\tau = 1 \cdot 513\,304 V \tag{21.19}$$

where V is the forward speed of the vehicle in m/sec.

Consider an impulse at the track, which at time $t = 0$, lies immediately below the foremost point of the vehicle carbody. Up until time T, when the front wheelset reaches the impulse, the vehicle suspension system plays no part in the carbody displacement relative to the track. This allows σ_d^2 to be written in the form

$$\sigma_d{}^2 = \frac{F^2}{\tau^2}\left[T + \frac{2}{\tau}(\mathrm{e}^{-\tau T} - 1) - \frac{1}{2\tau}(\mathrm{e}^{-2\tau T} - 1)\right] + \int_0^\infty \mathscr{I}(t)^2 \, \mathrm{d}t \tag{21.20}$$

where

$$T = \frac{1}{V}(l_{\mathrm{end}} - l - l_p) \tag{21.21}$$

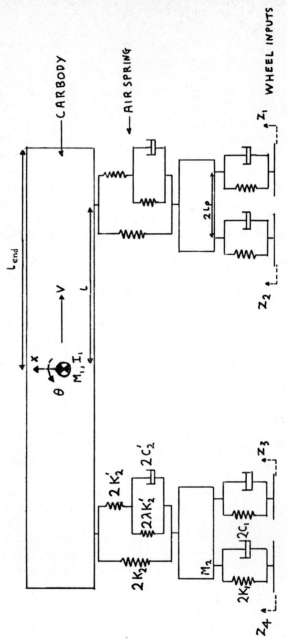

Fig. 21.1. Suspension system.

Only the integral term depends on the vehicle suspension, and provides a quadratic cost function for deriving a simple model of the system. $\mathscr{I}(t)$ has the Laplace transform,

$$\tilde{\mathscr{I}}(S) = \frac{4F(C_1 S + K_1)}{S(S + \tau)} \left[(K_2 + K_2')C_2 S + K_2'(\lambda K_2' + (1 + \lambda)K_2) \right]$$

$$\times \left\{ \frac{1 + e^{-2lS/V}}{\Delta(M_1; S)} + \frac{l_{\text{end}}(1 - e^{-2lS/V})}{l\Delta(I_1/l^2; S)} \right\} (1 + e^{-2lpS/V})$$

$$- \frac{F[S(1 - e^{-\tau T}) + \tau]}{\tau S(S + \tau)} \tag{21.22}$$

$\Delta(x; S)$ is the fifth order polynominal

$$\Delta(x; S) = xM_2 C_2 S^5 + x[4C_1 C_2 + (1 + \lambda)K_2' M_2]S^4$$

$$+ [4M_2 C_2(K_2 + K_2') + x\{(4K_1 + 2K_2')C_2$$

$$+ (2K_2 + 4(1 + \lambda)K_2')C_1\}]S^3$$

$$+ [4M_2((1 + \lambda)K_2 + \lambda K_2')K_2'$$

$$+ xK_2'\{(1 + \lambda)(4K_1 + 2K_2) + 2\lambda K_2'\}$$

$$+ 16C_1 C_2(K_2 + K_2')]S^2$$

$$+ [16K_1 C_2(K_2 + K_2') + 16K_2' C_1(\lambda K_2' + (1 + \lambda)K_2)]S$$

$$+ 16K_1 K_2'[\lambda K_2' + (1 + \lambda)K_2] \tag{21.23}$$

It was decided to approximate the integral

$$\int_0^\infty \mathscr{I}(t)^2 \, dt$$

by modelling $\tilde{\mathscr{I}}(S)$ by $\tilde{\mathscr{I}}_a(S)$, given by

$$\tilde{\mathscr{I}}_a(S) = \frac{A + {}_jB}{S + \zeta\omega - j(1 - \zeta^2)^{1/2}\omega} + \frac{A - {}_jB}{S + \zeta\omega + j(1 - \zeta^2)^{1/2}\omega} + \frac{C}{S + y} \tag{21.24}$$

The poles of the above model were selected by considering the third order system obtained by earthing the bogies. The complex conjugate poles of this model were used to define ζ and ω. The value of the real pole at $-y$ was chosen as a compromise between the real pole due to the airspring and the pole at $-\tau$ which occurs in the spectral input.

Taking the data

$$M_1 = 19\ 550\ \text{kg}$$
$$M_2 = 2\ 780\ \text{kg}$$
$$I_1 = 531\ 080\ \text{kg m}^2$$
$$K_1 = 1\ 500\ 000\ \text{N m}^{-1}$$
$$K_2 = -73\ 912\ \text{N m}^{-1}$$
$$K_2' = 381\ 798\ \text{N m}^{-1}$$
$$C_1 = 2\ 600\ \text{N s m}^{-1}$$
$$C_2 = 97\ 340\ \text{N s m}^{-1}$$
$$\lambda = 1{\cdot}2$$
$$l = 5{\cdot}9425\ \text{m}$$
$$l_p = 1{\cdot}144\ \text{m}$$
$$l_{\text{end}} = 9{\cdot}0275\ \text{m}$$
$$V = 20\ \text{m/s}$$

The parameters y, ζ, ω were selected as

$$y = 10$$
$$\zeta = 0{\cdot}25$$
$$\omega = 1\ \text{Hz}$$

The best values of A, B, C are given, from Section 21.2, as the solution of

$$\tilde{\mathscr{I}}_a(y)_a = \tilde{\mathscr{I}}(y) \tag{21.25}$$

$$\tilde{\mathscr{I}}_a(\zeta\omega - j(1 - \zeta^2)^{1/2}\omega) = \tilde{\mathscr{I}}(\zeta\omega - j(1 - \zeta^2)^{1/2}\omega) \tag{21.26}$$

Evaluating the right-hand sides of (21.25) and (21.26),

$$\tilde{\mathscr{I}}(y) = -1{\cdot}350\ 419\ 661 \times 10^{-3} \tag{21.27}$$

$$\tilde{\mathscr{I}}(\zeta\omega - j(1 - \zeta^2)^{1/2}\omega)$$
$$= -4{\cdot}638\ 739\ 062 \times 10^{-3} - j1{\cdot}238\ 867\ 379 \times 10^{-3} \tag{21.28}$$

Solving (21.25) and (21.26) yields

$$A = -1{\cdot}846\ 960\ 091 \times 10^{-2} \tag{21.29}$$

$$B = 2{\cdot}563\ 349\ 246 \times 10^{-3} \tag{21.30}$$

$$C = 2{\cdot}666\ 279\ 348 \times 10^{-2} \tag{21.31}$$

Now, (21.24) can readily be inverted and the integral

$$\int_0^\infty \mathscr{I}_a(t)^2 \, dt$$

is easily evaluated to give

$$\int_0^\infty \mathscr{I}(t)^2 \, dt \geqslant 1{\cdot}416\,966\,5 \times 10^{-4} \, m^2$$

Thus, from (21.20)

$$\sigma_d{}^2 \geqslant 1{\cdot}567\,061 \times 10^{-4} \, m^2 \tag{21.32}$$

The theory of Section 21.2 does not give any indication of the accuracy of the lower bound (21.32). To estimate this, $\sigma_d{}^2$ was also calculated by integrating $|\tilde{\mathscr{I}}(j\omega)|^2$ from 0–20 Hz numerically, using a step size of 0.1 Hz. This gives a value

$$\sigma_d{}^2 \simeq 1{\cdot}659\,640 \times 10^{-4} \, m^2 \tag{21.33}$$

from which

$$\int_0^\infty (t)^2 \, \tilde{\mathscr{I}} dt \simeq 1{\cdot}509\,546 \times 10^{-4} \, m^2 \tag{21.34}$$

Thus, the third order model calculated from the theory of Section 21.2 gives rise to a lower bound for

$$\int_0^\infty \mathscr{I}(t)^2 \, dt$$

which is accurate to approximately 6%.

21.4   CONCLUSIONS

A technique for deriving low order models of a system based on the Laplace transform has been derived. The models so derived give strict lower bounds to a quadratic cost function associated with the system. The simplicity and accuracy of the technique have been illustrated by application to the bounce dynamics of a railway vehicle subject to vertical track irregularities.

ACKNOWLEDGEMENT

The author would like to thank Mr S. F. Smith, Chief Mechanical Engineer, London Transport Executive, for permission to present this paper.

REFERENCES

1. Mitra, D. (1969). W matrix and the geometry of model equivalence and reduction, *Proc. IEE*, **116**, (6), 1101–1106, June.
2. Hedrick, J. K. 'A Summary of Optimisation Techniques that can be Applied to Suspension System Design', Report No. DOT-TSC-OST-73-9.
3. Chuang, S. C. 'A Method for Linear Systems Order Reduction', Pub. 72/53, Dept. of Computing and Control, Imperial College, London.
4. Plesner, A. I. (1969). *Spectral Theory of Linear Operators*, Ungar, New York, Vol. 1.
5. Pollard, M. G. 'Power Spectra of Track Roughness Obtained from the "APT Survey"', BR Tech. Note DT2, Oct. 1969.

22

The Use of Dynamic Strain Records to Estimate the Fatigue Life of a Semi-trailer Chassis

P. W. SHARMAN
Loughborough University of Technology

SUMMARY

The paper describes an experiment in which the strain was recorded at critical points on the chassis of a 16 ton GVW semi-trailer, operating on various road surfaces. Vertical acceleration was also recorded in the region of the suspension.

Statistical analysis of the records in terms of design factors and load spectra is then used to determine suitable maximum stress levels for the maximum static load and then to estimate the fatigue life. Since many chassis are of welded steel construction, the S–N curves used are appropriate to the class of joint. Miner's law is used to estimate the cumulative effect of the various load spectra.

The final section draws some general conclusions on the effect of increasing static stress levels on the fatigue life, and describes methods of weight reduction in the chassis while maintaining an adequate fatigue life.

22.1 INTRODUCTION

The continuously varying displacements imposed at the tyre contact points of a vehicle travelling along a road, may be thought of as a random signal exciting a dynamic system of masses, spring and dampers. By removing occasional extreme events (potholes, crash stops, etc.) the response may be treated by random process theory and is therefore amenable to a mathematical interpretation of use to the designer. In this paper, only the structural aspects of such an interpretation will be made and illustrated by a limited series of experiments on a semi-trailer.

In practice, some difficulties arise in the gathering and interpretation of such random data. Not the least of these is the selection of a representative stretch of road or track and the similar problem of the selection of a portion of the data recorded on the track. To ensure the signal is stationary and ergodic, lengthy portions of data should be analysed, but of course this is expensive in terms of the cost of time taken in analysis. Since no

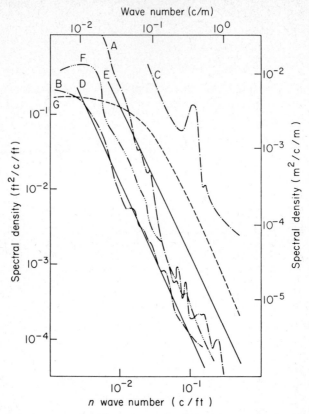

Fig. 22.1. Road profile spectra from ref. 1. A, country road, England; B, motorway, England; C, pavé track, England; D, black top on concrete, Germany; E, black top. Germany; F, runway, U.S.A.; G, cobbled surface, smooth, U.S.S.R.

automatic signal analysis equipment was available for the experiment, the data was processed by hand, and therefore only short portions were tested; thus the limitations of experimental accuracy must be realised. It is hoped that the series of tests will be included in a wider range of tests using automatic signal processing equipment in the near future.

Other difficulties relate to the nature of the track and the quality of recording equipment. Regarding the track surface, there is some literature [1] on national and Continental road surfaces which expresses the spectral density as a function of wavelength. The relevant data are collected in Fig. 22.1. Clearly, the differing nature of these measured surfaces creates great difficulty in defining a single spectrum suitable for design purposes.

From the designer's point of view, it would be excessively pessimistic to take the worst envelope. A better solution would be to work a 'bad' surface, thus giving good service under average conditions, and trust that some form of derating would be acceptable for worse conditions.

The quality of the recording (and subsequent analysis) equipment affects the results in several ways, the main effect being due to backlash and noise (electrical or mechanical) in the system. An analysis of these effects [2] shows that noise may have considerable influence on the distribution of exceedences; thus, every effort should be directed to using high-quality recording equipment.

22.2 EXPERIMENTAL OBJECTIVES AND EQUIPMENT

The main object of the experiment was to record the dynamic strain at various positions on a semi-trailer supplied by the Pitt Trailer Co Ltd, and denoted by 16 tons GVW. The positions were judged to be highly stressed areas, and the dynamic vertical accelerations at several positions were also recorded.

As a preliminary, a static stress analysis was carried out at the given payload weight. This gave the position of the most highly stressed section on the longitudinal beams and the distribution of stress along the length according to simple beam theory. Figure 22.2 shows the positions of the gauges and the results of the stress analysis.

Conventional foil strain gauges were attached to the inner surfaces of the upper and lower flanges of the I-section longitudinal beams and wired as a half-bridge circuit. Low resistance leads were carried to the forward end of the vehicle where the amplifiers and magnetic tape recording

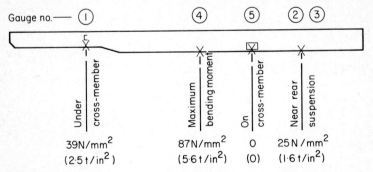

FIG. 22.2. Positions of strain gauges and static stress levels.

equipment were mounted in a small 'shed' structure on the forward end of the semi-trailer. However, the severity of the ride, particularly on the pavé surface, made its safety and accuracy somewhat doubtful and caused discomfort to the operator. Subsequently, the equipment was mounted in an estate car which travelled on a smoother track parallel to the pavé, the connections being made via a long multi-core wire carried on a flexible rod.

Continuous recordings were made in this manner for portions of various test tracks at the Motor Industries Research Institute, Nuneaton. The vehicle was driven at the maximum speed that the driver could maintain control, which varied between 25 mph and 35 mph. It was regretted that more control on speed was not enforced, since there is evidence [3] to show that the dynamic forces in suspension parts increase with increasing speed. Thus, it is reasonable to presume that the strains in the chassis are also dependent on speed and this restricts a general interpretation of the results. Figure 22.3 shows typical pen recorder results obtained from magnetic tape.

Calibration signals were added to the recordings by adding a known

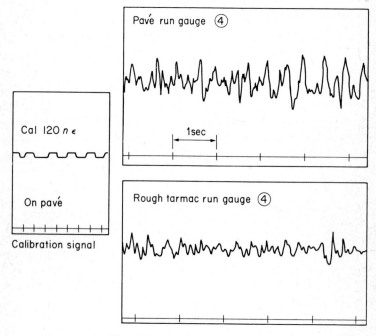

FIG. 22.3. Typical signal records.

resistance in parallel with one of the gauges in each circuit. This was converted to strain, and hence stress, thus establishing a stress scale on each record. Also added to the records were audio signals of the comments on test track surface.

22.3 STATISTICAL ANALYSIS OF RESULTS

A full and mathematically rigorous analysis of the many yards of strain records is clearly a formidable task, even if some automatic processing equipment is available. In this case, no such equipment was available, and hence only comparatively short sections of the records were analysed. The magnetic tape signal, with calibration steps, was transferred to a pen record and a portion was then selected.

The height of each 'peak' and 'valley' was measured from a suitable datum, over several hundred undulations. The length of the portion of record analysed thus corresponded to approximately one minute of real time. The mean was then calculated from:

$$\bar{h} = \frac{1}{N} \sum_{i=1}^{N} \{(h_{\text{peak}} + h_{\text{valley}})_i\} \tag{22.1}$$

The root mean square or standard deviation was then calculated from:

$$S = \left\{ \frac{\sum (h_{\text{peak}} - \bar{h})^2 + \sum (h_{\text{valley}} - \bar{h})^2}{N} \right\}^{1/2} \tag{22.2}$$

In order to assess fatigue damage, the number of exceedences was also counted for between six and ten differing stress levels. This counting must be done with some care, and was only done for stress levels above the mean. For a Gaussian distribution, the counts should be symmetrical about the mean. This was only checked in one case, in which the two distributions, above and below the mean, agreed to within about 8%. A hint which the author found useful is only to count those crossings of the chosen level which were in the same sense, in this case, of increasing stress with time.

The results are summarised in Table 22.1.

22.4 RESULTS IN TERMS OF A DESIGN FACTOR

It is usual in statistical work [2,3] to relate the probability of encountering a given level of signal, in this case stress, to the standard deviation. For

TABLE 22.1

Distribution of exceedences

Road condition	Stress level (N/mm²)	No. of exceedences
Smooth tarmac	115	4
	112	12
	109	20
	107	48
	104	112
	101	120
	99	132
Coarse tarmac	120	43
	117	8
	115	12
	112	25
	109	40
	107	88
	104	155
	101	180
	99	205
Ride and handling track	146	3
	136	8
	130	12
	125	17
	120	29
	115	84
	109	144
	104	195
	99	250
Pavé track	185	4
	173	27
	160	72
	148	100
	136	150
	123	188
	110	208
	99	208

instance, if a Gaussian distribution of signal is assumed, then 99·9% of the events will be in the band $\pm 3S$, where S is the standard deviation. Thus, the chance of exceeding $3S$ is about 1 in 1000. This level of probability is commonly accepted in many industrial situations and will be used to derive design factors.

The design factor in this case is a numerical factor greater than unity which multiplies the static (1 g) load to give a load which is used in subsequent design and analysis. Using the '3S' criterion, the design factor is therefore

$$DF = \frac{1 + 3S}{\bar{h}} \qquad (22.3)$$

where $\bar{h}$ is the mean signal level, e.g. static stress.

Since the response to various types of road surface was recorded, different design factors are derived and are given in Table 22.2. Several companies which design commercial vehicles use a design factor of 2·0, which in these tests was only exceeded in very severe situations, such as

TABLE 22.2

Design factors derived from (1 + 3S) *criterion*

Road condition	Design factor
Smooth tarmac	1·2
Coarse tarmac	1·25
Ride and handling track	1·6
Short bumps on ride and handling track	1·9
Long waves on ride and handling track	1·4
Level crossing	2·2
Pavé surface	2·4

railway level crossings, skew ridges, and on the pavé surface. It should be remembered that these factors are appropriate to a particular speed, judged by a single driver as the maximum possible for full payload on the observed surface. It is quite likely that other drivers may produce different results, and thus not too much significance should be placed on the precise numerical magnitude. The factors are given to three significant figures, which is consistent with the quality of the records, but certainly the final digit should not be used out of context and considerable latitude must be allowed on the figures after the decimal point when comparing with other data.

In retrospect, much more control on the speed should have been exercised, possibly with repeated runs on the same surface at different speeds.

22.5   FATIGUE LIFE PREDICTION

In order to estimate the fatigue life of the chassis, assuming that failure will occur at the point of maximum measured stress, the following information is required: (a) a stress life (SN) curve for the material; (b) a suitable cumulative damage law; (c) a spectrum of operational use.

The material used for the flanges of this particular semi-trailer was to the specification BS 4360, Grade 50B, and since no stress-life curves for this material could be located, the information contained in BS 153 was used. Basically, this specifies stress-life curves for various types of welded joints for structural steel used in bridge construction, which is to a less exacting specification than BS 4360, Grade 50B, so that the life calculations would be conservative. The presence of welded joints, however, degrades the steel in the region of the weld, making the data more appropriate. The results are meaningful relative to each other, which is probably the most that can be expected from fatigue life prediction in any case. A further utility of BS 153 is that the life is given in terms of mean stress and 'stress ratio'—the minimum stress divided by the maximum—thus accounting for mean stress, presumably by the 'modified Goodman diagram' method. In terms of the measured stresses, it can be seen that the stress ratio is given by:

$$\text{Stress ratio} = \frac{2 \times \text{Mean stress} - \text{Max. stress}}{\text{Max. stress}}$$

For assessing damage caused by cumulative cycles of stress at differing levels, Miner's law was used, i.e. fatigue failure occurs when

$$\sum \left(\frac{n}{N}\right) = 1$$

where n is the number of cycles at a given stress level and N the number of cycles which would cause failure at that stress level.

Whilst this law takes no account of the order of the stress cycles and ignores stress rate and frequency effects, it is commonly accepted in practice [4] for use in the absence of any other easily applied method.

The operational aspect is one in which some standards should be set on the basis of comparative design. The only suggestion found in the literature [6] is 25% rough road operation and 75% smooth road, with special events occurring with the frequency shown in Table 22.3.

As these data are relevant to the operational conditions in the USA and did not correspond in any way to the recording made in this series of tests,

TABLE 22.3

Event	Distance during which event occurs once (miles)
Tractor–trailer engagement	500
Backing into shipping dock (severe jolt)	4000
Hitting pothole or curb	1500
Tight turn up ramp	3000
Brake stop from 15 mph—hard	1000
—normal	100

the life was calculated separately for each test track condition, and no attempt was made to combine these sectors.

The general problem of special events may be treated from a statistical point of view [5], in combination with the continuous degradation of the strength of the structure due to the growth of fatigue cracks. However, as no numerical quantities were readily available for the various parameters (crack propagation rate, scatter characteristics, etc.), the application of such theory is not possible to this series of tests.

Table 22.4 shows the results of these calculations in which the life has been given in terms of the hours of operational use. This is the most direct result to derive from the experimental data, as the length of the record analysed was 60 sec in real time. This gave a total of several hundred exceedences, which was judged to be sufficient for reasonable accuracy balanced with time required for counting.

TABLE 22.4

Fatigue life estimates

Road condition	Life (h)	
	Class D	Class E
Smooth tarmac	$2 \cdot 7 \times 10^7$	$1 \cdot 2 \times 10^6$
Coarse tarmac	$2 \cdot 7 \times 10^7$	$1 \cdot 2 \times 10^6$
Ride and handling track	$1 \cdot 5 \times 10^4$	$1 \cdot 7 \times 10^3$
Pavé	110	25

The life was calculated for both Class D and Class E welded joints in BS 153, which are defined as:

Class D—Longitudinal manual fillet welds. Transverse butt welds made in the flat position with no undercut.
Class E—Other tranverse butt welds and transverse butt welds made on backing strip. Cruciform butt welds.

The lives on smooth tarmac and rough tarmac are given as identical, since the stress levels involve extrapolation of the stress–life curves, which are very flat in this region, being close to the fatigue limit.

In terms of an eight-hour operational day for 360 days per year, the working year is approximately 3×10^3 h. Thus, the ride and handling track represents the limiting surface to which the trailer should be subjected in the fully laden condition. Class E joints would also be unsatisfactory in this condition.

For tarmac road operation, the trailer may be judged to be overstrength, even with Class E joints, where the life is two to three orders of magnitude in excess of the normal requirement—about 10 years. Thus, the mean stress may be raised to around 120 N/mm² (7·8 T/in²) according to these calculations. This corresponds to the stress encountered on the ride and handling track, with Class D joints.

To accommodate more severe environments, less than the maximum payload would be used for a reasonable fatigue life, and the yield stress for the material should not be less than $2·4 \times 120$, i.e. 288 N/mm² (18·8 T/in²), which is well within the specification.

22.6   CONCLUSIONS

For operation on normal trunk roads the design factors should not exceed 1·3, but factors of almost 2·4 were encountered on rough surfaces such as Continental pavé.

To obtain a reasonable fatigue life on normal trunk roads, the mean (1 g) stress at maximum payload should not exceed 120 N/mm² (7·8 T/in²).

Close attention should be paid to welded joints in the region of the maximum stress.

REFERENCES

1. Robson, J. D. and Dodds, C. H. 'The Response of Vehicle Components to Random Road Surface Undulations', FISITA 1970, Paper 17.2D.

2. Whittaker, M. W. and Macaulay, M. A. 'Vehicle Service Loads—A Survey of Analysis Techniques', MIRA Report 1967–3.
3. Andrew, S. and Whittaker, M. W. 'Vehicle Service Loads—Suspension Components Loads in Four Passenger Cars', MIRA Report 1969–10.
4. Grace, G. (1971). Design for finite life—part 1, accelerated fatique testing, *ADE*, **12**, March.
5. Matolcsy, M. (1971). Design for finite life—part 2, life and reliability of vehicle frame structures, *ADE*, **12**, May.
6. Sidelko, W. J. 'An Objective Approach to Highway Truck Frame Design', SAE Paper No. SP 276, Dec. 1965.

23

Design Data for Heavy Vehicles

C. C. Woodley and B. R. Piggott
The Welding Institute

SUMMARY

Vehicles which are required to carry very heavy concentrated loads, e.g. up to 400 ton, need to be designed to a minimum gross weight to enable them to operate as far as possible within the limitation of roads, bridges, etc. The basic vehicle weight could be minimised by using high strength materials. Welded joints in such materials tend to have the same fatigue strength as the lower strength materials, so that if fatigue strength is already a design criterion it might not be possible to take full advantage of high strength materials.

The investigation described in the paper was carried out to measure fluctuating stresses on a trailer with a 300-ton load during a delivery movement. This required the installation of strain gauges and mobile recording equipment for retrieving full data over long periods of the journey which included a journey by sea. Assessment of the measurements required that the speed of travel was known accurately and it was found that existing devices were insufficiently accurate at the low speeds employed. A much more accurate speed measuring device was therefore developed for this operation.

The results demonstrated the importance of correct loading and adjustment of the vehicle suspension system. The final conclusions of the exercise were that fatigue damage was unlikely to be a design criterion in respect of high strength materials.

23.1 INTRODUCTION

This paper describes the results of a strain measurement exercise on a 300-ton transporter owned by Robert Wynn & Sons Ltd, during a typical heavy load movement. The trailer was designed and manufactured by Crane Fruehauf Trailers Ltd of Dereham, Norfolk. The investigation showed that the actual static stresses induced by the load were in very good agreement with those predicted by the designers for this particular loading condition. The fluctuating stress ranges measured in the trailer, as it was travelling along a reasonably straight course, were very small when compared with the very high static mean stress induced by the load. The fluctuating stress ranges showed a marked increase when the trailer was negotiating severe right- or left-hand bends or manoeuvring round roundabouts. The test results also show that approximately 25% of load is effectively removed from the frame of the trailer when the 'hoverskirt' is in operation, and the measured values are again in good agreement with the predictions of the British Hover Craft Co. It can be concluded from the computer analysis that fluctuating stress ranges were small enough to indicate that the trailer should not suffer from fatigue failure during a working life of about 30 years, provided that the service loading conditions remain similar to those encountered during this test.

The analysis indicates that fatigue failure would be detected in the bolster after about 400 000 miles; the main beams and the swan neck would have lives of 1 500 000 and 28 000 000 miles, respectively. The loading condition can be considered as a high mean stress application which has a small fluctuating stress range superimposed, and therefore this particular condition makes the use of a high yield steel very attractive. It is recommended that the material used for future applications should be a high yield steel, which possesses good weldability and adequate notch toughness at the minimum expected service temperature.

A similar strain measurement exercise was carried out on the 300-ton transporter operated by Pickfords Heavy Haulage Ltd, when it was moving a similar load to the Dungeness B Power Station. The results obtained from this exercise were similar to those obtained in the earlier investigation, but this time the stresses recorded in the bolster units were smaller.

23.2 TRANSPORTATION OF HEAVY LOADS

The transport of heavy indivisible loads has always been considered as a job for the specialist haulage contractor, and right from the early days to the present time the number of recognised hauliers who were capable of carrying out these duties efficiently could just about be counted on the fingers of one hand. In the late 1920s and early 1930s, a 100-ton load hauled by a pair of Fowler B6 Road Locomotives would then have been considered by many as the ultimate in capacity, but in fact loads have continued to increase both in size and weight to a present-day maximum of about 300 ton. During this period of progress the hauliers have had to produce suitable transporters to carry these loads, and designers have been faced with the task of producing sophisticated trailers which were capable of carrying the maximum anticipated load and yet still meet the legal requirements and the haulier's terms of reference with respect to their limits of vehicle weight and overall dimensions. The designers have been able to achieve this objective only by manufacturing the frames from a weldable high yield steel, which enables them to use design stress levels which will accommodate the high service stresses.

Power station designers are well aware of the increased efficiencies they would be able to obtain from their plants if they could increase the physical size of the individual components. Their designers could produce individual components which would weigh between 300 and 500 ton, but before they can produce these designs they must be sure that suitable routes which have bridges strong enough to carry these loads are available for moving these objects and, most important, that the hauliers are able to transport these loads on their vehicles.

Great interest is being shown at present in the possibility of producing a new generation of trailers which would be capable of handling loads which were well in excess of 300 ton. Limitations on gross weight require that the weight of the trailer itself is kept as low as possible. One contributing factor to the trailer weight is the strength of the material and a natural development would be to use steels of higher strength. However, it has been established that the fatigue behaviour of steels, in the as-welded condition, is independent of the strength of the steel.

If it can be shown that fatigue strength is not a limiting design criterion, then the use of higher strength steels is feasible. To examine this question a series of strain measurements were recorded on Robert Wynn & Sons 300-ton transporter, whilst it was transporting a 265-ton transformer from GEC's Stafford Works to the CEGB's Pomona Dock in Manchester.

23.3   INSTRUMENTATION

Electrical resistance strain gauges were bonded to the transporter structure at the locations shown on the gauge plan which is presented in Fig. 23.1.

Temperature-compensated strain gauges, of 10 mm gauge length and nominal resistance 120 Ω, were used in a $\frac{1}{4}$-bridge 3-wire configuration for both static and dynamic tests.

For static loading tests all gauges were connected to a multipoint switch box and switched in turn to a portable strain indicator of the null balance type.

For the road tests the strain gauge circuits were first fed into signal conditioning units which contained bridge completion circuitry and which facilitated bridge balancing and circuit sensitivity adjustment. The bridge outputs were then recorded on two direct writing oscillographs having specially modified chart drives to provide slow paper speeds. The gauges

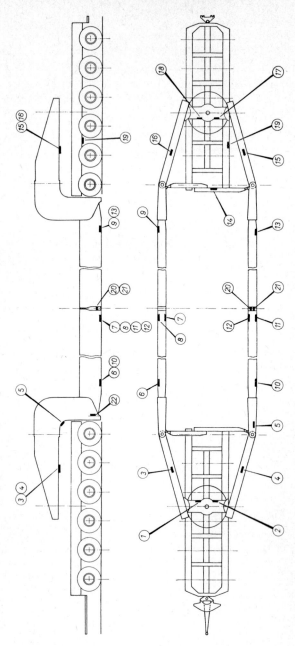

Fig. 23.1. Gauge plan for road test on Wynn 300-ton trailer.

bonded to the beams were recorded on a 12-channel NEP recorder and the remainder on a Bell & Howell 18-channel instrument. This equipment was housed in the front tractor cab and powered from an electrical generator mounted on the front bogie.

Road speed was also recorded continuously on both recorder charts. Use was made of a fifth wheel on which was mounted a magnetic pick-up and a toothed wheel to provide a pulsed voltage output. Conversion of this signal was used to provide a suitable galvanometer input for each recorder and an additional dial indication of road speed for quick reference in the cab.

The slow speed recording was designed and manufactured at The Welding Institute, because no suitable commercial instrument could be obtained that would measure to the required accuracy.

23.4 TEST PROGRAMME AND PROCEDURE

23.4.1 Programme of Work

A complete history of the working stress levels of all the gauges was obtained as the load was lowered on to the transporter beams in the GEC's Works at Stafford and throughout the four-day journey to Pomona Dock.

The route taken was of the order of 60 miles, following the A34 via Stone to a point 5 miles north of Newcastle-under-Lyme, where it changed to the A50 through Holmes Chapel, Knutsford and on to the A556 at Mere, through Altrincham taking the A560 and A5103 into Manchester.

The general road condition over this route could be described as typical for this transporter with the major manoeuvres taking place at roundabouts, sharp right-angle turns and the 17 bridges requiring the use of the 'hoverskirt'.

23.5 TEST PROCEDURES

23.5.1 Static Tests

These tests were carried out in the loading bay of the GEC's Works as the load was lowered on to the transporter beams.

A set of static indicator readings were noted for all gauges with the trailer in its unladen state. Indicator readings were again noted after the load had been placed on the transporter. This procedure was carried out three times to ensure that repeatable strain readings were obtained.

At the end of the journey the indicator readings were noted for all gauges before and after the load had been lowered to the ship's deck.

23.5.2   Road Tests

A continuous record of strain was made throughout the journey from Stafford to Pomona Dock. Calibration of the recorder channels was frequently carried out when the transporter was stationary and on near level surfaces.

Notes of the route conditions were compiled and correlated with the recorder charts, with 5-minute timing intervals. Additional notes were added to the chart as and when necessary.

23.6   RESULTS AND DISCUSSION OF TESTS

Strain gauge measurements were recorded from various locations on the transporter, both when the vehicle was in its unladen state and when it was carrying the 265-ton transformer.

When the static stresses were studied it was found that in all cases their agnitude was less than two-thirds of the yield point of the Fortiweld material (Fortiweld has a yield strength of about 29 ton/in^2 at $1\frac{1}{2}$ in thickness.) These stress levels were also in very good agreement with the designers' predictions for the loading system adopted for this particular movement. If designers consider this form of transporter as a statically loaded structure, the current design codes would recommend the use of design stress in the order of two-thirds the yield point of the material. This condition, of course, assumes that there is no significant fluctuating stress range superimposed on to this static stress.

A continuous record of strain data was recorded during a typical heavy load movement from Stafford to Manchester, in order to determine the magnitude of the fluctuating stresses which occur in the transporter. The journey of some 60 miles was considered as a typical run for these heavy vehicles, and most of the hazards they encounter during their daily work would occur several times on a route of this nature. The data collected during the journey were at first analysed manually to obtain values of the maximum and minimum fluctuating stresses which were recorded at each gauge station.

In order to get a realistic prediction of the fatigue life of the structure, it was necessary to analyse the random stress distribution obtained from the traces by computer. A computer program, which was based on the cumulative damage clauses given in BS 153, 'Steel Girder Bridges', was used for the analysis. These design clauses are based on the Miner's cumulative damage rule, which states that the fatigue damage at any stress level is directly proportional to the number of cycles of that stress applied and accumulates linearly until failure occurs. This leads to the following formula:

$$\sum \frac{n}{N} = \frac{n_1}{N_1} + \frac{n_2}{N_2} + \frac{n_3}{N_3} + \cdots + \frac{n_r}{N_r} = 1$$

where n_1 represents the number of cycles of stress S_1 which, by itself, would cause failure in N_1 cycles. The values of N are derived from the appropriate S–N curve.

The cumulative damage data are presented in Table 23.1 in the form of life predictions for the beams, the bolsters and the swan necks, which were the highest stressed members in the structure. The analysis makes the assumption that, in the trailer's future life, these parts of the structure do not encounter any higher degree of fatigue loading than experienced on this particular journey. For convenience, the fatigue life of each component is given in miles travelled by the transporter.

TABLE 23.1

Cumulative damage fatigue analysis (Robert Wynn & Sons 300-ton transporter: strain data from journey Stafford–Manchester (60 miles) with 265-ton load)

Part of structure	Strain gauge number	Fatigue damage for 60-mile journey	Predicted fatigue life in miles (assuming $\sum n/N = 1$)	Predicted fatigue life in load cycles
Main beams	11	0·000 036 31	1 660 000	$23\cdot2 \times 10^6$
Bolster	2	0·000 131 45	460 000	$11\cdot5 \times 10^6$
Swan neck	5	0·000 002 15	28 000 000	170×10^6

The fatigue analysis carried out highlighted that the bolster units were subjected to the greatest fatigue damage, and a failure in these components could be expected after the trailer had travelled approximately 400 000 miles (approximately 100 years life), provided that the trailer continues to receive the same pattern of loading as received on this particular journey. Under similar loading conditions the main beams would have a service life of about 1 500 000 miles and the swan necks 28 000 000 miles.

It was somewhat surprising to see that the most serious fatigue damage would occur on the bolster units, as the designer had always believed that the main beam would be the most vulnerable from this aspect.

From Table 23.1 it can be seen that the bolster is subjected to nearly twice as many cycles as the beams, whereas the swan neck only sees half the number of cycles which the beams encounter.

During the journey the BHC 'hoverskirt' equipment was used on several occasions to protect various bridges. This apparatus uses an air cushion effect to distribute the load and, in fact, effectively 'removes' load from the structure as the transporter passes over the bridge. The amount of load 'removed' from the main beams was in good agreement with the predictions given by the BHC.

It is interesting to note that changes in road speed within the rated limits of the transporter, road undulations and the effect of starting and stopping had no major effect on the magnitude of the fluctuating stresses which were recorded.

23.7 CONCLUSIONS

1. The stresses induced in the transporter by the application of the 265-ton transformer were all less than two-thirds of the yield point of the Fortiweld material. The actual values of the stresses were in very good agreement with the predictions of the designers for the loading pattern under consideration.

2. The fluctuating stress ranges recorded during the journey were very small indeed when compared with the very high mean stresses induced by the transformer.

3. The analysis of the strain data predicted that the transporter could be operated for at least 400 000 miles, under service loading conditions which were similar to those encountered during the investigation, before a fatigue failure would be expected to occur in any individual part of the transporter.

4. The bolster units suffered the highest degree of fatigue damage during the journey. The fatigue life of this detail would be about 100 years, based on the current annual mileage of the transporters.

5. In the future, designers will be able to consider the service loading to which heavy transporters are subjected as a stress cycle which is made up of a small fluctuating component which has to be superimposed on to a very high mean stress.

6. As fatigue failure is not now expected to be a major problem, it is recommended that future trailers are made from high yield steel, but care must be taken to ensure that the selected steel has good weldability and adequate notch toughness at the minimum expected service temperature.

7. When the 'hoverskirt' is in operation the stresses in the main beams are reduced by approximately 25%. Thus, the effective 'removal' of load from the beams would also be about 25%.

8. Changes in road speed, road undulation and the effect of starting and stopping had little effect on the range of fluctuating stress recorded.

ACKNOWLEDGEMENTS

This paper is based on the results of an investigation which was sponsored by Crane Fruehauf Trailers Ltd, Pickfords Heavy Haulage, and Robert Wynn & Sons Ltd, in conjunction with the CEGB, and the authors wish to acknowledge their thanks to the sponsors for allowing them to publish this paper.

Index

Automotive components, 21
  diesel injector nozzle, 24
  handbrake linkage lever, 32
  roller clutch sleeve, 37

Beams, torsion constants, 70
BERSAFE, 22
Brakes. See under Disc brakes.
Bus, static analysis, 376
Bus, active suspension
  active mode, 269
  advantage, 275
  application to Route Master buses,
    273
  concept, 257
  gas spring dynamics, 276
  passive mode, 266
  sensor/actuator valve dynamics,
    278
  theoretical analysis, 253
  vehicle dynamics, 260

Chassis
  experiments, 463
  fatigue life, 461
  fatigue life prediction, 468
  semi-trailer-design factor, 465
Computer programs
  BERSAFE, 22
  NEWPAC, 4
  PAFEC, 77
Cooling fans
  blade vibration, 231
  effects of environment, 222
  noise level, 217
  sources of noise, 219
Cumulative fatigue damage
  heavy vehicles, 478
  semi-trailer chassis, 468

Diesel engine
  frames, 112
  noise, 201
  photoelastic stress analysis, 111
  solution of equation of motion,
    441
  torsional vibration, 439
  vibration equation of motion,
    441
Diesel injector nozzle, 24
Disc brakes, squeal noise, 237
  See also Pin-disc system.
Disc type wheel
  design for static load, 107
  eccentric radial load, 101
  effect of design variations, 102
  finite element modelling, 99
  impact, 105
  symmetrical radial load, 100
  theoretical analysis, 91
Drive line vibration, 165
  experiments, 166
  modes, 169
  relation to internal noise, 173
Dynamic strain records, 461
  statistical analysis, 465

Earthmoving vehicles, 149
  major noise sources, 156
  modification for noise reduction,
    152
Engine inertia measurements, 416
Engine mount stiffness, measurement,
  418
Engine noise
  crankcase and cylinder block, 207
  diesel engines, 201
  methods of control, 202
  valve gear covers and sump, 210

Engine shake, 413
  centre of percussion system, 431
  different mounting systems, 425
  engine inertia, 416
  input excitation measurement 422
  mount stiffness, 418
  outline of theory, 415
Environmental noise
  earthmoving vehicles, 156
  railway vehicles, 13

Fans, cooling 217
Flywheel
  analysis, 75
  design requirements, 84
  finite element mesh design, 79
  finite element model, 77
  restraint conditions, 82
  spin test, 86
  variable material properties, 84

Handbrake linkage lever, 32
Heavy vehicles
  design data, 473
  instrumentation, 475
  test procedures, 477
High order linear systems
  simplified modelling, 451
  theoretical background, 452

Interior noise
  cars, 165
  earthmoving vehicles, 155
  railway vehicles, 13

Light truck frame
  analysis, 47
  idealisation, 59
  testing, 53
Light van body
  computer programs, 285
  dynamic tests, 286, 294
  idealisations, 288
  static and dynamic analysis, 283
  static tests, 285
London Transport vehicles, 351
  analysis using NEWPAC, 354
  dynamic analysis of car body, 366

static analysis of car body, 357
See also under Bus.
Long wheelbase vehicles, 123
  asymmetric load, 126
  cornering forces, 131
  design examples, 134
  lateral acceleration, 128
  loading cases, 124
  torsion, 125
  torsional displacement, 127

MAMA system, 310
Models, diesel engine, 111, 113

NEWPAC, 4, 320, 354
Noise measurement, earthmoving
  vehicles, 150
Noise reduction, earthmoving
  vehicles, 149

PAFEC, 77, 320
Photoelasticity
  deformation measurement, 116
  diesel engine models, 111
  model manufacture, 113
Pin-disc system
  analytical description, 240
  experimental arrangement, 239

Railway vehicles
  body structure design, 4
  bounce dynamics, 455
  design criteria, 2
  environmental noise, 12
  fatigue, 3
  interior noise, 13
  simplified analysis, 6
  testing, 9
  See also Underground railway
    coach and London Transport
    vehicles.
Roller clutch sleeve, 37

Suspension, active. See under Bus,
  active suspension.

Torsional constants of beams, 70, 145
Torsional vibration, diesel engines,
  439

Transmission noise, cars, 165
Transmission vibration, cars, 169
Truck frame, light, 47
Tyre, road noise, 181
  influencing factors, 187
  noise generation mechanisms, 190
  real time analysis, 193
  road surface effects, 194
  test methods, 183
  wet grip, 196

Undercarriage characteristics, 389
  computer simulation, 408
  dynamic equations, 398
  ground reaction forces, 398
  mathematical model, 393
  method of analysis, 391
  non-linearities, 395

performance index, 401
Underground railway coach,
    319
  analysis, 357
  structural behaviour, 313
  structural idealisation, 319
  test series, 321

Van body. See Light van body.
Vehicles
  earthmoving, 149
  heavy. See Heavy vehicles.
  long wheelbase, 123
Vibration analysis, pin-disc system,
    237

Wheels, disc type, 91
WKBJ approximation, 439